C. VAN EATON

MATHEMATICALLY
SPEAKING

ROBERT C. BINGHAM
PROFESSOR OF ECONOMICS
KENT STATE UNIVERSITY

MATHEMATICALLY SPEAKING

McGRAW-HILL BOOK COMPANY

NEW YORK ST. LOUIS SAN FRANCISCO DÜSSELDORF JOHANNESBURG
KUALA LUMPUR LONDON MEXICO MONTREAL NEW DELHI PANAMA
RIO DE JANEIRO SINGAPORE SYDNEY TORONTO

ECONOMICS, MATHEMATICALLY SPEAKING

Library of Congress Catalog Card Number 74-38975

07-005293-X

1 2 3 4 5 6 7 8 9 0 BABA 7 9 8 7 6 5 4 3 2

This book was set in Vega Light by York Graphic Services, Inc., and printed and bound by George Banta Company, Inc. The designer was Betty Binns; the drawings were done by B. Handelman Associates, Inc. The editors were Jack R. Crutchfield, Michael Elia, and Edwin Hanson. Ted Agrillo supervised production.

FOR MY FRIENDS AT THE
ROYAL UNIVERSITY OF MALTA
AND ESPECIALLY FOR
ALBERT, VICTORIA, JANE, AND CATHY

CONTENTS

PREFACE

Economics, Mathematically Speaking is intended primarily (though not exclusively) for students taking a course in principles of economics. It translates the economic theory found in the first course in economics into the language of mathematics.

A growing number of instructors in the principles course prefer to teach the principles of economics mathematically. Until now there has been no book suitable for students who had not completed a course in calculus.

Students who use *Economics, Mathematically Speaking* are not expected to have gone beyond a course in college algebra. Students who have finished the first course in calculus, however, will find this book valuable because it utilizes the mathematics learned in calculus courses to teach the principles of economics. The mathematics in this volume is limited to that needed to translate into simple mathematics the economic theory found in such introductory economics texts as Campbell R. McConnell's *Economics: Principles, Problems, and Policies*.

No mathematics is taught in this book for its own sake. Students are not presumed to be especially proficient in mathematics. The mathematics the student needs to understand economics is presented with or just before its application. This text differs from other first books in mathematical economics in that the necessary mathematics is not taught in its entirety prior to the economics.

The topics chosen for inclusion are those found in most on principles of economics textbooks. Subjects which do not lend themselves to mathematical treatment are, of course, omitted. Each topic is generally presented first in terms of the mathematics alone: letters rather than numbers are used. Then the student is given numerical examples: numbers rather than letters are used. Finally, a set of exercises (there are 46 in the book) involving both the mathematics and numerical applications is given so that the student may test and reinforce his understanding of the topic. The exercises are placed at convenient points within each chapter; answers will be found at the end of the book.

While meant mainly for students in principles of economics courses, this book may also be used by students in the junior-senior level courses in economic theory and even by students taking graduate courses in theory. It may be used to supplement any of a number of different principles of economics texts and texts in microeconomic and macroeconomic theory.

Being self-taught in mathematics, the author feels that the student will find, as he has done, that the following books are helpful to anyone wanting to go beyond the elementary mathematical economics found in these pages.

Clark Lee Allen: *Elementary Mathematics of Price Theory* (Belmont, Calif.: Wadsworth Publishing Company, Inc., 1962).

Clark Lee Allen: *The Framework of Price Theory* (Belmont, Calif.: Wadsworth Publishing Company, Inc., 1967).

R. G. D. Allen: *Mathematical Analysis for Economists* (London: Macmillan & Co., rev. ed., 1962).

W. L. Crum and Joseph Al Schumpeter: *Rudimentary Mathematics for Economists and Statisticians* (New York: McGraw-Hill Book Company, 1946).

Daniel Kleppner and Norman Ramsey: *Quick Calculus* (New York: John Wiley & Sons, Inc., 1965).

Silvanus P. Thompson: *Calculus Made Easy* (London: Macmillan & Co., 3d ed., 1945).

The author's debt to these books and their authors is great. He also recognizes his indebtedness to the colleagues whose brains he picked: Richard Bennett, Randall Mount, Harold Williams, and Henry Woudenberg, all of Kent State University. From Campbell McConnell came the suggestion that this book be written and faith in the author's ability to do it. But without John Huffnagle of Kent State University, who checked the mathematics at every step of the way, this book could not have been completed.

Robert C. Bingham

MATHEMATICALLY SPEAKING

INTRODUCTION

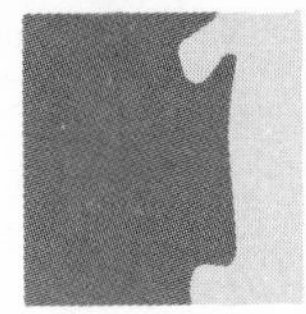

ECONOMICS AND MATHEMATICS

MATHEMATICS AS A LANGUAGE

A large part of economics deals with things that can (or might be) measured. Economics examines such things as price, cost, production, consumption, income, employment, wages, the interest rate, and so forth. All these are measurable.[1] The *relations* between these measurable things also concern economists. Economics is interested in such relations as that between the price of a commodity and the consumption of that commodity, that between the production of a good and the cost of producing it, and that between the wage rate of workers and the number of workers who find employment.

When an economist examines the relations between things that are measurable, he enters the world of mathematics: the world of geometry, algebra, and the other branches of mathematics. Instead of talking of "things that are measurable," economists speak of *quantities, magnitudes, variables,* and *parameters*. And instead of speaking of relations, they speak of *equations, functions, identities,* and *inequalities*.

The language of mathematics is different from the language used in ordinary conversation, but economists who use mathematics look at the same things as the economists who do not. Using mathematics does not change the subject matter of economics. Whether mathematics is used or not, the things economists study remain the same.

[1] While economics deals with measurable things, many of them have not actually been measured (and probably never will be). *Econometrics* is the branch of economics that measures the size of things.

The difference between economists who use mathematics and those who do not is simply a difference in approach, a difference in the tools and the kinds of symbols used. Those who use no mathematics (and they are very rare) are often called *verbal* or *literary* economists because the symbols they employ are words. Mathematical economists and mathematical economics use a different set of symbols: numbers, letters of the alphabet that stand for numbers, and the special symbols employed by mathematicians, for example, $+$, $-$, and $=$. Each symbol has a verbal counterpart or equivalent. The symbol $=$ means, in words, "is equal to." Many of the words employed by the literary economist have a mathematical equivalent. The relationship "is greater than" can be expressed by the sign $>$. In short, the difference between the mathematical and the nonmathematical economist is the language or symbols employed to express relations between measurable things.

The purpose of this book

The purpose of this book is not to teach you mathematics so that you can learn economics. This book relies primarily upon the mathematics you already know to teach that part of economics which can be taught in the language of mathematics. Its purpose is to translate the economics taught with words in textbooks and courses on the principles of economics into the relatively simple mathematics taught in high school or first-year college algebra courses.

Along the way you will learn some more mathematics, but this book will introduce additional mathematics only when it is to be put to immediate use, i.e., only when it is needed to understand some essential part of economics. Learning this additional mathematics will be worth the effort because the trouble is slight and the benefits are great. In the language of the economist, the benefits outweigh the costs.

The purpose of this first chapter

The literary economist expresses economics in words, sentences, and paragraphs. The mathematical economist expresses economics in variables and parameters, equations and inequalities, and models or systems of equations.

In this first chapter we review some of the mathematics you already know and define the fundamental terms to be used throughout this book. In the section that follows we look at variables and equations and examine the different kinds of equations used in this book. The last section shows how two or more equations can constitute an *economic model* and how an economic model determines the sizes economically measurable things take on.

VARIABLES AND EQUATIONS

In that part of economics which can be studied with the use of mathematics, the concepts of a variable and an equation are basic. For this reason, we examine both these concepts and several closely related ones in some detail. This examination (it turns out) is a review of some of the fundamentals of algebra.

Variables

As we noted earlier, much of economics deals with things we can (or, at least, might be able to) measure. For example, we can measure the price of a commodity, the output of an industry, or the number of employed workers in a nation. When we discuss price, output, or workers, these measurements are given various names—the *magnitude*, the *value*, or the *size* of the thing measured. We shall use all these terms to mean the same thing. Later we shall call these magnitudes or values by more specific names such as price, output, and employment.

A *variable* is any magnitude that is capable of changing or varying. The price of a commodity is variable if it can rise or fall and is not fixed in some way. If the output of an industry can increase or decrease, it is a variable; or if the number of employed workers in the economy can expand or contract, the level of employment is a variable. To say that these are variables does not mean that they will or must change but only that they can change. A variable, in short, is any magnitude or measurement which may vary.

The symbols for variables Following the practice of mathematicians, economists use letters of the alphabet to represent the different values an economic variable may have. If the price of some commodity is variable, the letter P, say, may be used to symbolize the different possible prices of this commodity. The letter P does not stand for any particular price ($15 or $1.98) but for *all possible* prices of this commodity. Often another letter written below (called a *subscript*) is added to the symbol for a variable to make the meaning clearer. For example, when there are two commodities, X and Y, we might use the symbols P_X and P_Y to mean the price of commodity X and the price of commodity Y, respectively.

A special symbol is the Greek capital letter delta, Δ. This symbol has a simple meaning. Delta, in words, means "a small change in." As a symbol, delta never appears alone but is always followed by some other symbol. What follows may be either a letter representing a variable or a letter representing some other kind of measurable magnitude. Thus, if P stands for the variable price of some commodity, then ΔP means "a small change in the price" of that commodity; or when N stands for the level of employment in the economy, ΔN means "a small change in the level of employment in the economy."

Just as a variable is a measurable magnitude, a change in the magnitude of a variable is also measurable; for example, if we can say the price of a certain commodity is so many dollars and cents, then we can also say that a change in the price of this commodity is so many dollars and cents. If it is possible for the price of this commodity to be either $4 or $5, this price may either increase from $4 to $5 or decrease from $5 to $4. If this price increases from $4 to $5, the change in price or ΔP is +$1; if it decreases from $5 to $4, the change in price is −$1.

Because ΔP stands for a measurable magnitude in exactly the same way that P stands for a measurable magnitude, we can add and subtract it and multiply and divide by it. We can also square it or take its square roots. Since both P and ΔP are expressed in numbers and represent numbers, we can do everything with them that we can do with numbers.

All we need remember at this point is that delta is a symbol meaning a small change in the value or magnitude of the symbol that follows it and that a change in the value or magnitude of a measurable thing is also measurable. Throughout this book we shall be much concerned with small changes in the values of measurable things: the delta symbol will represent a small change in such values.

Very few of the magnitudes with which economics is concerned are incapable of changing. It is difficult—perhaps impossible—to think of an economic magnitude that cannot change, and it would seem that there is no such thing in economics as a magnitude incapable of changing. Later in this chapter we shall point out that those magnitudes which we *assume* to remain unchanged are either *parameters* or *exogenous variables* (terms which we subsequently define).

In economics one frequently encounters the expression *ceteris paribus*. This Latin phrase means literally "other things being equal." An an expression, *ceteris parabus* means that the magnitude of all other variables is assumed to be constant. It is a short way of saying that the values of the variables other than those being discussed or examined are assumed to remain unchanged, i.e., we assume that other magnitudes are constant.

Equations

An equation is a statement that something is equal to something else. Each of the following is a simple equation:

$$S = Y - C$$
$$C = a + bY$$
$$S = I$$

These three equations have several characteristics in common. They all contain the symbol $=$, which means, in words, "is equal to" or "equals." Without this symbol we do not have an equation.

Each of the three equations have something to the left and something to the right of the equals sign. The something to the left we call the *left side* (or the left member) of the equation, and the something to the right we call the *right side* (or member). Such equations as

$$S - I = 0$$
$$0 = R - C$$

also have right and left sides, but the something on one side is zero.

The somethings that appear on the two sides of an equation are made up of variables and parameters. They are also made up of one or more terms. *Terms* we define as those parts of the right and left sides of an equation which are separated by plus or minus signs. In the equation $S = Y - C$, there is one term, S, on the left side and two terms, Y and C, on the right side. The equation $C = a + bY$ has one term, C, on the left side and two terms, a and bY, on the right side. It should be noted that bY is a single term because b and Y are not separated by a plus or a minus sign. The term bY means b times Y (or b multiplied by Y). Likewise, Y/S is a single term because it means Y divided by S.

A variable, we know, is a magnitude that is capable of changing. A *parameter* is a magnitude which is assumed to remain constant or unchanged. It is customary in mathematics to use letters from the beginning of the alphabet to indicate parameters. Letters such as *a, b, c,* and *d* usually indicate that a magnitude is a parameter. Letters from the end of the alphabet often indicate the magnitude is a variable. *X* and *Y* are usually variables. It is important to realize, however, that there are no real rules here. A particular letter may serve as either a variable or a parameter, or it may have some other meaning. To determine whether a particular letter is a parameter, a variable, or something else, it is necessary to consult the nonmathematical language accompanying the equation. The careful economist employing mathematics will tell you in words whether a particular letter is a parameter, a variable, or a *functional notation* (which we shall examine below).

An equation, then, is a collection of variables and parameters separated by an equals sign. If we let *capital* letters indicate variables and *lowercase* letters indicate parameters, the equation $S = I$ contains two variables and no parameters. The equation $S = Y - C$ has three variables and no parameters. $C = a + bY$ has two variables and two parameters. In the equations in which zero appears, zero is a parameter.

Kinds of equations

The equations employed in economics fall into one of three categories: (1) functional (or behavioral) equations, (2) definitional (or identity) equations, and (3) equilibrium equations. Simply looking at an equation is seldom enough to tell us which kind it is. Determining the kind of equation usually depends upon a verbal explanation.

Functional equation When the magnitude of one variable depends in some way upon the magnitude of another variable (or other variables), the variables are functionally related. The equation that tells us *how* one variable depends upon others is a functional equation. This kind of equation is also called a *behavioral* equation because the behavior of one variable (how it varies) depends upon the magnitudes of the other variable or variables.

Often we know enough to be able to say that one variable depends *in some way* upon the value of another variable, but we do not want to be or cannot be specific about how one depends upon the other. If, for example, the magnitude of *C* depends in some way upon the magnitude of *Y*, we write

$$C = f(Y)$$

In this equation *f* is neither a variable nor a parameter. It is a *functional notation* and means "is a function of" or "depends in some way upon." One should read this equation as "*C* is a function of *Y*" or "*C* depends upon *Y*." Other letters frequently used to indicate a functional or behavioral relation between variables are the Roman letters *F*, *g*, and *h*, and the Greek letters ϕ (phi) and ψ (psi). Any letter, in fact, may be employed to indicate a functional relationship. We might write $C = C(Y)$. The *C* on the left side is a variable, but the *C* on the right side is a functional notation. But because of the confusion it might cause, this book never uses the same symbol for both a variable and a functional notation.

To write $C = f(Y)$ does not mean that *C* depends solely upon the value of

Y. It does mean that Y is the *only variable* upon which C depends. The magnitude of C also depends upon the magnitude of the parameters in the equation. If, for example,

$$C = a + bY$$

the magnitude of C is related to the magnitude of the parameters a and b as well as to the magnitude of the variable Y. If we are more specific and say that

$$C = 10 + 0.8Y$$

then for any value we assign to Y, we can determine the value of C. And if

$$C = 10 + 0.8Y$$

or

$$0.8Y = C - 10$$

then dividing this last equation through by 0.8 gives

$$Y = \frac{C - 10}{0.8}$$

For any value we assign to C, we can now determine the value of Y. Table 1-1 indicates some of the values of C and Y that "go together."

Note that we do not necessarily assume that the value of Y is the *cause* of the value of C. It may or it may not be. C may be the cause of Y. To say that two variables are functionally related (or to say that one variable is a function of another) implies nothing about which variable is cause and which is effect.

We may wish to change the assumed value of one or more of the *parameters* in a functional equation. For example, if the equation

$$C = 10 + 0.8Y$$

changes to

$$C = 10 + 0.75Y$$

or to

$$C = 15 + 0.8Y$$

or to

$$C = 15 + 0.75Y$$

then the relation between C and Y has changed. Because a change in the assumed values of the parameters has taken place, this kind of change is called

TABLE 1-1

C	Y
50	50
90	100
170	200
330	400

a *parametric shift* or a *parametric change*. In our example, the magnitude of C associated with any particular value of Y is no longer the same; the magnitude of Y associated with any particular value of C is different from what it was

Definitional equation Not all equations are functional equations. Some are definitional (or identity) equations. If we define a firm's profit π as its revenue R less its cost C, we can write

$$\pi = R - C$$

In this book we shall indicate a definitional equation by using the identity sign $\equiv$ instead of the equality sign $=$. We therefore write the equation above as

$$\pi \equiv R - C$$

which says that the firm's profit is *defined* as being equal to its revenue minus its costs.

It is true that a firm's profit depends upon the magnitude of its revenue and the magnitude of its costs. This does not mean, however, that this is a functional equation. A definitional equation is a statement that the right and left sides of the equation are equal by definition. It is a statement that cannot be untrue. No matter what a firm's revenue and costs are, its profit is always equal to revenue minus costs. The definition of profit is true for *all* possible values of R and C.

A functional equation, on the other hand, is not true for all possible values of the variables. The right and left sides of the equation are equal only when the variables have *particular* values. If, for example, the functional equation is

$$C = 10 + 0.8Y$$

the right and left sides of the equation are equal only when C and Y are both 50, Y is 100 and C is 90, Y is 200 and C is 170, Y is 400 and C is 330, etc. The two sides of the equation are not equal when Y is 50 and C is 40, when Y is 110 and C is 90, when Y is 200 and C is 180, and so on.

Often it is not clear whether a particular equation is functional or definitional. It is for this reason that we use the identity sign to indicate that an equation is a definition.

Equilibrium equation The third kind of equation used in economics, the equilibrium equation, enables us to determine what the magnitudes of particular variables will be. With the equation

$$C = 10 + 0.8Y$$

we can determine how much C will be *if* we know Y or how much Y will be *if* we know C. But to determine *both* C and Y we need another equation. The equilibrium equation tells us the condition that must prevail before we can determine what the magnitude of each variable will be.

If with equation $C = 10 + 0.8Y$ we have a statement that the values of C and Y must be equal, we can write the equilibrium equation

$$C = Y$$

Now we can determine what *both* C and Y will be in the following way. For C

in the equation $C = 10 + 0.8Y$ we can substitute Y because the equilibrium equation tells us that Y must equal C. We now have the equation $Y = 10 + 0.8Y$. Subtracting $0.8Y$ from both sides of this equation leaves

$$Y - 0.8Y = 10 + 0.8Y - 0.8Y$$

or

$$0.2Y = 10$$

Dividing both sides of this equation by 0.2, we have

$$\frac{0.2Y}{0.2} = \frac{10}{0.2}$$

or

$$Y = 50$$

This value of Y we can then substitute into the equation $C = 10 + 0.8Y$ to find that

$$\begin{aligned} C &= 10 + 0.8(50) \\ &= 10 + 40 \\ &= 50 \end{aligned}$$

We might also substitute 50 for Y in the equilibrium equation ($C = Y$) to find C equal to 50.[2]

Exercise 1-1

1 A magnitude that is capable of changing is called a ____________

2 The symbol used for a variable represents the different possible ________ of the variable.

3 The symbol Δ means ______________________________

a Thus ΔR means a ____________ in ____________

b If R increases from 0.20 to 0.30, ΔR will equal ____________

c If R decreases from 0.15 to 0.10, ΔR will equal ____________

4 To express the idea that the magnitudes of all variables except W and Z are assumed to remain unchanged we might use the expression ____________

5 An equation is a statement that something is ____________ something else.

a The something on the left side of an equation is called the left ____________ or ____________, and the something on the right side is called the ____________ or ____________

[2] The curious student may be interested in knowing why this third kind of equation is called an *equilibrium* equation. The dictionary definition of the term equilibrium means a state of balance between opposing forces. In economics this means that the forces that would increase the value of a variable balance or equal the forces that decrease the value of that variable. Equilibrium, therefore, is achieved when the value of a variable shows no tendency either to rise or to fall. (Disequilibrium is a state of *im*balance between opposing forces and in economics means that the forces increasing the value of a variable do *not* balance or equal the forces decreasing the value of the variable. When the value of a variable shows a tendency to rise or to fall, there is *dis*equilibrium.) The values that concern us in economics are the values of variables when there is equilibrium. The equilibrium equation tells us what the values of these variables will be when they show no tendency to rise or to fall.

b Each side of an equation contains one or more ____________, each of which is made up of one or more ____________ and ____________

c A term contains variables and parameters not separated by ____________ or ____________ signs

6 The three kinds of equations used in economics are:

a ____________, or ____________, equations

b ____________, or ____________, equations

c ____________ equations

7 When a functional equation is:

a $W = f(Z)$

(1) We say in words that W is a ____________ of Z.

(2) The letter f is a ____________

(3) If the value of either variable changes, the value of the other variable will ____________

b $W = 20 + 0.5Z$

(1) If Z is equal to 100, $W =$ ____________

(2) If W is equal to 60, $Z =$ ____________

(3) If Z is equal to 0, $W =$ ____________

(4) If W is zero, $Z =$ ____________

(5) If the values of the two parameters are changed there will be a parametric ____________ or ____________

8 To indicate that the two sides of an equation are equal by definition, the symbol ____________ is employed. This kind of equation is called a ____________ or ____________ equation.

9 An equilibrium equation is the equation that enables us to find or determine ____

10 Suppose that a functional equation is $W = 20 + 0.5Z$ and that the equilibrium equation is $Z = 3W$. The actual value of W will be ____________, and the actual value of Z will be ____________

Inequalities

Some of the statements we wish to make cannot be expressed in equations. We cannot express the idea that Robert is taller than William in an equation. The verbal term "is greater than" is not expressed by an equals sign but by the symbol $>$. If we wish to say that Robert's height R is greater than William's height W, we can write

$$R > W$$

This inequality statement also implies that W is less than R. When we wish to say more explicitly that W is less than R, we write

$$W < R$$

where the symbol $<$ means "is less than." (It also implies that R is greater than W.)

Often in economics we want to say that one thing is *either* greater than *or* equal to something else. When we wish to say that X is greater than or equal to Y, we write $X \geqq Y$

To say that X is *either* less than *or* equal to Y, we write

$$X \leqq Y$$

Occasionally we want to say that X may be greater than, or less than, or equal to Y. We would make this statement by writing

$$X \gtreqqless Y$$

When two or more symbols such as $<$, $>$, or $=$ separate two somethings, the word "or" is understood to stand between the symbols.

Linear and nonlinear equations

The functional equations we employ in economics[3] can be divided into two groups, linear and nonlinear equations. A *linear* equation is an equation in which the greatest exponent (or power) of any variable in the equation is 1 *and* the variables are not multiplied by each other. All equations that do not fit these two requirements are nonlinear equations. A *nonlinear* equation is an equation in which a variable with an exponent (or power) greater than 1 appears *or* variables with exponents of 1 are multiplied by each other. Linear equations are also called *first-degree* equations because the largest exponent of any variable is 1. Nonlinear equations are second-, third-, fourth-, and higher-degree equations.

The following is an example of a first-degree equation:

$$Y = a + bX$$

but each of

$$Y = a + bX^2$$
$$XY = c$$

is a nonlinear equation. These are both second-degree equations. $Y = a + bX^2$ is a second-degree equation because the greatest exponent appearing is 2. $XY = c$ is a second-degree equation because the *sum* of the exponents of the two variables, X and Y, is 2. Equations such as

$$Y = a - y^3$$
$$XY^2 = c$$

are third-degree equations for similar reasons.

Because the functional equations used in the first part of this book are linear, or first-degree, equations, it is worth examining the characteristics of a linear equation.

The linear equation A linear equation is the following kind of equation:

$$Y = a + bX$$

[3] In this book we shall employ only algebraic functions and not concern ourselves with the transcendental functions found in trigonometry.

The variables are Y and X, and the parameters are a and b. The parameters may be positive, zero, or negative; or in the language of mathematics

$$a \gtreqless 0$$

$$b \gtreqless 0$$

When b is negative we shall write this equation as

$$Y = a - bX$$

and when a is negative, we shall indicate it by placing a minus sign in front, as

$$Y = -a + bX$$

With both a and b negative, the linear equation is

$$Y = -a - bX$$

When a is equal to zero, we write

$$Y = bX$$

or

$$Y = -bX$$

If b is zero, we have

$$Y = a$$

or

$$Y = -a$$

The values of a and b in the linear equation, then, *are their absolute values,* their values of magnitudes without regard to their sign.

We should note that the linear equation has two terms, the term equal to the parameter a and the term equal to the parameter b multiplied by the variable X. Either of these terms may equal zero.

The first-degree equation is called a linear equation or function because when it is plotted on a graph the curve that results is a straight line, or linear. It is customary (though not necessary) to plot the variable appearing on the left side of an equation on the vertical axis (called the *ordinate*) and to plot the variable from the right side on the horizontal axis (called the *abscissa*). When we plot the linear equation

$$Y = 20 + 0.8X$$

we obtain the curve shown in Fig. 1-1. In this example the parameter a is equal to 20, and the parameter b is equal to 0.8. We should observe that the constant term (the a term) in the linear equation is the value which Y would have *if X were zero.* [If X were zero, Y would equal $20 + 0.8[0]$ or $20 + 0$.] Graphically, the constant term is the point at which the curve crosses or intersects the Y axis. In our example Y is 20 when X is zero, and the curve crosses the Y axis at 20.

The parameter b in a first-degree equation is equal to the slope (or steepness) of the curve. The slope of any curve is equal to the distance we move up or down as we move along the curve *divided by* the distance we move to the right

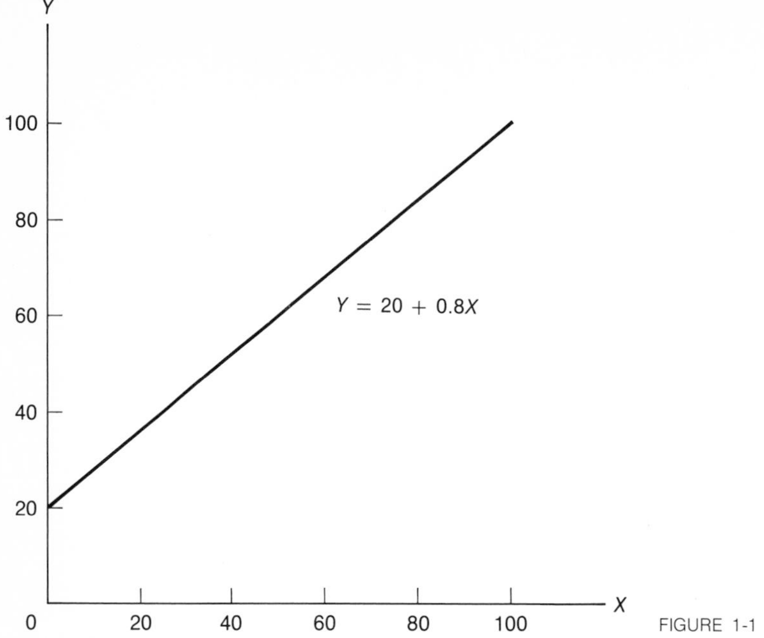

FIGURE 1-1

or to the left in moving along the curve. With Y measured on the vertical (or up-and-down) axis and X measured on the horizontal (or left-and-right) axis, the slope of the curve is equal to the change in Y divided by the change in X. Recalling that we use the symbol Δ to mean "a small change in," the slope of the curve is equal to $\Delta Y/\Delta X$.

When we have a linear equation of the form

$$Y = a + bX$$

and X changes by an amount equal to ΔX, Y changes by an amount equal to ΔY. Because Y depends upon X, when X changes by ΔX to become $X + \Delta X$, Y will change by ΔY to become $Y + \Delta Y$. In symbols we write

$$Y + \Delta Y = a + b(X + \Delta X)$$

or

$$Y + \Delta Y = a + bX + b\,\Delta X$$

From this last equation we can subtract the equation $Y = a + bX$. When we subtract one equation from another, we usually subtract the left side of one equation from the left side of the other and the right side of one from the right side of the other equation. Therefore to subtract the equation $Y = a + bX$ from the equation $Y + \Delta Y = a + bX + b\,\Delta X$, we subtract Y from $Y + \Delta Y$ to obtain ΔY and we subtract $a + bX$ from $a + bX + b\,\Delta X$ to obtain $b\,\Delta X$. Because we have subtracted equals from equals, the differences are also equal, and we can write

$$\Delta Y = b\,\Delta X$$

Now if we divide both sides by ΔX, we have

$$\frac{\Delta Y}{\Delta X} = b$$

$\Delta Y/\Delta X$ is the slope of the curve, and in a linear equation $\Delta Y/\Delta X$ is equal to b. The slope of the curve, therefore, is equal to the parameter b in the equation for a linear function.

Most but not all of the variables we deal with in economics have only positive magnitudes—magnitudes which may be zero or greater. Economics does not concern itself with negative employment, negative output, negative prices, negative wage rates, etc. Some of the variables in economics, however, may take on negative values. Total saving in the economy, for example, may be less than zero. In this case we might have a linear function such as

$$S = -a + bX$$

an example of which would be

$$S = -10 + 0.4X$$

This equation is graphed in Fig. 1-2. Notice that the vertical (or S) axis intercept is -10 because the parameter a has a negative value of 10. Because b is 0.4 in this example, the slope of the curve is 0.4.

In both these examples of linear functions the parameter b was preceded by a plus sign. Both these functions are *increasing* functions: when the magnitude of one variable increases, the magnitude of the other variable also increases; and if one variable decreases, the other variable decreases. The two variables increase and decrease together. Put another way, the two variables are *directly* related. In addition, both of the curves we drew had a *positive* slope: as we move from left to right along either curve, we also move upward.

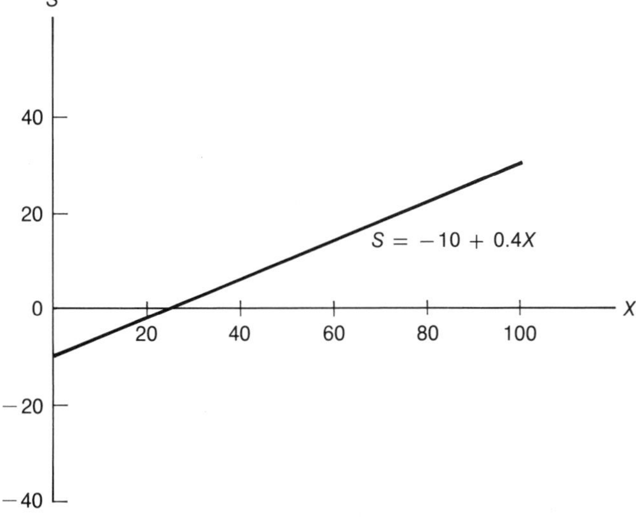

FIGURE 1-2

Not all linear functions in economics are increasing functions. Many are *decreasing* functions: as one variable increases, the other variable decreases (and as one decreases, the other increases). The two variables are *inversely* related. The following equation, in which L and R are variables, is a decreasing function:

$$L = j - kR$$

The second term on the right side is preceded by a minus sign, and when R increases, L will decrease (and when R decreases, L will increase). This can be seen if we let R change by ΔR to become $R + \Delta R$. L will then change by ΔL to become $L + \Delta L$. We can write

$$L + \Delta L = j - k(R + \Delta R)$$

or

$$L + \Delta L = j - kR - k\,\Delta R$$

From this equation we can subtract the equation $L = j - kR$ to find

$$\Delta L = -k\,\Delta R$$

And if we divide through by ΔR, we are left with

$$\frac{\Delta L}{\Delta R} = -k$$

This last equation tells us that $\Delta L/\Delta R$ is negative, which means that the relation between L and R is an inverse one. And because $\Delta L/\Delta R$ is the slope of the graph of this function, we know that the graph of the function has a *negative* slope. When j equals 10 and k equals 3, this function is

$$L = 10 - 3R$$

We have plotted this function in Fig. 1-3. Because the term containing the variable on the right side is preceded by a minus sign, the graph of this function has a negative slope: as we move from left to right, the curve slopes downward.

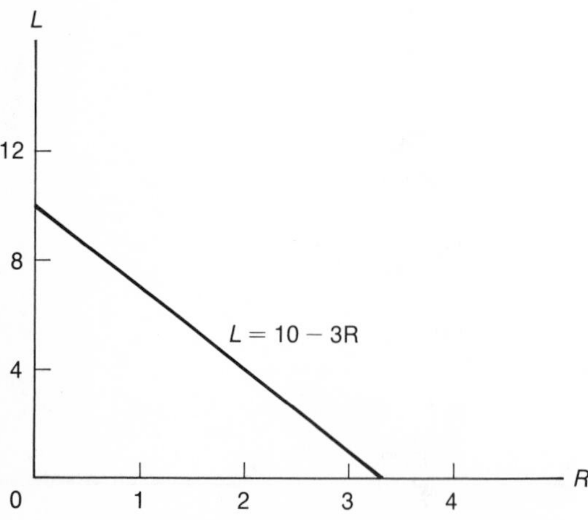

FIGURE 1-3

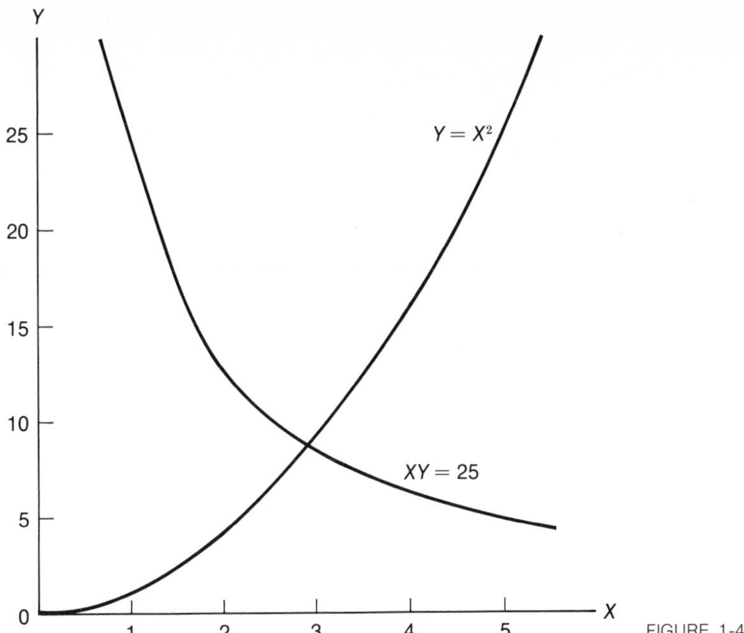

FIGURE 1-4

Nonlinear equations Not all equations in economics are linear equations. The relations between some economic variables can be faithfully described only by nonlinear equations. Equations of a degree greater than 1 are nonlinear because the graphs of these equations do not result in straight lines.

Graphs of the two nonlinear second-degree equations

$$Y = X^2$$
$$XY = 25$$

appear in Fig. 1-4. We can observe again that neither equation results in a straight line. Both curves are nonlinear, or curvilinear. The first equation shows (where X is positive) a direct relation between X and Y: when X increases, Y also increases (and vice versa). The second equation, on the other hand, indicates an inverse relation between the two variables: when X increases, Y decreases (and vice versa).

In the first part of this book we use only linear equations. In the latter part, however, we need second- and third-degree equations. As we encounter these nonlinear equations, we shall define the slope of the graph of a nonlinear function.

Functions with more than two variables

Just as not all behavioral equations are linear, not all equations contain just two variables. We have already seen a definitional equation such as

$$S \equiv Y - C$$

which contains three variables, S, Y, and C. We might also have a functional equation such as

$$L = j - kR + cY$$

containing three variables, L, R, and Y, and three parameters, j, k, and c. We shall have little difficulty with either functional or definitional equations with three or more variables and need not be concerned with how to graph them.

Exercise 1-2

1 When we wish to express the idea that:

a W is less than Z, we write W __________ Z.

b W is greater than Z, we write W __________ Z.

c W is greater than or equal to Z, we write W __________ Z.

d W is less than or equal to Z, we write W __________ Z.

2 A linear equation is also called a __________-degree equation. Such an equation is defined as ______________________________

3 An equation in which a variable with an exponent of 2 appears or in which two variables, each with an exponent of 1, are multiplied by each other is a __________ equation. If we graph such an equation, we obtain a curve that is __________ or __________

4 Indicate the degree of each of the following equations:

a $\frac{Z - W}{5} = 30$

b $\frac{Z}{5W} = -30$

c $-W = -50 + 3Z$

d $W = 50 + 3Z^2$

e $W = 50^2 - 2Z$

5 The equation $W = c + eZ$ is a linear equation in which the variables are W and Z.

a The parameter c is the value of W when Z is equal to __________

b The parameter c, graphically, is the point at which the graph of the equation crosses the __________ axis.

c The parameter e, graphically, is the __________ of the curve of this equation when it is plotted on a graph.

d Show that $\Delta W/\Delta Z$ is equal to the parameter e.

6 Suppose that $U = -100 + 0.6T$.

a When T is zero, $U =$ __________

b If U equals zero, T is equal to __________

c The ratio $\Delta U/\Delta T$ is equal to __________

d When we graph this equation:

(1) -100 is ______

(2) 0.6 is ______

7 If:

a $W = c + eZ$:

(1) $W + \Delta W =$ ______

(2) $\Delta W =$ ______

(3) $\Delta W/\Delta Z =$ ______

b $P = g - hQ$:

(1) $P + \Delta P =$ ______

(2) $\Delta P =$ ______

(3) $\Delta P/\Delta Q =$ ______

c $U = -100 + 0.6T$:

(1) $U + \Delta U =$ ______

(2) $\Delta U =$ ______

(3) $\Delta U/\Delta T =$ ______

d $S = 150 - 3V$:

(1) $S + \Delta S =$ ______

(2) $\Delta S =$ ______

(3) $\Delta S/\Delta V =$ ______

8 Plot each of the following equations on the accompanying graph.

a $U = -100 + 0.5T$

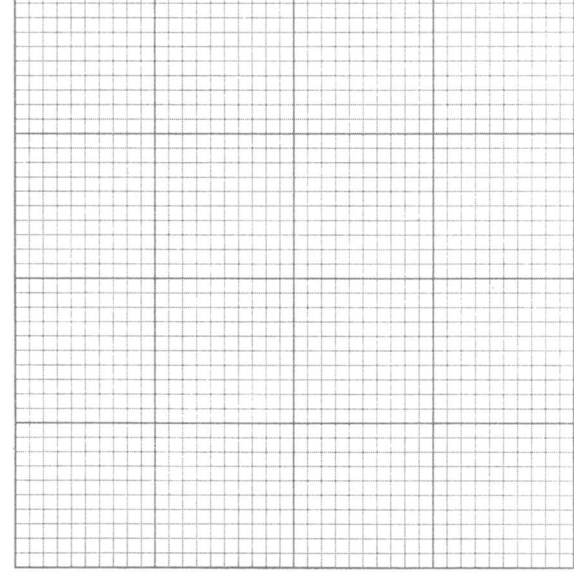

b $U = 75 + 0.6T$

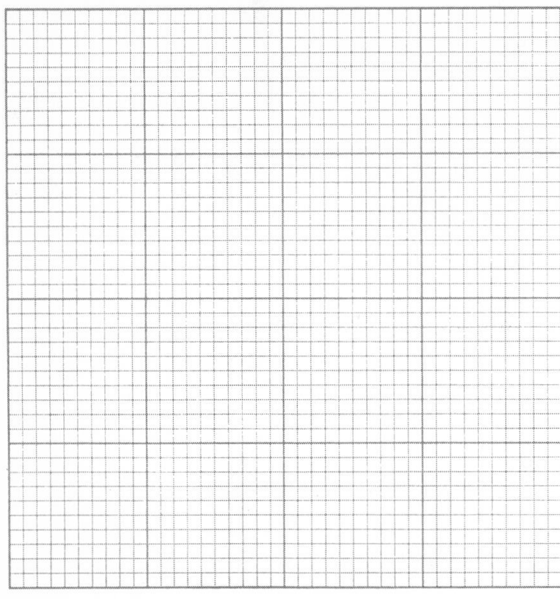

c $U = 80 - 0.3T$

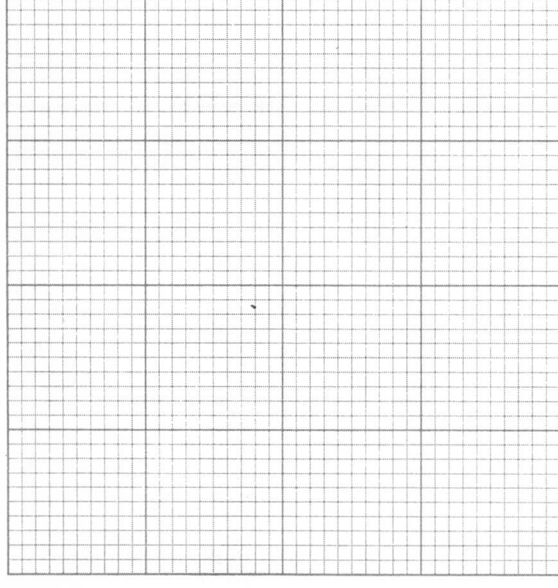

d $U = -10 - 0.2T$

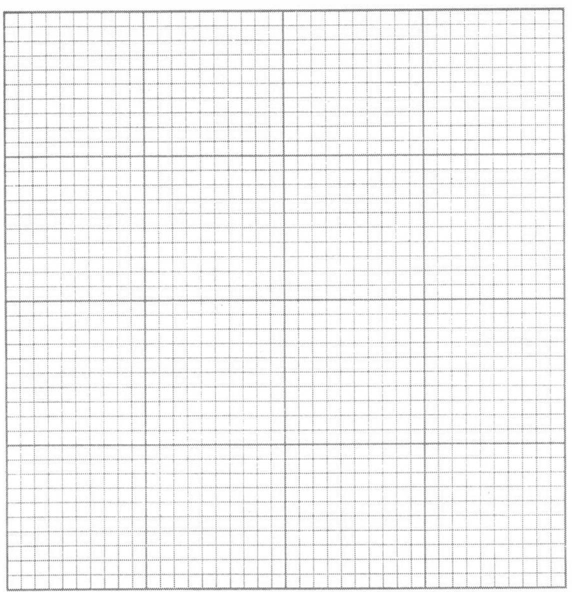

9 Using the four equations in question 8:

a Which of these equations are increasing functions? ____________

b Indicate in the table the value of U when T is zero and the value of $\Delta U/\Delta T$ for each equation.

EQUATION	WHEN $T = 0$, $U =$	$\frac{\Delta U}{\Delta T} =$
$U = -100 + 0.5T$	____________	____________
$U = 75 + 0.6T$	____________	____________
$U = 80 - 0.3T$	____________	____________
$U = -10 - 0.2T$	____________	____________

ECONOMIC MODELS

We have examined equations in detail because an economic model or theory is a collection of equations. Such a collection is also called a *system* of equations. The simplest kind of model contains a single equation. Very few economic models contain only one equation; most of our models will have two, three, or more equations. Some economic models contain more than 500 equations!

Regardless of the number of equations making up an economic model, no model or system of equations is ever completely realistic. Even models with more than 500 equations are abstractions—simplifications of reality. To present reality completely such a model would require millions of equations and would be too complex to be useful. Therefore the models we employ in economics, including those with hundreds of equations, are all simplifications of the world we actually live in. They do not and cannot explain the values of all variables in an economy.

For this reason, most models concern themselves with a limited number of variables. The magnitudes of those variables which do not appear in the equations making up any model are assumed to remain unchanged, i.e., constant. This assumption of constancy is summed up by the phrase *ceteris paribus*. The variables that appear in the equations of any model fall into two categories, *endogenous* variables and *exogenous* variables.

Endogenous and exogenous variables

Variables whose magnitudes are determined by the model are *endogenous* variables; those whose magnitudes are *not* determined by the model are *exogenous* variables.

Exogenous variables are not the same as parameters. A parameter is a magnitude which is assumed to be constant. An exogenous variable *is* a variable. It is not constant, and it may vary. But a model containing exogenous variables does not determine or explain what the magnitudes of the exogenous variables will be. As with a parameter, it is necessary to know the magnitudes of the exogenous variables in order to determine the values of the endogenous variables in the model.

Because it is necessary to know the magnitudes of the exogenous variables to determine the magnitudes of the endogenous variables, the values of the exogenous variables are often *assumed* to be *given*. Then the values of the endogenous variables can be determined. This does not mean that the values of the exogenous variables are assumed to be constant. All that is assumed is that the exogenous variables can vary, that the model does not tell us what their values will be, and that if they vary, the values of the endogenous variables will also vary. The values of the endogenous variables will be different if the values of the exogenous variables change. Therefore we can work out the magnitudes of the endogenous variables only by assigning some given values to the exogenous variables. In this book we shall indicate that a variable is exogenous by placing a bar over the symbol for that variable. Thus, if a variable, say I, is exogenous, it will appear in the equations as $\bar{I}$.

Closed economic models

To determine the magnitude of all the variables, exogenous and endogenous, in an economic model requires that there be as many equations as there are variables. A model in which the number of equations and the number of variables are equal is termed a *closed* model or system. In order to find the magnitudes of all the variables in the model, not only must there be an equal number of variables and equations but the equations must also be both different and consistent.

To say that they must be *different* means that no two equations say the same thing. For example, the two equations

$$Z = X + Y$$
$$Y = Z - X$$

say exactly the same thing: the first equation can be converted to the second, and the second can be converted to the first. If we subtract X from both sides of the first equation we have

$$Z - X = X + Y - X$$

or

$$Z - X = Y$$

which is precisely what the second equation says. And if we add X to both sides of the second equation, we have

$$Y + X = Z - X + X$$

or

$$Y + X = Z$$

which is just what the first equation says.

To say that the equations must be *consistent* means that no one equation contradicts or is inconsistent with any other equation. For example, if we have

$$X = Y + 3$$
$$Y = X - 2$$

we have two contradictory or inconsistent equations. To see that they are inconsistent, add 2 to both sides of the second equation to obtain

$$\begin{aligned} Y + 2 &= X - 2 + 2 \\ &= X \end{aligned}$$

The second equation says that $X = Y + 2$, but the first says that $X = Y + 3$. X may equal either $Y + 2$ or $Y + 3$, but it cannot equal both. Shown another way, if we substitute $X - 2$ (from the second equation) for Y in the first equation we have

$$\begin{aligned} X &= (X - 2) + 3 \\ &= X - 2 + 3 \\ &= X + 1 \end{aligned}$$

This, of course, is impossible. For if we now subtract X from both sides of this last equation we are left with

$$0 = 1$$

To determine the magnitude of all variables in an economic model there must be, in short, an equal number of *different* and *consistent* equations

As an example of a closed system we might have the following set of equations:

$$C = a + bY \qquad (1\text{-}1)$$
$$S \equiv Y - C \qquad (1\text{-}2)$$
$$S = I \qquad (1\text{-}3)$$
$$I = \bar{I} \qquad (1\text{-}4)$$

There are in this system four different equations. There are also six different symbols, C, a, b, Y, S, and I. The lowercase letters, a and b, are parameters. The variables in the model, then, are C, Y, S, and I. The fourth equation indicates that I is an exogenous variable, one whose magnitude is not determined or explained by the model. The endogenous variables are C, Y, and S. We can find the magnitude of each of these three variables from the model once we have assigned a value to I. And for every different value we assign to I, there are different values for C, Y, and S.

The second equation is a definitional one. The sign $\equiv$ indicates that S is defined as being equal to $Y - C$. The first, third, and fourth equations are either functional or equilibrium equations. Which is which we cannot tell by merely looking at them, but an equation (like the first) containing one or more parameters is usually functional, and an equation (like the fourth) which tells us that a variable is exogenous is not often an equilibrium equation. We are left, in this case, with the third equation as the equilibrium equation.

Notice that we have started assigning numbers to equations. The number is shown at the extreme right and is made up of two numbers separated by a hyphen, the first number being that of the chapter and the second that of the equation itself. Only important equations or equations to which we wish to refer later will be assigned numbers. When an equation number is repeated out of sequence, it is indented from the margin:

$$I = \bar{I} \qquad (1\text{-}4)$$

Open economic models

As an example of an open model take the following set of equations:

$$L \equiv L_a + L_t \qquad (1\text{-}5)$$
$$L_t = cY \qquad (1\text{-}6)$$
$$L_a = j - kR \qquad (1\text{-}7)$$
$$M = L \qquad (1\text{-}8)$$
$$M = \bar{M} \qquad (1\text{-}9)$$

The parameters, we assume, are c, j, and k, leaving us with six variables L, L_a, L_t, Y, R, and M. Equation 1-9 tells us that M is an exogenous variable and that L, L_a, L_t, Y, and R are the endogenous variables. From equation 1-5 we know that L is defined as the sum of L_a and L_t.

Because the number of equations (five) is less than the number of variables (six), this is called an *open* model or system. It cannot tell us the values of all six variables. All it can tell us is the assigned value of the exogenous variable M. Of what use is it then? If we give a value to *any one* of the five endogenous variables, we can determine the values of the other four endogenous variables. If, for example, we assign a magnitude to R, we can then determine the magnitudes of L, L_a, L_t, and Y. Or if we assign a value to Y, we can find the values of L, L_a, L_t, and R. It is often useful in economics to know what the values of some variables will be when we assign a value to the other variables and to know how the magnitudes of some variables change when the values of the others change. It might be useful to know, for example, what Y will be if we give different values to R and how Y will change if we change R.

Solution equations

In both open and closed economic models we are able to obtain *solution* equations for each endogenous variable.

Solution equations in closed systems Any closed system of equations can be reduced to a set of solution equations. There are as many solution equations in a model as there are endogenous variables. If, as in the closed model above (equations 1-1 to 1-4), there are three endogenous variables, C, Y, and S, there are also three solution equations—one each for C, Y, and S.

Each solution equation expresses the magnitude of one variable as a function *of the parameters and exogenous variables in the model.* On one side of the equation is an endogenous variable, and on the other side there are parameters and exogenous variables. To see what a solution equation is and how it is obtained, let us reconsider the following closed model:

$$C = a + bY \qquad (1\text{-}1)$$
$$S \equiv Y - C \qquad (1\text{-}2)$$
$$S = I \qquad (1\text{-}3)$$
$$I = \bar{I} \qquad (1\text{-}4)$$

which has three endogenous variables, C, Y, and S.

To obtain the solution equation for Y we substitute $\bar{I}$ for I in equation 1-3 and obtain

$$S = \bar{I} \qquad (1\text{-}10)$$

Then for S in equation 1-1 we substitute $Y - C$ (from equation 1-2) and get

$$Y - C = \bar{I} \qquad (1\text{-}11)$$

For C we now substitute $a + bY$ from equation 1-1 and have

$$Y - (a + bY) = \bar{I} \qquad (1\text{-}12)$$

Adding the parameter a to both sides of 1-12, we have

$$Y - bY = a + \bar{I}$$

or

$$Y(1 - b) = a + \bar{I} \qquad (1\text{-}13)$$

Now we can divide both sides of equation 1-13 by $1 - b$ to get

$$\frac{Y(1 - b)}{1 - b} = \frac{a + \bar{I}}{1 - b}$$

$$Y^* = \frac{a + \bar{I}}{1 - b} \qquad (1\text{-}14)$$

On the left side we have the endogenous variable Y alone and on the right side nothing but parameters (a, b, and 1) and exogenous variables ($\bar{I}$). To indicate that this is the solution value of Y we star Y and write Y^*.

In a similar way we can obtain solution equations for C and S. The solution equation for C is found in the following way. From equation 1-2, if $S = Y - C$, then adding C to both sides

$$S + C = Y$$

or

$$Y = C + S$$

We can therefore substitute $C + S$ for Y in equation 1-1 to get

$$C = a + b(C + S) \tag{1-15}$$

For S in equation 1-15 we substitute, from equation 1-3, I:

$$C = a + b(C + I) \tag{1-16}$$

For I we next substitute, from equation 1-4, $\bar{I}$ to obtain

$$C = a + b(C + \bar{I})$$

or

$$C = a + bC + b\bar{I} \tag{1-17}$$

Subtracting bC from both sides of equation 1-17 gives us

$$C - bC = a + b\bar{I}$$

or

$$C(1 - b) = a + b\bar{I} \tag{1-18}$$

Dividing through by $1 - b$ gives us the solution for equation C.

$$C^* = \frac{a + b\bar{I}}{1 - b} \tag{1-19}$$

Again on the left side we have a single endogenous variable and on the right side nothing but parameters and exogenous variables. (The student can prove for himself that the solution equation for S is $S^* = \bar{I}$.)

Solution equations in open systems In models which contain more variables than equations we can also obtain solution equations for each of the variables. Solution equations in open systems express the magnitude of each endogenous variable as a function of the parameters and exogenous variables in the model *and the magnitude of at least one other endogenous variable*. If an open model has one more variable than it has equations, the solution value of each variable will be a function of the parameters, exogenous variables, and one endogenous variable. When the number of variables exceeds by 2 the number of equations, the solution value of each variable is a function of the parameters, exogenous variables, and two endogenous variables.

In the open system containing the equations

$$L \equiv L_a + L_t \tag{1-5}$$
$$L_t = cY \tag{1-6}$$
$$L_a = j - kR \tag{1-7}$$
$$M = L \tag{1-8}$$
$$M = \bar{M} \tag{1-9}$$

there are six variables and only five equations. The magnitude of any one of the five endogenous variables, such as Y, can be made a function of the three parameters (c, j, and k), the exogenous variable $\bar{M}$, and any one of the other endogenous variables. We find Y^* by first substituting $\bar{M}$ for M and $L_a + L_t$ for L in equation 1-8:

$$\bar{M} = L_a + L_t \tag{1-20}$$

For L_a we substitute (from equation 1-7) $j - kR$, and for L_t we substitute (from equation 1-6) cY:

$$\bar{M} = (j - kR) + cY \tag{1-21}$$

Subtracting $j - kR$ from both sides of this last equation gives us

$$\bar{M} - (j - kR) = c\bar{Y}$$

or

$$cY = \bar{M} - (j - kR) \tag{1-22}$$

Dividing through by c, we obtain

$$Y^* = \frac{\bar{M} - j + kR}{c} \tag{1-23}$$

The magnitude of Y, this last equation tells us, equals the exogenous variable $\bar{M}$ less the parameter j plus the product of the parameter k and the endogenous variable R all divided by the parameter c. For each of the other four endogenous variables we can also obtain a solution equation by similar methods. But each of the five solution equations will contain an endogenous variable on both sides of the equation.

The solution to a second-degree equation. We often find that the solution equation for an endogenous variable is a second-degree equation. Such equations as

$$X^2 - 3X = 12$$

and

$$2X^2 - 6X = -49$$

containing the endogenous variable X are examples of second-degree solution equations.

Finding the numerical value (or values) of the variable which satisfies a second-degree equation entails two steps. First, the equation should be rewritten so that one side of the equation (usually the right side) is equal to zero. The equation $X^2 - 3X = 12$ (by subtracting 12 from both sides of the equation) can be rewritten as

$$X^2 - 3X - 12 = 0$$

And (by adding 49 to both sides) the equation $2X^2 - 6X = -49$ can be rewritten as

$$2X^2 - 6X + 49 = 0$$

In rewriting a second-degree equation so that the right side of the equation is equal to zero it is useful (though not necessary) to arrange the terms on the left side of the equation so that the term containing the variable squared is the first term, the term containing the variable to the first power is next, and the term not containing the variable is the third.

The second step is to employ the formula, developed in basic algebra, to find the solution to a second-degree equation. Once we have rewritten a second-degree equation so that one side of the equation is equal to zero, a second-degree equation containing one variable (X) has the form

$$aX^2 + bX + c = 0$$

The parameters in the equation are a, b, and c; and these, respectively, are the coefficients of X^2 and of X and the constant term. The only restriction we must make is that the coefficient a cannot be zero. (If the coefficient of X^2 were zero, the value of the term containing X^2 would also be zero. We would not have a second-degree equation but a first-degree equation because the equation would not have a term of a power greater than 1.) The coefficients b and c may be zero. From algebra the formula that tells us the value of X in a second-degree equation is

$$X = \frac{-b \pm \sqrt{b^2 - 4ac}}{2a}$$

Applying this formula to the equation $X^2 - 3X - 12 = 0$ gives:

- a is 1.
- b is -3.
- c is -12.

and

$$X = \frac{-3 \pm \sqrt{(-3)^2 - 4(1)(-12)}}{2(1)}$$

$$= \frac{3 \pm \sqrt{9 + 48}}{2}$$

$$= \frac{3 \pm \sqrt{57}}{2}$$

From a table of square roots we find that the square root of 57 is approximately 7.55, and so

$$X = \frac{3 \pm 7.55}{2}$$

This tells us that X has two values. One value of X (call it X_1) is equal to $(3 + 7.55)/2$; and the other value of X (call it X_2) is equal to $(3 - 7.55)/2$. In mathematics it is usual to express the notion that a variable has two values by writing

$$X_1 = \frac{3 + 7.55}{2} \qquad X_2 = \frac{3 - 7.55}{2}$$

and, continuing,

$$X_1 = \frac{10.55}{2} \qquad X_2 = \frac{-4.55}{2}$$

$$= 5.275 \qquad = -2.275$$

A second-degree equation ordinarily has two solutions.[4] Only infrequently, however, does this mean that an economic model gives us two solutions for an endogenous variable. Often we can discard one of the solution values because it is economic nonsense. For example, if one of the solution values is negative and the value of that variable cannot possibly be negative (as the employment of labor or the output of a commodity cannot be negative), we can discard it. Sometimes, however, we do obtain two solutions both of which are plausible. Neither is nonsense nor impossible. In these cases we need some other rule, usually in the form of an inequality, that tells which solution to accept and which to reject.

In the second half of this book, when we examine the economic models of microeconomic theory, we shall frequently encounter solution equations of the second degree. But our models will contain an inequality that tells us which solution to accept. For the present all you need to keep in mind is that there is an algebraic formula to which you will want to refer later that gives the two potential solution values of any second-degree equation containing one endogenous variable.

Changes in exogenous variables

Having found the solution equations in any closed model, we can discover the relations between changes in any one of the exogenous variables (or parameters) and the resulting change in the endogenous variables. Suppose, for example, that in a closed system the solution equation for Y is

$$Y^* = \frac{a + \bar{I}}{1 - b} \tag{1-14}$$

and we are interested in what will happen to the magnitude of Y^* when the magnitude of the exogenous variable $\bar{I}$ changes. Since we designate a change in the magnitude of a variable (or a parameter) by the symbol Δ, $\Delta\bar{I}$ is the change in the magnitude of $\bar{I}$ and ΔY^* is the change in the magnitude of Y^*. (Δa would be a change in the value of the parameter a.)

If we let $\bar{I}$ change by $\Delta\bar{I}$, there will be a change in Y^* equal to ΔY^*. Using the solution equation for Y^*, we can write

$$Y^* + \Delta Y^* = \frac{a + (\bar{I} + \Delta\bar{I})}{1 - b} \tag{1-24}$$

What we have done is rewrite equation 1-14, replacing $\bar{I}$ with $\bar{I} + \Delta\bar{I}$ and Y^* with $Y^* + \Delta Y^*$. Of what value is an equation like 1-24? We can find out what effect the change in $\bar{I}$ has upon Y^*. How? By subtracting equation 1-4 from equation 1-24. Both these equations have the same denominator, $1 - b$, and the subtraction is fairly simple. When we subtract one equation from another we subtract the left side of one from the left side of the other and the right side

[4] All second-degree equations have two solutions if we allow for solutions containing an *imaginary* number (a number equal to the square root of a negative number). But if we allow only for solutions containing *real* numbers (numbers that are not imaginary), a second-degree equation has either two solutions or no solutions. It will have no solutions when the term under the radical sign ($\sqrt{\ }$) is negative.

of one from the right side of the other. Thus if we subtract equation 1-14 from equation 1-24, we subtract Y^* from $Y^* + \Delta Y^*$ to obtain ΔY^*, and if we subtract $(a + \bar{I})/(1 - b)$ from $(a + \bar{I} + \Delta\bar{I})/(1 - b)$, we obtain $\Delta\bar{I}/(1 - b)$. Then we can write the remainders as the equation

$$\Delta Y^* = \frac{\Delta\bar{I}}{1 - b} \qquad (1\text{-}25)$$

This equation tells us that the change in the magnitude of Y^* is equal to the magnitude of the change in $\bar{I}$ divided by 1 minus the value of parameter b. If b is equal to 0.8 and $\bar{I}$ changed by 10, using equation 1-25, we would find the change in Y^* to be

$$\Delta Y^* = \frac{10}{1 - 0.8}$$

$$= \frac{10}{0.2}$$

$$= 50$$

Y^* changes by 50 when $\bar{I}$ changes by 10 and the parameter b is equal to 0.8.

In economics we are often interested in the ratio of one change to another. An equation like 1-25 enables us to determine the ratio of the change in Y^* (when $\bar{I}$ changes) to the change in $\bar{I}$. This ratio is found by dividing both sides of equation 1-25 by $\Delta\bar{I}$. ΔY^* divided by $\Delta\bar{I}$ leaves us with $\Delta Y^*/\Delta\bar{I}$ on the left side; and $\Delta\bar{I}/(1 - b)$ divided by $\Delta\bar{I}$ leaves us with $1/(1 - b)$ on the right side. We can therefore write

$$\frac{\Delta Y^*}{\Delta I} = \frac{1}{1 - b} \qquad (1\text{-}26)$$

The ratio of the change in Y^* to the change in $\bar{I}$ is equal to 1 divided by 1 minus the parameter b.

Even when an economic model is open, we can employ solution equations to determine the relation between a change in either an exogenous variable or an endogenous variable (or a parameter) and the resulting change in another endogenous variable. The solution for Y^* in our example of an open model was

$$Y^* = \frac{\bar{M} - j + kR}{c} \qquad (1\text{-}23)$$

The two endogenous variables are Y and R, and the exogenous variable was $\bar{M}$. When $\bar{M}$ changes by $\Delta\bar{M}$, Y^* changes by ΔY^*, or

$$Y^* + \Delta Y^* = \frac{\bar{M} + \Delta\bar{M} - j + kR}{c} \qquad (1\text{-}27)$$

Subtracting equation 1-23 from 1-27, we have

$$\Delta Y^* = \frac{\Delta\bar{M}}{c} \qquad (1\text{-}28)$$

The change in the endogenous variable Y^* equals the change in the exogenous variable $\bar{M}$ divided by the parameter c. If, for example, c is 0.25 and $\bar{M}$ changed by 5, Y^* would change by 5/0.25, or 20. Dividing equation 1-28 through by $\Delta\bar{M}$, we obtain

$$\frac{\Delta Y^*}{\Delta \bar{M}} = \frac{1}{c} \tag{1-29}$$

The ratio of the change in Y^* to the change in $\bar{M}$ is equal to 1 divided by the parameter c.

We can also determine from the solution equation (1-23) the relation between the two endogenous variables Y and R. For when R changes by ΔR, Y^* will change by ΔY^*; and we can write

$$Y^* + \Delta Y^* = \frac{\bar{M} - j + k(R + \Delta R)}{c}$$

or

$$Y^* + \Delta Y^* = \frac{\bar{M} - j + kR + k\,\Delta R}{c} \tag{1-30}$$

Now we subtract equation 1-23 from equation 1-30 to obtain

$$\Delta Y^* = \frac{k\,\Delta R}{c} \tag{1-31}$$

The change in Y^* equals the parameter k multiplied by the change in R divided by the parameter c. Dividing through by ΔR gives

$$\frac{\Delta Y^*}{\Delta R} = \frac{k}{c} \tag{1-32}$$

The ratio of the change in Y^* to the change in R equals the ratio of the parameter k to the parameter c. If c equals 0.25 and k is 30, this ratio will be 30/0.25, or 120. If R changes by 0.01, the change in Y^* will be

$$\Delta Y^* = \frac{30(0.01)}{0.25}$$

$$= \frac{0.30}{0.25}$$

$$= 1.2$$

Exercise 1-3

1 An economic model or theory consists of one or more __________; for this reason a model is also called a __________ of __________

2 The variables appearing in an economic model are either:

a __________ variables, the magnitudes of which are determined by the model.

b or __________ variables, the magnitudes of which are not determined by the model and which are identified by placing __________ over the symbol for the variable.

3 A closed economic model consists of an __________ number of equations and __________. Each of the equations must be __________ and __________

4 Why would each of the following pairs of equations not be found in the same economic model?

a $C = 20 + 0.8Y;\ Y = -25 + 1.25C$

b $C = 20 + 0.9Y;\ Y = -25 + 1.25C$

c $D = 100 - 3P;\ P = 50 - D/3$

d $D = 100 - 3P;\ P = 33\frac{1}{3} - D/3$

5 If we let lowercase letters represent parameters and uppercase letters represent variables:

a The following system of different and consistent equations constitutes a(n) ____________ system or model because there are three equations and ____________ variables:

(1) $D = a - bP$

(2) $S = -c + eP$

(3) $S = D$

b The value of P that we obtain when we solve this system of equations can be expressed by the equation $P^* =$ ____________

c Employing your answer to part *b* (above), if the parameter a changes by Δa, the value of P^* will change by ΔP^*:

(1) $\Delta P^* =$ ____________

(2) $\Delta P^*/\Delta a =$ ____________

6 Suppose that

$D = 100 - 3P$

$S = -10 + 2P$

$D = S$

Then:

a $P^* =$ ____________

b Both D^* and $S^* =$ ____________

c If the parameter 100 in the first equation decreases to 90:

(1) $\Delta P^* =$ ____________

(2) $\Delta D^* = \Delta S^* =$ ____________

7 If we let lowercase letters indicate parameters and uppercase letters indicate variables:

a The following system of equations constitutes a(n) ____________ system or model because there are three equations and ____________ variables

$S = -a + cY$

$S = I + G$

$G = \bar{G}$

b The set of equations indicates that only the variable ____________ is an ____________ variable.

c In order to determine:

(1) S^* we need to know the value of either ____________ or ____________

(2) I^* we need to know the value of either ____________ or ____________

(3) Y^* we need to know the value of either ____________ or ____________

d Write one solution equation for each of the following variables:

(1) $Y^* =$ ____________

(2) $I^* =$ ____________

(3) $S^* =$ ____________

8 Assume that
$S = -10 + 0.2Y$
$S = I + G$
$G = 50$

a Determine:

(1) S^* as a function of I: $S^* =$ ______

(2) I^* as a function of S: $I^* =$ ______

(3) Y^* as a function of I: $Y^* =$ ______

b Employing your answers to part *a* and assuming that G increases by 10:

(1) $\Delta S^* =$ ______

(2) $\Delta I^* =$ ______

(3) $\Delta Y^* =$ ______

c With G equal to 50 again, if the -10 in the first equation becomes -20:

(1) $\Delta S^* =$ ______

(2) $\Delta I^* =$ ______

(3) $\Delta Y^* =$ ______

THE REMAINING FOURTEEN CHAPTERS

The remainder of this book is divided into Parts 2 and 3. The models of macroeconomics are examined in Chapters 2 to 7. Chapters 8 to 15 examine the models of microeconomics.

Part 2: macroeconomics

Chapter 2 introduces the student to macroeconomic analysis by examining an economy in which governments make no expenditures for goods and services, collect no taxes, and do not engage in international trade. Government expenditures and taxation are added in Chapter 3, and international trade is added in Chapter 4 to make the analysis more realistic and more useful. Chapter 5 looks at the demand for, and the supply of, money in order to explain the rate of interest. The analysis of Chapters 2 to 5 is combined in a single model in Chapter 6. The study of macroeconomic analysis is concluded in Chapter 7 with an examination of the economics of growth.

Part 3: microeconomics

The examination of microeconomics begins in Chapter 8 with a look at demand and supply. This examination continues in Chapter 9, where the marginal revenue and elasticity concepts are introduced. Chapter 10 looks behind demand to explain why individual consumers behave as they do. In Chapter 11 the student will find an explanation of the costs of production. Chapters 12 and 13 examine two different kinds of product markets, pure monopoly and pure competition. The tools needed for the analysis of resource markets are presented in Chapter 14 and utilized in Chapter 15 to explain the price and employment of resources.

Enough has been said *about* economics and mathematics. It is time now to use mathematics to study economics!

MACROECONOMICS

A CLOSED AND GOVERNMENTLESS ECONOMY

In this chapter we examine the forces that determine the equilibrium level of national output and income in an economy that engages in no international trade and has no government spending or taxation.

After defining certain terms and explaining the basic assumptions in the first section, three economic models are developed. All these models assume that consumer spending is an increasing and linear function of national income. In the first of the three models it is assumed that investment spending is an exogenous variable. In the second model investment spending is assumed to be an increasing and linear function of national income. In the third model, investment spending is assumed to be a function of an exogenous variable, the rate of interest.

Our aim in each of the three models is to develop formulas for finding the equilibrium national income and to discover the relations between changes in the exogenous variables and parameters and the resulting changes in equilibrium national income.

DEFINITIONS AND ASSUMPTIONS

Throughout this chapter we shall make use of certain definitions and assumptions. The first is that the economy engages in no international trade; that governments in the economy make no expenditures for goods and services, make no transfer payments, and collect no taxes; and that all saving in the economy is personal saving. There are three important consequences of this assumption.

1 Net national product, national income, personal income, and disposable income in the economy are identical.

$$\text{NNP} \equiv \text{NI} \equiv \text{PI} \equiv \text{DI}$$

The variable which is equal to NNP, NI, PI, and DI we call national output and label Y. Because a nation's total output and its total income are, by definition, equal to each other, we sometimes refer to Y as *national output* and at other times *national income*.

2 The aggregate quantity of goods and services D demanded in the economy has only two components: the consumption component C and the net investment component I;

$$D \equiv C + I \tag{2-1}$$

3 There are only two things that receivers of the national income Y can do with their income: spend for consumer goods and services C or save S.

$$Y \equiv C + S \tag{2-2}$$

It follows from this that we can define saving as national income less consumption.

$$S \equiv Y - C \tag{2-3}$$

Equilibrium national output

In addition to the first assumption we assume that the economy will tend to produce that national output at which the aggregate quantity of goods and services demanded D and national output are equal. The equilibrium output (or income) is the output at which

$$D = Y \tag{2-4}$$

Because D is, by definition, equal to $C + I$ (2-1), we can write equation 2-4 as

$$C + I = Y \tag{2-5}$$

And because $Y = C + S$ (equation 2-2), we can write equation 2-5 as

$$C + I = C + S \tag{2-6}$$

Subtracting C from both sides of the above equation, we find that the equilibrium output is also the output at which

$$I = S \tag{2-7}$$

The consumption function

The third assumption used throughout this chapter is that consumption is an increasing and linear function of national income. This means that the consumption function can be written

$$C = C_0 + bY \tag{2-8}$$

C_0 we define as *autonomous consumption,* the consumption that would occur if national income were zero, i.e., the part of total consumption expenditures that is not affected by the level of national income. We assume that C_0 is a positive figure, that at a zero national income consumers will still spend some amount for consumption.

$$C_0 > 0 \tag{2-9}$$

In equation 2-8, b is the parameter that links the level of national income to the level of consumption. It is assumed that b is greater than zero and less than one.

$$0 < b < 1 \tag{2-10}$$

The saving function Once we have expressed consumption as a function of national income, we can also express saving as a function of national income. Our definition of saving is

$$S \equiv Y - C \tag{2-3}$$

Into this equation we substitute the consumption function (equation 2-8) for C

$$\begin{aligned} S &= Y - (C_0 + bY) \\ &= -C_0 + Y - bY \\ &= -C_0 + (1 - b)Y \end{aligned} \tag{2-11}$$

If we assume that b is greater than zero and less than one, then $1 - b$ is less than one and greater than zero.

As an example of the linear consumption function we might have

$$C = \$97.5 + 0.75Y \tag{2-12}$$

The saving function would then be

$$S = -\$97.5 + 0.25Y \tag{2-13}$$

Equations 2-12 and 2-13 tell us that:

- If Y is zero, C is \$97.5 and S is $-$\$97.5.
- We can find C at any level of Y by adding \$97.5 to $0.75Y$.
- We can find S at any level of Y by subtracting \$97.5 from $0.25Y$.

The marginal propensities Both C and S depend upon the level of Y; therefore when Y changes, C and S will also change. We define the *marginal propensity to consume* (MPC) as the ratio of the small change in consumption ΔC that occurs when income changes to the small change in national income ΔY that brings about the change in consumption:

$$\text{MPC} = \Delta C / \Delta Y \tag{2-14}$$

To find the value of the MPC we start with the consumption function.

$$C = C_0 + bY \tag{2-8}$$

When Y changes by ΔY, C will change by ΔC. At the new level of Y

$$C + \Delta C = C_0 + b(Y + \Delta Y) \tag{2-15}$$

$$C + \Delta C = C_0 + bY + b\,\Delta Y \tag{2-16}$$

We now subtract equation 2-8 from equation 2-16 to find that

$$\Delta C = b\,\Delta Y \qquad (2\text{-}17)$$

Solving for the MPC ($\Delta C/\Delta Y$), we obtain

$$\frac{\Delta C}{\Delta Y} = b \qquad (2\text{-}18)$$

It turns out that when the consumption function is linear, the MPC is equal to the parameter b.

In a similar fashion we can find the *marginal propensity to save* (MPS), that is, the ratio of the small change in savings ΔS that occurs when there is a small change in national income to the change in national income ΔY. Starting with the saving function,

$$S = -C_0 + (1 - b)Y \qquad (2\text{-}11)$$

we assume that when Y changes by ΔY, S will change by ΔS. At the new level of Y

$$S + \Delta S = -C_0 + (1 - b)(Y + \Delta Y) \qquad (2\text{-}19)$$
$$S + \Delta S = -C_0 + (1 - b)Y + (1 - b)\,\Delta Y \qquad (2\text{-}20)$$

Subtracting equation 2-11 from equation 2-20,

$$\Delta S = (1 - b)\,\Delta Y \qquad (2\text{-}21)$$

and solving for the MPS ($\Delta S/\Delta Y$), we obtain

$$\frac{\Delta S}{\Delta Y} = 1 - b \qquad (2\text{-}22)$$

The MPS is equal to 1 minus b or 1 minus the MPC.

In our examples of the consumption and saving functions (equations 2-12 and 2-13), the MPC is 0.75, and the MPS is 1 − 0.75, or 0.25.

The average propensities The *average propensity to consume* (APC) is the ratio of consumption at any level of national income to that level of income.

$$\text{APC} = \frac{C}{Y} \qquad (2\text{-}23)$$

Substituting the consumption function for C in the equation above,

$$APC = \frac{C_0 + bY}{Y}$$

we find that

$$\frac{C}{Y} = \frac{C_0}{Y} + \frac{bY}{Y}$$

$$= \frac{C_0}{Y} + b \qquad (2\text{-}24)$$

The APC equals the ratio of autonomous consumption to the level of income plus the MPC.

From equation 2-24 we can discover that as long as autonomous consumption is greater than zero and the MPC is greater than zero and less than one, the APC will *decrease* as Y increases (and vice versa). The APC decreases as Y increases because:

- C_0/Y decreases because C_0 remains constant, and Y increases.
- b remains constant.
- With C_0/Y decreasing and b remaining constant, the sum of C_0/Y and b will therefore decrease.

Suppose that the consumption function is

$$C = \$97.5 + 0.75Y \tag{2-12}$$

When Y has the values given in column 1 of Table 2-1, C will have the values shown in column 2. The values for C_0/Y, b, and the APC ($= C_0/Y + b$) at each of the income levels are shown in columns 3, 4, and 5, respectively.

The *average propensity to save* (APS) is the ratio of saving at any level of income to the level of income:

$$\text{APS} = \frac{S}{Y} \tag{2-25}$$

Into equation 2-25 we substitute the saving function, equation 2-11:

$$\text{APS} = \frac{-C_0 + (1 - b)Y}{Y}$$

$$\frac{S}{Y} = \frac{-C_0}{Y} + \frac{(1 - b)Y}{Y}$$

$$= \frac{-C_0}{Y} + (1 - b) \tag{2-26}$$

The APS is equal to the negative ratio of autonomous consumption to income plus the MPS.

In equation 2-26 we can see that the APS will *increase* as income increases (and vice versa) provided autonomous consumption is greater than zero and the MPS is less than one and greater than zero. As Y increases:

- $-C_0$ remains constant and Y increases; $-C_0/Y$ therefore increases (becomes a smaller *negative* number).
- $1 - b$ remains constant.

TABLE 2-1

(1) Y	(2) C	(3) $\frac{C_0}{Y}$	(4) b	(5) APC = $\frac{C_0}{Y} + b$
300	322.5	0.325	0.75	1.075
400	397.5	0.244	0.75	0.994
500	472.5	0.195	0.75	0.945
600	547.5	0.163	0.75	0.913
700	622.5	0.139	0.75	0.889

TABLE 2-2

(1) Y	(2) S	(3) $-\frac{C_0}{Y}$	(4) $1-b$	(5) APS = $-\frac{C_0}{Y}+(1-b)$
300	−$22.5	−0.325	0.25	−0.075
400	2.5	−0.244	0.25	0.006
500	27.5	−0.195	0.25	0.055
600	52.5	−0.163	0.25	0.087
700	77.5	−0.139	0.25	0.111

■ The sum of $-C_0/Y$ and $1 - b$ therefore increases.

If our savings function is

$$S = -\$97.5 + 0.25Y \tag{2-13}$$

the values of S, $-C_0/Y$, $1 - b$, and the APS at various levels of Y are as shown in Table 2-2.

The sums of the propensities The sum of the MPC and the MPS is equal to unity. From equations 2-18 and 2-22 we have found that

$$\text{MPC} = b$$
$$\text{MPS} = 1 - b$$

If we add b and $1 - b$, the sum is 1.

Similarly, the sum of the APC and the APS is 1. We know that

$$\text{APC} = \frac{C_0}{Y} + b \tag{2-24}$$

$$\text{APS} = \frac{-C_0}{Y} + (1 - b) \tag{2-26}$$

We can see that

$$\left(\frac{C_0}{Y} + b\right) + \left[\frac{-C_0}{Y} + (1 - b)\right] = 1$$

$$\frac{C_0}{Y} + b - \frac{C_0}{Y} + 1 - b = 1$$

Exercise 2-1

1 In the models in this chapter the following definitions are used:

a NNP ≡ NI ≡ PI ≡ DI ≡ ____________ (use the symbol)

b $D \equiv$ ____________ + ____________

c $Y \equiv$ ____________ + ____________

d $S \equiv$ ____________ − ____________

2 There are several different ways of expressing the equilibrium output. In this chapter we say that it is the Y at which:

a ____________ = ____________

b ____________ + ____________ = ____________ + ____________

c ____________ = ____________

3 When the consumption function is $C = C_0 + bY$:
a What assumption is made about the size of C_0?
b What assumption is made about the size of b?
c What assumption is made about the size of $1 - b$?
d Show that the saving function is $S = -C_0 + (1 - b)Y$.

4 Define (in symbols):

a MPC ≡ ____________ / ____________

b MPS ≡ ____________ / ____________

c APC ≡ ____________ / ____________

d APS ≡ ____________ / ____________

5 Show that when the consumption function is $C = C_0 + bY$:
a The MPC = b.
b The MPS = $1 - b$.

6 Suppose the consumption function is $C = \$100 + 0.80Y$.

a The saving function is $S =$ ____________

b The MPC is ____________

c The MPS is ____________

d When $Y = \$200$:

(1) The APC = ____________

(2) The APS = ____________

e Autonomous consumption is $____________

7 Suppose the consumption function is linear, that autonomous consumption is greater than zero, and the MPC is greater than zero and less than one.
a Show that the APC must increase as Y decreases.
b Show that the APS must decrease as Y decreases.

8 Show that:
a MPC + MPS = 1
b APC + APS = 1

9 Below is a consumption schedule.

Y	C	S
$100	$110	________
200	200	________
300	290	________
400	380	________
500	470	________

a Draw up, by filling in the *S* column, the saving schedule that is derived from this consumption schedule.
b Write the linear consumption function from which this schedule is drawn.
c Write the linear saving function from which the saving schedule is drawn.
d On the graph below plot and label the consumption and saving curves.

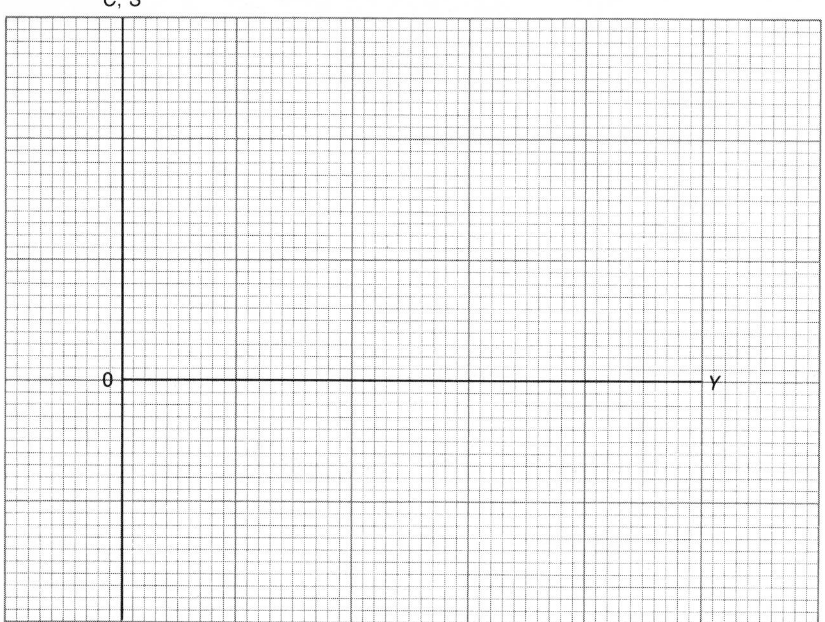

10 Assume that the consumption function is $C = \$150 + 0.70Y$.
a Write the formula that will enable us to compute the APC for any given level of *Y*. APC = __________
b Write the formula that will enable us to compute the APS for any given level of *Y*. APS = __________

THE FIRST MODEL: EXOGENOUS INVESTMENT

In this first model we assume that the investment component of aggregate demand is an exogenous variable. Our aim is to find an equation which will tell us what the equilibrium level of national income will be. To find this equation we can follow either of two approaches. No matter which approach we use the result is the same: we obtain the same equation for the equilibrium level of national income.

The aggregate demand–aggregate supply approach

If we assume that investment is an exogenous variable, we may write

$$I = \bar{I} \tag{2-27}$$

We assume that consumption is an increasing and linear function of income.

$$C = C_0 + bY \qquad (2\text{-}8)$$

The aggregate quantity of goods and services demanded is defined as the sum of consumption and investment spending.

$$D \equiv C + I \qquad (2\text{-}1)$$

The equilibrium national income is the income at which the aggregate quantity of goods and services demanded is equal to the aggregate quantity of goods and services supplied, or

$$D = Y \qquad (2\text{-}4)$$

This simple model contains the four equations given above. It also has four variables. Three of the variables (C, D, and Y) are endogenous, and one (I) is exogenous. The first two equations are functional, the third is definitional, and the fourth is the equilibrium equation.

To find an equation which tells us what the equilibrium level of Y will be we substitute the right side of equation 2-1 for D in equation 2-4 to obtain

$$C + I = Y$$

For C and I we substitute the right sides of equations 2-8 and 2-27, respectively, and solve for Y.

$$C_0 + bY + \bar{I} = Y$$
$$C_0 + \bar{I} = Y - bY$$
$$= Y(1 - b)$$

$$Y^* = \frac{C_0 + \bar{I}}{1 - b} \qquad (2\text{-}28)$$

Equation 2-28 is the solution equation for Y and tells us that the equilibrium level of national income is equal to autonomous consumption plus exogenous investment divided by 1 minus the MPC, that is, by the MPS. If, for example, investment is \$30 and $C = \$97.5 + 0.75Y$, we find that

$$Y^* = \frac{\$97.5 + \$30}{1 - 0.75}$$
$$= \frac{\$127.5}{0.25}$$
$$= \$510$$

Once we have found Y^*, we can also find the amount of consumption C^* and the amount of saving S^* that will take place in the economy. For Y in equation 2-9 we substitute Y^* and solve for C^*. To find S^* we subtract C^* from Y^* (equation 2-3). In our example Y^* is \$510. If we substitute \$510 for Y in the consumption equation, we find

$$C^* = \$97.5 + 0.75(\$510)$$
$$= \$97.5 + \$382.5$$
$$= \$480$$
$$S^* = \$510 - \$480$$
$$= \$30$$

D^* is (from equation 2-1) equal to $C^* + \bar{I}$ or \$480 + \$30 = \$510.

The saving-investment approach

We can discover the same equation for the equilibrium level of national income by employing a somewhat different approach. As before, we assume that investment is given and constant

$$I = \bar{I} \tag{2-27}$$

Instead of the consumption function we use the saving function

$$S = -C_0 + (1 - b)Y \tag{2-11}$$

The equilibrium level of national income is the level of national income at which saving and investment are equal.

$$S = I \tag{2-7}$$

This approach has three equations and three variables, S, I, and Y. I is an exogenous variable. The first two equations are functional, and the third equation is the equilibrium equation. To find the equilibrium level of Y we substitute equations 2-27 and 2-11 for I and S, respectively, in equation 2-7 and solve for Y.

$$-C_0 + (1 - b)Y = \bar{I}$$

$$(1 - b)Y = C_0 + \bar{I}$$

$$Y^* = \frac{C_0 + \bar{I}}{1 - b} \tag{2-28}$$

This is exactly the same solution equation we obtained using the aggregate demand–aggregate supply approach: the equilibrium national income equals autonomous consumption plus investment divided by 1 minus the MPC (or divided by the MPS).

Changes in autonomous consumption and investment: the multiplier

We would now like to find out what effect a change in either autonomous consumption or investment will have on the equilibrium level of national income. Let us look first at the effect of a change in autonomous consumption.

The autonomous consumption multiplier Assume that the parameter we call autonomous consumption C_0 changes by ΔC_0 and that as a result national income changes by ΔY^*. From equation 2-28 for the equilibrium value of Y, the new value of Y^* is equal to $Y^* + \Delta Y^*$; and we can write

$$Y^* + \Delta Y^* = \frac{C_0 + \Delta C_0 + \bar{I}}{1 - b} \tag{2-29}$$

To find the amount ΔY^* by which Y^* changes we subtract equation 2-28 from equation 2-29.

$$\Delta Y^* = \frac{\Delta C_0}{1 - b} \tag{2-30}$$

Equation 2-30 says that the change in Y^* is equal to the change in C_0 divided by 1 minus the MPC.

The ratio of the change ΔY^* in the equilibrium national income to the change ΔC_0 in autonomous consumption we call the *autonomous consumption multiplier.* We label the autonomous consumption multiplier k_C. Thus

$$k_C = \frac{\Delta Y^*}{\Delta C_0} \tag{2-31}$$

If we divide both sides of equation 2-30 by ΔC_0, we obtain

$$\frac{\Delta Y^*}{\Delta C_0} = \frac{1}{1 - b} \tag{2-32}$$

The value of the autonomous consumption multiplier is equal to 1 divided by 1 minus the MPC.

As an example, suppose the value of b is 0.75. Then 1 minus b is 0.25, and 1 divided by 0.25 is equal to 4. This means that whenever autonomous consumption changes by \$1, the equilibrium level of Y will change by \$4. This we can see if we use equation 2-30 and substitute \$1 for ΔC_0 and 0.75 for b. Notice also that the sign of this multiplier is positive. Thus a \$1 *increase* in autonomous consumption will *increase* equilibrium Y by \$4; and a \$1 *decrease* in autonomous consumption will *decrease* equilibrium Y by \$4.

The investment multiplier What is the effect upon equilibrium Y of a change in the exogenous variable $\bar{I}$? If $\bar{I}$ changes by $\Delta\bar{I}$, equilibrium Y will change by ΔY^*.

$$Y^* + \Delta Y^* = \frac{C_0 + \bar{I} + \Delta\bar{I}}{1 - b} \tag{2-33}$$

From equation 2-33 we subtract equation 2-28

$$\Delta Y^* = \frac{\Delta\bar{I}}{1 - b} \tag{2-34}$$

The change in equilibrium Y is equal to the change in $\bar{I}$ divided by 1 minus the MPC.

The *investment multiplier* k_I is defined as the ratio of the change in equilibrium Y to the change in $\bar{I}$.

$$k_I = \frac{\Delta Y^*}{\Delta\bar{I}} \tag{2-35}$$

To find the value of the investment multiplier we divide both sides of equation 2-34 by $\Delta\bar{I}$ and obtain

$$\frac{\Delta Y^*}{\Delta\bar{I}} = \frac{1}{1 - b} \tag{2-36}$$

The value of the investment multiplier:

- Is equal to 1 divided by 1 minus the MPC.
- Has a positive sign.
- Has the same value and sign as the autonomous consumption multiplier.

Suppose, for example, that b is equal to 0.80. Then 1 minus 0.80 is 0.20, and 1 divided by 0.20 is 5. A \$1 increase in investment would increase equilibrium Y by \$5, and a \$1 decrease in investment would decrease equilibrium Y by \$5. This is evident if we use equation 2-34 and substitute \$1 for $\Delta\bar{I}$ and 0.80 for b.

Exercise 2-2

1 With the aggregate demand–aggregate supply approach, the four equations in the first model are

$C =$ ____________

$I =$ ____________

$D \equiv$ ____________ + ____________

$D =$ ____________

2 In the model above:

a The endogenous variables are ____________, ____________, and ____________

b The exogenous variable is ____________

c The first two equations are ____________ equations, the third equation is a ____________ equation, and the fourth equation is the ____________ equation.

3 Show, using the aggregate demand–aggregate supply approach, that

$$Y^* = \frac{C_0 + \bar{I}}{1 - b}$$

4 If we employ the saving-investment approach, the equations in the model are

$S =$ ____________

$I =$ ____________

$S =$ ____________

There are in this model ____________ variables. The endogenous variables are ____________ and ____________

5 Using the saving-investment approach, show that

$$Y^* = \frac{C_0 + \bar{I}}{1 - b}$$

6 Suppose that

$I = \$50$
$C - \$40 + 0.8Y$
Then:

a $Y^* = \$$____________

b $C^* = \$$____________

c $S^* = \$$____________

d $D^* = \$$____________

7 In symbols:

a The autonomous consumption multiplier is ________ and equals ________ / ________

b The investment multiplier is ________ and equals ________ / ________

8 Show that:

a $\Delta Y^* = \dfrac{\Delta C_0}{1 - b}$ and $\dfrac{\Delta Y^*}{\Delta C_0} = \dfrac{1}{1 - b}$

b $\Delta Y^* = \dfrac{\Delta \bar{I}}{1 - b}$ and $\dfrac{\Delta Y^*}{\Delta \bar{I}} = \dfrac{1}{1 - b}$

9 Assume that $C = \$60 + 0.6Y$.

a If $\bar{I}$ increases by \$10, Y^* will (increase, decrease) by \$________

b If $\bar{I}$ decreases by \$18, Y^* will ________ by \$________

c If C_0 increases by \$8, Y^* will ________ by \$________

d If C_0 decreases by \$6, Y^* will ________ by \$________

10 Employing the equations in question 9, by how much would $\bar{I}$ have to change to bring about:

a A \$25 increase in Y^*? \$________

b A \$18 decrease in Y^*? \$________

THE SECOND MODEL: INDUCED INVESTMENT

Like consumption, net investment may also be a function of national income. We assume in this model that investment is an increasing and linear function of national income

$$I = I_0 + mY \tag{2-37}$$

where I_0 is *autonomous investment,* i.e., the investment that would take place if Y were zero, and m is the parameter that relates I to the level of Y. It is assumed that

$$0 < m < 1$$

and that

$$I_0 \geqq 0$$

The marginal propensity to invest (MPI) is defined as the ratio of the small change in investment ΔI that occurs when Y changes to the small change in national income (ΔY) that brings about the change in I.

$$\text{MPI} = \frac{\Delta I}{\Delta Y} \tag{2–38}$$

We can find the value of the MPI in the following way. When Y changes by ΔY, I will change by ΔI. At the new level of Y, using equation 2-37,

$$\begin{aligned} I + \Delta I &= I_0 + m(Y + \Delta Y) \\ &= I_0 + mY + m\,\Delta Y \end{aligned} \tag{2-39}$$

From equation 2-39 we subtract equation 2-37.

$$\Delta I = m\,\Delta Y \tag{2-40}$$

The term $m\,\Delta Y$ (which is equal to ΔI) is the *induced investment* because it is the change in investment that is induced by, or results from, a change in Y. From equation 2-40 we can solve for $\Delta I/\Delta Y$, the MPI.

$$\frac{\Delta I}{\Delta Y} = m \tag{2-41}$$

The MPI, in short, is equal to the parameter m.

The equilibrium level of national income

As in the first model, we can find the equilibrium of Y using either the aggregate demand–aggregate supply approach or the saving-investment approach. Both approaches yield the same result.

The aggregate demand–aggregate supply approach We continue to assume that C is an increasing and linear function of Y.

$$C = C_0 + bY \tag{2-8}$$

We also assume that

$$I = I_0 + mY \tag{2-37}$$
$$D \equiv C + I \tag{2-1}$$
$$D = Y \tag{2-4}$$

This model has four equations, four endogenous variables (C, Y, D, and I), and a solution.

Into equation 2-4 we substitute equations 2-8 and 2-37 for C and I, respectively.

$$C + I = Y$$
$$(C_0 + bY) + (I_0 + mY) = Y$$

Then we solve for Y.

$$\begin{aligned} C_0 + bY + I_0 + mY &= Y \\ C_0 + I_0 &= Y - bY - mY \\ &= Y(1 - b - m) \end{aligned}$$

$$Y^* = \frac{C_0 + I_0}{1 - b - m} \tag{2-42}$$

This tells us that equilibrium Y is equal to the sum of autonomous consumption and autonomous investment divided by 1 minus the MPC minus the MPI.

The saving–investment approach This approach employs the saving function

$$S = -C_0 + (1 - b)Y \tag{2-11}$$

the investment function

$$I = I_0 + mY \tag{2-37}$$

and the equilibrium equation

$$S = I \tag{2-7}$$

This approach has three equations, three endogenous variables, and a solution.

Substituting the saving and investment functions for S and I, respectively, in equation 2-7 we have

$$-C_0 + (1 - b)Y = I_0 + mY$$
$$(1 - b)Y - mY = C_0 + I_0$$
$$Y - bY - mY = C_0 + I_0$$
$$Y(1 - b - m) = C_0 + I_0$$

$$Y^* = \frac{C_0 + I_0}{1 - b - m} \tag{2-42}$$

This is the same solution obtained from the aggregate demand–aggregate supply approach.

Once we have found Y^*, we can find the values of C^*, S^*, I^*, and D^*. C^* is found by inserting the Y^* into the consumption equation (2-8), and I^* is found by inserting Y^* into the investment equation (2-37). D^* is the sum of C^* and I^* (equation 2-1). S^* is equal to Y^* minus C^* (equation 2-3).

An example Suppose

$$C = \$97.5 + 0.75Y$$
$$I = \$2.5 + 0.15Y$$

Using equation 3-42, we find that

$$Y^* = \frac{\$97.5 + \$2.5}{1 - 0.75 - 0.15}$$
$$= \frac{\$100}{0.10}$$
$$= \$1{,}000$$

Consumption, using the consumption equation, is

$$C^* = \$97.5 + 0.75(\$1{,}000) = \$97.5 + \$750 = \$847.5$$

Investment, using the investment equation, is

$$I^* = \$2.5 + 0.15(\$1{,}000) = \$2.5 + \$150 = \$152.5$$

The aggregate quantity of goods and services demanded is

$$D^* = \$847.5 + \$152.5 = \$1{,}000$$

D^* is equal to Y^*. Saving is income minus consumption, or

$S^* = \$1{,}000 - \$847.5 = \$152.5$

Notice that saving and investment are equal.

The supermultipliers

In the earlier model we saw that when either C_0 or $\bar{I}$ changed, equilibrium Y would change by a multiple (of the change in C_0 or $\bar{I}$) equal to $1/(1 - \text{MPC})$. We defined the autonomous consumption multiplier as $\Delta Y^*/\Delta C_0$ and the investment multiplier as $\Delta Y^*/\Delta \bar{I}$. This earlier model assumed that investment is an exogenous variable.

We now want to discover the value of the autonomous consumption and investment multipliers when investment is not exogenous but an increasing and linear function of the level of national income. These multipliers we shall call *supermultipliers* and use capital K as symbols for them.

The autonomous consumption multiplier The equilibrium equation in this model is

$$Y^* = \frac{C_0 + I_0}{1 - b - m} \tag{2-42}$$

If autonomous consumption changes by C_0, the equilibrium income will change by ΔY^*. We write

$$Y^* + \Delta Y^* = \frac{C_0 + \Delta C_0 + I_0}{1 - b - m} \tag{2-43}$$

and solve for ΔY^* by subtracting equation 2-42 from equation 2-43.

$$\Delta Y^* = \frac{\Delta C_0}{1 - b - m} \tag{2-44}$$

This tells us that the change in equilibrium Y equals the change in autonomous consumption divided by 1 minus the MPC minus the MPI. We can now solve for the value of the autonomous consumption supermultiplier K_c.

$$K_c = \frac{\Delta Y^*}{\Delta C_0} = \frac{1}{1 - b - m} \tag{2-45}$$

The value of the autonomous consumption supermultiplier is 1 divided by 1 minus the MPC minus the MPI.

The investment multiplier When autonomous investment changes by ΔI_0, equilibrium national income will change by ΔY^*. Thus

$$Y^* + \Delta Y^* = \frac{C_0 + I_0 + \Delta I_0}{1 - b - m} \tag{2-46}$$

Subtracting equation 2-42 from equation 2-46, we find

$$\Delta Y^* = \frac{\Delta I_0}{1 - b - m} \tag{2-47}$$

and the investment supermultiplier K_I is

$$K_I = \frac{\Delta Y^*}{\Delta I_0} \frac{1}{1 - b - m} \tag{2-48}$$

The investment supermultiplier has the same value as the autonomous consumption supermultiplier. Note also that they both have a positive sign (if the sum of b and m is less than 1). This tells us that an *in*crease in either C_0 or I_0 will *in*crease Y^* and that a *de*crease in either C_0 or I_0 will *de*crease Y^*.

We should also observe that when I is an increasing function of Y, these multipliers have a greater value than when I is a constant amount. Why is this? Because the investment that is induced by a change in income has, in turn, a further multiplier effect on the level of income.

A numerical example of the multipliers Let us again suppose that

$$C = \$97.5 + 0.75Y$$
$$I = \$2.5 + 0.15Y$$

Employing equations 2-45 and 2-48, the value of the autonomous consumption and investment supermultiplier is equal to 1/(1 − 0.75 − 0.15), which is equal to 1/0.10, or 10. This means that a \$1 increase in either autonomous consumption or autonomous investment will increase Y^* by \$10 and a \$1 decrease in either C_0 or I_0 will bring about a \$10 decrease in Y^*.

We should observe that a \$1 increase in I_0 results in a \$1.5 increase in mY. The value of m is 0.15, and the \$1 increase in I_0 causes Y^* to increase by \$10. So (from equation 2-40) the induced change in I is 0.15(\$10), or \$1.5. The *total* change in I that results from the \$1 change in I_0 is equal to the \$1 increase in I_0 *plus* the \$1.5 increase in mY or a \$2.5 increase in I. The student should be able to show that a \$2 decrease in I_0 will bring about a \$20 decrease in Y^*, a \$3 decrease in mY, and a total decrease in I of \$5.

Exercise 2-3

1 In the second model it is assumed that investment is a __________ and __________ function of __________

2 If the investment function is $I = I_0 + mY$:

a I_0 is called __________ investment.

b mY is called __________ investment.

c $\Delta I/\Delta Y$ is called the __________ __________ to __________ and is equal to __________

3 Suppose that $I = \$5 + 0.0625Y$.

a The marginal propensity to investment = __________

b Autonomous investment = __________

c If Y increases by \$16, I will (increase, decrease) __________ by \$__________

d If Y decreases by \$40, I will __________ by \$__________

4 With the aggregate demand–aggregate supply approach, the equations of the second model are

$C =$ ___________

$I =$ ___________

$D =$ ___________ $+$ ___________

___________ $=$ ___________

The four endogenous variables are ___________, ___________, ___________, and ___________

5 If we employ the saving-investment approach, the equations are

$S =$ ___________

$I =$ ___________

___________ $=$ ___________

6 Show that

$$Y^* = \frac{C_0 + I_0}{1 - b - m}$$

7 Suppose that
$C = \$90 + 0.60Y$
$I = \$30 + 0.10Y$

Then:

a $Y^* = \$$___________

b $C^* = \$$___________

c $S^* = \$$___________

d $I^* = \$$___________

e $D^* = \$$___________

8 Definitions:

a The autonomous consumption supermultiplier = ___________ / ___________, and its symbol is ___________

b The investment supermultiplier = ___________ / ___________, and its symbol is ___________

9 Show that:

a $\Delta Y^* = \dfrac{\Delta C_0}{1 - b - m}$ and $\dfrac{\Delta Y^*}{\Delta C_0} = \dfrac{1}{1 - b - m}$

b $\Delta Y^* = \dfrac{\Delta I_0}{1 - b - m}$ and $\dfrac{\Delta Y^*}{\Delta I_0} = \dfrac{1}{1 - b - m}$

10 Using the functions in question 7:

a K_C and $K_I =$ ___________

b If C_0 increases by \$21, y^* will (increase, decrease) ___________ by \$ ___________

c If C_0 decreases by \$6, Y^* will ___________ by \$___________

d If I_0 increases by \$18, Y^* will __________ by \$__________

e If I_0 decreases by \$24, Y^* will __________ by \$__________

THE THIRD MODEL: THE RATE OF INTEREST

In this model we shall continue to assume that

$$C = C_0 + bY \tag{2-8}$$

that

$$D \equiv C + I \tag{2-1}$$

and that

$$D = Y \tag{2-4}$$

Investment in this model, however, is assumed to be a decreasing and linear function of the rate of interest i in the economy, or

$$I = I_0 - ji \tag{2-49}$$

The rate of interest is an exogenous variable, and we write

$$i = \bar{i} \tag{2-50}$$

In the investment equation (2-49), I_0 is the number of dollars that would be spent for investment if the rate of interest were zero. We assume that I_0 is positive.

The parameter j relates the interest rate to the level of investment spending. We call it the *interest rate–investment coefficient*. If the rate of interest changes by $\Delta\bar{i}$, the level of investment spending will change by ΔI. Thus, employing equation 2-49, we can write

$$I + \Delta I = I_0 - j(\bar{i} + \Delta\bar{i})$$

or

$$I + \Delta I = I_0 - j\bar{i} - j\,\Delta\bar{i}$$

From this last equation we subtract equation 2-49 to find that

$$\Delta I = -j\,\Delta\bar{i} \tag{2-51}$$

And if we divide equation 2-51 by $\Delta\bar{i}$, we find that

$$\frac{\Delta I}{\Delta\bar{i}} = -j \tag{2-52}$$

Equation 2-52 tells us that the ratio of the small change in investment (when there is a small change in the interest rate) to the change in the rate of interest is equal to the parameter j. It also tells us that this ratio is negative: decreases in i bring about increases in I, and increases in i result in decreases in I.

The unit for measuring the rate of interest is the percentage point. The parameter j is measured in dollars (of investment spending) divided by the percentage point. As an example of investment demand we might have an equation like

$$I = \$60 - 5\frac{\$}{\%}i$$

If the rate of interest is 5 percent, investment will be

$$I = \$60 - 5\frac{\$}{\%}(5\%)$$

$$= \$60 - \$25$$
$$= \$35$$

Equilibrium national income

Our third model has five equations,

$$C = C_0 + bY \quad (2\text{-}8)$$
$$D \equiv C + I \quad (2\text{-}1)$$
$$D = Y \quad (2\text{-}4)$$
$$I = I_0 - ji \quad (2\text{-}49)$$
$$i = \bar{i} \quad (2\text{-}50)$$

It has four endogenous variables (C, Y, I, and D), one exogenous variable (i), and a solution. Solving for the equilibrium national income, we obtain by substitution

$$D = Y \quad (2\text{-}4)$$
$$C + I = Y$$
$$(C_0 + bY) + (I_0 - ji) = Y$$
$$C_0 + I_0 - j\bar{i} = Y - bY$$
$$= Y(1 - b)$$

$$Y^* = \frac{C_0 + I_0 - j\bar{i}}{1 - b} \quad (2\text{-}53)$$

As a numerical example, suppose that

$$C = \$97.5 + 0.75Y$$

$$I = \$60 - 5\frac{\$}{\%}i$$

$$I = 6\%$$

From equation 2-53, the equilibrium national income is

$$Y^* = \frac{\$97.5 + \$60 - 5\frac{\$}{\%}(6\%)}{1 - 0.75}$$

$$= \frac{\$97.5 + \$60 - \$30}{0.25}$$

$$= \frac{\$127.5}{0.25}$$

$$= \$510$$

Having found Y^*, we can also find the equilibrium values of the three other endogenous variables from the equations in the model. $C^* = C_0 + bY^*$. $I^* = I_0 - j\bar{i}$. $D^* = C^* + I^*$. (We can also find S^* by subtracting C^* from Y^*.)

In our example,

$$C^* = \$97.5 + 0.75(\$510) = \$97.5 + \$382.5 = \$480$$

$$I^* = \$60 - 5\frac{\$}{\%}(6\%) = \$60 - \$30 = \$30$$

$$D^* = \$480 + \$30 = \$510$$
$$S^* = \$510 - \$480 = \$30$$

Notice that $Y^* = D^*$ and that $S^* = I^*$.

The multipliers

In a model containing two parameters (C_0 and I_0) and an exogenous variable (i) we have three multipliers: the autonomous consumption multiplier, the investment multiplier, and the interest rate multiplier.

Consumption and investment multipliers The autonomous consumption and investment multipliers have the same values they had in our first model. The autonomous consumption multiplier k_c is defined as $\Delta Y/\Delta C_0$ (equation 2-31). The equilibrium equation 2-53 shows that when C_0 changes by ΔC_0, Y^* will change by ΔY^*. We can therefore write

$$Y^* + \Delta Y^* = \frac{C_0 + \Delta C_0 + I_0 - j\bar{i}}{1 - b}$$

From this equation we subtract equation 2-53 to find that

$$\Delta Y^* = \frac{\Delta C_0}{1 - b} \tag{2-54}$$

and, dividing through by ΔC_0, that

$$\frac{\Delta Y^*}{\Delta C_0} = \frac{1}{1 - b} \tag{2-55}$$

In a similar way we can find the value of the investment multiplier. In this model, however, we define the investment multiplier as the ratio of the change in Y^* to the change in I_0: $k_i = \Delta Y^*/\Delta I_0$. Again employing equation 2-53, when I_0 changes by ΔI_0 there will be a change in ΔY^*, so that

$$Y^* + \Delta Y^* = \frac{C_0 + I_0 + \Delta I_0 - j\bar{i}}{1 - b}$$

From this equation we subtract 2-53 to obtain

$$\Delta Y^* = \frac{\Delta I_0}{1 - b} \tag{2-56}$$

and

$$\frac{\Delta Y^*}{\Delta I_0} = \frac{1}{1 - b} \tag{2-57}$$

Notice that when there is no investment induced by changes in national income, the consumption and investment multipliers have the same values they had in our first model, in which investment was an exogenous variable.

The interest rate multiplier In this model the rate of interest is an exogenous variable, but we are interested in discovering the effect of a change in $\bar{i}$ upon Y^*. We want to know the value of the interest rate multiplier K_i, which is defined as

$$K_i = \frac{\Delta Y^*}{\Delta \bar{i}} \tag{2-58}$$

The interest rate multiplier is the ratio of the small change in equilibrium national income (when the rate of interest changes) to the small change in the rate of interest.

Starting with the equilibrium equation for this model (2-53), a change in $\bar{i}$ equal to $\Delta\bar{i}$ will bring about a change in Y^* equal to ΔY^*:

$$Y^* + \Delta Y^* = \frac{C_0 + I_0 - j(\bar{i} + \Delta\bar{i})}{1 - b}$$

or

$$Y^* + \Delta Y^* = \frac{C_0 + I_0 - j\bar{i} - j\,\Delta\bar{i}}{1 - b}$$

From this last equation we subtract equation 2-53 and obtain

$$\Delta Y^* = \frac{-j\,\Delta\bar{i}}{1 - b} \tag{2-59}$$

Dividing through by $\Delta\bar{i}$

$$\frac{\Delta Y^*}{\Delta\bar{i}} = \frac{-j}{1 - b} \tag{2-60}$$

The value of the interest rate multiplier, equation 2-60 tells us, is negative and equals the value of the parameter j (the interest rate–investment coefficient) divided by 1 minus the parameter b (the marginal propensity to consume). The negative value of the interest rate multiplier means that increases in i decrease Y^* and that decreases in i increase Y^*.

Examples of the multipliers Let

$$C = \$97.5 + 0.75Y$$

$$I = \$60 - 5\,\frac{\$}{\%}\,i$$

The value of the parameter b is 0.75, and the value of j is 5 \$/%; thus $1 - b$ is equal to 0.25. If either C_0 (\$97.5) or I_0 (\$60) increased by \$1, applying equations 2-54 or 2-56, respectively, shows that the equilibrium national income would increase by \$4 (= \$1/0.25). A \$1 decrease in either C_0 or I_0 would decrease Y^* by \$4. The autonomous consumption and investment multiplier is 4.

Suppose $\bar{i}$ changed by 1 percentage point, for example from 6 to 7 percent. What would be the effect on Y^*? From equation 2-59,

$$\begin{aligned}\Delta Y^* &= \frac{-5\ \$/\%\ (1\%)}{1 - 0.75} \\ &= \frac{-\$5}{0.25} \\ &= -\$20\end{aligned}$$

The 1 percentage point increase in $\bar{i}$ decreased Y^* by \$20. The ratio of the change in Y^* to the change in $\bar{i}$ (the interest rate multiplier) is equal to $-\$20/1\%$, or 20.

Why did the 1 percentage point decrease in $\bar{i}$ increase Y^* by \$20? Because the 1 percent decrease in $\bar{i}$ brought about a \$5 increase in I and \$5 multiplied by the multiplier of 4, that is 1/0.25, is equal to \$20 increase in Y^*. Had $\bar{i}$ decreased by 2 percent, the change in Y^* would have been an increase of \$40 because

$$\Delta Y^* = \frac{-5\ \$/\%\ (-2\%)}{1 - 0.75}$$

$$= \frac{\$10}{0.25}$$

$$= \$40$$

The 2 percentage point decrease in $\bar{i}$ brought about a \$10 increase in I, and \$10 times the multiplier of 4 is the \$40 increase in Y^*.

Exercise 2-4

1 In the third model:

$C =$ ____________

$D \equiv$ ____________ + ____________

____________ = ____________

$I =$ ____________

$i =$ ____________

This model has four endogenous variables: ____________, ____________, ____________, and ____________

2 In the investment function:

a I_0 is the amount of investment that would occur if ____________ were zero.

b The parameter j is called the ________________________ coefficient.

c $\Delta I / \Delta \bar{i}$ is equal to ____________

3 Assume $I = \$100 - 4\ \$/\%\ (i)$.

a If i decreases by 2%, I will (increase, decrease) ____________ by \$____________

b If i increases by 3%, I will ____________ by \$____________

4 Show that

$$Y^* = \frac{C_0 + I_0 - j\bar{i}}{1 - b}$$

5 Suppose that

$$C = \$80 + 0.80Y$$

$$I = \$100 - 4\ \frac{\$}{\%}\ i$$

$$i = 4\%$$

a $Y^* = \$$__________

b $C^* = \$$__________

c $I^* = \$$__________

d $D^* = \$$__________

e $S^* = \$$__________

6 Show that:

a $\dfrac{\Delta Y^*}{\Delta C_0} = \dfrac{1}{1 - b}$

b $\dfrac{\Delta Y^*}{\Delta I_0} = \dfrac{1}{1 - b}$

c $\dfrac{\Delta Y^*}{\Delta \bar{i}} = \dfrac{-j}{1 - b}$

7 Using the equations in question 5:

a The value of both the autonomous consumption and investment multiplier is __________.

b The value of the interest rate multiplier is __________

8 Still using the equations in question 5:

a If C_0 decreases by \$3, Y^* will __________ by \$__________

b If I_0 increases by \$5, Y^* will __________ by \$__________

c If $\bar{i}$ increases by 2%, Y^* will __________ by \$__________

d If $\bar{i}$ decreases by 1.5%, Y^* will __________ by \$__________

9 If $C = \$75 + 0.66\tfrac{2}{3}Y$ and $I = \$80 - 6\ \$/\%\ (i)$.

a By how much would $\bar{i}$ have to change to increase Y^* by \$18? __________%.

b By how much would $\bar{i}$ have to change to decrease Y^* by \$24? __________%.

10 Suppose, employing the equations in question 9, that C_0 increased by \$5, I_0 decreased by \$4, and $\bar{i}$ rose by 1 percent. What would be the total effect on Y^* of these three events? \$__________

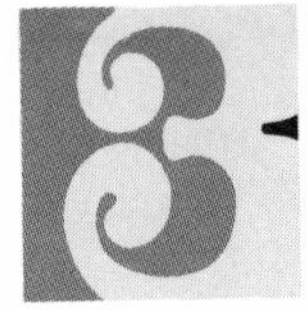

THE ECONOMY AND GOVERNMENT

The previous chapter examined an economy in which governments made no expenditures and collected no taxes. To add both realism and usefulness we turn now to an economy in which governments do spend and do collect taxes.

We begin in the first section by defining the new terms and by explaining the assumptions we employ. In the second section we develop a simple model for an economy in which governments spend and collect a fixed amount of taxes. A more advanced model is developed in the final section, where it is assumed that the taxes collected are an increasing and linear function of the level of national income.

In both these models we wish to find formulas that tell us what the equilibrium level of national income will be. We also wish to find formulas that tell us how changes in the exogenous variables will affect the equilibrium level of national income.

DEFINITIONS AND ASSUMPTIONS

In this chapter we use four of the definitions and assumptions employed in the last chapter, but because we are now studying an economy in which government participates by spending and taxing, some of the definitions and assumptions we use are different. Let us look first at the four which are the same.

Four old assumptions

The four definitions and assumptions used in Chapter 2 which are also used in this chapter are as follows:

1 The economy is a closed economy. It engages in no international trade. (Later, in Chapter 4, we shall examine the equilibrium national income in an economy which exports and imports goods and services.)

2 All saving in the economy is personal saving. There are no undistributed corporate profits.

3 For simplicity, in the models in this chapter we assume that net investment spending is an exogenous variable.

$$I = \overline{I} \tag{3-1}$$

4 The equilibrium level of national income is the national income Y, which is equal to the aggregate quantity of goods and services demanded D. The equilibrium equation is

$$D = Y \tag{3-2}$$

New definitions and assumptions

In this chapter we have introduced into our analysis the assumption that there are governments in the economy. This assumption means that governments do three things: (1) They spend for goods and services; (2) they collect taxes; and (3) they make transfer payments. The consequences of this assumption require additional explanation.

Aggregate demand If governments spend for goods and services, aggregate demand, instead of having just two components (consumption and investment), now has three components: the consumption component, the net investment component, and the *government spending for goods and services* component G. We therefore define aggregate demand as

$$D \equiv C + I + G \tag{3-3}$$

What determines the size of G? Our assumption is that G is an exogenous variable. It may increase or decrease, but its size depends upon political decisions. It is not related to, or dependent upon, any of the economic variables in our models. This we symbolize mathematically be writing

$$G = \overline{G} \tag{3-4}$$

Taxes, transfer payments, and disposable income We shall define taxes Tx as the sums collected by governments from persons in the economy for which these persons receive no goods or services in direct exchange. We shall assume that all taxes are personal taxes: they are collected from persons rather than from corporations.

Transfer payments Tr are just the opposite of taxes. They are equal to the sums paid out by governments to persons for which these persons provide governments with no goods or services in direct exchange. All transfer payments, we shall assume, are paid to persons rather than to corporate business firms.

Because a transfer payment is the reverse of a tax, we may combine these two concepts into one concept. Net taxes T we define as equal to taxes minus transfer payments.

$$T \equiv Tx - Tr \tag{3-5}$$

In most economies tax collections exceed transfer payments; and net taxes are therefore a positive amount.

Disposable income Y_d is defined as being equal to national income minus net taxes.

$$Y_d \equiv Y - T \tag{3-6}$$

In an economy in which governments collect no net taxes, Y and Y_d are equal; but if governments collect a positive amount of net taxes (because taxes are greater than transfer payments), then Y_d is less than Y by the amount of the net taxes.

Consumption In the last chapter we assumed that consumption was an increasing and linear function of *national* income. National income and disposable income in the last chapter were equal because there were no governments to collect taxes or make transfer payments. Thus when we assumed consumption was a function of national income, we were really assuming that consumption was a function of disposable income.

In this chapter, we explicitly assume consumption to be an increasing and linear function of *disposable* income. We write this consumption function as

$$C = C_0 + bY_d \tag{3-7}$$

We make the same kind of assumptions about this consumption function that we made about the consumption function in the previous chapter.

1 C_0, autonomous consumption, is positive

$$C_0 > 0$$

2 The parameter b is greater than zero and less than one.

$$0 < b < 1$$

3 Having made consumption a function of disposable income we must also make saving a function of disposable income. We now define saving S as being equal to disposable income less consumption.

$$S \equiv Y_d - C \tag{3-8}$$

Substituting the consumption function (equation 3-7) for C in the equation above, we obtain

$$S = Y_d - (C_0 + bY_d)$$

and find that

$$\begin{aligned} S &= Y_d - C_0 - bY_d \\ &= -C_0 + Y_d - bY_d \\ &= -C_0 + (1 - b)Y_d \end{aligned} \tag{3-9}$$

This tells us that S at any level of disposable income equals $(1 - b)$ times Y_d minus autonomous consumption. Since we have assumed b to be greater than zero and less than one, $1 - b$ is less than one and greater than zero.

4 In the definitions of the average and marginal propensities to consume and to save employed in the previous chapter the national income variable appeared. Because national income and disposable income were equal in the last chapter and are not equal in this chapter, we must substitute Y_d for Y in these definitions. We therefore have

$$\text{MPC} = \frac{\Delta C}{\Delta Y_d} \tag{3-10}$$

$$\text{MPS} = \frac{\Delta S}{\Delta Y_d} \tag{3-11}$$

$$\text{APC} = \frac{C}{Y_d} \tag{3-12}$$

$$\text{APS} = \frac{S}{Y_d} \tag{3-13}$$

Using these revised definitions, we find that the MPC is again equal to the parameter b in the consumption function and the MPS is equal to $1 - b$. The proof of this first proposition starts with our consumption function.

$$C = C_0 + bY_d \tag{3-7}$$

When Y_d changes by ΔY_d, C will change by ΔC.

$$C + \Delta C = C_0 + b(Y_d + \Delta Y_d) \tag{3-14}$$

Subtracting equation 3-7 from equation 3-14, we find

$$\Delta C = b\,\Delta Y_d \tag{3-15}$$

and solving for the MPC we get

$$\frac{\Delta C}{\Delta Y_d} = b \tag{3-16}$$

The proof that the MPS is equal to $1 - b$ is left to the student.

If we substitute the consumption function (equation 3-7) for C in our revised definition of the APC, we have

$$\frac{C}{Y_d} = \frac{C_0 + bY_d}{Y_d}$$

We find that

$$\frac{C}{Y_d} = \frac{C_0}{Y_d} + \frac{bY_d}{Y_d}$$

and that

$$\frac{C}{Y_d} = \frac{C_0}{Y_d} + b \tag{3-17}$$

This is similar to equation 2-24. Proof of the proposition that

$$\text{APS} = \frac{-C_0}{Y_d} + (1 - b) \tag{3-18}$$

is again left to the student, along with the proof of the following two propositions:

- The MPC plus the MPS equals 1.
- The APC plus the APS equals 1.

Exercise 3-1

1 Define each of the following in the spaces provided:

a $T \equiv$ __________ − __________

b $Y_d \equiv$ __________ − __________

c $S \equiv$ __________ − __________

d MPC $\equiv$ __________ / __________

e MPS $\equiv$ __________ / __________

f APC $\equiv$ __________ / __________

g APS $\equiv$ __________ / __________

2 Suppose the consumption function is $C = \$40 + 0.60Y_d$.

a The saving function is $S =$ __________

b The MPC is __________

c The MPS is __________

3 If $C = \$40 + 0.60Y_d$, and if T is \$50, when Y is \$600:

a $Y_d =$ __________

b $C =$ __________

c $S =$ __________

4 When the consumption function is $C = C_0 + bY_d$:
a What assumptions are made about C_0, b, and $1 - b$?
b Show that the saving function is $S = -C_0 + (1 - b)Y_d$.
c Show that the MPS $= 1 - b$.
d Show that the APS $= -C_0/Y_d + (1 - b)$.

5 Prove that:
a MPC + MPS = 1
b APC + APS = 1

6 Suppose the consumption function is $\$30 + 0.70Y_d$.
a Write the equations that will enable us to compute the APC and the APS at any level of Y_d.

(1) APC = __________

(2) APS = __________

b When Y_d is \$500, the APC is __________ and the APS is __________

7 The equilibrium national income is the national income which is equal to __________

8 D in this chapter is equal to __________ + __________ + __________

9 If $C = C_0 + bY_d$, $C_0 > 0$, and $0 < b < 1$:
a Show that the APC decreases as Y_d increases.
b Show that the APS increases as Y_d increases.

10 In this chapter we assume that both G and I are __________ variables.

A SIMPLE MODEL: EXOGENOUS TAXES

So far we have said nothing about what determines the amount of net taxes paid in the economy. There are two assumptions we might make about net taxes: (1) We might assume that net taxes are an exogenous variable, or (2) we might assume that they are a function of national income. In this simple model we shall assume that they are exogenous. (In the more advanced model that follows it is assumed that net taxes are an increasing and linear function of national income.) In both models we look for an equation that tells us what the equilibrium national income is and for the equations that tell us what the values of the various multipliers are.

Equilibrium national income

If we assume that net taxes are an exogenous variable, we may write

$$T = \bar{T} \tag{3-19}$$

We add to this assumption the assumptions that both I and G are also exogenous variables.

$$I = \bar{I} \tag{3-1}$$
$$G = \bar{G} \tag{3-4}$$

Consumption is an increasing and linear function of disposable income.

$$C = C_0 + bY_d \tag{3-7}$$

Disposable income is defined as

$$Y_d \equiv Y - T \tag{3-6}$$

Aggregate demand is the sum of its three components:

$$D \equiv C + I + G \tag{3-3}$$

Finally, the equilibrium national income is the national income which equals the aggregate quantity of goods and services demanded:

$$Y = D \tag{3-2}$$

These seven equations are our model. Equations 3-6 and 3-3 are definitional equations; 3-2 is the equilibrium equation; and the remaining four equations are behavioral equations. The model has four endogenous variables (Y, Y_d, C, and D) and three exogenous variables (T, I, and G); therefore, it has a solution for all the variables. We are primarily interested in the equilibrium value of Y.

To find the equilibrium value of Y we start with the equilibrium equation

$$Y = D \tag{3-2}$$

We then substitute the right side of equation 3-3 for D

$$Y = C + I + G$$

For C in this equation we substitute the consumption equation (3-7)

$$Y = (C_0 + bY_d) + I + G$$

For Y_d we substitute the definition of Y_d (equation 3-6)

$$Y = C_0 + b(Y - T) + I + G$$

indicate that T, I, and G are exogenous, and expand the equation to

$$Y = C_0 + bY - b\overline{T} + \overline{I} + \overline{G}$$

Moving all terms containing Y to the left side and all other terms to the right side, we have

$$Y - bY = C_0 - b\overline{T} + \overline{I} + \overline{G}$$

Now we solve for Y

$$Y(1 - b) = C_0 - b\overline{T} + \overline{I} + \overline{G}$$

$$Y^* = \frac{C_0 - b\overline{T} + \overline{I} + \overline{G}}{1 - b} \tag{3-20}$$

This tells us that the equilibrium Y is equal to the quantity autonomous consumption less the MPC times net taxes plus I plus G divided by the quantity 1 minus the MPC.

Suppose, for example, the consumption function is $C = \$40 + 0.60Y_d$, net taxes are \$50, I is \$60, and G is \$45. The equilibrium Y would be

$$\begin{aligned} Y^* &= \frac{\$40 - 0.60(\$50) + \$60 + \$45}{1 - 0.60} \\ &= \frac{\$40 - \$30 + \$60 + \$45}{0.40} \\ &= \frac{\$115}{0.40} \\ &= \$287.5 \end{aligned}$$

Having found Y^*, we can also find Y_d^*, C^*, and D^* by using the other equations in the model.

$$\begin{aligned} Y_d^* &= Y^* - \overline{T} = \$287.5 - \$50 = \$237.5 \\ C^* &= \$40 + 0.60Y_d^* = \$40 + 0.60(\$237.5) = \$182.5 \\ D^* &= C^* + \overline{I} + \overline{G} = \$182.5 + \$60 + \$45 = \$287.5 \end{aligned}$$

We can also find S^* by subtracting C^* from Y_d^*

$$S^* = Y_d - C = \$237.5 - \$182.5 = \$55$$

Note that Y^* and D^* are equal.

An alternative approach

There is a second approach we can use to get the same results. This alternative corresponds to the saving-investment approach we employed in the last chapter. There we found that the equilibrium Y is the Y at which S and I are equal. When governments that collect net taxes and spend for goods and services are introduced into the analysis, the equilibrium Y is no longer the Y at which S

is equal to I. There is, however, a relation between S, I, G, and T that enables us to find Y^* by using another approach.

To use this alternative approach we need one additional equation. When governments tax, there are no longer two things people can do with the national income (spend for consumption or save) but three: spend for consumption, save, and pay their net taxes. Thus

$$Y \equiv C + S + T \tag{3-21}$$

Using the equilibrium equation ($Y = D$), we substitute $C + S + T$ for Y and $C + I + G$ for D:

$$C + S + T = C + I + G \tag{3-22}$$

This is another way of stating that Y is at its equilibrium level when $C + S + T$ and $C + I + G$ are equal. Because C appears on both sides of this equation we can subtract C from both sides of the equation and obtain

$$S + T = I + G \tag{3-23}$$

The equilibrium national income is the income at which saving plus net taxes equals investment plus government spending for goods and services.

Using this statement of the equilibrium national income, we now substitute the saving equation 3-9 for S.

$$[-C_0 + (1 - b)Y_d] + T = I + G$$

For Y_d we substitute its definition (equation 3-6) and indicate that T, I, and G are exogenous variables.

$$-C_0 + (1 - b)(Y - \bar{T}) + \bar{T} = \bar{I} + \bar{G}$$

Expanding this equation, we have

$$-C_0 + (1 - b)Y - (1 - b)\bar{T} + \bar{T} = \bar{I} + \bar{G}$$
$$-C_0 + Y - bY - \bar{T} + b\bar{T} + \bar{T} = \bar{I} + G$$

Moving all expressions with Y in them to the left side and all other expressions to the right side, we obtain

$$Y - bY = C_0 - b\bar{T} + \bar{T} - \bar{T} + \bar{I} + \bar{G}$$

The $+\bar{T}$ and the $-\bar{T}$ offset each other, and we now have

$$Y - bY = C_0 - b\bar{T} + \bar{I} + \bar{G}$$

When we solve for Y, we have

$$Y^* = \frac{C_0 - b\bar{T} + \bar{I} + \bar{G}}{1 - b} \tag{3-20}$$

This is exactly the same equation for the equilibrium value of Y we obtained originally.

The important thing to note is that when Y is at its equilibrium level, not only do we find that

$$Y = D$$

or

$$Y = C + I + G$$

but we also find that

$S + T = I + C$

In the numerical example worked about above, the equilibrium Y was \$287.5, and S was \$55. It was assumed that T was \$50, that I was \$60, and G was \$45. Therefore

$$S + T = I + G$$
$$\$55 + \$50 = \$60 + \$45$$
$$\$105 = \$105$$

The multipliers

If any of the three exogenous variables (I, G, or T) or if the parameter C_0 changes, the equilibrium level of Y will also change. We are particularly interested in this chapter in what happens to Y^* if G or T changes. Let us take these in turn and first find the relationship between a change in G and the resulting change in Y^* and then find the relation between a change in T and the resulting change in Y^*. [We leave it to the student to show that both the consumption and the investment multipliers equal $1/(1 - b)$.]

The government expenditures multiplier If G changes by $\Delta\bar{G}$, Y^* will change by ΔY^*. Using our equilibrium equation (4-20), we can write

$$Y^* + \Delta Y^* = \frac{C_0 - b\bar{T} + \bar{I} + \bar{G} + \Delta\bar{G}}{1 - b}$$

From this we subtract the equilibrium equation and obtain

$$\Delta Y^* = \frac{\Delta\bar{G}}{1 - b}$$

If we divide through by $\Delta\bar{G}$, we have

$$\frac{\Delta Y^*}{\Delta\bar{G}} = \frac{1}{1 - b} \tag{3-24}$$

This expression, $\Delta Y^*/\Delta\bar{G}$, we define as the government expenditures multiplier k_G, that is, the ratio of the change in Y^* (brought about by a change in $\bar{G}$) to the change in $\bar{G}$

$$k_G \equiv \frac{\Delta Y^*}{\Delta\bar{G}} = \frac{1}{1 - b} \tag{3-25}$$

The value of this multiplier is equal to 1 divided by the quantity 1 minus the MPC.

In our numerical example, where the MPC was 0.60, the multiplier would be $1/(1 - 0.60)$ or $1/0.40$, which is equal to $2\frac{1}{2}$; a change in $\bar{G}$ would have brought about a change in Y^* $2\frac{1}{2}$ times the change in $\bar{G}$. It should be noted that the sign of this multiplier is positive. Therefore, when $\bar{G}$ increases, Y^* will increase, and when $\bar{G}$ decreases, Y^* will also decrease. When the multiplier is $2\frac{1}{2}$, a \$10 increase in $\bar{G}$ will increase Y^* by \$25 and a \$10 decrease in $\bar{G}$ will decrease Y^* by \$25.

The tax multiplier When taxes change, the equilibrium national income will also change. A change in $\bar{T}$ equal to $\Delta\bar{T}$ results in a change in Y^* equal to ΔY^*.

Using our equilibrium equation (3-20), we can therefore write

$$Y^* + \Delta Y^* = \frac{C_0 - b(\overline{T} + \Delta\overline{T}) + \overline{I} + \overline{G}}{1 - b}$$

$$= \frac{C_0 - b\overline{T} - b\,\Delta\overline{T} + \overline{I} + \overline{G}}{1 - b}$$

By subtracting the equilibrium equation we obtain

$$\Delta Y^* = \frac{-b\,\Delta\overline{T}}{1 - b}$$

The tax multiplier k_T is the ratio of the change in Y^* (brought about by a change in $\overline{T}$) to the change in $\overline{T}$. To obtain this ratio we divide through by $\Delta\overline{T}$ in the equation above

$$k_T \equiv \frac{\Delta Y^*}{\Delta\overline{T}} = \frac{-b}{1 - b} \tag{3-26}$$

We find that the tax multiplier equals the negative ratio of the MPC to the quantity 1 minus the MPC.

There are several important things to note about the tax multiplier:

1 The tax multiplier is a negative number (in contrast with the government expenditures multiplier which is a positive number). This means that an increase in taxes results in a decrease in equilibrium Y, and a decrease in taxes brings about an increase in equilibrium Y.

2 The tax multiplier is not of the same absolute value as the government expenditures multiplier or the investment or consumption multipliers. These multipliers have an absolute value, i.e., a value that ignores their sign, of $1/(1 - b)$, and the tax multiplier has a value of $b/(1 - b)$.

3 The tax multiplier has an absolute value which is exactly 1 less than the government expenditures, investment, and consumption multipliers. This is to say that, ignoring the minus sign in front of the tax multiplier,

$$k_T = k_G - 1 \tag{3-27}$$

or

$$\frac{b}{1 - b} = \frac{1}{1 - b} - 1 \tag{3-28}$$

This we can prove in the following way. We start with

$$\frac{1}{1 - b} = \frac{1}{1 - b} - 1$$

To the numerator on the left side of the equation we add 1 and then subtract 1. We do not change the value of this numerator when we add zero to it; and +1 and −1 equal 0.

$$\frac{b + 1 - 1}{1 - b} = \frac{1}{1 - b} - 1$$

We can now separate the left expression into two parts.

$$\frac{1}{1 - b} - \frac{1 - b}{1 - b} = \frac{1}{1 - b} - 1$$

The term $(1 - b)/(1 - b)$ is equal to 1, and we may now write

$$\frac{1}{1-b} - 1 = \frac{1}{1-b} - 1$$

The value of the tax multiplier is 1 less than the value of the government expenditures, investment, and consumption multipliers.

4 The value of the tax multiplier is negative and 1 less than the other multipliers for a fairly simple set of reasons.

a There is a tax multiplier because a change in taxes changes the disposable income of consumers. When T *increases* by some amount, Y_d *decreases* by that same amount; and when T *decreases*, Y_d *increases* by that amount.

b When Y_d decreases, consumers decrease their consumption expenditures by an amount equal to their MPC times the decrease in Y_d; and when Y_d increases, consumers increase C by an amount that equals their MPC times the increase in Y_d. Thus:

- $+\Delta\overline{T}$ results in a $-\Delta C$ equal to $-b\,\Delta\overline{T}$.
- $-\Delta\overline{T}$ results in a $+\Delta C$ equal to $+b\,\Delta\overline{T}$.

c If we take the decrease in consumption $-b\,\Delta\overline{T}$ that results from an increase in taxes $+\Delta\overline{T}$ and multiply this decrease in consumption by the consumption multiplier, we find that the change in Y^* is

$$\Delta Y^* = -b\,\Delta\overline{T}\frac{1}{1-b}$$

$$= \frac{-b\,\Delta\overline{T}}{1-b}$$

$$\frac{\Delta Y^*}{\Delta\overline{T}} = \frac{-b}{1-b}$$

This again tells us that the ratio of the change in Y^* to the change in taxes, i.e., the tax multiplier, is equal to the negative ratio of the MPC to 1 minus the MPC.

d Similarly, when we multiply the increase in consumption $b\,\Delta\overline{T}$ that results from a decrease in taxes $-\Delta\overline{T}$ by the consumption multiplier, we have the change in Y^*.

$$\Delta Y^* = b\,\Delta\overline{T}\frac{1}{1-b}$$

$$= \frac{b\,\Delta\overline{T}}{1-b}$$

Dividing through by the negative change in taxes $-\Delta\overline{T}$, we find that the tax multiplier is

$$\frac{\Delta Y^*}{\Delta\overline{T}} = \frac{-b}{1-b}$$

In short, the tax multiplier is a negative figure and 1 less than the other multipliers because the effect of a change in taxes is to change consumption in the opposite direction by an amount equal to the change in taxes times the MPC.

5 In this model the tax multiplier can always be found by multiplying the government expenditures multiplier by $-b$. This can be done because these other multipliers have a value of $1/(1-b)$; and $1/(1-b)$ times $-b$ is equal to $-b/(1-b)$, which is the value of the tax multiplier.

To continue our numerical example, if b is 0.60, the k_G will be $2\frac{1}{2}$. We can find the tax multiplier in three different ways. It equals $-0.60/(1-0.60)$, which is $-(0.60/0.40)$, or $-1\frac{1}{2}$. It also equals the government expenditures multiplier of $2\frac{1}{2}$ minus 1, which (with the sign changed) is $-1\frac{1}{2}$. And it equals the government expenditures multiplier of $2\frac{1}{2}$ multiplied by $-b$, -0.60; and $2\frac{1}{2}$ times -0.60 is again $-1\frac{1}{2}$.

The balanced budget multiplier Imagine that government increases both government expenditures for goods and services *and* taxes by equal amounts. What will be the effect on the equilibrium national income? The effect will be to increase Y^* by an amount that equals the increases in $\bar{G}$ and in $\bar{T}$.

To see that this is true, suppose we let the equal increases in $\bar{G}$ and $\bar{T}$ be ΔX. Thus

$$\Delta\bar{G} = \Delta\bar{T} = \Delta X$$

When $\bar{G}$ changes by ΔX and $\bar{T}$ changes by ΔX, Y^* will change by ΔY^*, and we can write (using equilibrium equation 3-20),

$$Y + \Delta Y^* = \frac{C_0 - b(\bar{T} + \Delta X) + \bar{T} + \bar{G} + \Delta X}{1-b}$$

$$= \frac{C_0 - b\bar{T} - b\,\Delta X + \bar{T} + \bar{G} + \Delta X}{1-b}$$

From the latter equation we subtract the equilibrium equation and obtain

$$\Delta Y^* = \frac{-b\,\Delta X + \Delta X}{1-b}$$

$$= \frac{\Delta X(-b+1)}{1-b}$$

$$= \frac{\Delta X(1-b)}{1-b}$$

$$= \Delta X$$

If we wish to know the ratio of the change in Y^* to the equal changes in $\bar{G}$ and $\bar{T}$ we divide the equation above by ΔX and get

$$\frac{\Delta Y^*}{\Delta X} = 1 \qquad (3\text{-}29)$$

This tells us that equal changes in $\bar{G}$ and $\bar{T}$ have a multiplier effect of 1 upon the equilibrium Y: they increase Y^* by an amount equal to 1 times the change in $\bar{G}$ and in $\bar{T}$.

Another way of seeing the truth of this proposition is to take the multiplier effect of the change in $\bar{G}$ and of the change in $\bar{T}$ separately and then add the results. Again let $\Delta\bar{G} = \Delta\bar{T} = \Delta X$. The multiplier effect of the change in $\bar{G}$ is

$$\Delta Y^* = \Delta X \frac{1}{1-b}$$

The multiplier effect of the change in $\bar{T}$ is

$$\Delta Y^* = \Delta X \frac{-b}{1-b}$$

Adding to find the total effect on Y^*,

$$\Delta Y^* = \Delta X \frac{1}{1-b} + \Delta X \frac{-b}{1-b}$$

$$= \frac{\Delta X}{1-b} + \frac{-b\,\Delta X}{1-b}$$

$$= \frac{\Delta X - b\,\Delta X}{1-b}$$

$$= \frac{\Delta X(1-b)}{1-b}$$

$$= \Delta X$$

If b is 0.60, the k_G will be $2\frac{1}{2}$ and the k_T will be $-1\frac{1}{2}$. A \$10 increase in $\bar{G}$ *by itself* increases Y^* by \$25. An equal increase in $\bar{T}$ of \$10 will, *by itself,* decrease Y^* by \$15. The \$25 increase and the \$15 decrease add up to a \$10 increase in Y^*. The short cut, of course, is to know that we can find the effect on equilibrium Y by multiplying the \$10 increase in $\bar{G}$ and in $\bar{T}$ by 1: a \$10 increase in $\bar{G}$ or in $\bar{T}$ times 1 is equal to a \$10 increase in Y^*.

There are two other things to note about equal changes in $\bar{G}$ and in $\bar{T}$: (1) If $\bar{G}$ and $\bar{T}$ both *decrease* by some amount, the effect will be to *decrease* Y^* by that amount. (2) We obtain these effects on Y^* regardless of the size of the MPC. It does not matter whether the MPC is 0.99, 0.50, or 0.01. Equal increases (or decreases) in $\bar{G}$ and in $\bar{T}$ will result in an equal increase (or decrease) in Y^*.

Exercise 3-2

1 Assume that
$C = \$20 + 0.80Y_d$
$I = \$40$
$G = \$30$
$T = \$30$

a The other equations needed to complete this model and to compute the equilibrium values of the seven variables are

$Y_d \equiv$ ________ $-$ ________

$D \equiv$ ________ $+$ ________ $+$ ________

________ $=$ ________

b In equilibrium:

(1) $Y^* =$ ________

(2) $Y_d^* =$ ________

(3) $C^* =$ ________

(4) $S^* =$ ________

(5) $D^* =$ ________

2 Using the equations in the question above, show that in equilibrium $S^* + T^* = I^* + G^*$.

3 Show that the investment multiplier $\Delta Y^*/\Delta \bar{I}$ and the consumption multiplier $\Delta Y^*/\Delta C_0$, when taxes are an exogenous variable, are equal to $1/(1 - b)$.

4 Suppose the MPC has the values shown in column 1 in the table below. Complete the table by computing the government expenditures multiplier and the tax multiplier and entering them in columns 2 and 3.

(1) MPC	(2) k_G	(3) k_T
0.90	________	________
0.80	________	________
0.75	________	________
$0.66\frac{2}{3}$	________	________
0.60	________	________
0.50	________	________

---

5 Assume the MPC is 0.70. To increase Y^* by \$100:

a $\bar{G}$ would have to (increase, decrease) ________ by \$________

b $\bar{T}$ would have to (increase, decrease) ________ by \$________

c Both $\bar{G}$ and $\bar{T}$ would have to ________ by \$________

6 Prove that

$$Y^* = \frac{C_0 - b\bar{T} + \bar{I} + \bar{G}}{1 - b}$$

7 Show that:

a The tax multiplier has a value equal to $-b/(1 - b)$.

b The government expenditures multiplier has a value equal to $1/(1 - b)$.

c The tax multiplier has a value 1 less than the government expenditures multiplier.

d The balanced budget multiplier is equal to 1.

A MORE ADVANCED MODEL: INDUCED TAXES

We shall assume in this more advanced model that net taxes, instead of being an exogenous variable, are an increasing and linear function of national income. We express this mathematically as

$$T = T_0 + tY \qquad (3\text{-}30)$$

T_0 we call *autonomous taxes,* the taxes that would be levied even if Y were zero. The parameter t relates changes in Y to changes in T. The expression tY we call *induced taxes,* the taxes that are levied because Y is greater than zero.

When Y changes by ΔY, T will change by ΔT.

$$\begin{aligned} T + \Delta T &= T_0 + t(Y + \Delta Y) \\ &= T_0 + tY + t\Delta Y \end{aligned}$$

From this last equation we subtract equation 3-30 and obtain

$$\Delta T = t\Delta Y \qquad (3\text{-}31)$$

Dividing through by ΔY, we find

$$\frac{\Delta T}{\Delta Y} = t \qquad (3\text{-}32)$$

The expression $\Delta T/\Delta Y$ we define as the *marginal tax rate* (MTR), the ratio of a change in taxes (that results from a change in national income) to the change in national income. In our linear tax function, t is the MTR, and we assume it is a positive number, indicating that as Y increases, so will T. We also assume that t is less than 1.

$$0 < t < 1$$

Equilibrium national income

The only way our more advanced model differs from our simple model is in the tax function. Taxes are now a function of Y rather than being an exogenous variable. The other equations in this more advanced model are the same as they were in the simple model:

$$\begin{aligned} C &= C_0 + bY_d && (3\text{-}7) \\ I &= \bar{I} && (3\text{-}1) \\ G &= \bar{G} && (3\text{-}4) \\ Y_d &\equiv Y - T && (3\text{-}6) \\ D &\equiv C + I + G && (3\text{-}3) \\ Y &= D && (3\text{-}2) \end{aligned}$$

These six equations plus the tax function (equation 3-30) give us a total of seven equations, five endogenous variables (Y, Y_d, C, T, and D), and two exogenous variables (I and G). The model, therefore, should have a solution.

To find the equilibrium Y we start with equation 3-2 and substitute equation 3-3 into it.

$$\begin{aligned} Y &= D && (3\text{-}2) \\ Y &= C + I + G \end{aligned}$$

For C we substitute the consumption function (equation 3-7), and for I and G we substitute their exogenous values.

$$Y = (C_0 + bY_d) + \bar{I} + \bar{G}$$

For Y_d we substitute its definition (equation 3-6).

$$Y = C_0 + b(Y - T) + \bar{I} + \bar{G}$$

Finally, for T we substitute the tax function

$$\begin{aligned} y &= C_0 + bY - b(T_0 + tY) + \bar{I} + \bar{G} \\ &= C_0 + bY - bT_0 - btY + \bar{I} + \bar{G} \end{aligned}$$

and solve for Y.

$$Y - bY + btY = C_0 - bT_0 + \bar{I} + \bar{G}$$
$$Y(1 - b + bt) = C_0 - bT_0 + \bar{I} + \bar{G}$$
$$Y^* = \frac{C_0 - bT_0 + \bar{I} + \bar{G}}{1 - b + bt} \tag{3-33}$$

This solution equation tells us that equilibrium Y equals the quantity autonomous consumption minus the MPC times autonomous taxes plus investment plus government expenditures for goods and services divided by the quantity 1 minus the MPC plus the MPC times the MTR.

An alternative approach We might have sought the level of Y at which

$$S + T = I + G \tag{3-23}$$

substituted the saving function (equation 3-9) for S and the tax function (equation 3-30) for T, inserted the exogenous values of I and G, and solved for Y as follows:

$$S + T = I + G$$
$$[-C_0 + (1 - b)Y_d] + (T_0 + tY) = \bar{I} + \bar{G}$$
$$[-C_0 + (1 - b)(Y - T)] + (T_0 + tY) = \bar{I} + \bar{G}$$
$$[-C_0 + (1 - b)(Y - T_0 - tY)] + (T_0 + tY) = \bar{I} + \bar{G}$$
$$(-C_0 + Y - bY - T_0 + bT_0 - tY + btY) + (T_0 + tY) = \bar{I} + \bar{G}$$
$$-C_0 + Y - bY + bT_0 + btY = \bar{I} + \bar{G}$$
$$Y - bY + btY = C_0 - bT_0 + \bar{I} + \bar{G}$$
$$Y(1 - b + bt) = C_0 = bT_0 + \bar{I} + \bar{G}$$
$$Y^* = \frac{C_0 - bT_0 + \bar{I} + \bar{G}}{1 - b + bt} \tag{3-33}$$

This result is the same as that originally obtained, but the alternative approach is somewhat more complicated.

A numerical example Assume that

$$C = \$40 + 0.50Y_d$$
$$I = \$60$$
$$G = \$55$$
$$T = \$10 + 0.20Y$$

The equilibrium Y is

$$Y^* = \frac{\$40 - 0.50(\$10) + \$60 + \$55}{1 - 0.50 + 0.50(0.20)}$$
$$= \frac{\$40 - \$5 + \$60 + \$55}{1 - 0.50 + 0.10}$$
$$= \frac{\$150}{0.60}$$
$$= \$250$$

We can also find T^*, Y_d^*, C^*, D^*, and S^*.

$$T^* = \$10 + 0.20(250) = \$10 + \$50 = \$60$$
$$Y_d^* = \$250 - \$60 = \$190$$

$C^* = \$40 + 0.50(\$190) = \$40 + \$95 = \$135$
$D^* = \$135 + \$60 + \$55 = \$250$
$S^* = \$190 - \$135 = \$55$

We can observe that $Y^* = D^*$ and that

$$S^* + T^* = I^* + G^*$$
$$\$55 + \$60 = \$60 + \$55$$
$$\$115 = \$115$$

The multipliers

Just as in the earlier model we found that when T or G changes, equilibrium Y also changes, we find in this more advanced model that a change in either $\bar{G}$ or in the tax *function* brings about a change in Y^*. (We again leave it to the student to work out the investment and consumption multipliers.)

The government expenditures multiplier When $\bar{G}$ changes by $\Delta\bar{G}$, Y^* changes by ΔY^*. Using our equilibrium equation 3-33, we can write

$$Y + \Delta Y^* = \frac{C_0 - bT_0 + \bar{I} + \bar{G} + \Delta\bar{G}}{1 - b + bt}$$

and subtract from this equation the equilibrium equation (3-33) to obtain

$$\Delta Y^* = \frac{\Delta\bar{G}}{1 - b + bt} \qquad (3\text{-}34)$$

Dividing through by ΔG to obtain the government expenditures multiplier $\Delta Y^*/\Delta G$, we get

$$k_G \equiv \frac{\Delta Y^*}{\Delta G} = \frac{1}{1 - b + bt} \qquad (3\text{-}35)$$

When taxes are a function of Y (rather than an exogenous variable), the government expenditures multiplier is equal to 1 divided by the quantity 1 minus the MPC plus the MPC times the MTR. In our numerical example, in which b was 0.50 and t was 0.20, the value of k_G is

$$k_G = \frac{1}{1 - 0.50 + 0.50(0.2)}$$
$$= \frac{1}{0.60}$$
$$= 1\tfrac{2}{3}$$

The fact that this number is positive means that an increase in $\bar{G}$ of \$15 would result in Y^* increasing by \$15 times $1\tfrac{2}{3}$, or \$25 and that a decrease in $\bar{G}$ of \$15 would result in Y^* decreasing by \$15 times $1\tfrac{2}{3}$, or \$25.

Taxes and the government expenditures multiplier The careful observer will note that the \$15 increase in government expenditures for goods and services did *not* bring about a \$15 government deficit. It is true that $\bar{G}$ increased by \$15, but it is also true that this \$15 increase in G brought about a \$25 increase in Y^*. And as a result of the \$25 increase in Y^*, T increased by an amount equal to t times the increase in Y^*.

$$\Delta T = t\,\Delta Y \qquad (3\text{-}31)$$

In our example the increase in T was 0.20($25), or $5. So while $\bar{G}$ increased by $15, T increased by $5. And the $15 increase in $\bar{G}$ brought about a government deficit of only $10: the $15 increase in G less the $5 increase in tax collections.

Is there a formula that tells us the change that will take place in the government budget ΔB as a result of a change $\Delta\bar{G}$ in $\bar{G}$? The change in the budget is by definition equal to the change in $\bar{G}$ less the change in T^*.

$$\Delta B \equiv \Delta\bar{G} - \Delta T^*$$

Because ΔT equals t times ΔY^*, we can write

$$\Delta B = \Delta\bar{G} - t\,\Delta Y^*$$

The change in Y^* is equal to the change in $\bar{G}$ times the government expenditures multiplier.

$$\Delta Y = \Delta G \frac{1}{1 - b + bt}$$

We can therefore write

$$\Delta B = \Delta\bar{G} - \frac{t\,\Delta\bar{G}}{1 - b + bt}$$

$$= \Delta\bar{G}\left(1 - \frac{t}{1 - b + bt}\right) \qquad (3\text{-}36)$$

The change in the budget equals the change in $\bar{G}$ times the quantity 1 minus the MTR divided by 1 minus the MPC plus the MPT times the MTR.

In our example, where $\bar{G}$ is $15, b is 0.50, and t is 0.20,

$$\Delta B = \$15\left(1 - \frac{0.20}{1 - 0.50 + 0.50(0.20)}\right)$$

$$= \$15\left(1 - \frac{0.20}{0.60}\right)$$

$$= \$15(1 - \tfrac{1}{3})$$

$$= \$15(\tfrac{2}{3})$$

$$= \$10$$

The positive sign in front of the $10 here means that the government deficit has *increased* by $10.

The tax multiplier We do not expect that the value or the sign of the tax multiplier k_T will be the same as k_G. To find the tax multiplier when

$$T = T_0 + tY \qquad (3\text{-}30)$$

we must first define what we mean by a change in taxes. We shall *define* a change in taxes as a change in autonomous taxes (T_0, rather than a change in the tax rate t, or a change in total taxes, $T_0 + tY$). Our tax multiplier is therefore

$$k_T \equiv \frac{\Delta Y}{\Delta T_0} \qquad (3\text{-}37)$$

To find the value of this tax multiplier we use the equation for the equilibrium national income. When T_0 changes by ΔT_0, Y^* changes by ΔY^*.

$$Y^* + \Delta Y^* = \frac{C_0 - b(T_0 + \Delta T_0) + \bar{I} + \bar{G}}{1 - b + bt}$$

From this we subtract the equilibrium equation to obtain

$$\Delta Y^* = \frac{-b\,\Delta T_0}{1 - b + bt} \qquad (3\text{-}38)$$

Dividing through by ΔT_0, we obtain the tax multiplier.

$$k_T \equiv \frac{\Delta Y^*}{\Delta T_0} = \frac{-b}{1 - b + bt} \qquad (3\text{-}39)$$

We note several things about this multiplier:

1 It has a negative sign: changes in autonomous taxes result in a change in Y^* in the opposite direction.

2 Its value is not equal to the value of the government expenditures multiplier, which is $1/(1 - b + bt)$.

3 The value of k_T is equal to the government expenditures multiplier multiplied by the MPC.

$$\frac{1}{1 - b + bt}\,b = \frac{b}{1 - b + bt}$$

4 Because b is less than unity, the value of k_T is less than the value of k_G. For example, if k_G is $2\frac{1}{2}$ and the MPC is 0.80,

$$\begin{aligned} k_T &= 2.5(0.8) \\ &= 2.0 \end{aligned}$$

and 2.0 is less than 2.5.

The multipliers and the MTR The government expenditures multiplier is equal to $1/(1 - b + bt)$. Because t is both in the denominator of this expression and positive, as t increases, the value of k_G decreases (and vice versa). To illustrate this relationship between the value of k_G and t, assume that the MPC is constant and equal to 0.80. k_G would have the values shown in Table 3-1 as t varies.

The values of k_T are also shown in column 3 of Table 3-1. They also decrease in value as t increases. Note again that the value of k_T is equal to k_G times the MPC, which is 0.80 in this example.

This relationship between t and the two multipliers is important for at least two reasons:

1 The most obvious reason is that the smaller t is, the greater the effect of a change in $\bar{G}$, $\bar{T}$, C_0, or T_0 upon the equilibrium Y; and the larger t is, the smaller the effect of these changes on Y^*.

TABLE 3-1

(1) t	(2) k_G	(3) k_T
0.1	3.57	−2.86
0.2	2.78	−2.22
0.3	2.27	−1.82
0.4	1.92	−1.54
0.5	1.67	−1.33

2 If the tax function is a function in which the MTR increases as Y increases (as it does in the American personal income tax system), the size of the multipliers will decrease as Y rises and increase as Y falls.

The balanced budget multiplier again In our *simple* model in which taxes were an exogenous variable we saw that:

- If taxes and government expenditures increase by an equal amount, the equilibrium national income will increase by the same amount.
- This result was achieved because the tax multiplier was negative and 1 less in value than the government expenditures multiplier.

We now ask two questions about our model in which taxes are a function of national income: (1) Is the tax multiplier (defined as $\Delta Y^*/\Delta T_0$) 1 less in value than the government expenditures multiplier $\Delta Y^*/\Delta \bar{G}$? (2) Will equal increase in taxes and government expenditures increase the equilibrium national income by the same amount?

To dispose of the first question first: Is k_T 1 less than k_G? Does

$$\frac{\Delta Y^*}{\Delta T_0} = \frac{\Delta Y^*}{\Delta \bar{G}} - 1$$

and, therefore, does

$$\frac{b}{1 - b + bt} = \frac{1}{1 - b + bt} - 1$$

The answer to this question is no. *As we have defined the tax multiplier,* it does not have a value 1 less than the government expenditures multiplier.

We can show that they are not equal by substituting $(1 - b + bt)/(1 - b + bt)$ for 1 in the equation above.

$$\frac{b}{1 - b + bt} \neq \frac{1}{1 - b + bt} - \frac{1 - b + bt}{1 - b + bt}$$

$$\neq \frac{1 - (1 - b + bt)}{1 - b + bt}$$

$$\neq \frac{b - bt}{1 - b + bt}$$

The two sides are not equal unless t, the MTR, is equal to zero. If t is greater than zero, b and $b - bt$ are not equal and therefore the two fractions are not equal. When the MTR is greater than zero, the tax multiplier (the change in equilibrium Y divided by the change in autonomous taxes) is not 1 less in value than the government expenditures multiplier.

Our second question is whether an equal increase in taxes and government expenditures will increase equilibrium national income by the same amount. The answer to this question depends upon what we mean by an increase in taxes:

- If by an increase in taxes we mean an increase in autonomous taxes, the answer is that an equal increase in T_0 and $\bar{G}$ will not increase Y^* by the same amount.
- If by an increase in taxes we mean an increase in autonomous taxes *plus* the increase in taxes that is induced by the increase in Y, the answer is yes: an equal increase in T and $\bar{G}$ will increase Y^* by the same amount.

To demonstrate these two propositions, let us go back to an equation we used earlier to find Y^* in this model

$$Y^* = C_0 + bY - b(T_0 + tY) + \overline{I} + \overline{G}$$
$$= C_0 + bY - bT_0 - btY + \overline{I} + \overline{G}$$

Suppose both T_0 and $\overline{G}$ change by an amount equal to ΔX.

$$\Delta T_0 = \Delta\overline{G} = \Delta X$$

When they both change by ΔX, Y^* will change by ΔY^* and we can write

$$Y^* + \Delta Y^* = C_0 + b(Y^* + \Delta Y^*) - b(T_0 + \Delta X) - bt(Y + \Delta Y^*) + \overline{I} + (\overline{G} + \Delta X)$$
$$= C_0 + bY^* + b\,\Delta Y^* - bT_0 - b\,\Delta X - btY^* - bt\,\Delta Y^* + \overline{I} + \overline{G} + \Delta X$$

From this last equation we subtract the equilibrium equation above and obtain

$$\Delta Y^* = b\,\Delta Y^* - b\,\Delta X - bt\,\Delta Y^* + \Delta X$$

Moving all the terms with ΔY^* to the left and all other terms to the right, we have

$$\Delta Y^* - b\,\Delta Y^* + bt\,\Delta Y^* = -b\,\Delta X + \Delta X$$
$$\Delta Y^*(1 - b + bt) = \Delta X(1 - b)$$

$$\Delta Y^* = \frac{\Delta X(1 - b)}{1 - b + bt}$$

$$\frac{\Delta Y^*}{\Delta X} = \frac{1 - b}{1 - b + bt}$$

If t should equal zero, $\Delta Y^*/\Delta X$ *would be* $(1 - b)/(1 - b)$, or 1. But as long as t is greater than zero, $\Delta Y^*/\Delta X$ is not 1 (and is, in fact, less than 1).

To demonstrate that an equal increase in *total* taxes and in government expenditures will increase equilibrium national income by the same amount we start with this version of the equilibrium equation

$$Y^* = C_0 + b(Y - T) + \overline{I} + \overline{G}$$
$$= C_0 + bY - bT + \overline{I} + \overline{G}$$

Now we let both $\overline{G}$ and total taxes T increase by ΔX so that Y^* increases by ΔY^* and write

$$Y^* + \Delta Y^* = C_0 + b(Y^* + \Delta Y^*) - b(T + \Delta X) + \overline{I} + (\overline{G} + \Delta X)$$
$$= C_0 + bY^* + b\,\Delta Y^* - bT - b\,\Delta X + \overline{I} + \overline{G} + \Delta X$$

From this last equation we subtract the original equilibrium equation and obtain

$$\Delta Y^* = b\,\Delta Y^* - b\,\Delta X + \Delta X$$

Moving all terms with ΔY^* in them to the left and leaving all other terms on the right, we have

$$\Delta Y^* - b\,\Delta Y^* = -b\,\Delta X + \Delta X$$

Factoring,

$$\Delta Y^*(1 - b) = \Delta X(1 - b)$$

and dividing through by $1 - b$, we have

$$\Delta Y^* = \Delta X\frac{1 - b}{1 - b}$$
$$= \Delta X$$

The change in equilibrium Y, this tells us, is equal to the equal changes in $\bar{G}$ or T.

If we divide the last equation through by ΔX, we obtain

$$\frac{\Delta Y}{\Delta X} = 1$$

This tells us that the ratio of a change in equilibrium Y to the amount that equals the change in $\bar{G}$ and in T is 1. The multiplier effect of equal changes in *total* taxes and government expenditures is 1.

Summary

When by a change in taxes we mean a change in autonomous taxes, the value of the tax multiplier is not 1 less than the government expenditures multiplier; the multiplier effect of equal changes in autonomous taxes and government expenditures is not 1 (but less than 1); and an equal increase in autonomous taxes and government expenditures will not increase equilibrium income by that amount (but by a smaller amount).

When by a change in taxes we mean a change in total taxes, the value of the tax multiplier is 1 less than the value of the government expenditures multiplier; the multiplier effect of equal changes in taxes and government expenditures is 1; and an equal increase in taxes and government expenditures will increase equilibrium income by that amount.

To illustrate this summary, suppose the MPC is 0.8 and the tax function is $T = \$20 + 0.5Y$. Now imagine $\bar{G}$ and autonomous taxes increase by \$15 (while the MTR remains a constant 0.5). The effect of the change in $\bar{G}$, by itself, is to increase Y by \$25. The effect of the change in autonomous taxes by itself is to decrease Y^* by \$20. The combined effect of the two changes is to increase Y^* by \$5 (= +\$25 − \$20). This increase of \$5 is less than the equal increase of \$15 in $\bar{G}$ and autonomous taxes.

Suppose now we let $\bar{G}$ increase by \$15, as before, and let total taxes increase by \$15. The effect of the increase in $\bar{G}$, by itself, is again to increase Y^* by \$25. Now let autonomous taxes increase by \$7.50. This, by itself, would decrease Y^* by \$10 (equal to the change in autonomous taxes times the autonomous tax multiplier of $\frac{4}{3}$). So far these two events have increased Y by \$15. But when Y^* increases by \$15, taxes go up by another \$7.50 because the MTR is 0.5; so a \$15 increase in $\bar{G}$ accompanied by an equal increase in total taxes of \$15 (equal to the \$7.50 increase in autonomous taxes plus the \$7.50 increase in induced taxes) did increase Y^* by \$15. The multiplier effect was 1; and an equal increase in $\bar{G}$ and T results in the same increase in Y^*.

Exercise 3-3

1 How does this more advanced model differ from the simple model?

2 Suppose that the tax function is $T = T_0 + tY$.

a Define the marginal tax rate. MTR ≡ ____________ / ____________
b Show that the MTR = t.

c T_0 is called ____________

3 The equations in this model are

$C =$ ____________

$T =$ ____________

$I =$ ____________

$G =$ ____________

$Y_d \equiv$ ____________ $-$ ____________

$D \equiv$ ____________ $+$ ____________ $+$ ____________

$Y =$ ____________

a The endogenous variables are ____________, ____________, ____________, ____________, and ____________

b We can also find saving because $S \equiv$ ____________ $-$ ____________

4 Show that

$$Y^* = \frac{C_0 - bT_0 + \bar{I} + \bar{G}}{1 - b + bt}$$

5 Assume that
$C = \$100 + 0.75Y_d$
$T = \$20 + 0.33\tfrac{1}{3}Y$
$I = \$80$
$G = \$60$

a What is the saving function? $S =$ ____________
b What are the values of:

(1) $Y^* = \$$____________

(2) $C^* = \$$____________

(3) $T^* = \$$____________

(4) $Y_d^* = \$$____________

(5) $D^* = \$$____________

(6) $S^* = \$$____________

c Government has a (surplus, deficit) ____________ of $____________
d Show that $S^* + T^* = I^* + G^*$.

6 Using the equations in question 5, what is the value of:

a The government expenditures multiplier? $K_G =$ ______

b The tax multiplier? $K_T =$ ____________

7 Show that in this model:
a The consumption multiplier equals $1/(1 - b + bt)$.
b The investment multiplier is $1/(1 - b + bt)$.

8 Employing the functions in question 5, what is the value of:

a The consumption multiplier? $K_C =$ ____________

b The investment multiplier? $K_I =$ ____________

9 Assume that
$C = C_0 + 0.90Y_d$
$T = T_0 + 0.30Y$

What would be the effect of each of the following upon Y^*?

a $\bar{G}$ decreases by \$10: ___________

b $\bar{T}$ increases by \$20: ___________

c C_0 decreases by \$30: ___________

d T_0 increases by \$50: ___________

10 Show that:
a $K_G \cdot b = K_T$
b $K_G > K_T$

11 Why is the tax multiplier less than the government expenditures multiplier?

12 What is the relationship between the value of t and the values of the tax and government expenditures multipliers?

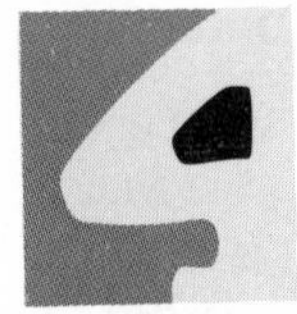

INTERNATIONAL TRADE AND NATIONAL INCOME

In the macroeconomic models of Chapters 2 and 3 we assumed that the economy was closed: it neither imported nor exported goods and services. But the American economy (and every other economy in our modern world) is, in fact, an open economy. Its households, business firms, and governments buy and sell goods and services in other economies.

To make our macroeconomic analysis still more realistic and useful we look in this chapter at an open economy. We discard the assumption that the economy is closed and assume instead that it both exports and imports goods and services. Our attention will be focused on the effect that the exportation and importation of goods and services has upon the equilibrium national income of the economy. We shall also introduce the foreign trade multiplier and the balance of trade.

The first section of the chapter explains the definitions and assumptions we employ and then uses them to determine the equilibrium national income in an open economy. In the second section we use our model to find the value of the foreign trade multipliers and the effects upon the balance of trade of changes in exports and in other exogenous variables.

THE MODEL OF AN OPEN ECONOMY

To construct our model of an open economy we use most of the same assumptions and definitions we employed in the last chapter to build our models of a closed economy. Let us look first at these definitions and assumptions. Then we can find the equilibrium national income.

Definitions and assumptions

As in our earlier macroeconomic models, we shall make the following simplifying assumptions: (1) There are no undistributed corporate profits. All corporate profits are distributed to stockholders and become their personal income. This means that whatever saving is done in the economy is done by households and is personal saving. (2) All taxes levied are personal taxes, and all government transfer payments are personal transfer payments. Taxes are not collected from firms, and transfer payments are not made to firms. (3) As a result of these two assumptions, the economy's net national product, national income, and personal income are equal to each other. For this variable we shall again use the terms national income and national output and the symbol Y. (4) We define disposable income Y_d as equal to national income less net taxes T. Net taxes, as before, are equal to taxes less government transfer payments. The first equation in our model, therefore, is a definitional equation.

$$Y_d \equiv Y - T \qquad (4\text{-}1)$$

The exogenous variables Our model will contain three variables whose values are not explained by the model. These three exogenous variables are the economy's exports of goods and services X; the level of government expenditures for goods and services G; and the rate of interest in the economy i. In the language of mathematics we assume that

$$X = \bar{X} \qquad (4\text{-}2)$$
$$G = \bar{G} \qquad (4\text{-}3)$$
$$i = \bar{i} \qquad (4\text{-}4)$$

The consumption, investment, and net tax functions We utilize three functional equations which we used in our earlier macroeconomic models. Consumption is assumed to be an increasing and linear function of disposable income, or

$$C = C_0 + bY_d \qquad (4\text{-}5)$$

The parameters in this function are C_0 and b. C_0 is autonomous consumption, and it is assumed to have a positive value. The parameter b is the marginal propensity to consume $\Delta C/\Delta Y_d$, and it is assumed to be greater than zero and less than one.

The level of net investment spending in the economy I is assumed to be a decreasing and linear function of the rate of interest, or

$$I = I_0 - ji \qquad (4\text{-}6)$$

The parameters I_0 and j are, respectively, autonomous investment (the level of investment spending that would be approached as the rate of interest approached zero) and the interest rate–investment coefficient (equal to $\Delta I/\Delta i$, the ratio of the change in investment to the change in the interest rate). It is assumed that I_0 is positive. No particular assumption is made about the value of the parameter j. Unlike one of our earlier models,[1] this model does not assume that the level of I is related to or depends upon the size of Y.

Net taxes are assumed to be an increasing and linear function of national income.

$$T = T_0 + tY \tag{4-7}$$

The parameter t is the marginal propensity to tax and is equal to $\Delta T/\Delta Y$ (the ratio of the change in taxes to the change in the national income). We assume that t is greater than zero but less than one. T_0 is the level of tax collections that would be approached as national income fell toward zero, and it is assumed to be greater than zero.

Aggregate demand When an economy is able to export goods and services, a part of the total demand for its national output comes from abroad. Aggregate demand D in an open economy, therefore, is the sum of consumer demand, investment demand, the demand of government, and the demand from the rest of the world. Demand from the rest of the world we may call *export demand* and label X. The aggregate demand in such an economy might then be written

$$D \equiv C + I + G + X$$

In writing this definition of aggregate demand we have failed to take account of the fact that a part of consumer demand, investment demand, and government demand is for goods and services produced in foreign countries. If we wish to know the aggregate demand for goods and services produced at home—in the domestic economy—we must deduct or subtract the consumer demand, the investment demand, and the government demand for products produced abroad.

The *total* of consumer, business, and government demand for goods and services produced in foreign countries we may call the *import demand* and label M. The aggregate demand, then, for goods and services produced in the economy (at home) is the sum of consumer, investment, and government demand for goods and services, no matter where these goods and services are produced, plus the demand for goods and services from abroad (export demand) *less* the total consumer, business, and government demand for goods and services from abroad (the import demand). We may write our aggregate demand definition

$$D \equiv C + I + G + X - M \tag{4-8}$$

The import function The demand for goods and services from abroad, as we have just pointed out, comes from consumers, businesses, and governments. We shall assume that this import demand is an increasing and linear function of the level of national income in the economy. This import function we write as

$$M = N_0 + mY \tag{4-9}$$

This import demand function contains two parameters, N_0 and m. The parameter N_0, which we call *autonomous imports,* is that part of the demand for imported goods and services which is not related to the level of national income (or is not influenced by changes in national income). Put another way, it is the

[1] See pages 49 to 53.

level of import demand that would be approached as the level of national income approaches zero. Our assumption is that N_0 may be zero or greater but cannot be less than zero: an economy cannot import a negative quantity of goods and services, and so

$$N_0 \geqq 0$$

The symbol m is the parameter that relates changes in the import demand to changes in national income. If Y were to change by an amount equal to ΔY, M would change by an amount equal to ΔM. Employing equation 4-9, when Y changes by ΔY to become $Y + \Delta Y$, the import demand changes from M to $M + \Delta M$ and

$$M + \Delta M = N_0 + m(Y + \Delta Y)$$

or

$$M + \Delta M = N_0 + mY + m\,\Delta Y$$

From this last equation we now subtract equation 4-9 to find

$$\Delta M = m\,\Delta Y \qquad (4\text{-}10)$$

Any change in import demand, equation 4-10 tells us, is equal to the parameter m multiplied by the change in national income; or when national income changes, the change in the import demand will equal the change in national income multiplied by the parameter m.

Dividing both sides of equation 4-10 by ΔY, we find

$$\frac{\Delta M}{\Delta Y} = m \qquad (4\text{-}11)$$

The parameter m, it turns out, is equal to the ratio of the change in import demand (that occurs when national income changes) to the change in national income. This ratio, $\Delta M/\Delta Y$, is called the *marginal propensity to import;* and the parameter m in the import demand function, as we can see in Equation 4-11, is equal to the marginal propensity to import. Verbally, the marginal propensity to import is the percentage of any increase in national income that is spent for imported goods and services.

We shall assume that the marginal propensity to import is greater than zero and less than one, or

$$0 < m < 1$$

In the American economy we would expect m to be fairly small and much closer to zero than one. While the marginal propensity to import has varied from year to year, it has been between 4 and 8 percent (between 0.04 and 0.08) in recent years.

Equilibrium in the economy In the models for a closed economy the equilibrium level of national income Y^* was the level of national income which was equal to the aggregate quantity of goods and services demanded. We employ the same equilibrium equation in a model of an open economy: the economy will produce the national income at which the aggregate quantity of goods and services supplied Y and the aggregate quantity of goods and services demanded

D are equal. Our equilibrium equation is

$$Y = D \tag{4-12}$$

There are two other methods we might employ to express the condition that prevails when the economy is producing its equilibrium national output.

The saving-investment approach Saving in an open economy is defined in exactly the same way as in a closed economy. Saving is equal to disposable income less consumption, or

$$S \equiv Y_d - C \tag{4-13}$$

We already know (from equation 4-1) that

$$Y_d \equiv Y - T \tag{4-1}$$

Substituting $Y - T$ for Y_d in equation 4-13, saving is

$$S \equiv (Y - T) - C$$

or

$$S \equiv Y - T - C$$

If we now add $T + C$ to both sides of this last equation, we find

$$S + (T + C) \equiv Y - T - C + (T + C)$$
$$S + T + C \equiv Y \tag{4-14}$$

The national income in the economy is equal to saving plus net taxes plus consumption.

Returning to the equilibrium equation, 4-12, we may substitute (from equation 4-14) $C + S + T$ for Y; and for D we may substitute (from equation 14-8) $C + I + G + X - M$.

$$C + S + T = C + I + G + X - M$$

Subtracting C from both sides, we have

$$S + T = I + G + X - M$$

Adding M to both sides, the equilibrium equation becomes

$$S + T + M = I + G + X \tag{4-15}$$

The equilibrium national income is the national income at which saving plus net taxes plus imports equals investment plus government expenditures for goods and services plus exports.

The balance of trade approach A second way of viewing the condition that prevails when the economy is in equilibrium involves the relation between the economy's exports and imports. Let us return to equation 4-15 and subtract $I + G$ from both sides of the equation to obtain

$$S + T + M - (I + G) = I + G + X - (I + G)$$

or

$$S + T + M - I - G = X$$

From both sides we now subtract M so that

$$S + T - I - G = X - M \quad (4\text{-}16)$$

When the economy is in equilibrium, saving plus net taxes minus investment minus government expenditures for goods and services equals exports minus imports.

We define the difference between an economy's exports and imports of goods and services as its *balance of trade,* $X - M$. Equation 4-16 tells us that in equilibrium the economy's balance of trade equals saving plus net taxes less investment and government expenditures. In the second section of the chapter we shall return to the economy's balance of trade to learn what causes the balance of trade to change and to discover the effects upon the balance of trade of changes in the national income.

The Equations and the Variables

We now have all the definitions and assumptions we need to determine the equilibrium national income in an *open* economy. Our model consists of ten equations and ten variables. Three of the variables are exogenous, and seven are endogenous. The ten equations are

$$C = C_0 + bY_d \quad (4\text{-}5)$$
$$T = T_0 + tY \quad (4\text{-}7)$$
$$I = I_0 - ji \quad (4\text{-}6)$$
$$M = N_0 + mY \quad (4\text{-}9)$$
$$X = \overline{X} \quad (4\text{-}2)$$
$$G = \overline{G} \quad (4\text{-}3)$$
$$i = \overline{i} \quad (4\text{-}4)$$
$$Y_d \equiv Y - T \quad (4\text{-}1)$$
$$D \equiv C + I + G + X - M \quad (4\text{-}8)$$
$$Y = D \quad (4\text{-}12)$$

The first four equations are functional equations and relate each of four different variables to other variables in the model. The next three are also functional equations and assign values to three more of the variables in the model. Equations 4-1 and 4-8 are definitional equations. The last equation, 4-12, is the equilibrium equation. The seven endogenous variables are C, Y_d, T, Y, I, M, and D. The variables X, G, and i are exogenous. The model has an equal number of different equations and variables, and we should be able to find the values of the seven endogenous variables. We can also find the equilibrium level of saving in the economy by employing the equation which defines saving (equation 4-13).

The equilibrium national income To find the equilibrium national income we start with the equilibrium equation

$$Y = D \quad (4\text{-}12)$$

For D we substitute the right side of equation 4-8

$$Y = C + I + G + X - M$$

For C, I, and M we substitute the right sides of equations 4-5, 4-6, and 4-9, respectively. And for G and X we substitute from equations 4-2 and 4-3 to get

$$Y = (C_0 + bY_d) + (I_0 - ji) + \bar{G} + \bar{X} - (N_0 + mY)$$

Next we substitute (from equation 4-1) $Y - T$ for Y_d and (from equation 4-4) $\bar{i}$ for i

$$Y = C_0 + b(Y - T) + I_0 - j\bar{i} + \bar{G} + \bar{X} - N_0 - mY$$

For T we substitute the right side of equation 4-7 to obtain

$$Y = C_0 + bY - b(T_0 + tY) + I_0 - j\bar{i} + \bar{G} + \bar{X} - N_0 - mY$$

and

$$Y = C_0 + bY - bT_0 - btY + I_0 - j\bar{i} + \bar{G} + \bar{X} - N_0 - mY$$

Transferring all terms containing Y to the left side, we have

$$Y - bY + btY + mY = C_0 - bT_0 + I_0 - j\bar{i} + \bar{G} + \bar{X} - N_0$$

or

$$Y(1 - b + bt + m) = C_0 - bT_0 + I_0 - j\bar{i} + \bar{G} + \bar{X} - N_0$$

Dividing both sides of the last equation by $1 - b + bt + m$ gives us the solution equation for the equilibrium national income.

$$Y^* = \frac{C_0 - bT_0 + I_0 - j\bar{i} + \bar{G} + \bar{X} - N_0}{1 - b + bt + m} \tag{4-17}$$

We should note that Y^* depends upon the parameters (C_0, b, T_0, I_0, N_0, j, t, and m) and the exogenous variables (i, G and X) in the model.

Having found Y^*, we can find the equilibrium values of the other six endogenous variables in the model:

- Equation 4-7 will tell us the equilibrium value of T.
- Equation 4-9 gives the equilibrium value of M.
- From equation 4-1 we find the equilibrium Y_d.
- Then we can determine equilibrium C from equation 4-5.
- Equation 4-6 yields equilibrium I.
- The equilibrium value of D can be found from equation 4-8.

A special assumption In examining the consumption, net tax, and import functions earlier we assumed that the parameters b, t, and m were each greater than zero and less than one. To these assumptions we must add a further assumption: *the value of $b - bt - m$ is less than 1.*

To understand why we make this special assumption, let us first rewrite equation 4-17

$$Y^* = \frac{C_0 - bT_0 + I_0 - j\bar{i} + \bar{G} + \bar{X} - N_0}{1 - (b - bt - m)} \tag{4-18}$$

If $b - bt - m$ were greater than 1, the denominator of equation 4-18 would be negative. Given the assumptions we have made about the values of the parameters and exogenous variables appearing in the numerator of equation 4-18, we would then find that the equilibrium national income was also negative. Preventing this kind of economic nonsense is one reason for assuming $b - bt - m$ is less than 1. As long as $b - bt - m$ is less than 1, the equilibrium national income in our model is positive.

But there is a second and more complex reason for making this special assumption. We assume $b - bt - m$ is less than 1 to ensure that any change in national income results in a change in aggregate demand that is *smaller than* the change in national income. In our model for an open economy aggregate demand is

$$D \equiv C + I + G + X - M \tag{4-8}$$

G and X are exogenous variables and are assumed to remain unchanged. I depends upon the exogenous variable i, which is also assumed to remain unchanged; and, as a consequence, I is assumed to remain unchanged. Only C and M are endogenous variables, and so we can write

$$\Delta D = \Delta C - \Delta M \tag{4-19}$$

If our consumption function is

$$C = C_0 + bY_d \tag{4-5}$$

then substituting $Y - T$ (equation 4-1) for Y_d

$$C = C_0 + b(Y - T)$$

or

$$C = C_0 + bY - bT$$

For T we substitute the tax function (equation 4-7) to obtain

$$C = C_0 + bY - b(T_0 + tY)$$

or

$$C = C_0 + bY - bT_0 - btY$$

C_0 and T_0 are parameters and assumed constant. C changes, therefore, only when Y changes; and the change in C is

$$\Delta C = b\,\Delta Y - bt\,\Delta Y \tag{4-20}$$

We know from equation 4-10 that

$$\Delta M = m\,\Delta Y \tag{4-10}$$

Now we can substitute the right sides of equations 4-20 and 4-10 for ΔC and ΔM, respectively, in equation 4-19 to find that the change in aggregate demand is

$$\Delta D = b\,\Delta Y - bt\,\Delta Y - m\,\Delta Y$$

or

$$\Delta D = \Delta Y(b - bt - m) \tag{4-21}$$

As long as $b - bt - m$ is less than 1, we can see from equation 4-21 that any change in D will be less than the change in Y.

It is fair to ask why we wish the change in aggregate demand to be smaller than the change in national income. As long as ΔD is less than ΔY, the equilibrium national income will be *stable*. Equilibrium national income is stable if when the national income is not equal to its equilibrium value, national income will move *toward* its equilibrium value. (The equilibrium is *un*stable if when national income is not equal to its equilibrium value, it moves *away from* its equilibrium level.) As long as $b - bt - m$ is less than 1, ΔD is smaller than ΔY; and when ΔD is less than ΔY, national income has a stable and positive equilibrium value.

A numerical example Let us assume that

$$C = \$100 + 0.08Y_d$$
$$T = \$10 + 0.2Y$$
$$I = \$30 - \$200i$$
$$M = \$5 + 0.04Y$$
$$X = \$15$$
$$G = \$50$$
$$i = 0.06$$

These seven functional equations along with the two definitional equations (4-1 and 4-8) and the equilibrium equation (4-12) constitute our model.

Employing the equation for the equilibrium national income (4-17),

$$Y^* = \frac{C_0 - bT_0 + I_0 - j\bar{i} + \bar{G} + \bar{X} - N_0}{1 - b + bt + m} \qquad (4\text{-}17)$$

$$Y^* = \frac{\$100 - 0.8(\$10) + \$30 - \$200(0.06) + \$50 + \$15 - \$5}{1 - 0.8 + 0.16 + 0.04}$$

$$= \frac{\$100 - \$8 + \$30 - \$12 + \$50 + \$15 - \$5}{1 - 0.8 + 0.16 + 0.04}$$

$$= \frac{\$170}{0.40}$$

$$= \$425$$

Having found the equilibrium national income to be \$425, we can find the equilibrium values of the other six endogenous variables.

$$T^* = \$10 + 0.2Y = \$10 + 0.2(\$425) = \$10 + \$85 = \$95$$
$$Y_d^* \equiv Y - T = \$425 - \$95 = \$330$$
$$C^* = \$100 + 0.8Y_d = \$100 + 0.8(\$330) = \$100 + \$264 = \$364$$
$$M^* = \$5 + 0.04Y = \$5 + 0.04(\$425) = \$5 + \$17 = \$22$$
$$I^* = \$30 - \$200(0.06) = \$30 - \$12 = \$18$$
$$D^* \equiv C + I + G + X - M = \$364 + \$18 + \$50 + \$15 - \$22$$
$$= \$425$$

Notice that when Y is at its equilibrium level, not only is Y equal to D but both equations 4-15 and 4-16 are satisfied. Employing equation 4-13, saving in the economy is

$$S \equiv Y_d - C \qquad (4\text{-}13)$$
$$S^* = \$330 - \$364 = -\$34$$

Equation 4-15 is

$$S + T + M = I + G + X \tag{4-15}$$

and in the numerical example

$$-\$34 + \$95 + \$22 = \$18 + \$50 + \$15 = \$83$$

The balance of trade, from equation 4-16, is

$$S + T - I - G = X - M \tag{4-16}$$

$$-\$34 + \$95 - \$18 - \$50 = \$15 - \$22 = -\$7$$

The economy's balance of trade is −$7. Its exports exceed its imports by $7. Put another way, investment plus government expenditures for goods and services exceed saving plus net taxes by $7.

Exercise 4-1

1 We make the following two assumptions in our model of an open economy.

a There are no ____________ corporate profits, and all saving, therefore, is ____________ saving.

b All taxes are ____________ taxes, and all transfer payments are ____________ payments.

This means that the economy's ____________, ____________, and ____________ are equal.

2 Our definition of:

a Net taxes is $T \equiv$ ____________ − ____________

b Aggregate demand is $D \equiv$ ____________ + ____________ + ____________ + ____________ − ____________

3 The exogenous variables in the model are ____________, ____________, and ____________

4 The following functional equations are employed in the model:

a $C =$ ____________ + ____________

b $I =$ ____________ − ____________

c $T =$ ____________ + ____________

d $M =$ ____________ + ____________

5 In the import demand function:

a N_0 is the economy's ____________ imports and is ____________ or ____________ zero.

b m is equal to Δ____________ / Δ____________ and is called the ____________ ____________ to ____________

c m is assumed to be greater than ____________ and less than ____________

6 Equilibrium is achieved in the economy when ____________ = ____________.

When the economy is in equilibrium we also find that:

a ______ + ______ + ______ =

______ + ______ + ______

b ______ + ______ − ______ −

______ = ______ − ______

7 We define saving as $S \equiv$ ______ − ______. Show that when the economy is in equilibrium:

a $S + T + M = I + G + X$
b $S + T - I - G = X - M$

8 Write the ten equations that make up the model of an open economy.

$C =$ ______

$I =$ ______

$T =$ ______

$M =$ ______

$Y_d =$ ______

$i =$ ______

$G =$ ______

$X =$ ______

$D =$ ______

______ = ______

a The endogenous variables are ______.
b Show that

$$Y^* = \frac{C_0 - bT_0 + I_0 - j\bar{i} + \bar{G} + \bar{X} - N_0}{1 - b + bt + m}$$

c To ensure that the equilibrium national income is positive and stable we make the special assumption that ______ < ______

9 Assume that
$C = \$50 + 0.75Y_d$
$I = \$20 - \$160i$
$T = \$20 + 0.40Y$
$M = \$11 + 0.05Y$
$X = \$20$
$G = \$40$
$i = 0.05$

Then:

a $Y^* = \$$ ______

b $T^* = \$$ ______

c $Y_d^* = \$$ ______

d $C^* = \$$ ______

e $I^* = \$$ ______

f $M^* = \$$ ______

g $D^* = \$$__________

h $S^* = \$$__________

10 Using the equations in question 9, when the economy is in equilibrium:

a $S + T + M = \$$__________

b $I + G + X = \$$__________

c $S + T - I - G = \$$__________

d $X - M = \$$__________

CHANGES IN EXPORTS AND THE BALANCE OF TRADE

Armed with the equation for the equilibrium national income, we can find the effect of a change in the economy's exports upon its national income: we can determine its foreign trade or export multiplier. We can also determine the effects of changes in the values of the exogenous variables and parameters in the model upon the balance of trade.

The foreign trade multiplier

If exogenous exports $\overline{X}$ change by an amount equal to $\Delta\overline{X}$, Y^* will change by ΔY^*. Using equation 4-17, we can write

$$y^* + \Delta Y^* = \frac{C_0 - bT_0 + I_0 - j\overline{i} + \overline{G} + (\overline{X} + \Delta\overline{X}) - N_0}{1 - b + bt + m} \tag{4-22}$$

From equation 4-22 we subtract equation 4-17 to find that

$$\Delta Y^* = \frac{\Delta\overline{X}}{1 - b + bt + m} \tag{4-23}$$

The change in Y^* that results from a change in exports is equal to the change in exports divided by 1 minus the marginal propensity to consume plus the marginal propensity to consume times the marginal tax rate plus the marginal propensity to import.

When we divide both sides of equation 4-23 by $\Delta\overline{X}$, we find that

$$\frac{\Delta Y^*}{\Delta\overline{X}} = \frac{1}{1 - b + bt + m} \tag{4-24}$$

The ratio of the change in equilibrium national income (that results from a change in exogenous exports) to the change in exogenous exports is called the *foreign trade* (or export) *multiplier*. Equation 4-24 says that the value of the foreign trade multiplier is equal to $1/(1 - b + bt + m)$, the inverse, or reciprocal, of $1 - b + bt + m$. We should note that as long as $b - bt - m$ is less than one and b, t, and m are each greater than zero and less than one, $1 - b + bt + m$ is also less than positive one and the value of the foreign trade multiplier is positive and greater than one.

Numerical example Using the parameters of our earlier example, in which

$b = 0.8$, $t = 0.2$, and $m = 0.04$,

$$\frac{\Delta Y^*}{\Delta \bar{X}} = \frac{1}{1 - 0.8 + 0.8(0.2) + 0.04}$$

$$= \frac{1}{1 - 0.8 + 0.16 + 0.04}$$

$$= \frac{1}{0.40}$$

$$= 2.5$$

The ratio of the change in equilibrium national income to the change in exogenous exports is 2.5. This means that if exogenous exports increase by \$10, equilibrium national income increases by 2.5 times \$10, or \$25. It also means that if exogenous exports decrease by \$5, the equilibrium national income decreases by 2.5 times \$5, or \$12.50. Because 2.5 is positive, Y^* increases when $\bar{X}$ increases and decreases when $\bar{X}$ decreases.

Other multipliers in an open economy Using the same method employed to determine the value of the foreign trade multiplier, the student should be able to find the relation between a change in any of the other exogenous variables ($\bar{G}$ and $\bar{i}$) or parameters (C_0, T_0, I_0, and N_0) and the resulting change in the equilibrium national income. He will find that:

- The government expenditures multiplier is

$$\frac{\Delta Y^*}{\Delta \bar{G}} = \frac{1}{1 - b + bt + m} \tag{4-25}$$

- The consumption multiplier is

$$\frac{\Delta Y^*}{\Delta C_0} = \frac{1}{1 - b + bt + m} \tag{4-26}$$

- The investment multiplier is

$$\frac{\Delta Y^*}{\Delta I_0} = \frac{1}{1 - b + bt + m} \tag{4-27}$$

- The interest rate multiplier is

$$\frac{\Delta Y^*}{\Delta \bar{i}} = \frac{-j}{1 - b + bt + m} \tag{4-28}$$

- The tax multiplier is

$$\frac{\Delta Y^*}{\Delta T_0} = \frac{-b}{1 - b + bt + m} \tag{4-29}$$

- The autonomous import multiplier is

$$\frac{\Delta Y^*}{\Delta N_0} = \frac{-1}{1 - b + bt + m} \tag{4-30}$$

We can observe that the first three of these multipliers are positive. Increases in G, C_0, and I_0 will increase Y^*, and decreases in them will decrease Y^*. Each of these three has the same value and the same sign as the foreign trade multiplier.

The second three multipliers are negative. Increases in i, T_0, and N_0 will decrease Y^*, and decreases in them will increase Y^*.[2] Each of the last three multipliers has a different value. The sixth, the autonomous import multiplier, has the same value as the foreign trade and the first three multipliers, but it is negative instead of positive.

Retaining the values given the parameters in our earlier example, namely,

$b = 0.8$
$t = 0.2$
$m = 0.04$
$j = \$200$

$1/(1 - b + bt + m)$ is equal to 2.5. If either G, C_0, or I_0 increases by \$10, Y^* increases by \$25; and if either of them decreases by \$10, Y^* decreases by \$25.

If the rate of interest changes, the ratio of the change in Y^* to the change in $\bar{i}$ can be found by using equation 4-28. The value of the interest rate multiplier is

$$\frac{\Delta Y^*}{\Delta \bar{i}} = \frac{-\$200}{1 - 0.8 + 0.8(0.2) + 0.04}$$
$$= \frac{-\$200}{0.40}$$
$$= -\$500$$

This means that if the rate of interest increases by 0.01, the equilibrium national income will decrease by \$500 times 0.01, or \$5. Or if the rate of interest decreases by 0.02, the equilibrium national income will increase by \$500 times 0.02, or \$10.

The student should be able to determine for himself the effect of a given change in either autonomous taxes T_0 or autonomous imports N_0 upon Y^*. Using the values of the parameters given above, he can find that:

- The autonomous tax multiplier is equal to -2 and that a \$10 increase (decrease) in T_0 will result in a \$20 decrease (increase) in Y^*.
- The autonomous import multiplier is equal to -2.5 and that a \$10 increase (decrease) in M_0 will bring about a \$25 decrease (increase) in Y^*.

The balance of trade

The difference between an economy's exports and imports of goods and services is its balance of trade (also called its balance on the current account or its net exports). Let us use B for the balance of trade

$$B \equiv X - M \tag{4-31}$$

When X is greater than M, B is positive and the economy is said to have an

[2]The interest rate multiplier is negative because increases in the rate of interest decrease investment and decreased investment results in a smaller equilibrium national income. The tax multiplier is negative because increases in autonomous taxes decrease disposable income, decreased disposable income decreases consumption spending, and decreased consumption spending results in a smaller equilibrium national income. The autonomous import multiplier is negative because an increase in autonomous imports decreases the level of aggregate demand and a decreased level of aggregate demand brings about a smaller equilibrium national income.

export balance of trade; but when M exceeds X, B is negative and the economy has an import balance. If exports, for example, are \$35 and imports \$20, the balance of trade is \$5. If exports are \$32 and imports \$38, the balance of trade is $-\$6$.

The balance of trade changes when exports, imports, or both exports and imports change. The change in the balance of trade equals the change in exports less the change in imports; or

$$\Delta B \equiv \Delta X - \Delta M \tag{4-32}$$

The balance of trade will increase and ΔB will be positive whenever the increase in X is greater than the increase in M or the decrease in X is less than the decrease in M. If, for example, X increases by \$5 and M increases by \$4, then B will increase by \$1; and if X decreases by \$3 and M decreases by \$5, B will increase by \$2.

We assumed in equation 4-9 that an economy's imports were an increasing and linear function of its national income, or

$$M = N_0 + mY \tag{4-9}$$

N_0 (autonomous imports) and m (the marginal propensity to import) are the two parameters in the import demand function. A change in national income will bring about a change in M, and we saw in equation 4-10 that

$$\Delta M = m\,\Delta Y \tag{4-10}$$

But a change in the value of either of the two parameters will also bring about a change in the imports of the economy. We shall not be concerned with changes in the value of m and shall assume that it does not change. We are, however, concerned with changes in N_0 and the effect of a change in autonomous imports upon the balance of trade.

With the parameter m constant, the change in the economy's imports is equal to the change in autonomous imports plus the marginal propensity to import multiplied by the change in national income. Mathematically, we can say that

$$\Delta M = \Delta N_0 + m\,\Delta Y \tag{4-33}$$

For ΔM in equation 4-32 we may now substitute the right side of equation 4-33 to obtain

$$\Delta B = \Delta X - (\Delta N_0 + m\,\Delta Y)$$

or

$$\Delta B = \Delta X - \Delta N_0 - m\,\Delta Y \tag{4-34}$$

The change in the balance of trade, equation 4-34 tells us, is equal to the change in exports less the change in autonomous imports and the marginal propensity to import multiplied by the change in national income. We can now use equation 4-34 to determine the effect *on the balance of trade* of changes in the economy's exports and in the other exogenous variables and parameters of our model.

Changes in exports and the balance of trade Suppose the value of the exogenous variable $\overline{X}$ changes by an amount equal to $\Delta\overline{X}$ and that there are no changes in the other *exogenous* variables and parameters (including N_0) in the model. The change in balance of trade, we know from equation 4-34, is

$$\Delta B = \Delta\bar{X} - \Delta N_0 - m\,\Delta Y \tag{4-34}$$

With ΔN_0 equal to zero, the change in the balance of trade is

$$\Delta B = \Delta X - m\,\Delta Y \tag{4-35}$$

From equation 4-23 we know that a change in exports brings about a change in the equilibrium national income and that the change in national income is

$$\Delta Y^* = \frac{\Delta\bar{X}}{1 - b + bt + m} \tag{4-23}$$

For ΔY in equation 4-35 we may substitute the right side of equation 4-23 to obtain

$$\Delta B = \Delta\bar{X} - m\frac{\Delta\bar{X}}{1 - b + bt + m}$$

or

$$\Delta B = \Delta\bar{X}\left(1 - \frac{m}{1 - b + bt + m}\right) \tag{4-36}$$

The change in the balance of trade (that results from a change in exports) is equal to the change in exports times the quantity 1 minus the parameter m divided by 1 minus the marginal propensity to consume plus the marginal propensity to consume times the marginal tax rate plus the marginal propensity to import.

Since we assumed that $b - bt - m$ is less than 1, $1 - (b - bt - m)$ or $1 - b + bt + m$ is also less than 1 (and positive). The parameter m is also positive. This means that $m/(1 - b + bt + m)$ is positive. Furthermore, given the assumptions we have made about the values of b and t (greater than zero but less than one), $1 - b + bt + m$ must be greater than m. This means that the fraction $m/(1 - b + bt + m)$ is less than 1 and therefore $1 - m/(1 - b + bt + m)$ is also less than 1.

So, with $1 - m/(1 - b + bt + m)$ both positive and less than 1, a change in exports results in a change in the balance of trade that is *directly related to but smaller than the change in exports*. An increase in exports will increase the balance of trade by an amount smaller than the change in exports, and a decrease in exports will decrease the balance of trade by an amount smaller than the decrease in exports.[3]

To illustrate this conclusion, let us again suppose that

$b = 0.8$
$t = 0.2$
$m = 0.04$

and that the economy's exports increase by \$10. Applying equation 4-36, the

[3]The change in the balance of trade is smaller than the change in exports because the increase (decrease) in national income brought about by any increase (decrease) in exports results in some increase (decrease) in imports.

change in the balance of trade is

$$\Delta B = \$10\left[1 - \frac{0.04}{1 - .8 + 0.8(0.2) + 0.04}\right]$$
$$= \$10\left(1 - \frac{0.04}{0.40}\right)$$
$$= \$10(1 - 0.1)$$
$$= \$10(0.9)$$
$$= \$9$$

The \$10 increase in exogenous exports increased the balance of trade by \$9.

If the exogenous exports had decreased by \$5, the change in the balance of trade would have been

$$\Delta B = -\$5\left[1 - \frac{0.04}{1 - 0.8 + 0.8(0.2) + 0.04}\right]$$
$$= -\$5(0.9)$$
$$= -\$4.50$$

The balance of trade would have decreased by \$4.50 as a consequence of the \$5 decrease in exogenous exports.

A change in autonomous imports and the balance of trade Let us assume that autonomous imports change by an amount equal to ΔN_0 and that exogenous exports are constant. Utilizing equation 4-34, the change in the balance of trade (with $\Delta\overline{X}$ equal to zero) is

$$\Delta B = -\Delta N_0 - m\,\Delta Y \qquad (4\text{-}37)$$

For ΔY we may substitute, from equation 4-30, $-\Delta N_0/(1 - b + bt + m)$ to obtain

$$\Delta B = -\Delta N_0 - m\frac{-\Delta N_0}{1 - b + bt + m}$$

or

$$\Delta B = -\Delta N_0\left(1 - \frac{m}{1 - b + bt + m}\right) \qquad (4\text{-}38)$$

The expression inside the parentheses in equation 4-38 is exactly the same as the expression inside the parentheses in equation 4-36; and for the same reasons this expression is both positive and less than 1. Equation 4-38 therefore tells us that the change in the balance of trade is *inversely related to but smaller than the change in autonomous imports*. An increase (decrease) in autonomous imports brings about a smaller decrease (increase) in the balance of trade.[4]

Assuming once more that $b = 0.8$, $t = 0.2$ and $m = 0.04$, if N_0 increases by

[4] The change in the balance of trade is smaller than the change in autonomous imports because the decrease (increase) in national income brought about by any increase (decrease) in autonomous imports results in some decrease (increase) in the imports which depend upon the level of national income.

$8, the change in the balance of trade, using equation 4-34, will be

$$\begin{aligned}\Delta B &= -(+\$8)\frac{0.04}{1 - 0.8 + 0.8(0.2) + 0.04} \\ &= -\$8\left(1 - \frac{0.04}{0.40}\right) \\ &= -\$8(1 - 0.1) \\ &= -\$8(0.9) \\ &= -\$7.20\end{aligned}$$

The $8 increase in N_0 brought about a $7.20 decrease in the balance of trade. Had N_0 decreased by $9, the balance of trade would have increased by $8.10; for

$$\begin{aligned}\Delta B &= -(-\$9)(0.9) \\ &= \$8.10\end{aligned}$$

The effects of other changes on the balance of trade By employing equation 4-34 along with the equations for the values of the various multipliers (equations 4-25 to 4-29) we can find the effect on the balance of trade of changes in $\bar{G}$, C_0, I_0, T_0, and $\bar{I}$. We shall not work out the effects of all these changes. The student should be able to determine for himself the effects on the balance of trade by employing the same method we employed to find the effect of a change in autonomous imports. To illustrate how we can determine the effect of each of these changes, let us work out the effect of a change in government expenditures for goods and services on the balance of trade.

Starting with equation 4-34

$$\Delta B = \Delta\bar{X} - \Delta N_0 - m\,\Delta Y \tag{4-34}$$

if we assume that exogenous exports and autonomous imports are constant,

$$\Delta B = -m\,\Delta Y \tag{4-39}$$

From equation 4-25 we can see that if $\bar{G}$ changes by $\Delta\bar{G}$, the change in Y^* is

$$\Delta Y^* = \Delta\bar{G}\frac{1}{1 - b + bt + m} \tag{4-40}$$

The right side of equation 4-40 is now substituted for ΔY in equation 4-39. The change in the balance of trade is

$$\Delta B = -m\left(\Delta\bar{G}\frac{1}{1 - b + bt + m}\right)$$

or

$$\Delta B = \Delta\bar{G}\frac{-m}{1 - b + bt + m} \tag{4-41}$$

The fractional expression is negative because m in the numerator is preceeded by a minus sign, but it is less than 1 for reasons given earlier. Thus when government expenditures increase (decrease), the result is a decrease (an increase) in the balance of trade that is smaller than the change in government expenditures.

Using the same values for m, b, and t as in all our previous examples, if $\bar{G}$

increases by \$15, the change in the balance of trade will be

$$\Delta B = \$15\frac{-0.04}{1 - 0.8 + 0.8(0.2) + 0.04}$$

$$= \$15\frac{-0.04}{0.40}$$

$$= \$15(-0.1)$$
$$= -\$1.50$$

The \$15 increase in government expenditures decreases by the balance of trade by \$1.50.

Exercise 4-2

1 Define the foreign trade multiplier. ________________

2 Show that the foreign trade multiplier is equal to $1/(1 - b + bt + m)$.

3 If $b = 0.75$, $t = 0.4$, and $m = 0.05$:

a The value of the foreign trade multiplier is ________

b If exogenous exports increase by \$9, the equilibrium national income will (increase, decrease) ________ by \$________

c If exogenous exports decrease by \$15, the equilibrium national income will ________ by \$________

4 Demonstrate that:

a $$\frac{\Delta Y^*}{\Delta \bar{G}} = \frac{\Delta Y^*}{\Delta C_0} = \frac{\Delta Y^*}{\Delta I_0} = \frac{1}{1 - b + bt + m}$$

b $$\frac{\Delta Y^*}{\Delta \bar{i}} = \frac{-j}{1 - b + bt + m}$$

c $$\frac{\Delta Y^*}{\Delta T_0} = \frac{-b}{1 - b + bt + m}$$

d $$\frac{\Delta Y^*}{\Delta N_0} = \frac{-1}{1 - b + bt + m}$$

5 Assume that $b = 0.75$, $t = 0.40$, $m = 0.05$, and $j = \$160$. What would be the effect of each of the following upon the equilibrium national income?

a A \$12 increase in N_0: ________

b A \$9 decrease in T_0: ________

c A 1 percentage point increase in $\bar{i}$: ________

d A \$24 increase in $\bar{G}$: ________

6 Define:

a The balance of trade: $B \equiv$ ________

b A change in the balance of trade: $\Delta B \equiv$ ________

7 Show that:

a If N_0 can change
$\Delta B = \Delta X - \Delta N_0 - m\,\Delta Y$

b With N_0 constant
$\Delta B = \Delta X - m\,\Delta Y$

c $\Delta B = \Delta \overline{X}\left(1 - \frac{m}{1 - b + bt + m}\right)$

d $\Delta B = -\Delta N_0 \frac{m}{1 - b + bt + m}$

8 What assumptions must be made to ensure that $1 - 1/(1 - b + bt + m)$ is positive and less than 1?

9 Show that:

a $\Delta B = \Delta \overline{G} \frac{-m}{1 - b + bt + m}$

b $\Delta B = \Delta I_0 \frac{-m}{1 - b + bt + m}$

c $\Delta B = \Delta C_0 \frac{-m}{1 - b + bt + m}$

d $\Delta B = \Delta T_0 \frac{mb}{1 - b + bt + m}$

e $\Delta B = \Delta \overline{i} \frac{mj}{1 - b + bt + m}$

10 Let
$b = 0.75$
$t = 0.40$
$m = 0.05$
$j = \$160$

What would be the effect of each of the following on the balance of trade?

a A \$24 increase in $\overline{X}$: ____________

b A \$18 increase in N_0: ____________

c A \$9 decrease in T_0: ____________

d A \$6 increase in C_0: ____________

e A 1 percentage point increase in $\overline{i}$: ____________

f A \$12 decrease in I_0: ____________

MONEY AND THE RATE OF INTEREST

Our analysis has not yet explained what determines the level of interest rates in the economy. We recognized earlier that the interest rate helps to determine the amount of investment spending in the economy. The level of investment spending is one of the components of aggregate demand, and aggregate demand, in turn, determines the equilibrium national income of the economy. But we assumed that the rate of interest was an exogenous variable: it was given and was not explained.

We now introduce the rate of interest into our analysis as an endogenous variable. The rate of interest is the price paid for the use of money. Like other prices, the price paid for the use of money is determined by the supply of money and the demand for it. We examine the supply of money in the first section of this chapter, the demand for money in the second section, and how demand and supply together determine the equilibrium rate of interest in the economy in the third.

THE SUPPLY OF MONEY

The supply of money M_0 has two components, the currency component M_c, which includes paper money and coins, and the demand deposit component M_d, the checking accounts which the public has in commercial banks. We define the money supply, therefore, as

$$M_0 \equiv M_c + M_d \tag{5-1}$$

For simplicity we shall assume in this chapter that the currency component of the money supply is constant, i.e., that the amount of currency in the hands of the public does not change. This assumption means that changes in the money supply occur only as a result of changes in the demand deposit component. for if M_c is constant,

$$\Delta M_c = 0$$

and

$$\Delta M_0 = \Delta M_d \tag{5-2}$$

Put another way, a change in the demand deposit component brings about an equal change in the money supply.

Demand deposits, reserves, and the reserve ratio

Having assumed that M_0 changes only when M_d changes, we now wish to know what determines the size of M_d, what causes M_d to change, and the amount by which M_d can change.

In the banking system commercial banks are required by law to have reserves R in the form of either deposits at the Federal Reserve Banks or currency in their own vaults. The amount of reserves they must have depends upon the demand deposits the public has in their banks *and* the required (or legal) reserve ratio r. The required reserve ratio is a percentage set by the Federal Reserve Banks. It is the percentage of demand deposits which commercial banks must have in reserves.[1] Thus we can write the reserves required by law as a function of the demand deposits of commercial banks and the required reserve ratio

$$R = rM_d \tag{5-3}$$

For example, if commercial banks have demand deposits of \$150 and the required reserve ratio is 20 percent, the required reserve would be 20 percent of \$150, or \$30.

When we are interested in knowing what determines the maximum size of M_d (and of M_0) in the economy, a more useful form of equation 5-3 is found by dividing both sides of this equation by r

$$\frac{rM_d}{r} = \frac{R}{r}$$

$$M_d = \frac{R}{r} \tag{5-4}$$

This equation tells us that the amount of demand deposits in the economy may equal as much as the reserves of commercial banks divided by the required reserve ratio. If commercial banks had \$60 of reserves and the required reserve ratio was 25 percent, demand deposits in the economy could (at most) be \$60

[1] Commercial banks are also required to have a reserve for their time deposits; but because time deposits are not a part of the money supply, we shall ignore them and the reserves required by law for time deposits.

divided by 25 percent, or \$240. In using equation 5-4, we shall assume that demand deposits are always as large as allowed by the reserves and the required reserve ratio. This means we assume that commercial banks never have an excess reserve.

In summary, we assume that the demand deposits of an economy equal the reserves held by commercial banks divided by the required reserve ratio set by the Federal Reserve Banks.

Changes in reserves and the required reserve ratio

If demand deposits in the economy depend upon the reserves of commercial banks and the required reserve ratio, then a change in either reserves or the reserve ratio will bring about a change in demand deposits (and in the money supply). Let us look first at how a change in reserves affects demand deposits and then at how a change in the reserve ratio will alter demand deposits.

Changes in reserves When reserves change by ΔR, demand deposits change by ΔM_d. Using equation 5-4, we can write

$$M_d + \Delta M_d = \frac{R + \Delta R}{r} \tag{5-5}$$

From this equation we subtract equation 5-4 and obtain

$$\Delta M_d = \frac{\Delta R}{r}\left(= \Delta R \frac{1}{r}\right) \tag{5-6}$$

The change in demand deposits and in the money supply equals the change in reserves divided by the required reserve ratio (or the change in reserves multiplied by the reciprocal of the reserve ratio). Notice that the sign of $\Delta R/r$ is positive. When reserves increase, demand deposits will increase; and when R decreases, M_d also decreases.

Suppose, for example, that r is 20 percent and R increased by \$10. M_d would increase by an amount equal to \$10 times $1/0.20 =$ \$10 times 5, or \$50. If r is 25 percent and R decreased by \$5, M_d would decrease by \$5 times $1/0.25 =$ \$5 times 4, or \$20.

The reciprocal of the required reserve ratio is often called the *deposit multiplier*. In the two examples above, the reciprocal of 20 percent and the deposit multiplier is 5, and the reciprocal of 25 percent and the deposit multiplier is 4. The change in demand deposits that accompanies a change in the reserves of commercial banks is equal to the change in reserves times the deposit multiplier. We should note that the smaller the required reserve ratio, the larger the deposit multiplier and the larger the ratio, the smaller this multiplier.

Why and how do the reserves of commercial banks change? They change primarily because the Federal Reserve Banks want them to change in order to bring about a change in demand deposits and the money supply. The Federal Reserve alters reserves by two principal means. They may lower (or raise) the discount rate, the rate at which commercial banks can borrow reserves at the Federal Reserve Banks, to expand (or contract) the reserves of commercial banks. They may also buy (or sell) United States government securities in the open market for these securities to increase (or decrease) commercial bank reserves. The details of these two methods of changing commercial bank reserves we leave to your principles of economics textbook.

Changes in the required reserve ratio The formula for finding the effect of a change in r upon M_d is a bit more complicated than the formula for finding the effect of a change in R (equation 5-6), but it is just as specific and just as useful. Again we start with equation 5-4

$$M_d = \frac{R}{r} \tag{5-4}$$

When r changes by Δr, M_d changes by ΔM_d; and we may write

$$M_d + \Delta M_d = \frac{R}{r + \Delta r} \tag{5-7}$$

From equation 5-7 we subtract equation 5-4

$$\Delta M_d = \frac{R}{r + \Delta r} - \frac{R}{r}$$

Next we put the two terms on the right side over a common denominator.

$$\Delta M_d = \frac{r(R)}{r(r + \Delta r)} - \frac{(r + \Delta r)R}{r(r + \Delta r)}$$

$$= \frac{rR - rR - R\,\Delta r}{r(r + \Delta r)}$$

$$= \frac{-R\,\Delta r}{r(r + \Delta r)} \tag{5-8}$$

This equation tells us that the change in demand deposits (and the money supply) equals the negative quantity that is the reserves of banks times the change in the required reserve ratio divided by the original reserve ratio times the original reserve ratio plus the change in the reserve ratio. It is important to see that the right-hand expression is negative. This means that an increase in r will decrease M_d and a decrease in r will increase M_d.

As an example of the usefulness of equation 5-8, assume that commercial banks have reserves of \$200, that the reserve ratio is 20 percent, and demand deposits are therefore \$1,000. Now assume the reserve ratio increases to 25 percent, an increase of 5 percent. Applying equation 5-8,

$$\Delta M_d = \frac{-\$200(0.05)}{0.20(0.20 + 0.05)}$$

$$= \frac{-\$10}{0.20(0.25)}$$

$$= \frac{-\$10}{0.05}$$

$$= -\$200$$

The 5 percent increase in r decreases M_d by \$200.

As another example, suppose commercial banks have reserves of \$500 and the reserve ratio decreases from 30 to 20 percent. Plugging these figures into the equation 5-8,

$$\Delta M_d = \frac{-\$500(-0.10)}{0.30(0.30 - 0.10)}$$

$$= \frac{\$50}{0.30(0.20)}$$

$$= \frac{\$50}{0.06}$$

$$= \$833.33\tfrac{1}{3}$$

The reduction in r from 30 to 20 percent expanded M_d (and M) by $833.33⅓.

When and how does the reserve ratio change? It changes when the Federal Reserve Banks decide to change it, and it changes as a result of the announcement by the Federal Reserve that they are changing it. The Federal Reserve lowers the rate when they wish demand deposits and the money supply to expand, and they raise it when they wish to contract demand deposits and the supply of money.

Exercise 5-1

1 Using symbols, the money supply M_0 is equal to ________ + ________

2 In examining the money supply in this chapter it is assumed that:

a M_c is ____________

b When M_d changes, M_0 changes by an amount equal to the change in ____________

3 Suppose there is $50 in currency and $290 in demand deposits in the economy.

a The money supply is equal to $____________

b When demand deposits increase by $40, the money supply will (increase, decrease) ____________ by $____________

4 If commercial banks have the demand deposits shown in column 1 and the required reserve ratios shown in column 2, show the reserves they are required to have in column 3.

(1) DEMAND DEPOSITS	(2) REQUIRED RESERVE RATIO	(3) REQUIRED RESERVE
$1,000	0.30	$____________
2,400	0.16⅔	____________
3,000	0.15	____________
8,000	0.12½	____________
1,400	0.20	____________
9,000	0.33⅓	____________

5 Assuming commercial banks do not have an excess reserve, show the deposit multiplier in column 3 and demand deposits in column 4, given the reserves and the required reserve ratios shown in columns 1 and 2, respectively.

(1) RESERVES	(2) RESERVE RATIO	(3) DEPOSIT MULTIPLIER	(4) DEMAND DEPOSITS
$3,000	0.33⅓	________	$________
3,000	0.30	________	________
2,400	0.16⅔	________	________
2,400	0.15	________	________
2,000	0.12½	________	________
1,500	0.10	________	________
1,000	0.08⅓	________	________

6 Suppose the required reserve ratio is the percentage shown in column 1 and the amount the reserves of commercial banks change are shown in column 2. Place the changes in demand deposits in column 3.

(1) RESERVE RATIO	(2) CHANGE IN RESERVES	(3) CHANGE IN DEMAND DEPOSITS
0.08⅓	$900	$________
0.10	800	________
0.12½	700	________
0.15	600	________
0.16⅔	500	________
0.30	500	________
0.33⅓	200	________

7 The reserves of commercial banks are given in column 1 and the changes in the required reserve ratio in column 2. Show the changes in demand deposits that result in column 3.

(1) RESERVES	(2) CHANGES IN RESERVE RATIO	(3) CHANGES IN DEMAND DEPOSITS
$1,000	From 10 to 12½%	$________
800	From 15 to 12½%	________
600	From 15 to 16⅔%	________
400	From 16⅔ to 10%	________
200	From 33⅓ to 30%	________

8 Demonstrate that if $M_d = \frac{R}{r}$:

a $\Delta M_d = \frac{\Delta R}{r}$

b $\Delta M_d = \frac{-R\,\Delta r}{r(r + \Delta r)}$

9 What two things would the Federal Reserve Banks do if they wished to expand the money supply by increasing the reserves of commercial banks?

a ______________________________

b ______________________________

10 Why would the Federal Reserve Banks:

a Lower the reserve ratio? ______________________________

b Raise the reserve ratio? ______________________________

11 Suppose the money supply is $1,000, the reserves of commercial banks are $200, and the reserve ratio is 20 percent.

a Using equation 5-6, by how much would the reserves of commercial banks have to increase to bring about a $500 expansion in the money supply?

$__________

b Using equation 5-8, what should the reserve ratio be to induce a $500 expansion in the money supply? __________ %

THE DEMAND FOR MONEY

The demand for money has two components, and the total demand for money is their sum. The two components of the demand for money are the transactions demand L_t and the asset demand L_a. We use the symbol L for the total demand for money and express this relationship as

$$L \equiv L_t + L_a \tag{5-9}$$

The transactions demand

Money serves the economy as a medium of exchange. It is used by buyers to make purchases and is accepted by sellers in exchange for goods and services. Money is a means of effecting purchases and sales without the inconveniences of barter. To perform this function it is necessary for consumers and firms to have money on hand—in wallets and purses, in vaults and cash drawers, and in demand deposit accounts. This need or demand for money is called the *transactions demand.*

The amount of money the economy demands for transactions depends upon the volume or level of sales in the economy. It depends upon the level of national income Y. The higher the level of Y, the greater the transactions demand for money; and the lower the level of Y, the smaller the transactions demand. We may express this demand as an increasing and linear function

$$L_t = kY \tag{5-10}$$

The parameter k links the level of Y to the quantity of money demanded for transaction purposes. It is assumed that k is a positive number and that it is both greater than zero and less than one. Thus

$$1 < k < 0$$

We should note that there is no constant term on the right side of equation 5-10. This means that if Y is zero, the quantity of money demanded for transaction purposes will be zero.

The parameter k, it turns out, is the ratio of the change in L_t (when Y changes) to the change in Y. For if Y changes by ΔY, L_t will change by ΔL_t; and

$$\begin{aligned} L_t + \Delta L_t &= k(Y + \Delta Y) \\ &= kY + k\,\Delta Y \end{aligned}$$

From this last equation we subtract equation 5-10 to find ΔL_t.

$$\Delta L_t = k\,\Delta Y$$

Dividing through by ΔY,

$$\frac{\Delta L_t}{\Delta Y} = k$$

As an example of the transactions demand for money we might have $L_t = 0.2Y$. If the national income is \$100, the economy would demand 0.2 of \$100, or \$20, for transactions; if Y is \$200 the transactions demand would be 0.2 of \$200, or \$40, etc. The parameter k is equal to 0.2. The ratio of the change in L_t to the change in Y is equal to k, or to 0.2 in this example: for every change in Y, L_t changes by 0.2 of the change in Y; L_t changes by 20 cents for every dollar change in Y.

The asset demand

A second important function of money is its store of value of function. Consumers and business firms tend to hold some of their wealth in the form of money (currency and demand deposits) rather than in stocks and bonds, real estate and capital goods, and other property.

When firms and consumers choose to hold money instead of other forms of wealth, they must do without the income (dividends, interest, rent, profits, etc.) these other forms of wealth would provide them. They earn no income if they hold money because neither currency in a vault or billfold nor demand deposits in a commercial bank earn their owners any income. For this reason the greater the rate of interest that could be earned if the money were loaned, the greater the cost of holding on to money—the greater the interest income lost. The lower the rate of interest in the economy, the smaller the interest income a consumer or firm looses by choosing to hold money rather than another form of wealth.

Thus the amount of money the economy decides to hold on to as a form of wealth depends upon the rate of interest i. In general, the higher the i, the less money they will hold as wealth (because of the greater cost of, or loss from, holding money); the lower the i, the more money they will hold (because of the smaller cost of holding on to money). We can express this relationship between the asset demand for money as a decreasing and linear function

$$L_a = L_0 - ni \tag{5-11}$$

In this equation, the parameter L_0 is the amount of money the economy would hold as wealth if i were zero. We assume that L_0 is positive, that

$$L_0 > 0$$

The parameter n links changes in L_a to changes in i. The minus sign in front of ni indicates that when i decreases, L_a will increase and when i increases, L_a will decrease. The value of n (ignoring the negative sign preceeding it), it is assumed, is greater than zero.

$$n > 0$$

To see that n is the link between changes in i and the resulting changes in L_a, suppose that i changes by an amount equal to Δi. L_a will then change by ΔL_a. Using equation 5-11, we can write

$$\begin{aligned} L_a + \Delta L_a &= L_0 - n(i + \Delta i) \\ &= L_0 - ni - n\,\Delta i \end{aligned} \tag{5-12}$$

and then subtract equation 5-12 from equation 5-13

$$\Delta L_a = -n\,\Delta i \tag{5-13}$$

The change in the asset demand for money equals the negative quantity the parameter n times the change in i. Dividing through by Δi, we have

$$\frac{\Delta L_a}{\Delta i} = -n$$

The negative parameter n is the ratio of the change in L_a (that results from a change in i) to the change in i.

As an illustration of the asset demand for money we might have

$$L_a = \$40 - \$200i \tag{5-14}$$

Notice that L_0 is measured in dollars. The rate of interest i has no units attached to it. It is a pure number and expressed as a decimal. For the term ni to be dollars when i is a pure number, n must be measured in dollars. With a rate of interest of 6 percent (=0.06), the term ni would be $200 times 0.06, or $12. L_a would then be $40 minus $12, or $28. At 8 percent, ni is $200 times 0.08, or $16; and L_a is $40 less $16, or $24.

We should note in this example that because n is $200, the change in L_a equals −$200 times the change in i; and the ratio of the change in L_a to the change in i is −$200. We may also observe that if i were zero, ni would also be zero; and L_a would be $40. Thus $40 is the maximum number of dollars the economy wants as an asset (because zero is the lowest rate of interest possible).

It is possible that the economy, at some i, would have no asset demand for money. To find the i at which L_a would be zero, we let L_a be zero in equation 5–14

$$0 = \$40 - \$200i$$

and solve for i.

$$\$200i = \$40$$

$$i = \frac{\$40}{\$200}$$

$$= 0.20\ (=20\%)$$

In more general terms, the rate of interest at which L_a is zero is found by letting L_a be zero in equation 5-11

$$0 = L_0 - ni$$
$$ni = L_0$$
$$i = \frac{L_0}{n}$$

The rate of interest at which L_a is zero equals the number of dollars demanded for asset purposes when i is zero divided by the parameter n (the ratio of the change in L_a to the change in i).

The total demand for money

Earlier we saw that the total demand for money is the sum of the transaction and asset demands

$$L \equiv L_t + L_a \qquad (5\text{-}9)$$

For L_t and L_a in equation 5–9 we may substitute equations 5–10 and 5–11, respectively, and have

$$L = kY + (L_0 - ni)$$

or

$$L = L_0 + kY - ni \qquad (5\text{-}15)$$

This equation tells us that the total demand for money depends upon two variables, national income and the rate of interest, and three parameters, L_0, k, and n.

Equation 5-15 also tells us that the relation between the demand for money and Y is a direct one and the relation between the demand for money and the rate of interest is an inverse one: an increase in Y or a decrease in i will increase the quantity of money the economy wishes to have in its possession; and a decrease in Y or an increase in i decreases the amount of money firms and consumers wish to have on hand. In short, when we know the levels of Y and i in the economy, we also know the total demand for money.

Using our previous examples of the transactions demand and the asset demand for money

$$L_t = 0.2Y$$
$$L_a = \$40 - \$200i$$

the total demand for money is

$$L = \$40 + 0.2Y - \$200i$$

If Y is \$300 and i is 5 percent, the total quantity of money the economy would desire would be

$$\begin{aligned} L &= \$40 + 0.2(\$300) - \$200(0.05) \\ &= \$40 + \$60 - \$10 \\ &= \$90 \end{aligned}$$

Because $\Delta L_t/\Delta Y = k$ and $\Delta L_a/\Delta i = -n$, for every \$10 increase in Y, L_t and L increase by 0.2 times \$10, or \$2; and for every 0.01 that i increases, L_a and L decrease by \$200 times 0.01, or \$2. If Y were to increase by \$10 from \$300 to \$310 (with i constant), the total demand for money would be

$$\begin{aligned} L &= \$40 + 0.2(\$310) - \$200(0.05) \\ &= \$40 + \$62 - \$10 \\ &= \$92 \end{aligned}$$

or if i were to increase by 0.01 from 0.05 to 0.06 (with Y constant), the total demand for money would be

$$\begin{aligned} L &= \$40 + 0.2(\$300) - \$200(0.06) \\ &= \$40 + \$60 - \$12 \\ &= \$88 \end{aligned}$$

Exercise 5-2

1 Using symbols, define the total demand for money.

$L \equiv$ __________ + __________

2 Write the equation for the transaction demand for money.

$L_t =$ __________

a What assumption is made about the size of k? __________
b Show that $\Delta L_t/\Delta Y = k$.

3 Write the equation for the asset demand for money.

$L_a =$ __________

a What assumption is made about the size of L_0? __________

b What assumption is made about the size of n? __________
c Show that $\Delta L_a/\Delta i = -n$.

4 Suppose that
$L_t = 0.3Y$
$L_a = \$20 - \$300i$
a What would be:
(1) The quantity of money demanded for transaction purposes if Y were zero?

\$__________

(2) The quantity of money demanded for asset purposes if i were zero?
\$__________
b What would i have to be for the asset demand for money to be zero?
__________%
c Give the values of:
(1) $\Delta L_t/\Delta Y$: __________

(2) $\Delta L_a/\Delta i$: __________

d Write the total demand for money equation.

$L =$ __________

5 If the total demand for money equation is

$L = \$50 + 0.25Y - \$250i$

show the quantity of money demanded at each of the following sets of Y and i.

a \$500 and 6%: \$__________

b \$600 and 7%: \$__________

c \$700 and 5%: \$__________

6 Using the total demand for money equation in question 5:

a For every \$50 decreases in Y, L will (increase, decrease) __________ by \$__________

b For every 0.01 increase in i, L will __________ by \$__________

EQUILIBRIUM IN THE MONEY MARKET

The supply of money in the economy depends upon the required reserve ratio and the reserves of commercial banks, both of which are controlled by the Federal Reserve Banks. The demand for money depends upon the level of national income and the rate of interest. For there to be equilibrium in the money market the quantity of money supplied and the quantity of money demanded must be equal. The equilibrium equation is

$$M_0 = L \tag{5-16}$$

This equation, along with several additional assumptions, we use to determine the equilibrium rate of interest in the economy and to discover how changes in M_0, Y, and the demand for money affect the equilibrium interest rate.

Assumptions

We shall assume that there are four exogenous variables, Y, M_c, r, and R. In mathematical form we are assuming that

$$Y = \bar{Y} \tag{5-17}$$

and that

$$M_c = \bar{M}_c$$
$$M_c = \bar{C}$$
$$r = \bar{r}$$
$$R = \bar{R}$$

If M_c, r, and R are exogenous variables, then M will also be exogenous. This is true because

$$M_0 = M_c + M_d \tag{5-1}$$

and

$$M_d = \frac{R}{r} \tag{5-4}$$

By substituting equation 5-4 into equation 5-1,

$$M_0 = M_c + \frac{R}{r} \tag{5-18}$$

Once M_c, R, and r are given, so is M_0; if M_c, R, and r are exogenous, M_0 is exogenous and we can write

$$M_0 = \overline{M}_0 \tag{5-19}$$

Equilibrium

Given these assumptions, we can write our model for the money market in terms of the following set of equations.

$$L \equiv L_t + L_a \tag{5-9}$$
$$L_t = kY \tag{5-10}$$
$$L_a = L_0 - ni \tag{5-11}$$
$$M_0 = L \tag{5-16}$$
$$Y = \overline{Y} \tag{5-17}$$
$$M_0 = \overline{M}_0 \tag{5-19}$$

The first equation is a definition; the next two equations are behavioral; equation 5-16 is the equilibrium equation; and the last two equations are behavioral (telling us that Y and M are exogenous and given). We see that there are six equations in all and six variables (L, L_t, L_a, Y, i, and M_0). There are also three parameters in this system of equations, k, L_0, and n.

Because the number of equations and variables are equal, this set of equations should have a solution. Given the values of the three parameters and the two exogenous variables we ought to be able to find the values of the remaining four endogenous variables. We are primarily interested in knowing what the equilibrium value of i (or i^*) will be. Starting with the equilibrium equation,

$$M_0 = L \tag{5-16}$$

we substitute equation 5-19 for M and equation 5-9 for L.

$$\overline{M}_0 = L_t + L_a$$

For L_t and L_a we substitute equations 5-10 and 5-11, respectively,

$$\overline{M}_0 = k\overline{Y} + L_0 - ni$$

Finally, for Y we substitute equation 5-17 to obtain

$$\overline{M}_0 = k\overline{Y} + L_0 - ni$$

and solve for i by moving ni to the left side and $\overline{M}_0$ to the right side of the equation.

$$ni = k\overline{Y} + L_0 - \overline{M}_0$$

$$i^* = \frac{k\overline{Y} + L_0 - \overline{M}_0}{n} \tag{5-20}$$

Equation 5-20 says that the equilibrium rate of interest in the money market equals the quantity the parameter k times the given level of national income plus the parameter L_0 minus the given supply of money all divided by the parameter n. Once we have found i^*, we can find L_a by using equation 5–11, L_t by using equation 5-10 and the given Y, and L by using equation 5-9.

To illustrate, let us suppose that

$$L_t = 0.2Y$$
$$L_a = \$40 - \$200i$$
$$Y = \$500$$
$$M_0 = \$124$$

The parameter k is 0.2, L_0 is \$40, and n is \$200. Using equation 5-20,

$$i^* = \frac{0.2(\$500) + \$40 - \$124}{\$200}$$
$$= \frac{\$100 + \$40 - \$124}{\$200}$$
$$= \frac{\$16}{\$200}$$
$$= 0.08$$

If i is 0.08, then L_a is \$40 − \$200(0.08), or \$24. L_t is 0.2 times \$500, or \$100. L, therefore, is \$100 + \$24, or \$124, which is equal to the given supply of money.

Before going on to discover how changes in the exogenous variables and parameters affect i^*, it is essential to be aware that the model we have described above does not by itself really determine i^* in the economy. What it does do is *tell us what* i* *is in the money market if we know the level of national income.* But, recalling Chapters 2, 3, and 4, the level of national income depends upon the size of the investment component of aggregate demand, which in turn depends upon i. In the three previous chapters we assumed i was given in order to find the equilibrium national income in the market for goods and services—in the commodity market. In this chapter we assumed national income was given to find the equilibrium interest rate in the money market. Neither the model for finding Y^* in the last two chapters nor the model for finding i^* in this chapter is able to determine both Y^* and i^*. Each of the two models finds the value of one variable (Y^* or i^*) by assuming that the value of the other variable is given.

That neither of the models can determine both Y^* and i^*, that is, neither can find the value of one variable without assuming the other to be given, does not mean that these models are useless. In the next chapter we shall put the work we have already done together and combine the two models to obtain a complete model. This complete model will determine the equilibrium values of both Y and i. It is a model in which neither Y nor i is assumed given.

The effects of changes on the equilibrium interest rate

If we look again at the equation for the equilibrium rate of interest

$$i^* = \frac{k\bar{Y} + L_0 - \bar{M}_0}{n} \qquad (5\text{-}20)$$

we shall see that a change in k, $\bar{Y}$, L_0, $\bar{M}_0$, or n will alter i^*. What we wish to know is the effect of changes k, $\bar{Y}$, L_0, and $\bar{M}_0$ upon i^*. (We shall not concern ourselves with the effect of a change in n on i^*.)

A change in the money supply When $\bar{M}_0$ changes by $\bar{M}_0$, i^* changes by Δi^*. Using equation 5-20, we can write

$$i^* + \Delta i^* = \frac{k\bar{Y} + L_0 - (\bar{M}_0 + \Delta\bar{M}_0)}{n}$$

$$= \frac{k\bar{Y} + L_0 - \bar{M}_0 - \Delta\bar{M}_0}{n}$$

From this equation we subtract equation 5-20 and obtain

$$\Delta i^* = \frac{-\Delta\bar{M}_0}{n} \tag{5-21}$$

The change in i^* that results from a change in M_0 is equal to the negative quantity the change in M_0 divided by the parameter n. It is important to note that the minus sign means that an increase in M_0 will lower i^* (and vice versa).

Using our earlier example, in which n was \$200, if M_0 increases by \$10, the change in i^* will be

$$\Delta i^* = \frac{-(+\$10)}{\$200}$$

$$= \frac{-\$10}{\$200}$$

$$= -0.05$$

A \$10 increase in M_0 lowers i^* by 0.05. (When M_0 was \$124, i^* was 8 percent. Now with M_0 increased by \$10 to \$134, i^* decreases by 5 percent to 3 percent.)

A change in national income Using the equilibrium equation (5-20), when $\bar{Y}$ changes by $\Delta\bar{Y}$, i^* changes by Δi^*

$$i^* + \Delta i^* = \frac{k(\bar{Y} + \Delta\bar{Y}) + L_0 - \bar{M}_0}{n}$$

$$= \frac{k\bar{Y} + k\,\Delta\bar{Y} + L_0 - \bar{M}_0}{n}$$

Subtracting equation 5-20,

$$\Delta i^* = \frac{k\,\Delta\bar{Y}}{n} \tag{5-22}$$

The change in i^* is equal to the parameter k times the change in $\bar{Y}$ divided by the parameter n. We can see that $(k\,\Delta\bar{Y})/n$ is positive. When $\bar{Y}$ increases, i^* will also increase; and when $\bar{Y}$ decreases, i^* decreases.

The parameter k in our example is 0.2, and n is \$200. If $\bar{Y}$ increased by \$50, the change in i^* would be

$$\Delta i^* = \frac{0.2(\$50)}{\$200}$$

$$= \frac{\$10}{\$200}$$

$$= 0.05$$

With i^* equal to 8 percent when $\bar{Y}$ is \$500, i^* is now higher by 5 percent when $\bar{Y}$ is \$550. The equilibrium rate of interest is now 13 percent.

Changes in the demand for money Not only may the supply of money and national income change to alter i^*, but either the transactions demand or the asset demand for money may also change to affect i^*. We shall define:

- An increase in the transactions demand as an increase in the parameter k (and a decrease as a decrease in k)
- An increase in the asset demand as an increase in L_0 (and a decrease as a decrease in L_0)

Leaving the proofs to the student (using the same method we employed above),

$$\Delta i^* = \frac{\Delta k \, \bar{Y}}{n} \tag{5-23}$$

The change in i^* that results from a change in the transaction demand is equal to the change in the transactions demand times the given level of national income divided by the parameter n.

Were k to increase from 0.2 to 0.21, with $\bar{Y}$ equal to \$500 and with n equal to \$200,

$$\begin{aligned}\Delta i^* &= \frac{0.01(\$500)}{\$200} \\ &= \frac{\$5}{\$200} \\ &= 0.025\end{aligned}$$

The change in i^* would be $2\frac{1}{2}$ percent. The equilibrium rate of interest increased from 8 percent to $10\frac{1}{2}$ percent. Note that because the sign of $\Delta k \, \bar{Y}$ is positive, when k increases, i^* also increases (and vice versa).

It can also be shown by the student that

$$\Delta i^* = \frac{\Delta L_0}{n} \tag{5-24}$$

When the asset demand for money changes, the change in the equilibrium rate of interest that results is equal to the change in the asset demand (the change in L_0) divided by the parameter n. We see that the sign of $\Delta L_0/n$ is positive and that an increase in L_0 will increase i (and vice versa).

For example, if L_0 increased from \$40 to \$50 (an increase of \$10) and with n equal to \$200

$$\begin{aligned}\Delta i^* &= \frac{\$10}{\$200} \\ &= 0.05\end{aligned}$$

The \$10 increase in L_0 increased i^* by 5 percent: from 8 percent when L_0 was \$40 to 13 percent when L_0 was \$50.

Exercise 5-3

1 In symbols, there is equilibrium in the money market when ____________ = ____________

2 In finding equilibrium in the money market we have assumed that:

a On the supply side of the market the variables ____________, ____________, and ____________ are exogenous.

b On the demand side ____________ is an exogenous variable.

c As a result of the assumptions in part *a*, ____________ is exogenous.

3 To find equilibrium in the money market we employ six equations. These are (in symbols)

$L \equiv$ ____________ + ____________

$L_t =$ ____________

$L_a =$ ____________

____________ = ____________

$Y =$ ____________

$M_0 =$ ____________

4 Show, using the equations in question 3, that the equilibrium interest rate is equal to

$$\frac{k\bar{Y} + L_0 - \bar{M}_0}{n}$$

5 Assume that

$L_t = 0.15Y$
$L_a = \$50 - \$300i$
$Y = \$600$
$M_0 = \$125$

a What is the equilibrium rate of interest? ____________ %
b What are the equilibrium values of:

(1) L_t: \$____________

(2) L_a: \$____________

(3) L: \$____________

6 Prove that:

a $\Delta i^* = \dfrac{-\Delta\bar{M}_0}{n}$

b $\Delta i^* = \dfrac{k\,\Delta\bar{Y}}{n}$

c $\Delta i^* = \dfrac{\Delta k\,\bar{Y}}{n}$

d $\Delta i^* = \dfrac{\Delta L_0}{n}$

7 Employing the equations in question 5, what will be the effect in the money market of each of the following upon the equilibrium rate of interest?

a M_0 decreases by \$10: __________ %

b Y decreases by \$30: __________ %

c k decreases by 0.05: __________ %

d L_0 decreases by \$5: __________ %

EQUILIBRIUM IN THE ECONOMY

In Chapters 2 to 4 we developed models explaining the equilibrium national income of an economy. These models enabled us to find formulas for the equilibrium national income and to discover the relations between changes in the exogenous variables and the resulting changes in the national income. The rate of interest in all of these models was, however, an exogenous variable.

In Chapter 5 we developed a model that explained the equilibrium rate of interest in the economy. There we found formulas for the equilibrium rate of interest and discovered the relations between changes in the exogenous variables and the resulting change in the rate of interest. This model, however, assumed that the level of national income was an exogenous variable.

Chapter 6 brings together the models found in these earlier chapters. Our purpose is a single model for the economy in which neither national income nor the rate of interest is assumed to be given. In this model both national income and the rate of interest are endogenous variables. We shall be able to find the equilibrium national income *and* and equilibrium rate of interest.

The first section explains the assumptions we employ in this chapter. In the second section we develop a single model for the economy that enables us to find the equilibrium national income and rate of interest. Then in the final section we examine the relations between changes in the exogenous variables and the consequent changes in the equilibrium values of Y and i.

ASSUMPTIONS

To build an economic model requires us to state the conditions that must prevail if there is to be equilibrium and to explain the functions and definitions we use.

The Nature of Equilibrium

For there to be equilibrium in the economy as a whole there must be equilibrium *both* in the market in which goods and services are supplied and demanded *and* in the market in which money is demanded and supplied. This means that in the commodity market, i.e., the market for goods and services, the aggregate quantity of goods and services supplied or produced Y must be equal to the aggregate quantity of goods and services demanded D. It also means that in the money market the quantity of money demanded L must equal the supply of money M_0. Putting these two conditions into equation form, equilibrium in the economy as a whole requires that

$$Y = D \tag{6-1}$$

and

$$L = M_0 \tag{6-2}$$

Functions and definitions

In addition to the equilibrium conditions, we shall make the following assumptions:

1 Consumption is an increasing and linear function of disposable income.

2 Investment is a decreasing and linear function of the rate of interest.

3 Government spending for goods and services is an exogenous variable.

4 The aggregate quantity of goods and services demanded is the sum of consumption, investment, and government demand for goods and services.

5 Disposable income is defined as national income less net taxes.

6 Net taxes are an exogenous variable.

7 The transaction demand for money is an increasing and linear function of national income.

8 The asset demand for money is a decreasing and linear function of the rate of interest.

9 The total demand for money is the sum of the transaction demand and the asset demand.

10 The supply of money is an exogenous variable.

We should be aware that we are assuming that the economy is a closed one (that it neither exports nor imports goods and services) and that net taxes are a fixed amount (that taxes are not a function of national income). We have made these two assumptions to prevent our model from becoming too complex. While they reduce the realism of the model, they do not destroy its usefulness.[1]

[1] As in our earlier models, we again assume that all (net) taxes are personal taxes and that all saving is personal saving.

The ten assumptions we have made along with the equilibrium equations (6-1 and 6-2) give us the model that enables us to find the equilibrium national income and rate of interest in the economy and to find the values of the other endogenous variables in the model: consumption, investment, disposable income, the transaction, asset, and total demand for money, and the aggregate quantity of goods and services demanded. (We can also, if we wish, find the level of saving by subtracting consumption from disposable income.)

THE MODEL

Our model for the economy is a set of equations for the commodity market and a set of equations for the money market. Let us look at each set of equations separately before we join them together to find the equilibrium national income and interest rate.

The commodity market

In the commodity market our model consists of the following equations:

$$C = C_0 + bY_d \qquad (6\text{-}3)$$
$$I = I_0 - ji \qquad (6\text{-}4)$$
$$G = \bar{G} \qquad (6\text{-}5)$$
$$D \equiv C + I + G \qquad (6\text{-}6)$$
$$Y_d \equiv Y - T \qquad (6\text{-}7)$$
$$T = \bar{T} \qquad (6\text{-}8)$$
$$Y = D \qquad (6\text{-}1)$$

This model for the commodity market consists of seven equations.[2] There are in this model four parameters: C_0, b, I_0, and j. C_0 and I_0 are assumed to be positive; b is assumed to be greater than zero but less than one; and no special assumption is made about the value of j.

There are, however, eight variables (C, Y_d, Y, T, I, i, G, and D) in this model; and it is therefore an *open* model (or system of equations). We cannot find the equilibrium Y or i without assuming that one of the endogenous variables (C, Y_d, Y, I, i, or D) is given. What we are able to do is obtain a solution equation for the equilibrium Y in terms of the exogenous variables and parameters and the endogenous variable i. Alternatively, we can find a solution equation for i in terms of the exogenous variables and parameters and the endogenous variable Y.

Equilibrium *Y* equation To find the equation for the equilibrium national income, we start with the equilibrium equation

$$Y = D \qquad (6\text{-}1)$$

and substitute equation 6-6 for D

$$Y = C + I + G$$

[2]Equations 6-6 and 6-7 are definitional equations, and 6-1 is the equilibrium equation. The remaining equations are behavioral: 6-5 and 6-8 tell us which variables are exogenous, and 6-3 and 6-4 relate one endogenous variable to another.

For C, I, and G we substitute equations 6-3, 6-4, and 6-5, respectively.

$$Y = (C_0 + bY_d) + (I_0 - ji) + \bar{G}$$

Next we substitute equation 6-7 for Y_d.

$$Y = C_0 + b(Y - T) + I_0 - ji + \bar{G}$$

For T we substitute equation 6-8.

$$Y = C_0 + bY - b\bar{T} + I_0 + ji + \bar{G} \tag{6-9}$$

Moving all terms containing Y to the left side, we have

$$Y - bY = C_0 - b\bar{T} + I_0 - ji + \bar{G}$$

$$Y(1 - b) = C_0 - b\bar{T} + I_0 - ji + \bar{G}$$

Solving for the equilibrium national income,

$$Y_c^* = \frac{C_0 - b\bar{T} + I_0 - ji + \bar{G}}{1 - b} \tag{6-10}$$

Equilibrium *i* equation To find the equation for the equilibrium interest rate in the commodity market, we start with equation 6-9

$$Y = C_0 + bY - b\bar{T} + I_0 - ji + \bar{G} \tag{6-9}$$

and move the term containing i to the left and all other terms to the right side of the equation.

$$ji = C_0 + bY - b\bar{T} + I_0 + \bar{G} - Y$$

Rearranging terms, we have

$$\begin{aligned} ji &= C_0 - b\bar{T} + I_0 + \bar{G} - Y + bY \\ &= C_0 - b\bar{T} + I_0 + \bar{G} - Y(1 - b) \end{aligned}$$

Solving for the equilibrium interest rate gives

$$i_c^* = \frac{C_0 - b\bar{T} + I_0 + \bar{G} - Y(1 - b)}{j} \tag{6-11}$$

Numerical example To illustrate the use of these two equations, suppose that

$$\begin{aligned} C &= \$90 + 0.75Y_d \\ I &= \$50 - \$500i \\ T &= \$80 \\ G &= \$95 \end{aligned}$$

We find that the equilibrium national income in the commodity market is

$$\begin{aligned} Y_c^* &= \frac{\$90 - 0.75(\$80) + \$50 - \$500i + \$95}{1 - 0.75} \\ &= \frac{\$90 - \$60 + \$50 - \$500i + \$95}{0.25} \\ &= \frac{\$175 - \$500i}{0.25} \end{aligned}$$

If the rate of interest is 8 percent, then

$$Y_c^* = \frac{\$175 - \$500(0.08)}{0.25}$$
$$= \frac{\$175 - \$40}{0.25}$$
$$= \frac{\$135}{0.25}$$
$$= \$540$$

To find the equilibrium rate of interest in the commodity market as a function of national income, we use equation 6-11.

$$i_c^* = \frac{\$90 - 0.75(\$80) + \$50 + \$95 - Y(1 - 0.75)}{\$500}$$
$$= \frac{\$90 - \$60 + \$50 + \$95 - Y(0.25)}{\$500}$$
$$= \frac{\$175 - Y(0.25)}{\$500}$$

If the level of national income is \$540, then

$$i_c^* = \frac{\$175 - \$540(0.25)}{\$500}$$
$$= \frac{\$175 - \$135}{\$500}$$
$$= \frac{\$40}{\$500}$$
$$= 0.08$$

The equilibrium national income equation (6-10) tells us what national income in the commodity market will be if we know the rate of interest. The equilibrium interest rate (equation 6-11) tells us what the rate of interest in the commodity market must be if we are to obtain a known national income. Neither equation, however, can find both the equilibrium national income and the equilibrium interest rate.

Table 6-1 shows the equilibrium national incomes that accompany each of

TABLE 6-1

i_c^*, %	Y_c^*
10	\$500
9	520
8	540
7	560
6	580
5	600
4	620
3	640
2	660

nine different rates of interest in the commodity market. It also shows what the rate of interest must be if the commodity market is to achieve the nine different levels of national income.

It is important to note that as the rate of interest decreases, the equilibrium level of national income increases; and vice versa. And as the level of national income decreases, the interest rate increases; and vice versa. In short, the equilibrium national income is a decreasing function of the rate of interest, and the rate of interest is a decreasing function of national income. (This relationship is also linear because the functions we employed to obtain it are linear.)

Y_c^* and i_c^* are decreasing functions of each other because:

- In equation 6-10, the term ji appears with a negative sign in front of it, and the denominator $1 - b$ is positive.
- In equation 6-11, the term $Y(1 - b)$ also appears with a negative sign in front of it, and the denominator j is positive.

Graph of commodity equilibrium We can plot the data in the above table on a graph. On the vertical axis we plot the rate of interest and on the horizontal axis we plot national income. This curve (Figure 6-1) is called the *commodity-equilibrium curve* because it shows us what the equilibrium national income in the commodity market would be at each rate of interest and what the rate of interest would have to be for the commodity market to produce various national incomes.[3] The negative or downward slope of the commodity-equilibrium curve

[3] Often it is called the *IS* (eye ess) curve since it shows us the different combinations of Y and i at which investment I (including government expenditures for goods and services) and savings (including net taxes) are equal.

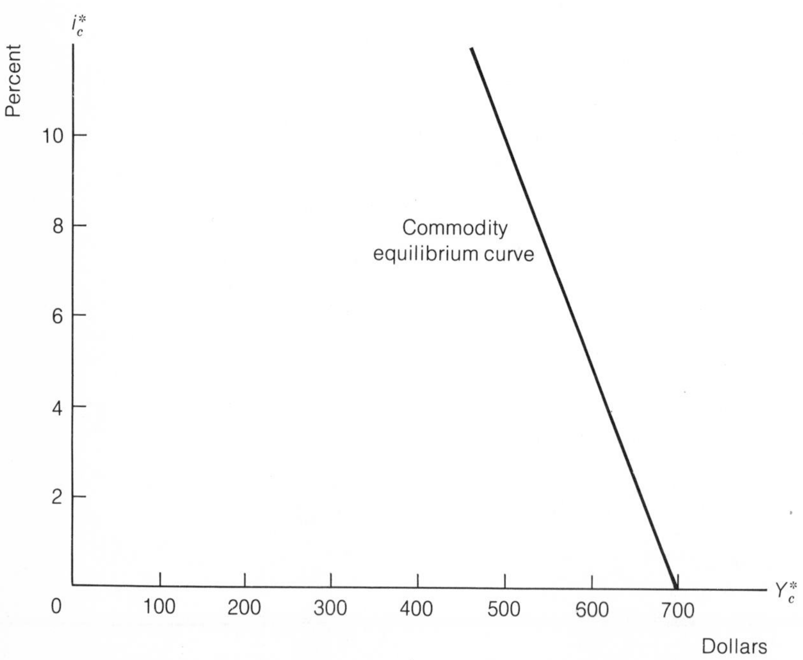

FIGURE 6-1

reflects the inverse relationship between the rate of interest and national income in the commodity market.

If we look at either Table 6-1 or the commodity-equilibrium curve, we see that whenever the rate of interest changes by 0.01, national income changes by \$20. (Or we see that when national income changes by \$20, the rate of interest changes by 0.01.) What determines the relationship between the changes in Y_c^* and i_c^*? Using equation 6-10, if i_c^* changes by Δi_c^*, Y_c^* will change by ΔY_c^*; and we can write

$$Y_c^* + \Delta Y_c^* = \frac{C_0 - b\overline{T} + I_0 - j(i_c^* + \Delta i_c^*) + \overline{G}}{1 - b}$$

From this equation we subtract equation 6-10 to find

$$\Delta Y_c^* = \frac{-j\,\Delta i_c^*}{1 - b} \tag{6-12}$$

and

$$\frac{\Delta Y_c^*}{\Delta i_c^*} = \frac{-j}{1 - b} \tag{6-13}$$

In our example, j is equal to \$500, and b is equal to 0.75. When the rate of interest changes by 0.01,

$$\Delta Y_c^* = \frac{-\$500(0.01)}{1 - 0.75} = \frac{-\$5}{0.25} = \$20$$

and

$$\frac{\Delta Y_c^*}{\Delta i_c^*} = \frac{-\$500}{1 - 0.75} = \frac{-\$500}{0.25} = \$2{,}000$$

For a change in i of 1.0, Y will change by \$2,000.

If $\Delta Y_c^*/\Delta i_c^* = -j/(1 - b)$, then $\Delta i_c^*/\Delta Y_c^* = -(1 - b)/j$. In our example, then, $\Delta i_c^*/\Delta Y_c^*$ is equal to $-(1 - 0.75)/\$500$, or $-0.25/\$500$, which is $-\$0.0005$. This means that for every \$1 change in equilibrium national income, the rate of interest will change by 0.0005.

The ratio $\Delta i_c^*/\Delta Y_c^*$, we should recognize, is the slope of the commodity-equilibrium curve. The slope of the curve is negative because the expression $(1 - b)/j$ is preceeded by a minus sign, and the slope of the curve depends upon the values of the parameters j and b. Were j to increase or b to decrease, the slope of the commodity-equilibrium curve would increase. Because it has a negative slope, an increase in the slope of the commodity-equilibrium curve means that it becomes flatter, or moves closer to a zero slope. Similarly, if j were to decrease or b to increase, the slope of the commodity equilibrium curve would decrease; it would become steeper and move closer to a curve that is a vertical line.

Before we go on to examine the money market, we should again be aware that the commodity market by itself is an open model: the number of variables is greater by 1 than the number of equations. We cannot find equilibrium Y or i in this open system. What we can do—and what we have done—is find equilibrium Y as a function of i and equilibrium i as a function of Y.

Exercise 6-1

1 There is equilibrium in the economy when (in symbols) __________ = __________ and __________ = __________.

2 Complete (in symbols) the model for the commodity market.

$C =$ __________

$I =$ __________

$G =$ __________

$D \equiv$ __________

$Y_d \equiv$ __________

$T =$ __________

$Y =$ __________

a This model has seven equations and __________ variables in addition to four parameters: __________, __________, __________, and __________

b This set of equations is an (open, closed) __________ system.

3 Show that:

a Equilibrium Y in the commodity market is equal to

$$\frac{C_0 - b\overline{T} + I_0 - ji + \overline{G}}{1 - b}$$

b Equilibrium i in the commodity market is equal to

$$\frac{C_0 - b\overline{T} + I_0 + \overline{G} - Y(1 - b)}{j}$$

4 Suppose that

$C = \$80 + 0.8Y_d$
$I = \$40 - \$600i$
$T = \$75$
$G = \$100$

Then:

a $i_c^* =$ __________

b $Y_c^* =$ __________

c $\Delta i_c^* =$ __________

d $\Delta Y_c^* =$ __________

5 Using the equations in question 4:

a Complete the table below.

i_c^*, %	Y_c^*
10	\$______
______	530
8	______
______	590
6	______
______	650
4	______
______	710
2	______

b Plot this table on the graph below.

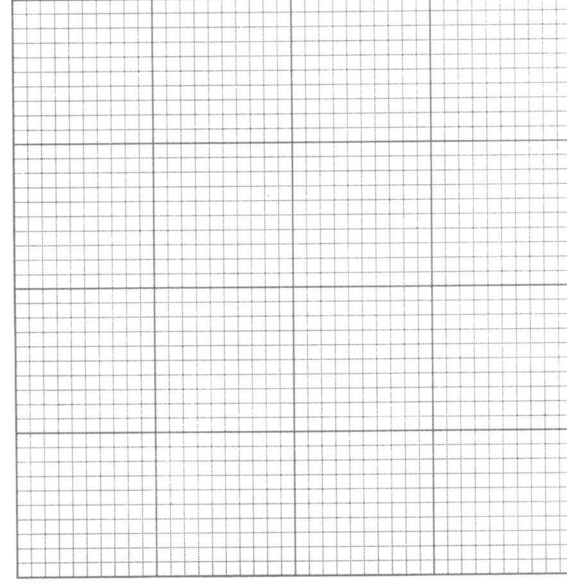

6 The slope of the commodity equilibrium plotted in question 5 is equal to

____

7 Explain why the slope of the commodity-equilibrium curve is negative.

The money market

Our model for the money market consists of the following equations:

$$L \equiv L_t + L_a \quad (6\text{-}14)$$
$$L_t = kY \quad (6\text{-}15)$$

$$L_a = L_0 - ni \tag{6-16}$$
$$M_0 = \bar{M}_0 \tag{6-17}$$
$$L = M_0 \tag{6-2}$$

The money market model consists of five equations[4] and six variables (L, L_t, L_a, Y, i, and M_0). It also contains three parameters: k is assumed to be greater than zero and less than one; L_0 is assumed to be positive; and no special assumption is made about the value of n. Because the number of variables exceeds the number of equations, this is an open model. We cannot solve for equilibrium Y or the equilibrium i without assuming that one of the endogenous variables (L, L_t, L_a, Y, or i) is given. But we can find a solution equation for Y in terms of the exogenous variables and parameters and the endogenous variable i or a solution equation for i in terms of the exogenous variables and parameters and the endogenous variable Y.

The equilibrium *Y* equation To find equilibrium Y in the money market Y_m^* as a function of the rate of interest, we start with the equilibrium equation for the money market.

$$L = M_0 \tag{6-2}$$

Substituting 6-14 for L and 6-17 for M_0, we have

$$L_t + L_a = \bar{M}_0$$

For L_t and L_a we substitute equations 6-15 and 6-16, respectively.

$$kY + L_0 - ni = \bar{M}_0 \tag{6-18}$$

Finally, we solve for Y.

$$kY = \bar{M}_0 - L_0 + ni$$

$$Y_m^* = \frac{\bar{M}_0 - L_0 + ni}{k} \tag{6-19}$$

Equilibrium *i* equation The equilibrium rate of interest equation can be found by going back to equation 6-18.

$$kY + L_0 - ni = \bar{M}_0 \tag{6-18}$$

We move kY and L_0 to the right side,

$$-ni = \bar{M}_0 - kY - L_0$$

multiply through by -1 and rearrange,

$$ni = kY + L_0 - \bar{M}_0$$

and finally divide through by n to find the equilibrium interest rate in the money market.

$$i_m^* = \frac{kY + L_0 - \bar{M}_0}{n} \tag{6-20}$$

[4] Equation 6-14 is definitional, and equation 6-2 is the equilibrium equation. The other three equations are functional.

Numerical example Suppose that

$$L_t = 0.2Y$$
$$L_a = \$20 - \$400i$$
$$M_0 = \$120$$

Equilibrium national income in the money market, using equation 6-19, is

$$Y_m^* = \frac{\$120 - \$20 + \$400i}{0.2}$$
$$= \frac{\$100 + \$400i}{0.2}$$

At an interest rate of 8 percent,

$$Y_m^* = \frac{\$100 + \$400(0.08)}{0.2}$$
$$= \frac{\$100 + \$32}{0.2}$$
$$= \frac{\$132}{0.2}$$
$$= \$660$$

Using equation 6-20, we can find the equilibrium interest rate in the money market.

$$i_m^* = \frac{(0.2)Y + \$20 - \$120}{\$400}$$
$$= \frac{0.2Y - \$100}{\$400}$$

If national income equaled $660,

$$i_m^* = \frac{0.2(\$600) - \$100}{\$400}$$
$$= \frac{\$132 - \$100}{\$400}$$
$$= \frac{\$32}{\$400}$$
$$= 0.08$$

We should note again that the equilibrium national income equation tells us what national income must be if we are to have equilibrium in the money market at various rates of interest; and the equilibrium interest rate equation tells us what the rate of interest must be in the money market if we are to obtain a known national income. Neither equation can find both the equilibrium national income and the equilibrium interest rate.

Table 6-2 shows the equilibrium national income that accompanies each of nine different rates of interest in the money market. It also shows what the rate of interest must be at each of nine national incomes if we are to have equilibrium in the money market.

We can observe that as the rate of interest decreases, national income also

TABLE 6-2

i^*_m, %	Y^*_m
10	$700
9	680
8	660
7	640
6	620
5	600
4	580
3	560
2	540

decreases; and vice versa. As national income decreases, the rate of interest decreases; and vice versa. Equilibrium national income is an increasing function of the interest rate in the money market, and the equilibrium interest rate is an increasing function of national income.

Y^*_m and i^*_m are increasing functions of each other because:

- In equation 6-19, there is a plus sign before the ni term and the denominator, k, is positive.
- In equation 6-20 there is a plus sign before the kY term and the denominator, k, is positive.

(Y^*_m and i^*_m are also linear functions of each other because the functions we employed to develop them are linear functions.)

Graph of money equilibrium The data from Table 6-2 are plotted in Figure 6-2. The rate of interest is again plotted on the vertical axis and national income on the horizontal axis. The curve is called the *money-equilibrium curve* because it shows us what the equilibrium interest rate would be in the money market at each level of national income and what the level of national income would have to be at each rate of interest for there to be equilibrium in the money market.[5] The positive or upward slope of the money-equilibrium curve indicates the direct relationship between the rate of interest and national income in the money market.

Looking either at the table or at the money-equilibrium curve we can see that whenever the rate of interest changes by 0.01, national income changes by $20; and when Y^*_m changes by $20, i^*_m changes by 0.01. We can discover the relationship between a change in i^*_m and a change in Y^*_m by using equation 6-19. When i^*_m changes by Δi^*_m, Y^*_m will change by ΔY^*_m. We therefore write

$$Y^*_m + \Delta Y^*_m = \frac{M_0 - L_0 + n(i^*_m + \Delta i^*_m)}{k}$$

[5]Frequently it is called the *LM* (el em) curve because it shows us the different combinations of Y and i at which the quantity of money demanded L and the quantity of money supplied M are equal.

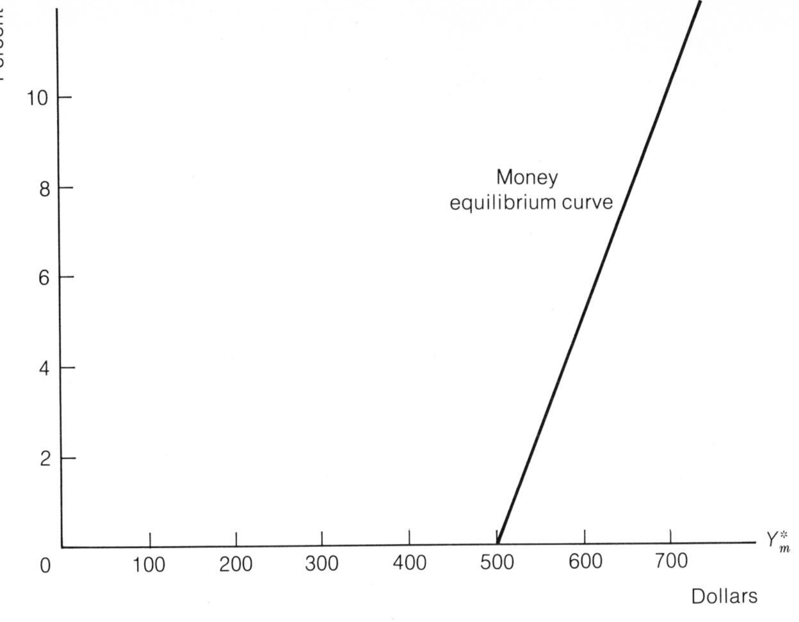
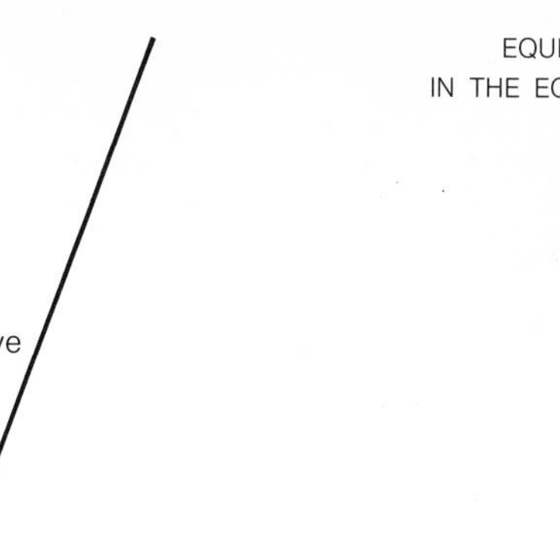

FIGURE 6-2

We then subtract equation 6-19 from this last equation to obtain

$$\Delta Y_m^* = \frac{n\,\Delta i_m^*}{k} \tag{6-21}$$

We also learn that

$$\frac{\Delta Y_m^*}{\Delta i_m^*} = \frac{n}{k} \tag{6-22}$$

Again we see that the expressions $(n\,\Delta i_m^*)/k$ and n/k are positive: the relation between Y_m^* and i_m^* is direct, and the money-equilibrium curve is upward-sloping.

In our example, n is equal to \$400 and k is equal to 0.2. If the interest rate changes by 0.01, Y_m^* will change by

$$\begin{aligned}\Delta Y_m^* &= \frac{\$400(0.01)}{0.2}\\ &= \frac{\$4}{0.2}\\ &= \$20\end{aligned}$$

$\Delta Y_m^*/\Delta i_m^*$ equals \$400/0.2, or \$2,000. For every change of 1.0 in the rate of interest, national income will change by \$2,000.

If $\Delta Y_m^*/\Delta i_m^*$ equals n/k, its inverse (or reciprocal) $\Delta i_m^*/\Delta Y_m^*$ equals k/n. In the numerical example, $\Delta i_m^*/\Delta Y_m^*$ is 0.2/\$400, or 0.005/\$1. This means that for every \$1 change in national income, the rate of interest in the money market must change by 0.0005.

We recognize that $\Delta i_m^*/\Delta Y_m^*$ is the slope of the money-equilibrium curve. Because $\Delta i_m^*/\Delta Y_m^*$ equals k/n, we see that the slope of the money-equilibrium curve equals the parameter k divided by the parameter n. The greater the value of k, the greater the slope; and the smaller the value of k, the smaller the slope of the money-equilibrium curve. And the greater the value of n, the smaller the slope; and the smaller the value of n, the greater the slope of the curve for money equilibrium.

Like the commodity market by itself, the money market by itself is an open system of equations. The number of variables exceeds by 1 the number of equations. In this open system we can find neither equilibrium Y nor equilibrium i. We did find, however, equilibrium Y as a function of i and equilibrium i as a function of Y.

Exercise 6-2

1 Complete (in symbols) the model for the money market.

$L \equiv$ __________ + __________

$L_t =$ __________

$L_s =$ __________ − __________

$M_0 =$ __________

__________ = __________

a This model has five equations and __________ variables in addition to three parameters: __________, __________, and __________

b This set of equations is a(n) (open, closed) __________ system.

2 Show that:

a Equilibrium Y in the money market equals

$$\frac{\bar{M}_0 - L_0 + ni}{k}$$

b Equilibrium i in the money market equals

$$\frac{kY + L_0 - \bar{M}_0}{n}$$

3 Suppose that

$L_t = 0.1Y$
$L_a = \$60 - \$600i$
$M_0 = \$86$

Then:

a $i_m^* =$ __________

b $Y_m^* =$ __________

c $\Delta i_m^* =$ __________

d $\Delta Y_m^* =$ __________

4 Using the equations in question 3:

a Complete the table below.

i_m^*, %	Y_m^*
10	\$_____
_____	800
8	_____
_____	680
6	_____
_____	560
4	_____
_____	440
2	_____

b Plot this table on the graph below.

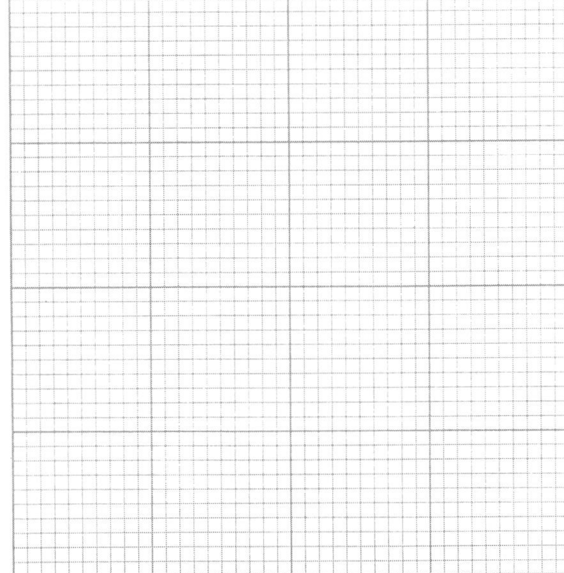

5 The slope of the money equilibrium curve on the graph above is equal to

____

6 Explain why the slope of the money equilibrium curve is positive.

Equilibrium in the two markets

In combining the two open systems, the commodity market and the money market, we have the following 12 equations.

$$C = C_0 + bY_d \tag{6-3}$$

$$I = I_0 - ji \quad (6\text{-}4)$$
$$G = \bar{G} \quad (6\text{-}5)$$
$$D \equiv C + I + G \quad (6\text{-}6)$$
$$Y_d \equiv Y - T \quad (6\text{-}7)$$
$$T = \bar{T} \quad (6\text{-}8)$$
$$Y = D \quad (6\text{-}1)$$
$$L \equiv L_t + L_a \quad (6\text{-}14)$$
$$L_t = kY \quad (6\text{-}15)$$
$$L_a = L_0 - ni \quad (6\text{-}16)$$
$$M_0 = \bar{M}_0 \quad (6\text{-}17)$$
$$L = M_0 \quad (6\text{-}2)$$

This set of twelve equations also has exactly 12 variables: C, Y_d, I, i, G, D, T, Y, L, L_t, L_a, and M_0. The set of equations, therefore, may have a solution; if it does, we can find values for all nine endogenous variables (C, Y_d, I, i, D, Y, L, L_t, and L_a).

The combined set of equations has a solution, while the sets for the commodity market and the money market did not have solutions. Why is this? When we combine the two sets of equations, we obtain 12 equations. When we add the 8 variables for the commodity market and the 6 variables for the money market, it would seem that we would obtain 14 variables. But 2 of the variables, Y and i, appear in both sets of equations, and we do not count them twice in the combined model. The arithmetic is as follows: we appear to have 14 variables, but 2 of them appear twice. So we subtract 2 to prevent the double counting of Y and i. The result is 12 different variables.

Equilibrium in the economy To find the values of all the variables and, in particular, to find the equilibrium values of Y and i, we employ the equilibrium equations we obtained earlier for the commodity and money markets. We found that

$$Y_c^* = \frac{C_0 - b\bar{T} + I_0 - ji + \bar{G}}{1 - b} \quad (6\text{-}10)$$

$$Y_m^* = \frac{\bar{M}_0 - L_0 + ni}{k} \quad (6\text{-}19)$$

Equation 6-10 tells us what Y must be at various interest rates if there is to be equilibrium in the commodity market, while equation 6-19 tells us what Y must be at various interest rates if there is to be equilibrium in the money market. For there to be equilibrium in both markets there must be the same equilibrium national income and equilibrium interest rate in both markets. In short, it is necessary that

$$Y_c^* = Y_m^*$$

and that

$$i_c^* = i_m^*$$

Said another way, the two equations 6-10 and 6-19 have two variables, Y^* and I^*. We can therefore solve these two equations to find both Y^* and i^*. We shall solve first for i^* and in the next section solve for Y^*.

Solving for i^*, Y_c^* must equal Y_m^*. Therefore, using equations 6-10 and 6-19, we write

$$\frac{C_0 - b\bar{T} + I_0 - ji + \bar{G}}{1 - b} = \frac{M_0 - L_0 + ni}{k}$$

Cross multiplying gives

$$k(C_0 - b\bar{T} + I_0 - ji + \bar{G}) = (1 - b)(\bar{M}_0 - L_0 + ni)$$

Segregating the terms containing i, we have

$$k(C_0 - b\bar{T} + I_0 + \bar{G}) - kji = (1 - b)(\bar{M}_0 - L_0) + (1 - b)ni$$

Now putting all terms containing i on the right and all other terms on the left,

$$k(C_0 - b\bar{T} + I_0 + \bar{G}) - (1 - b)(\bar{M}_0 - L_0) = (1 - b)ni + jki$$

isolating i,

$$k(C_0 - b\bar{T} + I_0 + \bar{G}) - (1 - b)(\bar{M}_0 - L_0) = i[n(1 - b) + jk]$$

and, finally, finding i,

$$i^* = \frac{k(C_0 - b\bar{T} + I_0 + \bar{G}) - (1 - b)(\bar{M}_0 - L_0)}{n(1 - b) + jk} \qquad (6\text{-}23)$$

This solution equation for the equilibrium rate of interest in the economy has only exogenous variables and parameters on its right side.

Equilibrium *Y* in the economy To solve for the equilibrium national income of the economy we shall use the equilibrium equations for i in the commodity and in the money markets of the economy.

$$i_c^* = \frac{C_0 - b\bar{T} + I_0 + \bar{G} - Y(1 - b)}{j} \qquad (6\text{-}11)$$

$$i_m^* = \frac{kY + L_0 - \bar{M}_0}{n} \qquad (6\text{-}20)$$

For there to be equilibrium in the entire economy it is necessary that

$$i_c^* = i_m^*$$

So that, substituting 6-11 for i_c^* and 6-20 for i_m^*, we have

$$\frac{C_0 - b\bar{T} + I_0 + \bar{G} - Y(1 - b)}{j} = \frac{kY + L_0 - \bar{M}_0}{n}$$

Cross multiplying gives

$$n[C_0 - b\bar{T} + I_0 + \bar{G} - Y(1 - b)] = j(kY + L_0 - \bar{M}_0)$$

and segregating the terms containing Y, we get

$$n(C_0 - b\bar{T} + I_0 + \bar{G}) - nY(1 - b) = jkY + j(L_0 - \bar{M}_0)$$

Putting all terms with Y in them on the right side and all other terms on the left side, we obtain

$$n(C_0 - b\bar{T} + I_0 + \bar{G}) - j(L_0 - \bar{M}_0) = nY(1 - b) + jkY$$

Isolating Y,

$$n(C_0 - b\bar{T} + I_0 + \bar{G}) - j(L_0 - \bar{M}_0) = Y[n(1 - b) + jk]$$

Finally, we find the solution equation for national income in the economy:

$$Y^* = \frac{n(C_0 - b\bar{T} + I_0 + \bar{G}) - j(L_0 - \bar{M}_0)}{n(1 - b) + jk} \tag{6-24}$$

Again the student should note that the right side of 6-24 contains only exogenous variables and parameters.

Equilibrium values of the other endogenous variables Once we have found Y^* and i^* for the economy as a whole, we can determine the equilibrium values of the other endogenous variables in the model.

1 Equation 6-7 defines Y_d.

2 Equation 6-3 enables us to find C.

3 Equation 6-4 determines I.

4 Equation 6-6 along with equation 6-5 gives us D. (D will also equal Y in equation 6-1.)

5 Equation 6-15 determines L_t.

6 Equation 6-16 enables us to find L_a.

7 Equation 6-14 gives us L. (L will also equal the M_0 given in equation 6-17 and $\dot{M}_0$ in equation 6-2.)

Numerical example Using the numerical examples we worked out above for both the commodity and money markets, we find that

$$i^* = 5\%$$
$$Y^* = \$600$$

To find i^* and Y^* we may employ the two tables we developed, the commodity-equilibrium and money-equilibrium curves, or the formulas for equilibrium i and Y.

Table 6-3 shows the equilibrium national income that accompanies each of

TABLE 6-3

i, %	Y_c^*	Y_m^*
10	\$500	\$700
9	520	680
8	540	660
7	560	640
6	580	620
5	600	600
4	620	580
3	640	560
2	660	540

nine different interest rates in the commodity market and the national incomes that result in equilibrium in the money market at the same nine interest rates. Observe that at 5 percent the equilibrium national income in the commodity market and the equilibrium national income in the money market are equal. Put another way, observe that at \$600, the equilibrium rates of interest in the commodity and money market are equal.

For finding i^* and Y^* we may also employ equations 6-23 and 6-24.

$$i^* = \frac{k(C_0 - b\overline{T} + I_0 + \overline{G}) - (1 - b)(\overline{M}_0 - L_0)}{n(1 - b) + jk} \tag{6-23}$$

$$\begin{aligned} i^* &= \frac{0.2[\$90 - (0.75)(\$80) + \$50 + \$95] - (1 - 0.75)(\$120 - \$20)}{\$400(1 - 0.75) + \$500(0.2)} \\ &= \frac{0.2(\$90 - \$60 + \$50 + \$95) - 0.25(\$100)}{\$400(0.25) + \$100} \\ &= \frac{0.2(\$175) - \$25}{\$100 + \$100} \\ &= \frac{\$35 - \$25}{\$200} \\ &= \frac{\$10}{\$200} \\ &= 0.05 \end{aligned}$$

$$Y^* = \frac{n(C_0 - b\overline{T} + I_0 + \overline{G}) - j(L_0 - \overline{M}_0)}{n(1 - b) + jk} \tag{6-24}$$

$$\begin{aligned} Y^* &= \frac{\$400[\$90 - (0.75)(\$80) + \$50 + \$95] - \$500(\$20 - \$120)}{\$400(1 - 0.75) + \$500(0.2)} \\ &= \frac{\$400(\$90 - \$60 + \$50 + \$95) - \$500(-\$100)}{(\$400)0.25 + \$100} \\ &= \frac{\$400(\$175) + 50{,}000 \text{ dollars}^2}{\$100 + \$100} \\ &= \frac{70{,}000 \text{ dollars}^2 + 50{,}000 \text{ dollars}^2}{\$200} \\ &= \frac{120{,}000 \text{ dollars}^2}{\$200} \\ &= \$600 \end{aligned}$$

The values of the other variables are

$$\begin{aligned} Y_d^* &= \$600 - \$80 + \$520 \\ C^* &= \$90 + 0.75(\$520) = \$90 + \$390 = \$480 \\ I^* &= \$50 - \$500(0.05) = \$50 - \$25 = \$25 \\ D^* &= \$480 + \$25 + \$95 = \$600 = Y^* \\ L_t^* &= 0.2(\$600) = \$120 \\ L_a^* &= \$20 - \$400(0.05) = \$20 - \$20 = \$0 \\ L^* &= \$120 + \$0 = \$120 = M_0 \end{aligned}$$

We may also find saving S^* in the economy. S is defined as $Y_d - C$. If Y_d^* is \$520 and C^* is \$480, then S^* is \$40. $S^* + T^*$ (= \$40 + \$80) = $I^* + G^*$ (= \$25 + \$95) = \$120.

Graphical analysis In Figure 6-3 we have plotted both the commodity-equilibrium and money-equilibrium curves that we plotted separately earlier. The reason we drew these curves earlier is now fairly obvious: the intersection of the commodity- and money-equilibrium curves determines the equilibrium rate of interest and the equilibrium national income. Note that the curves intersect at 5 percent and $600.

These curves also help us to understand exactly what equilibrium in the economy means. In the example 5 percent and $600 are the only set of values for *i* and *Y* that result in equilibrium in both the commodity and money markets.

- At 10 percent, *Y* would have to be $500 for there to be equilibrium in the commodity market, but at 10 percent, *Y* would have to be $700 for there to be money market equilibrium.
- At 2 percent, *Y* would have to be $660 in the commodity market and $540 in the money market.
- If *Y* were $560, *i* would have to be 7 percent for the commodity market to be in equilibrium; if *Y* were $560, *i* would have to be 3 percent to bring about equilibrium in the money market.
- If *Y* were $660, *I* would need to be 2 percent to have equilibrium in the commodity market; but with *Y* equal to $660, the equilibrium rate of interest in the money market is 8 percent.

The intersection of the commodity- and money-equilibrium curves and the equilibrium values of *Y* and *i* determined mathematically are the only values of *Y* and *i* that produce equilibrium in both markets. And for the economy to be in equilibrium, both markets must be in equilibrium.

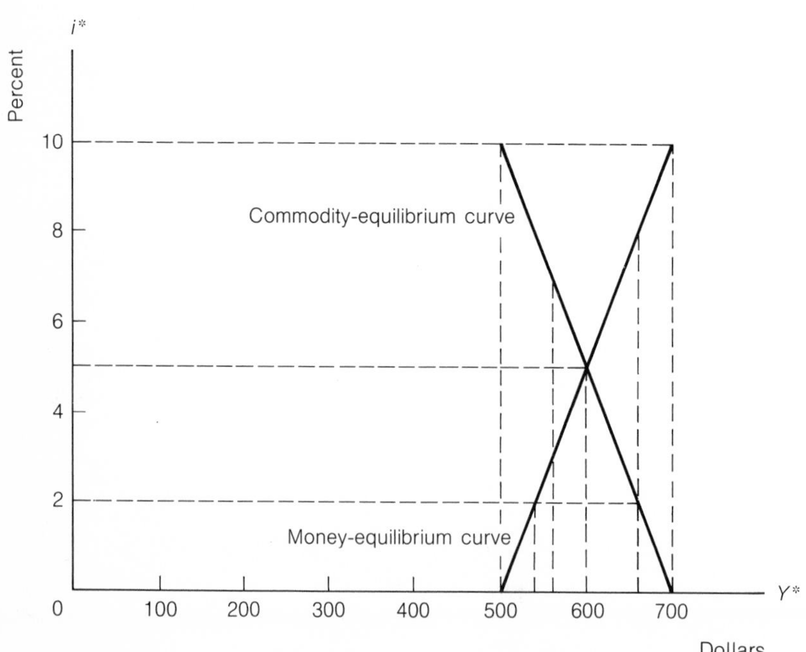

FIGURE 6-3

Exercise 6-3

1 For there to be equilibrium in the economy as a whole, it is necessary that $Y = D$ and $L = M$. This means (in symbols) that __________ = __________ and __________ = __________

2 Show that for the economy as a whole:

a $$i^* = \frac{k(C_0 - b\bar{T} + I_0 + \bar{G}) - (1 - b)(\bar{M}_0 - L_0)}{n(1 - b) + jk}$$

b $$Y^* = \frac{n(C_0 - b\bar{T} + I_0 + \bar{G}) - j(L_0 - \bar{M})}{n(1 - b) + jk}$$

3 For the economy

$C = \$80 + 0.8Y_d$
$T = \$75$
$I = \$40 - \$600i$
$G = \$100$
$L_t = 0.1Y$
$L_a = \$60 - \$600i$
$M_0 = \$86$

a What are the five remaining equations needed to complete this model?

$D \equiv$ __________ + __________ + __________

__________ = __________

$L \equiv$ __________ + __________

$Y_d =$ __________ − __________

__________ = __________

b Equilibrium

$i =$ __________%

$Y = \$$__________

c Plot on the graph below the commodity- and money-equilibrium curves.

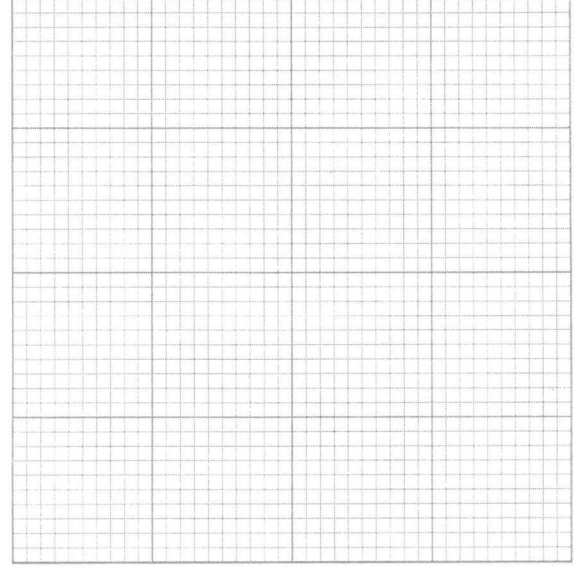

d These curves intersect at a(n):

(1) Interest rate of __________%.

(2) National income of $__________

4 Using the data in question 3, when the economy is in equilibrium:

a $Y_d^* = \$$__________

b $C^* = \$$__________

c $I^* = \$$__________

d $D^* = \$$__________

e $L_t^* = \$$__________

f $L_a^* = \$$__________

g $L^* = \$$__________

h $Y^* = \$$__________ $= D^* = \$$__________

i $L^* = \$$__________ $= M_0 = \$$__________

5

a At rates of interest greater than i^*, Y_c^* is __________ than Y_m^*.

b At rates of interest less than i^*, Y_c^* is __________ than Y_m^*.

c At national incomes greater than Y^*, i_c^* is __________ than i_m^*.

d At national incomes less than Y^*, i_c^* is __________ than i_m^*.

CHANGES IN THE EXOGENOUS VARIABLES

One purpose of working out formulas that tell us when the entire economy is in equilibrium is to be able to predict how changes in the exogenous variables in the model will affect the equilibrium national income, interest rate, and the other endogenous variables. In particular, we want to know what effect changes in government expenditures for goods and services, net taxes, and the money supply will have upon the economy. Knowing how changes in G, T, and M_0 affect Y^* and i^* makes it possible for the Federal government or the Federal Reserve to bring Y^* to a level consistent with full employment and stable prices by changing G, T, or M_0.

Changes in government expenditures for goods and services

To find the effects of changes in G (as well as the effects of changes in T and M) upon Y^* and i^*, we employ the two equilibrium equations, 6-23 and 6-24. Looking first at equation 6-23, when G changes by ΔG, i^* changes by Δi^*. We may therefore say

$$i^* + \Delta i^* = \frac{k[C_0 - b\overline{T} + I_0 + (\overline{G} + \Delta\overline{G})] - (1 - b)(M_0 - L_0)}{n(1 - b) + jk}$$

From this equation we subtract equation 6-23 to obtain

$$\Delta i^* = \frac{k\,\Delta\bar{G}}{n(1-b)+jk} \tag{6-25}$$

Using equation 6-24 enables us to find the effect of a change in G upon Y^*. For when G changes by ΔG, Y^* changes by ΔY^*.

$$Y^* + \Delta Y^* = \frac{n[C_0 - b\bar{T} + I_0 + (\bar{G} + \Delta\bar{G})] - j(L_0 - \bar{M})}{n(1-b)+jk}$$

Subtracting equation 6-24 from this equation, we have

$$\Delta Y^* = \frac{n\,\Delta\bar{G}}{n(1-b)+jk} \tag{6-26}$$

We should note that an increase in $\bar{G}$ increases both the equilibrium interest rate and the equilibrium national income. This can be seen to be true if we observe that in equation 6-25, n, j, k, and $1-b$ are all positive. The term $k/[n(1-b)+jk]$ is therefore positive. This means that an increase in $\bar{G}$ will also increase i^*; and a decrease in $\bar{G}$ will decrease i^*. Likewise in equation 6-26, n, j, k, and $1-b$ are positive; and therefore $n/[n(1-b)+jk]$ is positive. An increase in $\bar{G}$ will increase Y^*, and a decrease in $\bar{G}$ will decrease Y^*. It is also important to note that the size of the changes in i^* and Y^* depend upon the size of the change in $\bar{G}$ *and* upon the size of the four parameters n, b, j, and k.

Changes in net taxes

In a similar fashion we can find the effects of a change in net taxes upon equilibrium interest rate and the equilibrium national income. Letting $\bar{T}$ change by $\Delta\bar{T}$ in equation 6-23, i^* will change by Δi^*; and so

$$i^* + \Delta i^* = \frac{k[C_0 - b(\bar{T} + \Delta\bar{T}) + I_0 + \bar{G}] - (1-b)(\bar{M}_0 - L_0)}{n(1-b)+jk}$$

Now we subtract equation 6-23 from this last equation and find

$$\Delta i^* = \frac{-kb\,\Delta\bar{T}}{n(1-b)+jk} \tag{6-27}$$

In equation 6-24, Y^* will change by ΔY^*, so that

$$Y^* + \Delta Y^* = \frac{n[C_0 - b(\bar{T} + \Delta\bar{T}) + I_0 + G] - f(L_0 - \bar{M}_0)}{n(1-b)+jk}$$

Subtracting equation 6-24 gives

$$\Delta Y^* = \frac{-nb\,\Delta\bar{T}}{n(1-b)+jk} \tag{6-28}$$

The term $kb\,\Delta\bar{T}$ is preceeded by a minus sign: an increase in $\bar{T}$ will decrease i^*, and a decrease in $\bar{T}$ will increase i^*. The term nb is also preceeded by a minus sign: an increase in $\bar{T}$ will decrease Y^*, and a decrease in $\bar{T}$ will increase Y^*. The amounts that i^* and Y^* change as a result of a change in $\bar{T}$ again depend upon the magnitude of the tax change *and* the magnitude of the parameters n, b, j, and k.

Changes in the money supply

Changes in the money supply also bring about changes in the equilibrium interest rate and national income. Still using equations 6-23 and 6-24, when $\bar{M}_0$ changes by $\Delta\bar{M}_0$, i^* will change by Δi^*; and

$$i^* + \Delta i^* = \frac{k(C_0 - b\bar{T} + I_0 + \bar{G}) - (1 - b)[(\bar{M}_0 + \Delta\bar{M}_0) - L_0]}{n(1 - b) + jk}$$

Subtracting equation 6-23,

$$\Delta i^* = \frac{-(1 - b)\,\Delta\bar{M}_0}{n(1 - b) + jk} \tag{6-29}$$

When $\bar{M}_0$ changes by $\Delta\bar{M}_0$, Y^* changes by ΔY^*; and

$$Y^* + \Delta Y^* = \frac{n(C_0 - b\bar{T} + I_0 + \bar{G}) - j[L_0 - (\bar{M}_0 + \Delta\bar{M}_0)]}{n(1 - b) + jk}$$

Subtracting 6-24,

$$\Delta Y^* = \frac{j\,\Delta\bar{M}_0}{n(1 - b) + jk} \tag{6-30}$$

In equation 6-29 we see that an increase in $\bar{M}_0$ will decrease i^* because the term $(1 - b)\,\Delta\bar{M}_0$ is preceeded by a minus sign and the denominator is positive; and a decrease in $\bar{M}_0$ will increase i^*. But the term $j\,\Delta\bar{M}_0$ in equation 6-30 is positive, and an increase in $\bar{M}_0$ will increase Y^* while a decrease in $\bar{M}_0$ will decrease Y^*. The effect of the change in $\bar{M}_0$ depends upon the amount $\bar{M}_0$ changes and the values of the four parameters.

Numerical examples

In the numerical example we used earlier

$k = 0.2$
$n = \$400$
$b = 0.75$
$j = \$500$

With the values of these four parameters given, we can work out the effects of changes in $\bar{G}$, $\bar{T}$, and $\bar{M}_0$ upon i^* and Y^*.

Changes in *G* Suppose $\bar{G}$ increases by \$25. The change in the interest rate is

$$\Delta i^* = \frac{k\,\Delta\bar{G}}{n(1 - b) + jk} \tag{6-25}$$

$$\Delta i^* = \frac{0.2(\$25)}{\$400(1 - 0.75) + \$500(0.2)}$$

$$= \frac{\$5}{\$400(0.25) + \$100}$$

$$= \frac{\$5}{\$100 + \$100}$$

$$= 0.025 = 2\tfrac{1}{2}\%$$

The change in Y^* is

$$\Delta Y^* = \frac{n\,\Delta\bar{G}}{n(1-b)+jk} \tag{6-26}$$

$$\Delta Y^* = \frac{\$400(\$25)}{\$400(1-0.75)+\$500(0.2)}$$

$$= \frac{10{,}000 \text{ dollars}^2}{\$400(0.25)+\$100}$$

$$= \frac{10{,}000 \text{ dollars}^2}{\$100+\$100}$$

$$= \frac{10{,}000 \text{ dollars}^2}{\$200}$$

$$= \$50$$

The \$25 increase in G increased i^* by 2.5 percent and Y^* by \$50.

Changes in T Suppose $\bar{T}$ were to increase by \$20. The change in i^* is

$$\Delta i^* = \frac{-kb\,\Delta\bar{T}}{n(1-b)+jk} \tag{6-27}$$

Our denominator (to save steps) is again equal to \$200, and so

$$\Delta i^* = \frac{-0.2(0.75)(\$20)}{\$200}$$

$$= \frac{-3}{200}$$

$$= -0.015 = -1.5\%$$

The change in Y^* is

$$\Delta Y^* = \frac{-nb\,\Delta\bar{T}}{n(1-b)+jk} \tag{6-28}$$

$$\Delta Y^* = \frac{-\$400(0.75)(\$20)}{\$200}$$

$$= \frac{-6{,}000 \text{ dollars}^2}{\$200}$$

$$= -\$30$$

The \$20 increase in taxes decreased the rate of interest by 1.5 percent and national income by \$30.

Changes in M_0 If the supply of money increased by \$10, the effect on i^* would be

$$\Delta i^* = \frac{-(1-b)\,\Delta\bar{M}_0}{n(1-b)+jk} \tag{6-29}$$

The denominator is again \$200.

$$\Delta i^* = \frac{-(1-0.75)(\$10)}{\$200}$$

$$= \frac{-0.25(\$10)}{\$200}$$

$$= \frac{-\$2.5}{\$200}$$

$$= 0.0125 = 1\tfrac{1}{4}\%$$

And

$$\Delta Y^* = \frac{j\,\Delta\bar{M}_0}{n(1-b)+jk}$$

$$\Delta Y^* = \frac{\$500(\$10)}{\$200}$$

$$= \frac{5{,}000 \text{ dollars}^2}{\$200}$$

$$= \$25$$

The \$10 increase in the money supply decreased the equilibrium rate of interest by $1\frac{1}{4}$ percent and increased the equilibrium national income by \$25.

Changes in the other endogenous variables

Borrowing from Chapters 2 to 4 the formulas developed there, we can find the effects of changes in $\bar{G}$, $\bar{T}$, and $\bar{M}_0$ upon Y_d, C, I, L_t, and L_a. Each of these five endogenous variables depends either upon i or upon Y. When $\bar{G}$, $\bar{T}$, or $\bar{M}_0$ change, as we have seen, so do i^* and Y^*. Finding first the effects on Y^* and i^* of changes in an exogenous variable, we can then find the effects of the changes in i^* and Y^* upon Y_d^*, C^*, I^*, L_t^*, *and* L_a^*.

The formulas From earlier chapters we know that

$$\Delta C = b\,\Delta Y_d \qquad (3\text{-}15)$$

$$\Delta I = -j\,\Delta i \qquad (2\text{-}51)$$

$$\Delta L_t = k\,\Delta Y$$

$$\Delta L_a = -n\,\Delta i \qquad (5\text{-}13)$$

We also know that we define disposable income as

$$Y_d \equiv Y - T \qquad (6\text{-}8)$$

The change in disposable income is equal to the change in national income minus the change (if any) in net taxes, or

$$\Delta Y_d \equiv \Delta Y - \Delta T \qquad (6\text{-}31)$$

With the first four formulas in this section and equation 6-31 we can find the changes in Y_d^*, C^*, I^*, L_t^*, and L_a^* that result from changes in G, T, or M_0 *after* we have found the effects upon i^* and Y^*.

Numerical example In our example of the effect of a \$25 increase in $\bar{G}$, we found that:

- i^* would increase by 0.025.
- Y^* would increase by \$50.

Using equation 6-31, the change in disposable income is

$$\Delta Y_d^* = \$50 - \$0 = \$50$$

The changes in C^* and I^*, using equations 3-15 and 2-51, are

$$\Delta C^* = 0.75(\$50) = \$37.5$$
$$\Delta I^* = -\$500(0.025) = -\$12.5$$

The changes in L_t^* and L_a^* are

$$\Delta L_t^* = 0.2(\$50) = \$10$$
$$\Delta L_a^* = -\$400(0.025) = -\$10$$

It is interesting to note that because the supply of money M_0 has not changed, the total quantity of money demanded ($L \equiv L_t + L_a$) has not changed. But the transaction demand has increased as a result of the higher equilibrium national income and been offset by an equal decrease in the asset demand as a result of the higher equilibrium interest rate.

We may also observe that the change in Y^* is equal to the change in consumption plus the change in investment plus the change in government expenditures for goods and services, or

$$\Delta Y^* = \Delta C + \Delta I + \Delta G$$
$$\$50 = \$37.5 + (-\$12.5) + \$25$$
$$\$50 = \$50$$

Changes in parameters

We have not analyzed the effects on Y^* and i^* of changes in the parameters in our equations: changes in C_0, I_0, b, j, k, L_0, and n. To the interested student we leave the task of finding the relations between a change in each of these parameters and the resulting changes in the equilibrium national income and interest rate. These changes, despite the fact that we do not develop formulas for them, are as important in explaining changes in Y^* and i^* (and the other endogenous variables) as are changes in government expenditures, net taxes, and the supply of money.

Monetary and fiscal policy

Our knowledge of the relations between changes in G, T, M_0 and the resulting changes in Y^* can be used to determine what monetary and fiscal policies the economy should follow. The Federal Reserve Banks are responsible for monetary policy, and monetary policy involves control of the money supply to bring national income to a level consistent with both full employment of the labor force and stable prices. The Federal government is responsible for fiscal policy, and fiscal policy involves control of government expenditures and taxes to bring national income to the same level.

Monetary policy Suppose Y^* is greater or less than Y_f, the level of national income at which there are both full employment and stable prices. By decreasing or increasing M_0 the Federal Reserve can contract or expand Y^* to make it equal to Y_f. The amount the Federal Reserve should change M_0 to change Y^* by the desired amount can be determined from equation 6-30.

$$\Delta Y^* = \frac{j\,\Delta \bar{M}_0}{n(1-b) + jk} \qquad (6\text{-}30)$$

The required change in M_0 can be found by solving this equation for ΔM_0. Cross multiplying,

$$j\,\Delta M_0 = \Delta Y^*\,[n(1-b)+jk]$$

$$\Delta M_0 = \frac{\Delta Y^*\,[n(1-b)+jk]}{j} \tag{6-32}$$

If the Federal Reserve wants to increase Y^* by \$100 and

$k = 0.2$
$n = \$400$
$b = 0.75$
$j = \$500$

the change in the money supply necessary to bring about this result is

$$\Delta M_0 = \frac{\$100[\$400(1-0.75)+\$500(0.2)]}{\$500}$$
$$= \frac{\$100[\$400(0.25)+\$100]}{\$500}$$
$$= \frac{\$100(\$100+\$100)}{\$500}$$
$$= \frac{20{,}000 \text{ dollars}^2}{\$500}$$
$$= \$40$$

Fiscal policy By changing either G or T the Federal government can also contract or expand Y^* to make it equal to Y_f. The amount it should alter G to change Y^* by the desired amount is found in equation 6-26.

$$\Delta Y^* = \frac{n\,\Delta G}{n(1-b)+jk} \tag{6-26}$$

Solving for ΔG by cross multiplication,

$$n\,\Delta G = \Delta Y^*\,[n(1-b)+jk]$$

$$\Delta G = \frac{\Delta Y^*\,[n(1-b)+jk]}{n} \tag{6-33}$$

If the Federal government wishes to increase Y^* by \$100 (given the values of the parameters we used in the previous example), the change in G should be

$$\Delta G = \frac{\$100[\$400(1-0.75)+\$500(0.2)]}{\$100}$$
$$= \frac{\$100[\$400(0.25)+\$100]}{\$400}$$
$$= \frac{\$100(\$100+\$100)}{\$400}$$
$$= \frac{20{,}000 \text{ dollars}^2}{\$400}$$
$$= \$50$$

The change in T necessary to change Y^* and have it equal to Y_f is found in equation 6-28.

$$\Delta Y^* = \frac{-nb\,\Delta T}{n(1-b)+jk} \tag{6-28}$$

Solving for ΔT,

$$-nb\,\Delta T = \Delta Y^*\,[n(1-b)+jk]$$

$$\Delta T = \frac{-\Delta Y^*\,[n(1-b)+jk]}{nb} \tag{6-34}$$

Again, if the Federal government desired to increase Y^* by \$100 by changing T, the change in T should be

$$\begin{aligned}\Delta T &= \frac{-\$100[\$400(1-0.75)+\$500(0.2)]}{\$400(\$0.75)}\\ &= \frac{-\$100[\$400(0.25)+\$100]}{\$300}\\ &= \frac{-\$100(\$100+\$100)}{\$300}\\ &= \frac{-\$20{,}000\text{ dollars}^2}{\$300}\\ &= -\$66\tfrac{2}{3}\end{aligned}$$

It should decrease taxes by $\$66\frac{2}{3}$ to increase Y^* by \$100.

Exercise 6-4

1 Show that:

a $\Delta i^* =$

(1) $\dfrac{k\,\Delta G}{n(1-b)+jk}$

(2) $\dfrac{-bk\,\Delta T}{n(1-b)+jk}$

(3) $\dfrac{-(1-b)\,\Delta M_0}{n(1-b)+jk}$

b $\Delta Y^* =$

(1) $\dfrac{n\,\Delta G}{n(1-b)+jk}$

(2) $\dfrac{-nb\,\Delta T}{n(1-b)+jk}$

(3) $\dfrac{j\,\Delta M_0}{n(1-b)+jk}$

2 Suppose that

$k = 0.1$
$n = \$600$
$b = 0.8$
$j = \$600$

a Show the effects of a \$30 decrease in G on:

(1) i^*: ______%

(2) Y^*: \$______

(3) Y_d^*: \$______

(4) C^*: \$______

(5) I^*: \$______

(6) L_t^*: \$______

(7) L_a^*: \$______

b Show the effects of a \$40 decrease in T on:

(1) i^*: ______%

(2) Y^*: \$______

(3) Y_d^*: \$______

(4) C^*: \$______

(5) I^*: \$______

(6) L_t^*: \$______

(7) L_a^*: \$______

c Show the effects of a \$20 decrease in M on:

(1) i^*: ______%

(2) Y^*: \$______

(3) Y_d^*: \$______

(4) C^*: \$______

(5) I^*: \$______

(6) L_t^*: \$______

(7) L_a^*: \$______

3 Using the parameters in question 2 above, show the effects of a \$40 increase in either C_0 or I_0 upon:

a i^*: ______%

b Y^*: \$______

4 Still using the parameters in question 2 above, show the effects of a \$10 decrease in L_0 upon:

a i^*: \$______

b Y^*: \$______

5 Prove that:

a $$\Delta M = \frac{\Delta Y^*[n(1-b)+jk]}{j}$$

b $$\Delta G = \frac{\Delta Y^*[n(1-b)+jk]}{n}$$

c $$\Delta T = \frac{-\Delta Y^*[n(1-b)+jk]}{nb}$$

6 With $k = 0.1$, $n = \$600$, $b = 0.8$, and $j = \$600$, by how much must each of the following be changed to decrease the equilibrium national income by $80?

a M_0: $________

b G: $________

c T: $________

ECONOMIC GROWTH

Economic growth may mean either an increase in national income or an increase in per capita income as time passes. In this chapter we are interested only in increases in the total income of the economy that accompany the passage of time.[1]

In examining increases in national income, we are concerned with the answers to two questions: What determines how fast an economy is capable of growing? What must happen in the economy if it is to grow as rapidly as it is capable of growing?

As has been our practice in previous chapters, we explain our assumptions and definitions in the first section of the chapter. In the second section we examine an economy without government to discover how fast it can grow and what must happen if it is actually to grow that fast. We examine an economy with government in the third section to find out what determines how rapidly this economy is capable of growing and what conditions must prevail if it is to achieve all the growth of which it is capable.

DEFINITIONS AND ASSUMPTIONS

The definitions we employ and the assumptions we make throughout this chapter are basically the same as those used in earlier chapters, but a few differences require explanation.

[1] Economic growth may also refer to an increase in the total capacity (or ability) of the economy to produce goods and services. We shall not define growth as an increase in *potential* output but as an increase in the *actual* output of the economy.

Productive capacity and resources

The *maximum* output an economy is able to produce depends upon the quantities of the various resources available to it and the technology it employs to convert resources into products. Mathematically we may write that productive capacity P is a function of natural resources R, the size of the labor force N, the stock of capital K, and technology T.

$$P = f(R,N,K,T)$$

In this chapter we wish to focus our attention on the relation between changes ΔK in the capital stock of the economy and changes ΔP in its productive capacity. To concentrate on this relationship we assume that R, N, and T are constant, i.e., that while they are capable of changing, they do not change. So we are assuming that

$$P = f(K) \tag{7-1}$$

Given the quantity of natural resources and labor the economy has available and the technology it employs, its productive capacity depends on its capital stock.[2]

Investment and a change in the capital stock Since investment, as we learned in earlier chapters, is spending for additions to the economy's stock of capital goods, whenever we use the term investment I, we mean the same thing as an increase ΔK in the capital stock of the economy. These two terms may be used interchangeably, and we write the definition

$$I \equiv \Delta K \tag{7-2}$$

The capital-output ratio With natural resources, the labor force, and technology constant, the productive capacity of the economy, as we noted in equation 7-1, is a function of the stock of capital. We shall assume that this function is increasing and linear and that

$$P = \frac{1}{r}K \tag{7-3}$$

The parameter r is the capital-output ratio. For if $P = (1/r)K$, then dividing through by K,

$$\frac{P}{K} = \frac{1}{r}$$

and inverting both sides of the equation,

$$\frac{K}{P} = r \tag{7-4}$$

Equation 7-4 says that r is the ratio of the economy's capital stock to its productive capacity, just as equation 7-3 tells us that the maximum output an economy can produce is equal to $1/r$ times its stock of capital.

[2] Instead of assuming N constant, we might instead assume that the production of goods and services requires that N and K be employed in *fixed* proportions. This means that N/K is constant and that as K increases, N is assumed to increase at the same rate and to maintain the fixed ratio of N to K.

If, for example, an economy has a \$3,000 capital stock and its productive capacity is \$1,000, its capital-output ratio will be

$$r = \frac{\$3{,}000}{\$1{,}000}$$
$$= 3$$

Put another way, if r is 3 and its capital stock is \$3,000, then its productive capacity is

$$P = \tfrac{1}{3}(\$3{,}000)$$
$$= \$1{,}000$$

Our assumption about r is that it is constant and that it is greater than 1

$$r = \bar{r} \qquad (7\text{-}5)$$
$$r > 1$$

To the question: What determines the size of the parameter r? The answer is the quantities of the other two resources available to the economy (the quantities of natural resources and labor) and the technology the economy uses to produce products from resources. With the quantities of the other resources and technology given, the value of r is also given.

If K changes by ΔK, P will change by ΔP. Using equation 7-3, we can write

$$P + \Delta P = \frac{1}{r}(K + \Delta K)$$
$$= \frac{1}{r}K + \frac{1}{r}\Delta K$$

Subtracting equation 7-3 from the equation above, we find

$$\Delta P = \frac{1}{r}\,\Delta K \qquad (7\text{-}6)$$

Dividing through by ΔK,

$$\frac{\Delta P}{\Delta K} = \frac{1}{r}$$

and inverting the two sides of the equation gives

$$\frac{\Delta K}{\Delta P} = r \qquad (7\text{-}7)$$

The term $\Delta K/\Delta P$ is the *marginal capital-output ratio,* i.e., the ratio of the change in the capital stock to the change in the economy's productive capacity that accompanies the change in the capital stock. Equation 7-7 tells us that the marginal capital-output ratio is equal to the parameter r. If the capital stock increased by \$150 and as a result productive capacity increased by \$50, we know that

$$r = \frac{\$150}{\$50}$$
$$= 3$$

Or, if r is 3 and the capital stock increased by \$150, we know from equation

7-6 that the change in productive capacity would be

$$\Delta P = \tfrac{1}{3}(\$150)$$
$$= \$50$$

Instead of using equations 7-6 and 7-7, in which the term ΔK appears, we shall substitute for ΔK the other term which means exactly the same thing. For equation 7-6 we write

$$\Delta P = \frac{1}{r} I \qquad (7\text{-}8)$$

And for equation 7-7 we substitute

$$\frac{I}{\Delta P} = r \qquad (7\text{-}9)$$

Rates of growth

A rate of growth is expressed as a percentage or as a pure number. We shall define the rate of growth of any variable as the change in the value of the variable from one period of time to the next divided by the value of the variable in the first time period. Thus the rate of growth of the variable X is equal to $\Delta X/X$, where ΔX is the change in X between the earlier and later time period; and X is X in the earlier period. For example, if X in the first time period were \$100 and in the second period were \$120, the change in X would be +\$20. The rate of growth of X would therefore be +\$20/\$100, or 0.2, which is 20 percent.

Of particular concern to us are three different rates of growth. We are concerned with the rate of growth of national income or national output Y. The growth rate of Y is equal to $\Delta Y/Y$. The rate of growth of the productive capacity of the economy is equal to $\Delta P/P$. And the rate of growth of investment is $\Delta I/I$.

The price level

We assume, unless otherwise specified, that the prices of all goods and services are stable and that the price level is therefore stable or constant. The consequence of this assumption is that all changes in the values of the variables in our analysis are *real* changes and not the result of changes in the price of that variable.

The propensities to consume and save

For simplicity in this chapter we shall assume that the consumption equation is

$$C = bY_d \qquad (7\text{-}10)$$

We should note that unlike our earlier consumption equations, this one does not include the term C_0. This is another way of saying we assume that when disposable income is zero, consumption is also zero. As in earlier chapters, it is assumed that b is greater than zero and less than one. The parameter b we recognize as the marginal propensity to consume, i.e., the ratio of the change in C (when there is a change in Y_d) to the change in Y_d.

The average propensity to consume is still defined as the ratio of consumption (at any level of disposable income) to the level of disposable income. If we divide both sides of equation 7-10 by Y_d, we have

$$\frac{C}{Y_d} = b$$

The left side of this equation we recognize as the average propensity to consume. It tells us that the average propensity to consume is also equal to the parameter b. The consequence of assuming a consumption equation such as equation 7-10 in which autonomous consumption is zero is that the MPC and the APC are both equal to b. In short, we are assuming that the MPC and the APC are equal to each other.

We continue to define saving as equal to disposable income minus consumption.

$$S \equiv Y_d - C$$

For C in the equation above we substitute equation 7-10

$$S = Y_d - bY_d$$

and find

$$S = (1 - b)Y_d \tag{7-11}$$

Unlike previous saving equations, when Y_d is zero, saving is also zero. The term $1 - b$ we recognize as the marginal propensity to save, or the ratio of the change in saving (when there is a change in disposable income) to the change in disposable income. Since we have assumed that b is greater than zero and less than one, $1 - b$ must be less than one and greater than zero.

If we divide both sides of equation 7-11 by Y_d, we have

$$\frac{S}{Y_d} = 1 - b$$

The left side of this equation is the average propensity to save, and the equation says that the APS is equal to $1 - b$. Since the term $1 - b$ is the MPS, this equation says that the APS is equal to the MPS.

Our assumptions, then, about consumption and saving are that:

- The MPC and the APC are equal to each other and equal to b.
- The MPS and the APS are also equal to each other and equal to $1 - b$.

Equilibrium in the economy

In this chapter we deal with models in which government is and is not involved. In both models the equilibrium national income Y^* is the national income at which the aggregate quantity D of goods and services demanded is equal to the national income, or

$$Y^* = D$$

The model without government Aggregate demand in the model which does not involve government is

$$D \equiv C + I$$

At all levels of national income the economy uses the national income for either consumption or saving.

$$Y \equiv C + S$$

When national income is at its equilibrium value, therefore,

$$Y^* = C + I$$
$$C + S = C + I$$
$$S = I$$

From our work in Chapter 2 we recall the formula for the equilibrium national income:

$$Y^* = \frac{C_0 + I}{1 - b}$$

In a model such as ours, in which autonomous consumption C_0 is zero, the formula for the equilibrium national income is

$$Y^* = \frac{I}{1 - b} \qquad (7\text{-}12)$$

When I changes by ΔI, Y^* will change by ΔY^*.

$$Y^* + \Delta Y^* = \frac{I + \Delta I}{1 - b}$$

Subtracting equation 7-12, we have

$$\Delta Y^* = \frac{\Delta I}{1 - b} \qquad (7\text{-}13)$$

The model with government Aggregate demand in the model which does involve government is

$$D \equiv C + I + G$$

At all levels of national income the economy uses the national income for consumption, saving, and net taxes.

$$Y \equiv C + S + T$$

When national income is at its equilibrium value, therefore,

$$Y^* = C + I + G$$
$$C + S + T = C + I + G$$
$$S + T = I + G$$

From our work in Chapter 3, the formula for the equilibrium national income is

$$Y^* = \frac{C_0 - bT_0 + I + G}{1 - b + bt}$$

in which T_0 is autonomous taxation and t is the marginal tax rate. In the model involving government not only do we assume that autonomous consumption is zero, but, for simplicity, we also assume that autonomous taxation is zero.

The formula for the equilibrium national income is therefore

$$Y^* = \frac{I + G}{1 - b + bt} \qquad (7\text{-}14)$$

When $I + G$ change by $\Delta(I + G)$, Y^* will change by ΔY^*. Using equation 7-14,

$$Y^* + \Delta Y^* = \frac{I + G + \Delta(I + G)}{1 - b + bt}$$

Subtracting equation 7-14 gives

$$\Delta Y^* = \frac{\Delta(I + G)}{1 - b + bt} \qquad (7\text{-}15)$$

Full employment and productive capacity

If the economy is at full employment, it means that the economy's productive capacity P and its equilibrium national income Y^* are equal.

$$P = Y^* \qquad (7\text{-}16)$$

And if the economy is to remain at full employment as its productive capacity grows, it means that any increase in its productive capacity ΔP is matched by an equal increase in its equilibrium national income ΔY^*, or

$$\Delta P = \Delta Y^* \qquad (7\text{-}17)$$

Our assumption throughout this chapter is that the economy is always at full employment: that P always is equal to Y^* and any ΔP is equaled by ΔY^*. Our problem is to find this *rate* at which P *can* grow if full employment is maintained and the *rate* at which it *must* grow to maintain full employment.

Exercise 7-1

1 Define economic growth (in words) as the term is used in this chapter.

____

2 The productive capacity of the economy is a function of the following four variables:

a ____________________________

b ____________________________

c ____________________________

d ____________________________

In this chapter we assume three of these four variables are ____________

and that productive capacity is a function of ____________

3 A term that can be used in place of a change in the capital stock ΔK is

____________ or, in symbols, ____________

4 The parameter r is the ________________________________

a $r =$ ____________ / ____________

b $P =$ ____________ K

c r is assumed to be ____________ and ____________ than 1.

d r is also equal to Δ____________ / Δ____________

e $\Delta P =$ __________ ΔK or __________ I

5 Suppose:

a The capital-output ratio is 4:

(1) If P is \$1,000, K is \$ __________

(2) If K is \$3,000, P is \$ __________

(3) If ΔP is \$100, ΔK (or I) is \$ __________

(4) If ΔK (or I) is \$600, ΔP is \$ __________

b K is \$2,000 and P is \$400, r is __________

c ΔP is \$100 and ΔK is \$400, r is __________

6 Define (in symbols):

a The rate of growth of Y: __________

b The rate of growth of P: __________

c The rate of growth of I: __________

7 Suppose:

a Y is \$600, and ΔY is \$50. The rate of growth of Y is __________ %.

b P is \$1,000, and ΔP is \$200. The rate of growth of P is __________ %.

c I is \$200, and ΔI is \$10. The rate of growth of I is __________ %.

d The rate of growth of Y is 5%, and Y is \$600. ΔY is \$ __________

e The rate of growth of P is 10%, and P is \$1,000. ΔP is \$ __________

f The rate of growth of I is 4%, and I is \$200. ΔI is \$ __________

8 We assume in this chapter that the consumption and saving equations are

$C =$ __________ Y_d

$S =$ __________ Y_d

The consequences of these assumptions are that:

a Autonomous consumption is equal to __________

b When disposable income is zero, saving is equal to __________

c The MPC is equal to __________

d The MPS is equal to __________

e The APC is equal to __________

f The APS is equal to __________

g The MPC and the APC are __________

h The MPS and the APS are __________

9 For there to be equilibrium in the economy:

a In which there is no government:

(1) $Y^* =$ __________ + __________

(2) __________ + __________ = __________ + __________

(3) __________ = __________

b In which there is government:

(1) $Y^* =$ __________ + __________ + __________

(2) __________ + __________ + __________ = __________ + __________ + __________

(3) __________ + __________ = __________ + __________

10 Given the assumptions employed in this chapter:

a In an economy in which there is no government
$\Delta Y^* =$ __________

b In an economy in which there is government
$\Delta Y^* =$ __________

11 If there is to be full employment in the economy, __________ must equal __________. To maintain full employment as productive capacity grows it is necessary that __________ equal __________

THE MODEL WITHOUT GOVERNMENT

In this model we assume there is no government to spend for goods and services and to levy net taxes. The two questions for which we wish to find answers in this section (as well as in the next section, where we examine a model in which government does spend and tax) are:

- What determines how fast the economy is able to grow?
- What must happen to investment if the economy is in fact to grow as rapidly as it is able?

Equations, variables, and parameters

Our model consists of five equations and six variables. There are, in addition, two parameters.[3] Let us look first at the five equations:

$$P = Y^* \tag{7-16}$$
$$\Delta P = \Delta Y^* \tag{7-17}$$
$$\Delta Y^* = \frac{\Delta I}{1 - b} \tag{7-13}$$
$$Y^* = \frac{I}{1 - b} \tag{7-12}$$
$$\Delta P = \frac{1}{r} I \tag{7-8}$$

The first two equations tell us that we want an economy in which there is full employment at all times, that the equilibrium national income equals the productive capacity of the economy, and that any change in productive capacity is matched by an equal change in the equilibrium national income. Equation 7-13 says that the change in equilibrium income equals the change in investment

[3]Unlike some of our earlier models, this one does not employ a functional equation relating investment in the economy to other variables of the model. Investment is an endogenous variable, the value of which is unknown.

divided by 1 minus the MPC, that is, the change in investment times the multiplier. The equilibrium income, we find in equation 7-12, equals the level of investment divided by 1 minus the MPC. And equation 7-8 indicates that the change in productive capacity is equal to 1 divided by the capital-output rate times the level of investment.

In this model there are six variables, P, Y^*, ΔP, ΔY^*, I, and ΔI. In addition, there are two parameters, b, the marginal propensity to consume, and r, the capital-output ratio.

Because the number of variables exceeds the number of equations by 1 it seems that we cannot find the values for the six variables that will ensure full employment. This is true. But we do not want to find the values of these six variables. What we want to find are the rates of growth of national income ($\Delta Y^*/Y^*$) and investment ($\Delta I/I$) that ensure full employment and the rate at which the productive capacity of the economy is capable of growing ($\Delta P/P$). To find the values of each of the six variables that will ensure full employment in the economy all we need do is add a sixth equation that tells us either what P, Y, or I are or what the changes in P, Y, and I are.

Answers to the two questions

The two questions we wish to answer are: (1) At what rate can the productive capacity of the economy grow if full employment is maintained: and (2) What will ensure that full employment is maintained and the maximum rate of growth of national income is achieved?

At what rate can productive capacity grow? If full employment is maintained,

$$P = Y^* \tag{7-16}$$

and

$$\Delta P = \Delta Y^* \tag{7-17}$$

If we now divide the left side of equation 7-17 by the left side of equation 7-16 and the right side of equation 7-17 by the right side of equation 7-16, we find that

$$\frac{\Delta P}{P} = \frac{\Delta Y^*}{Y^*} \tag{7-18}$$

Equation 7-18 tells us that if the rate of growth of national income is equal to the rate of growth of productive capacity, the economy will be able to maintain full employment. But what is the rate of growth of productive capacity when full employment is maintained?

The change in the productive capacity of the economy, from equation 7-8, is I times $1/r$. At full employment, productive capacity and equilibrium national income are equal; and the equilibrium national income, from equation 7-12, is $I/(1 - b)$. So we can put down that

$$\frac{\Delta P}{P} = \frac{I(1/r)}{I/(1 - b)}$$

When we solve for $\Delta P/P$, we find

$$\frac{\Delta P}{P} = I\frac{1}{r}\,\frac{1-b}{I}$$

$$= \frac{1-b}{r} \tag{7-19}$$

The rate at which productive capacity is able to grow if there is always full employment in the economy equals $1 - b$ divided by the parameter r. The meaning of this is that productive capacity can grow at a rate which is equal to the *average* propensity to save divided by the capital-output ratio. For example, if b were 0.8 and r were 4, $1 - b$ would be 0.2; and 0.2 divided by 4 is 0.05. An economy with these parameters could grow at a rate of 5 percent. And if productive capacity grew at this rate, from equation 7-18, the equilibrium national income could also grow at this rate.

At what rate must investment grow to maintain full employment? To find the rate at which investment must grow we start with equation 7-17.

$$\Delta P = \Delta Y^* \tag{7-17}$$

For ΔP we substitute $(1/r)I$ (equation 7-8), and for ΔY^* we substitute $\Delta I/(1 - b)$ (equation 7-13). We then have

$$\frac{1}{r}I = \frac{\Delta I}{1-b}$$

Dividing through by I and multiplying through by $1 - b$, we have

$$\frac{\Delta I}{I} = \frac{1-b}{r} \tag{7-20}$$

To maintain full employment, investment must grow at a rate equal to the average propensity to save $(1 - b)$ divided by the capital-output ratio.

If an economy had a capital-output ratio of 4 and an average propensity to save of 0.2, investment would have to grow at a rate equal to 0.2 divided by 4, or by 5 percent, to maintain full employment in the economy.

Our conclusions in this section are:

- To maintain full employment national income must grow at the same rate as productive capacity.
- If full employment is maintained, productive capacity can grow at a rate equal to the average propensity to save divided by the capital-output ratio.
- Investment must grow at a rate equal to the average propensity to save divided by the capital-output ratio if productive capacity and national income are to grow as rapidly as they are able.

Numerical example

Suppose the average (and marginal) propensity to consume in an economy is 0.8. The average (and marginal) propensity to save will be 0.2. Assume that in this economy the capital-output ratio is 4. In the beginning—in period 1 (which may be a year or some shorter or longer period of time)—the equilibrium national

TABLE 7-1

TIME PERIOD	P	Y^*	C	S	I
1	$1,000	$1,000	$800	$200	$200
2	1,050	1,050	840	210	210
3	1,102.5	1,102.5	882	220.5	220.5

income is $1,000 because when Y is $1,000, S and I are both $200; and $C + I$ are $1,000. This $1,000 national income is a full-employment income because it is equal to the economy's productive capacity of $1,000. See Table 7-1.

Now P grows in period 2 by $50 because the $200 investment in period 1 divided by the capital-output ratio of 4 is $50. Note that the rate of growth of P between period 1 and period 2 is 5 percent ($50/$1,000 = 5%). If I grows by 5 percent, from $200 to $210, Y^* will increase by $10 (the increase in investment) divided by 0.2 (the marginal propensity to save). This higher Y^* of $1,050 will match the greater productive capacity of the economy and maintain full employment. The $50 increase in Y^* has increased Y^* by 5 percent because $\Delta Y^*/Y^*$ is $50/$1,000 or 5 percent.

In period 3, P grows by $52.5 because $210 (the level of investment in period 2) divided by 4 (the capital-output ratio) is $52.5. If I grows by 5 percent, from $210 to $220.5, Y^* will increase by $10.5 (the increase in investment) divided by 0.2 (the marginal propensity to save), or by $52.5. Again this Y^* is equal to the expanded P of the economy, and full employment is maintained.

We should be careful to note that in this example the average propensity to save of 0.2 divided by the capital-output ratio of 4 is 0.5, or 5 percent. Productive capacity and national income are both able to grow at this rate as long as investment grows at the same rate. (We may also observe that with Y^* growing at 5 percent, consumption and saving also grow at a 5 percent rate.) We see in this example that if investment increases at a rate equal to the average propensity to save divided by the capital-output ratio, productive capacity and national income will also grow at this rate and full employment will be maintained.

Improper investment growth rates

Let us suppose that in our example investment does *not* grow at 5 percent and that instead it grows at 1 or 10 percent, rates less than and greater than the rate which equals $(1 - b)/r$. What will be the consequences for the economy?

Table 7-2 shows I growing at a 1 percent rate, starting in period 1 with full employment and a Y^* (= P) of $1,000. The $200 I in period 1 has increased P by $50. But the $2 increase in I increases Y^* to only $1,010 in period 2, an increase of $10 (= $2/0.2). This Y^* of $1,010 is less than P by $40; and there is unemployment in the economy: national income is less than productive capacity. National income has grown by only 1 percent, the rate of growth of investment.

The $202 investment in period 2 increases P in period 3 to $1,100.5, a $50.5 increase. The increase in I of $2.02 results in Y^* increasing by $10.1

TABLE 7-2

TIME PERIOD	P	Y^*	C	S	I
1	$1,000	$1,000	$800	$200	$200
2	1,050	1,010	808	202	202
3	1,100.5	1,020.1	816.08	204.02	204.02

(= \$2.02/0.2) to \$1,020.1. This Y^* is again less than P—there is unemployment—and Y^* has grown by only 1 percent, the rate of growth of I. We observe that with the elapse of time Y^* grows by only 1 percent in each period because investment grew only at the 1 percent rate and that unemployment prevails because I did not grow at the 5 percent rate, the rate which equals the average propensity to save divided by the capital-output ratio. We should also note that C and S grow at this 1 percent rate too and that after period 2 the rate of growth of P slows down: in period 3, P did not grow by 5 percent but by about 4.7 percent (\$50.5/\$1,050 = 0.047).

Investment in Table 7-3 grows at a rate of 10 percent, starting in period 1 with P and Y^* equal at \$1,000. The I of \$200 in period 1 again adds \$50 to P in period 2. The 10 percent increase in I from period 1 to period 2 increases Y^* by \$100 (the \$20 increase in I divided by the MPS of 0.2). But the \$1,100 Y^* is greater than the P of \$1,050. How can this happen? Only if *P in dollar terms* is also valued at \$1,100, i.e., if there is inflation in the economy. If the price level rose by a little less than 4.8 percent, the value of the \$1,100 Y^* in period 2 at the prices prevailing in period 1 would be equal to

$$\frac{\$1{,}100}{1.048} = \$1{,}050$$

With a 4.8 percent rise in the price level the P in period 2 is equal to \$1,100, and there is full employment. While C, S, and I all apparently increase by 10 percent, the values of these three variables adjusted for the 4.8 percent rise in prices are still only \$840, \$210, and \$210, respectively. Thus, investment in dollar terms growing at a rate greater than $1 - b/r$ results in inflation in the economy, and in real terms P, Y^*, C, S, and I all grow at the rate which equals $(1 - b)/r$.

Inflation continues in period 3. The \$220 investment in period 2 increases P

TABLE 7-3

TIME PERIOD	P	Y^*	C	S	I
1	$1,000	$1,000	$800	$200	$200
2	1,050	1,100	880	220	220
3	1,105	1,210	968	242	242

by \$55 (= \$220/4) in period 3. But the \$22 and 10 percent increase in I in period 3 expands Y^* by \$110 (= \$22/0.2) to \$1,210. This Y^* is again greater than P and results in a rise in the price level of approximately 9.5 percent. The value of Y^* in period 3 adjusted for this price level increase is

$$\frac{\$1{,}210}{1.095} = \$1{,}105$$

Y^*, P, S, and I, when adjusted for the price increase, have increased by only 5 percent.

Summary

We have seen in this model containing no government that:

- The productive capacity and national income of an economy are able to grow at a rate which equals the average propensity to save divided by the capital-output ratio if full employment is maintained.
- To maintain full employment investment must grow at the rate which equals the average propensity to save divided by the capital-output ratio.
- If investment grows at less than this rate, national income, consumption, and saving will grow at this lower rate and there will be unemployment in the economy.
- If investment (in dollar terms) grows at a greater rate, inflation will result and national income, consumption, and saving (in real terms) will grow at the rate which equals the average propensity to save divided by the capital-output ratio.

Exercise 7-2

1 The model in this section contains the following five equations:

__________ = __________

Δ__________ = Δ__________

ΔY^* = __________

Y^* = __________

ΔP = __________

a This model contains six variables: __________, __________, __________, __________, __________, and __________. There are, in addition, two parameters: __________ and __________

b This is a(n) (open, closed) __________ system and we (can, cannot) __________ solve for the values of the six variables.

2 Show that:

a The rate at which productive capacity and national income are able to grow is $(1 - b)/r$.

b For productive capacity and national income to grow at this rate, investment must grow at a rate equal to $(1 - b)/r$.

3 Suppose $b = 0.9$ and $r = 5$.

a How rapidly are P and Y^* able to grow? __________ %

b How rapidly must I grow if P and Y^* are to grow at this rate? __________ %

c Assuming I grows at this rate, complete the table below to show the missing values.

TIME PERIOD	P	Y^*	C	S	I
1	\$5,000	\$5,000	\$_____	\$_____	\$_____
2	_____	_____	_____	_____	_____
3	_____	_____	_____	_____	_____

4 Still assuming $b = 0.9$ and $r = 5$:

a Complete the table below if I grows at a 5% rate.

TIME PERIOD	P	Y^*	C	S	I
1	\$5,000	\$5,000	\$_____	\$_____	\$_____
2	_____	_____	_____	_____	_____

(1) P, Y^*, C, I, and S in real terms will grow at a rate of __________ %.

(2) There will be __________ in the economy.

b Complete the table below if I grows at a 1% rate.

TIME PERIOD	P	Y^*	C	S	I
1	\$5,000	\$5,000	\$_____	\$_____	\$_____
2	_____	_____	_____	_____	_____

(1) Y^*, C, and S will grow at a rate of __________ %.

(2) There will be __________ in the economy.

THE MODEL WITH GOVERNMENT

It requires very little change in our model to take into account the existence of government that spends for goods and services G and levies net taxes T.

Our assumption about net taxes is that

$$T = tY \tag{7-21}$$

The parameter t is the marginal propensity to tax $\Delta T/\Delta Y$, the ratio of the change in net taxes (when national income changes) to the change in national income.

We assume that t is less than one and greater than zero.

$$0 < t < 1$$

We also assume that t is given and constant.

When we assume that $T = tY$, we are, in fact, assuming that autonomous taxes T_0 are zero: if Y were zero, net taxes would also be zero.

To help us understand the numerical examples of this model, we should also recall that disposable income Y_d equals national income minus net taxes.

$$Y_d \equiv Y - T$$

It is important to remember that when net taxes are levied, disposable income and national income are no longer equal and that, as a consequence, we cannot treat consumption and saving as functions of national income.

Equations, variables, and parameters

There are five equations and six variables in this model, the same as in the previous model, but in this model there are three instead of two parameters. The five equations are

$$P = Y^* \qquad (7\text{-}16)$$

$$\Delta P = \Delta Y^* \qquad (7\text{-}17)$$

$$\Delta Y^* = \frac{\Delta(I + G)}{1 - b + bt} \qquad (7\text{-}15)$$

$$Y^* = \frac{I + G}{1 - b + bt} \qquad (7\text{-}14)$$

$$\Delta P = \frac{1}{r}(I + G) \qquad (7\text{-}22)$$

Equations 7-16 and 7-17 are the same equations we used in the previous model. Equations 7-15 and 7-14 replace equations 7-13 and 7-12 and reflect the inclusion of government expenditures for goods and services as a component of aggregate demand and the inclusion of the marginal tax rate into the formulas for finding the equilibrium and changes in the equilibrium national income. The final equation, 7-22, is a different equation. It says that changes in productive capacity equal 1 divided by the capital-output ratio times the sum of investment expenditures and government expenditures for goods and services. The assumption we are making here is that government expenditures, as well as investment expenditures, add to the productive capacity of the economy.

This model has six variables, P, Y^*, ΔP, ΔY^*, $I + G$, and $\Delta(I + G)$.[4] The first four are the same ones we had in the model without government; the last two reflect the inclusion of government expenditures for goods and services as an element of aggregate demand and as an element that increases productive capacity. The two parameters[5] b and r are joined by a third parameter, t.

We cannot solve this model for the values of the variables unless we add an

[4] Just as in the previous model, in which I was an exogenous variable whose value was unknown, $I + G$ in this model is an exogenous variable with an unknown value.

[5] The value of r in this model will not be the same as in the previous model and can be expected to be greater. Many of the government expenditures will add little if anything to the productive capacity of the economy.

equation giving the value of one of these variables. But we can solve it to determine the rates of growth of productive capacity, national income, and investment plus government expenditures. The rate of growth of $I + G$ is

$$\frac{\Delta(I + G)}{I + G}$$

Answers to the two questions

We wish to find answers to the same questions we asked in the previous section: At what rate can the productive capacity (and national income) grow if full employment is maintained? What will ensure that full employment is maintained and the maximum rate of growth of national income is achieved? Our methods of finding answers to these two questions and the answers themselves are similar to those of the last section.

At what rate can productive capacity grow? Starting with equation 7-18, which we derived for the last model,

$$\frac{\Delta P}{P} = \frac{\Delta Y^*}{Y^*} \tag{7-18}$$

we substitute equation 7-22 for ΔP. For P we substitute Y^* because P and Y^* are equal (equation 7-17) when there is full employment; and for Y^* we substitute equation 7-14.

$$\frac{\Delta P}{P} = \frac{(1/r)(I + G)}{(I + G)/(1 - b + bt)}$$

Solving for $\Delta P/P$, we have

$$\frac{\Delta P}{P} = \frac{1}{r}(I + G)\frac{1 - b + bt}{I + G}$$

$$= \frac{1 - b + bt}{r} \tag{7-23}$$

The rate at which productive capacity can grow if there is full employment in an economy in which government spends and taxes is equal to 1 minus the MPC plus the MPC times the marginal tax rate all divided by the capital-output ratio. And if full employment is maintained, national output can grow at this same rate.

As an example, suppose that b is 0.8, r is 4, and t is 0.1. An economy with these parameters, applying equation 7-23, can grow at a rate equal to

$$\frac{\Delta P}{P} = \frac{1 - 0.8 + 0.8(0.1)}{4}$$

$$= \frac{0.2 + 0.08}{4}$$

$$= \frac{0.28}{4}$$

$$= 0.07 = 7\%$$

And if productive capacity grew at a 7 percent rate, national income would also grow at a rate of 7 percent.

At what rate must $I + G$ grow to maintain full employment? Starting with equation 7-17,

$$\Delta P = \Delta Y^* \qquad (7\text{-}17)$$

we substitute equation 7-22 for ΔP and equation 7-15 for ΔY^*

$$\frac{1}{r}(I + G) = \frac{\Delta(I + G)}{1 - b + bt}$$

Dividing through by $I + G$ and multiplying through by $1 - b + bt$, we have

$$\frac{\Delta(I + G)}{I + G} = \frac{1 - b + bt}{r} \qquad (7\text{-}24)$$

To maintain full employment in the economy, $I + G$ must grow at a rate equal to 1 minus the MPC plus the MPC times the marginal tax rate all divided by the capital-output ratio.

In an economy with a capital-output ratio of 4, an MPC of 0.8, and a marginal tax rate of 0.1, investment plus government expenditures would have to grow at a rate of 7 percent to maintain full employment in the economy. If investment plus government expenditures grow at this rate, productive capacity and national income will grow at the same rate.

Numerical example

Table 7-4 shows P, Y^*, T, Y_d, C, S, and $I + G$ over three periods of time, assuming that b is 0.8, r is 4, and t is 0.1. We start in period 1 with full employment in the economy and an equilibrium national income and productive capacity of \$1,000. The $I + G$ of \$280 in period 1 expands P in period 2 by \$70 to \$1,070, an increase of 7 percent. If $I + G$ increases by 7 percent, from \$280 to \$299.6, the \$19.6 in $I + G$ will increase Y^* by an amount equal to \$19.6 (the increase in $I + G$) times 1/0.28 [which is $1/(1 - b + bt)$, the multiplier], or by \$70. The \$70 increase in Y^* brings Y^* up to \$1,070, the new and higher P. Y^* is the equilibrium Y because at \$1,070, $Y = C + I + G$ (= \$1,070) and $S + T = I + G$ (= \$192.6 + \$107 = \$299.6).

Note that $I + G$ has increased by 7 percent and that $(1 - b + bt)/r$ in this example is 7 percent. With the 7 percent increase in $I + G$, P and Y^* also

TABLE 7-4

TIME PERIOD	P	Y^*	T	Y_d	C	S	$I + G$
1	\$1,000	\$1,000	\$100	\$900	\$720	\$180	\$280
2	1,070	1,070	107	963	770.4	192.6	299.6

increase by 7 percent, and full employment is maintained. It is also worth noting that T increases by 7 percent, Y_d increases by 7 percent, and C and S increase by 7 percent.

Improper $I + G$ growth rates

We shall not go to the trouble of working out the consequences of $I + G$ increasing at a rate less than or greater than $(1 - b + bt)/r$. These consequences are identical with the consequences worked out in the previous model of I increasing at a rate other than $(1 - b)/r$. If $I + G$ grows at a rate greater than $(1 - b + bt)/r$, the result is inflation and a real rate of growth for P, Y^*, and $I + G$ equal to $(1 - b + bt)/r$. If $I + G$ grows at a rate less than this, the consequence is unemployment and a rate of growth equal to the growth rate of $I + G$.

Summary

We have seen in this model containing government that:

- The productive capacity and national income of an economy are able to grow at a rate which equals the average propensity to save $(1 - b)$ plus the product of the marginal propensities to consume and to tax divided by the capital-output ratio.
- To maintain full employment, investment plus government expenditures must grow at this same rate.
- If investment plus government expenditures grow at a slower or a faster rate, the results are unemployment or inflation.

Three concluding observations

Throughout this section and the previous one three things have become apparent about economic growth.

The rate of growth in the economy If we refer to equations 7-19 and 7-23, we can see that the rate at which an economy is able to grow depends basically upon two parameters. One of these is r, the capital-output ratio. We can see in both equations that the smaller r is, the more rapidly the economy is able to grow. Put another way, the more a dollar of investment (or investment plus government expenditures) adds to the economy's productive capacity, the more rapidly it can increase its productive capacity and national income.

The other parameter is the percentage of its national income an economy is willing to save: $1 - b$ in the model without government and $1 - b + bt$ in the model with government. Here we see that the greater the percentage of its income the economy will save either directly (when consumers do not spend for consumption) or indirectly (when consumers do not consume or save but pay taxes), the more rapidly the economy will be able to grow.

In short, the more the economy will save and the more productive this saving is in creating added capacity to produce goods and services, the more rapidly it can grow. It is fair to say that if an economy wishes to grow at a more rapid rate, it must increase the percentage of its national income it saves, or increase the effectiveness of its saving as a producer of added capacity, or both.

The two sides of investment Investment (or investment plus government expenditures) plays two roles. It is a component of aggregate demand, and it also increases the productivity capacity of the economy. For there to be growth in productive capacity and national income, there must be investment. For the economy to have full employment and as much growth as is possible, the equilibrium national output must increase; and this requires an increase in the level of investment.

Said another way, as the full employment equilibrium level of national output increases, saving (plus net taxes) in the economy also increases. To maintain equilibrium at full employment requires an increasing level of investment (plus government expenditures) to offset the rising level of saving (plus net taxes).

The rate of growth and the amount of growth The tables of this chapter show that a constant *rate* of growth (in P, Y, I, or any of the other variables) requires that the *amount* of growth in each time period increase as time elapses. Starting with an I of \$1,000 in period 1, a 10 percent rate of growth in I means an increase in I of \$100 in period 2, an increase of \$110 in period 3, an increase of \$121 in period 4, etc. Maintaining full employment thus necessitates investment (or investment plus government expenditures) that increases by increasing amounts.

The corollary of this observation is that constant increases in the amount of growth result in a declining rate of growth. If I is \$1,000 in period 1 and increases by \$100 in period 2, the rate of growth is \$10 percent. Another \$100 increase in period 3 expands I from \$1,100 to \$1,200, but this is only an $8\frac{1}{3}$ percent growth rate. To maintain a constant growth rate requires an expanding amount of growth; and a constant amount of growth brings about a declining growth rate.

Exercise 7-3

1 The model in this section contains the following five equations:

$\_\_\_\_\_\_ = \_\_\_\_\_\_$

$\Delta\_\_\_\_\_\_ = \Delta\_\_\_\_\_\_$

$\Delta Y^* = \_\_\_\_\_\_$

$Y^* = \_\_\_\_\_\_$

$\Delta P = \_\_\_\_\_\_$

a The six variables are ______, ______, ______, ______, ______, and ______. The three parameters are ______, ______, and ______

b While we cannot solve for the values of the six variables, we can solve for the values of ______, ______, and ______

2 Show that:

a The rate at which productive capacity and national income are able to grow is $(1 - b + bt)/r$.

b For productive capacity and national income to grow at this rate, investment must grow at a rate of $(1 - b + bt)/r$.

3 Suppose $b = 0.6$, $t = 0.4$, and $r = 8$.

a How rapidly are P and Y^* able to grow? ____________ %

b How rapidly must $I + G$ grow if P and Y^* are to grow at this rate? ____________ %

c Assuming $I + G$ grows at this rate, complete the table below.

TIME PERIOD	P	Y^*	T	Y_d	C	S	$I + G$
1	$1,000	$1,000	$____	$____	$____	$____	$____
2	____	____	____	____	____	____	____
3	____	____	____	____	____	____	____

d How rapidly do T and Y_d grow? ____________ %

e How rapidly do C and S grow? ____________ %

4 Using the values of the parameters given in question 3:

a Complete the table below if $I + G$ grows at a 5% rate.

TIME PERIOD	P	Y^*	T	Y_d	C	S	$I + G$
1	$1,000	$1,000	$____	$____	$____	$____	$____
2	____	____	____	____	____	____	____

(1) P, Y^*, T, Y_d, C and S will grow at a rate of ____________ %.

(2) There will be ____________ in the economy.

b Complete the table below if $I + G$ grows at a 10% rate.

TIME PERIOD	P	Y^*	T	Y_d	C	S	$I + G$
1	$1,000	$1,000	$____	$____	$____	$____	$____
2	____	____	____	____	____	____	____

(1) P, Y^*, T, Y_d, C, S, and $I + G$ in real terms will grow at a rate of ____________ %.

(2) There will be ____________ in the economy.

5 What determines how fast an economy can grow if it maintains full employment?

a ____

b ____

6 What are the two roles of investment (or investment plus government expenditures) in economic growth?

a ____

b ____

7

a What is necessary if I is to grow at a constant rate? __________

b What will happen to Y^* and P if they grow at a constant rate? __________

8 Suppose that I grows by a constant amount each year.

a What happens to the rate of growth of investment? __________

b What happens to the rate of growth of productive capacity and national income? __________

MICROECONOMICS

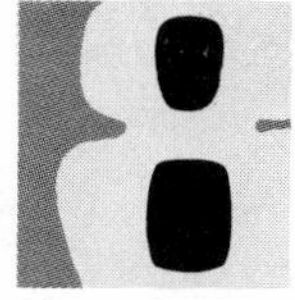

DEMAND AND SUPPLY

In the last six chapters, we examined a number of macroeconomic topics—national income and the growth of national income; the economy's money supply; the level of interest rates; and total consumption, investment, government spending, saving, taxes, and the balance of trade in the economy. We turn in this chapter and the next six to microeconomics, the study of individual markets, individual consumers, and individual firms and resource suppliers.

Demand and supply is the most useful microeconomic tool the economist possesses. It has more applications than any other tool used in economics. We undertake in this chapter to examine demand and supply mathematically. In the first section we look at demand, supply, and demand and supply together. We are interested in knowing what demand and supply are and how together they determine the price at which an economic good or service sells and the amount of the good or service that is bought and sold. In the second section we examine the effects of changes in demand and supply upon the price at which a commodity sells and the amount of the commodity sold.

DEMAND, SUPPLY, AND EQUILIBRIUM

Throughout this chapter we make three assumptions. First, we assume that markets are competitive. No one buyer and no one seller is able by himself to influence the price at which the good or service sells, and there is no collusion among buyers or sellers for the purpose of raising or lowering price or increasing or decreasing the amount of the good or service sold.

Second, the good or service may be either a product sold by business firms to consumers (or to other business firms) or the service of a resource sold by resource owners to firms. This means that demand and supply are useful in explaining the price and the quantity sold of any good or service, whether it is a product or a resource.

Third, we assume that demand and supply are the *market* (or total) demand and the *market* (or total) supply, and not individual demand and supply. This means that demand is the demand of all buyers of the good or service (and not the demand of just one buyer) and that supply is the supply of all sellers (and not the supply of just one seller).

The additional assumptions about demand and supply are contained in the remainder of this section of the chapter.

Demand

Demand is a function that relates the quantity of a commodity demanded D to the price P at which the commodity sells. We assume for simplicity that the demand function is linear. We also assume that the function is a decreasing one: the lower the price of the commodity, the greater the quantity demanded (and the higher the price, the smaller the quantity demanded).

The demand function we write as

$$D = a - bP \qquad (8\text{-}1)$$

The parameter a is the quantity that would be demanded if the price of the commodity were zero. We assume that a is a quantity greater than zero

$$a > 0$$

The negative sign in front of the parameter b indicates that increases in P decrease D and that decreases in P increase D. b is the parameter that relates changes in the quantity demanded to changes in the price of the commodity. When P changes by ΔP, D will change by ΔD; and we can write

$$D + \Delta D = a - b(P + \Delta P) \qquad (8\text{-}2)$$

Expanding gives

$$D + \Delta D = a - bP - b\,\Delta P$$

From this last equation we subtract the demand function (equation 8-1) and obtain

$$\Delta D = -b\,\Delta P \qquad (8\text{-}3)$$

The change in the quantity demanded is equal to $-b$ times the change in price. If we divide equation 8-3 by ΔP, we have

$$\frac{\Delta D}{\Delta P} = -b \qquad (8\text{-}4)$$

b is the ratio of the change in quantity demanded (when price changes) to the change in price. The minus sign preceding it means that an increase in price brings about a decrease in quantity demanded, and a decrease in price results in an increase in quantity demanded. This inverse relation between price and quantity demanded is called *the law of demand*.

In the real world, the amount of a good or service that consumers or business firms wish to purchase does not depend solely upon its price. Such variables as income and the prices of other commodities affect the amount of a particular commodity *consumers* want to buy. The demand for the product they produce and the prices at which they may employ other resources are variables that affect the amount of a particular resource *business firms* wish to employ. In making the quantity demanded a function of price alone we are assuming that all the other variables affecting D are constant. The values of these other variables determine the magnitudes of the parameters a and b in the demand equation. Changes in the other variables bring about changes in a and b. When we write a demand equation such as 8-1 which is to be a part of a model, we simplify our model by making the *ceteris paribus* assumption: all variables other than those appearing in the model remain unchanged.

Units of measurement The price of a commodity, we assume, is measured in dollars. Physical units such as pounds, quarts, bales, etc., are used to measure quantity demanded. The parameter a is also measured in physical units. The other parameter, b, is measured in neither physical units nor dollars but in both.

When we subtract bP from a to obtain D, the difference must be in physical units because D is measured in physical units, and so b times P must be physical units. If P is dollars, by what must we multiply P to obtain a physical unit? By a number which is *physical units per dollar*. The parameter b, therefore, is always measured by physical units per dollar; and b multiplied by P is measured in physical units because the dollars cancel each other.

A numerical example The demand for a commodity might be

$$D = 40 \text{ bushels} - 2\frac{\text{bushels}}{\text{dollar}}P$$

This equation tells us that:

- The physical unit for measuring quantity demanded is bushels.
- If P were zero, D would be 40 bushels.
- For every dollar increase in P, D will decrease by 2 bushels.

This demand equation enables us to find the quantity demanded at any price we select. If P is \$5, D will be

$$\begin{aligned} D &= 40 \text{ bushels} - 2\frac{\text{bushels}}{\text{dollar}}(\$5) \\ &= 40 \text{ bushels} - 10 \text{ bushels} \\ &= 30 \text{ bushels} \end{aligned}$$

We can also find what the price would have to be for buyers to demand some particular amount. Suppose we wished buyers to demand 20 bushels. For D

we substitute 20 bushels and then solve for P.

$$20 \text{ bushels} = 40 \text{ bushels} - 2\frac{\text{bushels}}{\text{dollar}}P$$

$$-20 \text{ bushels} = -2\frac{\text{bushels}}{\text{dollar}}P$$

$$20 \text{ bushels} = 2\frac{\text{bushels}}{\text{dollar}}P$$

Dividing through by 2 bushels/dollar, we have

$$P = \frac{20 \text{ bushels}}{2 \text{ bushels/dollar}}$$

$$= \$10$$

We can find the P at which buyers would demand zero bushels, that is, D would be zero, by letting D in our example be zero and solving for P.

$$0 = 40 \text{ bushels} - 2\frac{\text{bushels}}{\text{dollar}}P$$

$$-40 \text{ bushels} = -2\frac{\text{bushels}}{\text{dollar}}P$$

$$40 \text{ bushels} = 2\frac{\text{bushels}}{\text{dollar}}P$$

$$P = \$20$$

The demand curve In plotting the demand equation on a graph it is customary to plot D on the horizontal axis (the abscissa) and P on the vertical axis (the ordinate). We have plotted

$$D = 40 \text{ bushels} - 2\frac{\text{bushels}}{\text{dollar}}P$$

on the graph in Figure 8-1. Notice that:

- This curve slopes downward from left to right because b is preceded by a minus sign (and $\Delta D/\Delta P$ is therefore negative).
- The curve touches the quantity axis at 40 bushels (point D) because $a = 40$ bushels.
- The curve touches the price axis at \$20 (point A) because if P were \$20, D (as we found above) would be zero.
- Point C corresponds with the 30 bushels which we computed would be the quantity demanded at a price of \$5.
- Point B corresponds with the \$10 price which we computed would have to be charged if quantity demanded were to be 20 bushels.

To measure the slope of any straight line we divide the vertical displacement by the horizontal displacement. Because P is measured vertically and D horizontally in the graph above, the vertical displacement is ΔP and the horizontal displacement is ΔD. The slope of the demand curve is therefore

$$\text{Slope of demand curve} = \frac{\Delta P}{\Delta D} \tag{8-5}$$

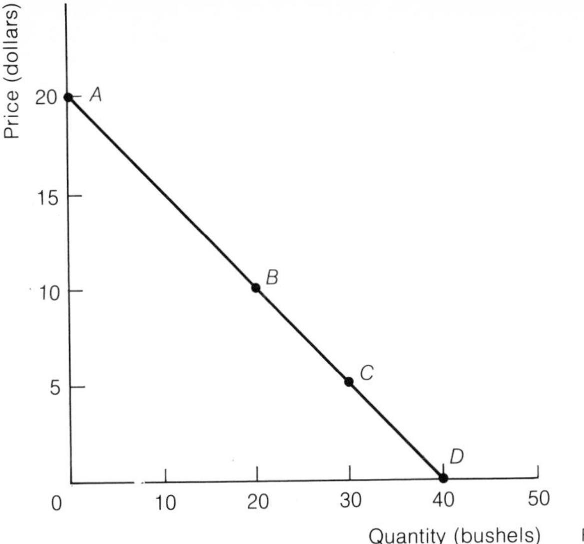

FIGURE 8-1

The inverse, or reciprocal, of $\Delta P/\Delta D$ is $\Delta D/\Delta P$, and we know that

$$\frac{\Delta D}{\Delta P} = -b \tag{8-4}$$

From this we may conclude that the parameter b is the reciprocal (or the inverse) of the slope of the demand curve. (Or we might say that the slope of the demand curve is equal to $-1/b$.) For if

$$\frac{\Delta D}{\Delta P} = -b$$

then

$$\frac{\Delta P}{\Delta D} = -\frac{1}{b}$$

and because

$$\text{Slope of demand curve} = \frac{\Delta P}{\Delta D} \tag{8-5}$$

we discover that

$$\text{Slope of demand curve} = -\frac{1}{b}$$

The time element Every demand function pertains to some period of time. When we write $D = a - bP$, we are saying that the quantity demanded *during a period of time* depends upon the price charged for the commodity *during that same period of time*. The period may be a year or longer, a month, week, day, hour, or even a second or split second. In writing the demand function we usually do not specify what the time period is, but it should be remembered that it is for some time period even if we neglect to say just how long that period is.

Supply

Like demand, supply is a function. Supply relates the quantity supplied S of a commodity to the price P at which the commodity sells. For simplicity, we assume that supply is a linear function. The supply function, it is also assumed, is an increasing function: the lower the price of the commodity, the smaller the quantity supplied; and the higher the price, the greater the quantity supplied.

For the supply function we write

$$S = c + eP \tag{8-6}$$

The parameter c is the quantity that would be supplied if the price of the commodity were zero. We make no particular assumption about the size of c. It may be greater than, less than, or equal to zero.

$$c \gtreqless 0$$

The plus sign in front of the parameter e indicates that when P increases, S increases; and when P decreases, S decreases. e is the parameter relating changes in the quantity supplied to changes in price. For when P changes by ΔP, S will change by ΔS.

$$\begin{aligned} S + \Delta S &= c + e(P + \Delta P) \\ &= c + eP + e\,\Delta P \end{aligned} \tag{8-7}$$

If we subtract equation 8-6 from this last equation, we have

$$\Delta S = e\,\Delta P \tag{8-8}$$

This tells us that the change in quantity supplied is equal to e times the change in P. Dividing through by ΔP, we have

$$\frac{\Delta S}{\Delta P} = e \tag{8-9}$$

The parameter e is the ratio of the change in quantity supplied (when price changes) to the change in price. The plus sign in front of e indicates that an increase in P results in an increase in S and a decrease in P results in a decrease in S. The direct relation between price and quantity supplied is called *the law of supply*.

In the real world the amount of a good or service that business firms or households offer to sell depends not only upon the price of that good or service but also upon other variables. Such variables as the costs of producing a particular product or the prices at which they are able to sell other products also affect the amount of a product *business firms* will put on the market. The prices that *consumers* must pay to obtain goods and services and the prices at which they are able to sell the services of other resources affect the amount of a particular resource they will make available in the marketplace. In writing a supply equation such as equation 8-6 we are again employing the *ceteris paribus* assumption: the values of all the other variables affecting S remain unchanged. The values of the other variables determine the magnitudes of c

and e in the supply function; and changes in these other variables result in changes in c and e. We assume when we write a supply equation that all other variables affecting S are given in order to simplify our study and our model of a competitive market.

As with demand, S and the parameter c are measured in physical units; P is measured in dollars; and the parameter e is measured in *physical units per dollar*. The supply function, like the demand function, pertains to some time period which is not usually specified. The quantity supplied in a given time period depends upon the price at which the commodity can be sold during the same period.

A numerical example We might have the supply equation

$$S = -10 \text{ bushels} + 3\frac{\text{bushels}}{\text{dollar}}P$$

This equation tells us that:

- The physical unit of measurement is bushels.
- As the price falls toward zero the quantity supplied would approach a negative 10 bushels.
- For every dollar increase in price, the quantity supplied would increase by 3 bushels.

The supply equation makes it possible to find the quantity supplied at any price we pick. If the price of this commodity is \$5, the quantity supplied will be

$$\begin{aligned} S &= -10 \text{ bushels} + 3\frac{\text{bushels}}{\text{dollar}}(\$5) \\ &= -10 \text{ bushels} + 15 \text{ bushels} \\ &= 5 \text{ bushels} \end{aligned}$$

The price at which the commodity would have to sell in order for a certain quantity to be offered for sale can also be found by using this equation. Suppose we want 50 bushels to be the quantity supplied. For S we substitute 50 bushels and then solve for P:

$$50 \text{ bushels} = -10 \text{ bushels} + 3\frac{\text{bushels}}{\text{dollar}}P$$

$$50 \text{ bushels} + 10 \text{ bushels} = 3\frac{\text{bushels}}{\text{dollar}}P$$

$$60 \text{ bushels} = 3\frac{\text{bushels}}{\text{dollar}}P$$

$$\frac{60 \text{ bushels}}{3 \text{ bushels/dollar}} = P$$

$$P = \$20$$

We can also find the price at which sellers would offer zero bushels for sale, that is, S would be zero, by letting S be zero and solving for P:

$$0 \text{ bushels} = -10 \text{ bushels} + 3\frac{\text{bushels}}{\text{dollar}}P$$

$$10 \text{ bushels} = 3\frac{\text{bushels}}{\text{dollar}}$$

$$P = \$3.33\tfrac{1}{3}$$

The supply curve In Figure 8-2 we have plotted

$$S = -10 \text{ bushels} + 3\frac{\text{bushels}}{\text{dollar}}P$$

In plotting the supply equation we have again plotted price on the vertical axis, and we have plotted quantity supplied on the horizontal axis.

Notice that:

- The curve slopes upward from left to right because the parameter e is preceded by a plus sign; that is, $\Delta S/\Delta P$ is positive.
- The curve intersects the quantity axis at -10 bushels because the parameter c is equal to -10 bushels.
- The curve touches the price axis at $\$3.33\frac{1}{3}$ (point B) because S would be zero, if the price were $\$3.33\frac{1}{3}$ (as computed above).
- Point C corresponds to the 5 bushels which would be supplied if P were \$5.
- Point E corresponds to the \$20 price which we computed would have to be the price if the quantity supplied were to be 50 bushels.

The slope of the supply curve is the vertical displacement ΔP divided by the horizontal displacement ΔS.

$$\text{Slope of supply curve} = \frac{\Delta P}{\Delta S} \qquad (8\text{-}10)$$

In equation 8-9 we found that

$$\frac{\Delta S}{\Delta P} = e \qquad (8\text{-}9)$$

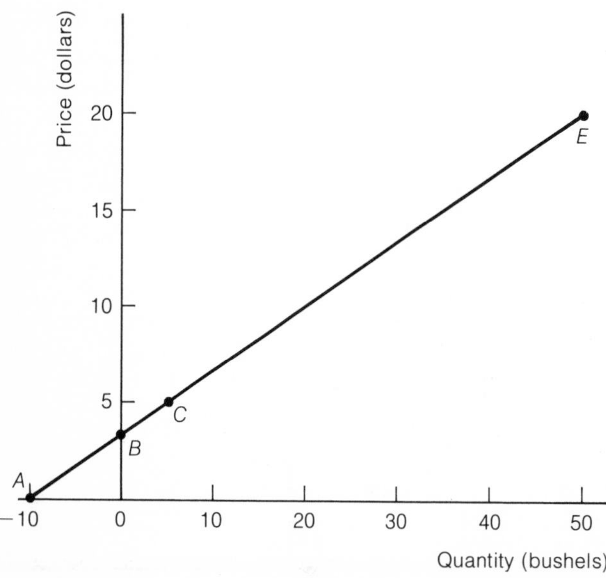

FIGURE 8-2

If $\Delta S/\Delta P = e$, then

$$\frac{\Delta P}{\Delta S} = \frac{1}{e}$$

$\Delta P/\Delta S$, which is the slope of the supply curve, is therefore equal to the reciprocal of e; and e is the reciprocal of the slope of the supply curve.

Equilibrium price and quantity

When we write both the demand and supply equations, we have just two equations:

$$D = a - bP \quad (8\text{-}1)$$
$$S = c + eP \quad (8\text{-}6)$$

These two equations have three variables, D, S, and P. To complete our model we need three equations. Our third equation is

$$D = S \quad (8\text{-}11)$$

The equilibrium price Equation 8-11 is the equilibrium equation. It says that the price which will be charged for this commodity in a competitive market is the price at which the quantity demanded D and the quantity supplied S are equal. We call the price at which D and S are equal the equilibrium price[1] and label it P^*.

We would like to have a solution equation to tell us what P^* will be. To find P^* we start with equation 8-11

$$D = S \quad (8\text{-}11)$$

and substitute the demand equation for D and the supply equation for S.

$$a - bP = c + eP \quad (8\text{-}12)$$

We can now solve for P by moving all terms containing P to one side of the equation and all other terms to the other side.

$$\begin{aligned} a - c &= bP + eP \\ &= P(b + e) \end{aligned}$$

$$P^* = \frac{a - c}{b + e} \quad (8\text{-}13)$$

Equation 8-13 tells us that the equilibrium price equals:

- a (the quantity demanded when P is zero) *minus* c (the quantity supplied when P is zero)
- Divided by b (the ratio $\Delta D/\Delta P$) *plus* e (the ratio $\Delta S/\Delta P$)

Notice that equation 8-13 is a solution equation for the variable P. It contains an endogenous variable on the left side and nothing but parameters on the right side. It should also be noted that this closed model of a competitive market

[1] The equilibrium price is the price at which the forces that would increase and the forces that would decrease price are balanced; or it is that price which would show no tendency either to rise or to fall. Prices other than the equilibrium price are disequilibrium prices.

contains three equations (8-1, 8-6, and 8-11), three endogenous variables (D, S, and P), four parameters (a, b, c, and e), and no exogenous variables.

In our numerical example

$$D = 40 \text{ bushels} - 2\frac{\text{bushels}}{\text{dollar}}P$$

$$S = -10 \text{ bushels} + 3\frac{\text{bushels}}{\text{dollar}}P$$

$$a = 40 \text{ bushels}$$

$$b = 2\frac{\text{bushels}}{\text{dollar}}$$

$$c = -10 \text{ bushels}$$

$$e = 3\frac{\text{bushels}}{\text{dollar}}$$

$$P^* = \frac{40 \text{ bushels} - (-10 \text{ bushels})}{2 \text{ bushels/dollar} + 3 \text{ bushels/dollar}}$$

$$= \frac{50 \text{ bushels}}{5 \text{ bushels/dollar}}$$

$$= \$10$$

Without using equation 8-13 we could have solved for P^* in the following way:

$$D = S \qquad (8\text{-}11)$$

$$40 \text{ bushels} - 2\frac{\text{bushels}}{\text{dollar}}P = -10 \text{ bushels} + 3\frac{\text{bushels}}{\text{dollar}}P$$

$$50 \text{ bushels} = 5\frac{\text{bushels}}{\text{dollar}}P$$

$$\frac{50 \text{ bushels}}{5 \text{ bushels/dollar}} = P$$

$$P^* = \$10$$

The equilibrium quantity Having found P^*, we can find the quantity that will be demanded and supplied at the equilibrium price by substituting P^* for P in either the demand or supply equations. P^* in our example is \$10. Using the demand equation,

$$D = 40 \text{ bushels} - 2\frac{\text{bushels}}{\text{dollar}}P$$

$$= 40 \text{ bushels} - 2\frac{\text{bushels}}{\text{dollar}}(\$10)$$

$$= 40 \text{ bushels} - 20 \text{ bushels}$$

$$= 20 \text{ bushels}$$

Using the supply equation we obtain the same result.

$$S = -10 \text{ bushels} + 3\frac{\text{bushels}}{\text{dollar}}P$$

$$= -10 \text{ bushels} + 3\frac{\text{bushels}}{\text{dollar}}(\$10)$$

$$= -10 \text{ bushels} + 30 \text{ bushels}$$

$$= 20 \text{ bushels}$$

The quantity demanded or quantity supplied (equal to each other at the equilibrium price) is called the *equilibrium quantity* and labeled Q^*. That is,

$$D = S = Q^* \tag{8-14}$$

In our example, Q^* is 20 bushels.

Instead of first finding P^* and then finding Q^* by substituting P^* in either the demand or supply equations, we might have found Q^* first by developing a solution equation for the equilibrium quantity. Starting with the demand equation

$$D = a - bP \tag{8-1}$$

we can express price as a function of quantity demanded.

$$D - a = -bP$$
$$a - D = bP$$

$$P = \frac{a - D}{b} \tag{8-15}$$

Now, using the supply equation

$$S = c + eP \tag{8-6}$$

we can also express price as a function of quantity supplied.

$$S - c = eP$$

$$P = \frac{S - c}{e} \tag{8-16}$$

Because a commodity has only one price, P in equation 8-15 is the same as the P in equation 8-16; and we write

$$\frac{a - D}{b} = \frac{S - c}{e}$$

Because $Q^* = D = S$ (equation 8-14) we can rewrite the last equation

$$\frac{a - Q^*}{b} = \frac{Q^* - c}{e}$$

and solve for Q^* (the equilibrium quantity). First we put both sides of this equation over a common denominator

$$\frac{e(a - Q^*)}{be} = \frac{b(Q^* - c)}{be}$$

$$\frac{ea - eQ^*}{be} = \frac{bQ^* - bc}{be}$$

$$\frac{ea}{be} - \frac{eQ^*}{be} = \frac{bQ^*}{be} - \frac{bc}{be}$$

Moving all terms with Q^* in them to the left and all other terms to the right,

$$-\frac{eQ^*}{be} - \frac{bQ^*}{be} = -\frac{bc}{be} - \frac{ea}{be}$$

If we multiply through by -1, we have

$$\frac{eQ^*}{be} + \frac{bQ^*}{be} = \frac{bc}{be} + \frac{ea}{be}$$

which we can rewrite as

$$\frac{Q^*(b + e)}{be} = \frac{bc + ea}{be}$$

Multiplying both sides of this equation by $be/(b + e)$ gives

$$Q^* = \frac{bc + ea}{be}\frac{be}{b + d}$$

$$= \frac{bc + ea}{b + e} \qquad (8\text{-}17)$$

This is our solution equation for the variables D and S. On the left is an endogenous variable. The right side contains only parameters.[2]

In our example we would have found Q^* to be

$$Q^* = \frac{(2 \text{ bushels/dollar})(-10 \text{ bushels}) + (3 \text{ bushels/dollar})(40 \text{ bushels})}{2 \text{ bushels/dollar} + 3 \text{ bushels/dollar}}$$

$$= \frac{-20 \text{ bushels}^2/\text{dollar} + 120 \text{ bushels}^2/\text{dollar}}{5 \text{ bushels/dollar}}$$

$$= \frac{100 \text{ bushels}^2/\text{dollar}}{5 \text{ bushels/dollar}}$$

$$= 20 \text{ bushels}$$

The development of equation 8-17 seems hardly worthwhile inasmuch as we have already found the equilibrium quantity by a much simpler method. But we shall need equation 8-17 in the next section, where we shall find it a useful means of discovering the effects of changes in demand and in supply on the equilibrium quantity.

Demand and supply curves In Figure 8-3 we have plotted

$$D = 40 \text{ bushels} - 2\frac{\text{bushels}}{\text{dollar}}P$$

and

$$S = -10 \text{ bushels} + 3\frac{\text{bushels}}{\text{dollar}}P$$

We can see that the two functions intersect at a price of \$10 and at a quantity of 20 bushels. Since we found that \$10 is the equilibrium price and 20 bushels is the equilibrium quantity, we may conclude that the demand and supply curves intersect at the equilibrium price and quantity. It should also be noted that:

- At prices other than P^*, D and S are not equal.

[2] To assure that the equilibrium quantity is not negative—an economic impossibility—we must assume that if c is negative (as it is in our example), bc is less than ea. If bc were greater than ea, the numerator on the right side of equation 8-17 would be negative, the right side of the equation would be negative, and Q^* would therefore be negative. But as long as bc is less than ea, the numerator on the right side, the right side of the equation, and Q^* are all positive.

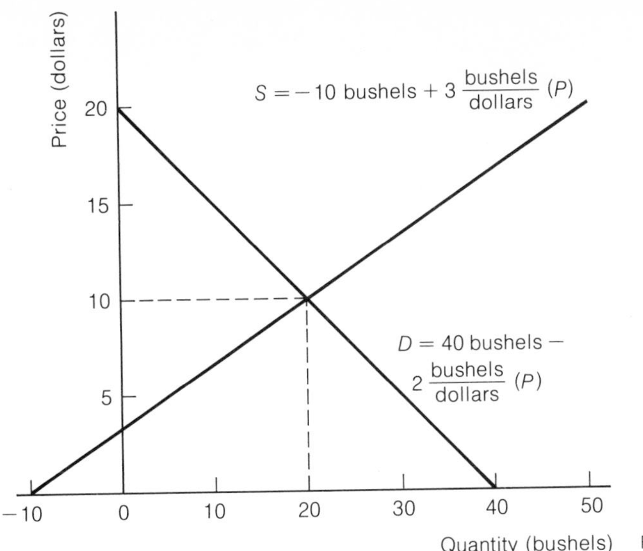

FIGURE 8-3

- At prices above P^*, S is greater than D.
- At prices below P^*, D is greater than S.

In our numerical example, at a price of \$15 (which is above the P^* of \$10) S is 35 bushels, and D is only 10 bushels. But at a price of \$5 (which is below the P^* of \$10) D is 30 bushels, and S is 5 bushels. (You can read D and S at each price directly off the graph, or you can compute D and S at each price by using the demand and supply functions.)

Exercise 8-1

1 If the demand function is $D = a - bP$:

a What assumption is made about the size of a?

b The parameter b is equal to __________

c What units are employed to measure:

(1) D: __________

(2) a: __________

(3) b: __________

(4) P: __________

d $\Delta D/\Delta P =$ __________. This relationship is called the __________

2 Suppose the demand function is

$$D = 100 \text{ bales} - 20 \frac{\text{bales}}{\text{dollar}} P$$

a What would be the quantity demanded if price were zero?

b At what price would quantity demanded be zero?

c When price increases by \$1, what happens to the quantity demanded?

d What is the quantity demanded when the price is:

(1) \$4: ___________ bales.

(2) \$3: ___________ bales.

(3) \$2: ___________ bales.

e Plot this demand function on the graph below.

f The slope of this demand curve equals ___________

3 If the supply function is $S = c + eP$:

a What assumption is made about the size of c?

b What assumption is made about e?

c The parameter e is equal to ___________

d The law of supply is ___________

4 Suppose the supply function is

$$S = -40 \text{ bales} + 30 \frac{\text{bales}}{\text{dollar}} P$$

a What would be the quantity supplied if the price were zero?

b What would be the price if the quantity supplied were zero?

c When price decreases by \$1, what happens to the quantity supplied?

d What is the quantity supplied when price is:

(1) \$4: ___________

(2) \$5: ___________

(3) \$6: ___________

e Plot the supply function on the graph on the next page.

f The slope of the supply curve equals ___________

5 If the demand and supply functions are

$D = a - bP$

$S = c + eP$

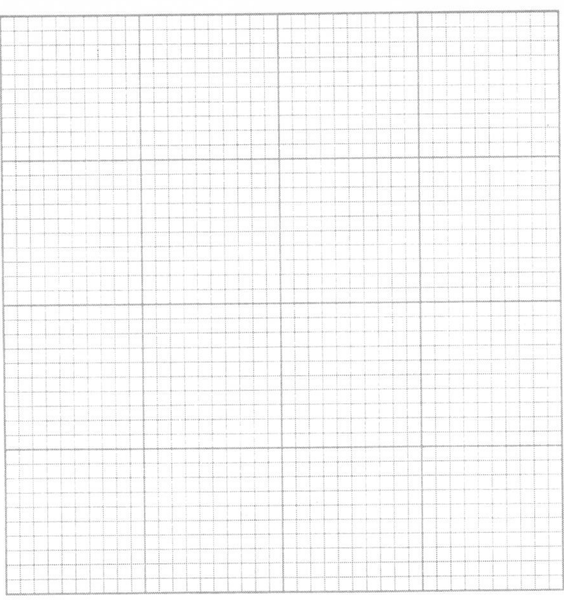

a What equation is needed to complete this system of equations? ________

b Show that

$$P^* = \frac{a - c}{b + e}$$

c Show that

$$Q^* = \frac{bc + ea}{b + e}$$

6 Using the demand function in question 2 and the supply function in question 4:

a $P^* = \$$____________

b $Q^* =$ ____________ bales.

7 In this chapter we have assumed that:

a The markets in which demand and supply meet are ____________ markets.
b The commodity bought and sold in these markets may be either a

____________ or a ____________

c The demand and supply we discuss are ____________ demand and supply.

8 Every demand and supply function pertains to a period of ____________

9 The price at which the demand and supply curves intersect is the

____________, and the quantity at which they intersect is the____________

10 If you have already found the equilibrium price, how can you find the equilibrium quantity without using the formula for equilibrium quantity?

CHANGES IN DEMAND AND SUPPLY

Having found the formulas for the equilibrium price and quantity, we can now discover how changes in demand, in supply, or in both will alter the equilibrium values of price and quantity. What we want to know is whether a change in demand (or in supply) will raise or lower the equilibrium price and whether it will increase or decrease the equilibrium quantity. In this section we first define a change in demand and a change in supply. Next, we look at the effects of changes in demand and the effects of changes in supply on P^* and Q^*. And finally we examine the effects of simultaneous changes in demand and supply.

Definitions

By a change in demand we shall mean a change in the parameter a in the demand function, the parameter b remaining constant. If Δa is positive, demand has increased, and if Δa is negative, demand has decreased. If the demand function is

$$D = 40 \text{ bushels} - 2\frac{\text{bushels}}{\text{dollar}}P$$

in which a is 40 bushels, and if the 40 bushels become 50 bushels (or any number more than 40) demand will have increased. If the 40 bushels became 30 bushels (or any number less than 40), demand will have decreased.

In Figure 8-4 we have plotted the demand function

$$D = 40 \text{ bushels} - 2\frac{\text{bushels}}{\text{dollar}}P \qquad \text{labeled } D_1$$

$$D = 50 \text{ bushels} - 2\frac{\text{bushels}}{\text{dollar}}P \qquad \text{labeled } D_2$$

$$D = 30 \text{ bushels} - 2\frac{\text{bushels}}{\text{dollar}}P \qquad \text{labeled } D_3$$

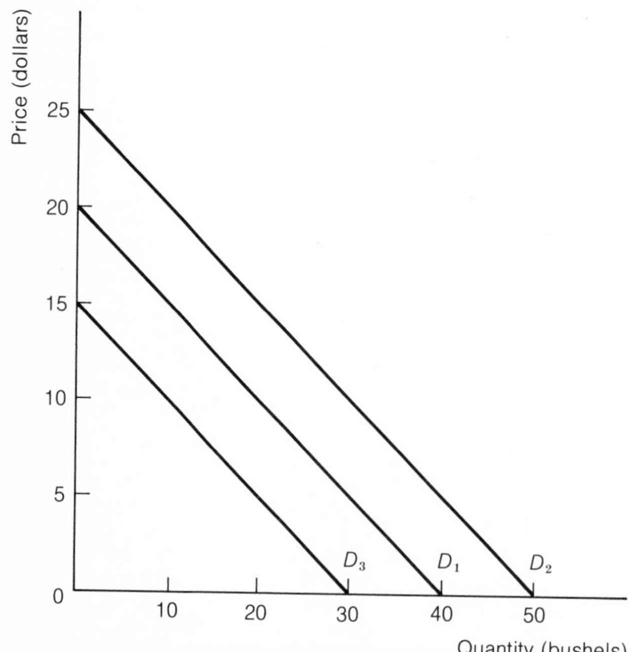

FIGURE 8-4

Graphically, an increase in demand (as we have defined it) means a parallel shift in the demand curve to the right, and a decrease in demand means a parallel shift in the demand curve to the left.

A change in supply is defined as a change in the parameter c in the supply function, the parameter e remaining constant. When Δc is positive, supply is said to have increased; and when Δc is negative, supply has decreased. Using our numerical example of the supply function

$$S = -10 \text{ bushels} + 3\frac{\text{bushels}}{\text{dollar}}P$$

in which c is -10 bushels, if c becomes -5 bushels (or any number of bushels greater than -10 bushels) supply will have increased. If c becomes -15 (or any number of bushels less than -10 bushels) supply will have decreased.

We have plotted three supply functions in Figure 8-5. S_1 is the original function

$$S = -10 \text{ bushels} + 3\frac{\text{bushels}}{\text{dollar}}P$$

S_2 is

$$S = -5 \text{ bushels} + 3\frac{\text{bushels}}{\text{dollar}}P$$

and S_3 is

$$S = -15 \text{ bushels} + 3\frac{\text{bushels}}{\text{dollar}}P$$

We can see that graphically an increase in supply (as we have defined it) means a parallel movement of the supply curve to the right and a decrease in supply means a parallel movement of the supply curve to the left.

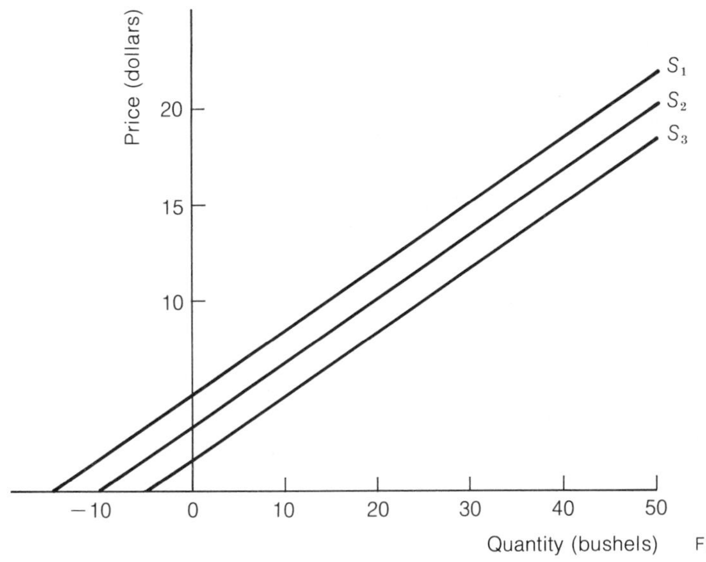

FIGURE 8-5

In summary:

- A change in demand is equal to Δa, and a change in supply is equal to Δc.
- When Δa is positive (negative), demand has increased (decreased).
- When Δc is positive (negative), supply has increased (decreased).

Before going on, we should note that there are more complicated changes in demand and supply that we might examine. A change in the parameter b in the demand function and a change in parameter e in the supply function are also changes in demand and supply, respectively. But since these changes require more time and effort than we wish to devote to them, we shall content ourselves with the simplest kind of changes in demand and supply: a change in a with b constant and a change in c with d constant.

The effects of changes in demand

To find the effect of changes in demand on equilibrium price and on equilibrium quantity we must make use of our formulas for P^* and Q^*, equations 8-13 and 8-17. Let us look first at the effects of changes in demand on P^*.

The effect on price The formula for P^* is

$$P^* = \frac{a - c}{b + e} \tag{8-13}$$

If demand changes by Δa, P^* will change by ΔP^*, and we write

$$P^* + \Delta P^* = \frac{(a + \Delta a) - c}{b + e}$$

$$= \frac{a + \Delta a - c}{b + e}$$

From this last equation we subtract the equilibrium equation (8-13) to find ΔP^*.

$$\Delta P^* = \frac{\Delta a}{b + e} \tag{8-18}$$

The change in the equilibrium price that results from a change in demand is equal to the change in demand divided by a quantity which is the sum of the values of the parameters b and d, that is, the values of $\Delta D/\Delta P$ and $\Delta S/\Delta P$.

If we divide equation 8-18 through by Δa, we have

$$\frac{\Delta P^*}{\Delta a} = \frac{1}{b + e} \tag{8-19}$$

The sum of the values of b and e is positive, and therefore $1/(b + e)$ is positive. This means that when Δa is positive, ΔP^* must also be positive if $\Delta P^*/\Delta a$ is to be positive. In short, an increase in demand results in an increase in P^*, and a decrease in demand brings about a decrease in P^*.

The effect on quantity Now let us look at the effect of a change in demand on the equilibrium quantity. The formula for Q^* is

$$Q^* = \frac{bc + ea}{b + e} \tag{8-17}$$

When demand changes by Δa, Q^* will change by ΔQ^*, and so

$$Q^* + \Delta Q^* = \frac{bc + e(a + \Delta a)}{b + e}$$

$$= \frac{bc + ea + e\,\Delta a}{b + e}$$

From this equation we subtract the equilibrium equation (8-17) to get

$$\Delta Q^* = \frac{e\,\Delta a}{b + e} \tag{8-20}$$

The change in the equilibrium quantity equals the quantity e times the change in demand divided by the quantity b plus e (which is the sum of $\Delta D/\Delta P$ and $\Delta S/\Delta P$).

Dividing equation 8-20 through by Δa, we have

$$\frac{\Delta Q^*}{\Delta a} = \frac{e}{b + e} \tag{8-21}$$

Since the sum of the values of b and e is positive and e itself is positive, $e/(b + e)$ is positive. For $\Delta Q^*/\Delta a$ to be positive, when Δa is positive, ΔQ^* must be positive; and when Δa is negative, ΔQ^* must be negative. This means that an increase in demand results in an increase in Q^* and a decrease in demand results in a decrease in Q^*.

Numerical examples Suppose, using the following demand and supply functions:

$$D = 40 \text{ bushels} - 2\frac{\text{bushels}}{\text{dollar}}P$$

$$S = -10 \text{ bushels} + 3\frac{\text{bushels}}{\text{dollar}}P$$

that the change in demand is +10 bushels. The effect on P^* is

$$\Delta P^* = \frac{\Delta a}{b + e} \tag{8-18}$$

In our example, b is 2 bushels/dollar, e is 3 bushels/dollar, and Δa is +10 bushels.

$$\Delta P^* = \frac{10 \text{ bushels}}{2 \text{ bushels/dollar} + 3 \text{ bushels/dollar}}$$

$$= \frac{10 \text{ bushels}}{5 \text{ bushels/dollar}}$$

$$= \$2$$

To find the effect on the equilibrium quantity we use

$$\Delta Q^* = \frac{e\,\Delta a}{b + e} \tag{8-20}$$

$$= \frac{(3 \text{ bushels/dollar})(10 \text{ bushels})}{2 \text{ bushels/dollar} + 3 \text{ bushels/dollar}}$$

$$= \frac{30 \text{ bushels}^2\text{/dollar}}{5 \text{ bushels/dollar}}$$

$$= 6 \text{ bushels}$$

The effects of this 10-bushel increase in demand are to increase the equilibrium price by $2 and to increase the equilibrium quantity by 6 bushels.

Suppose that demand had decreased by 20 bushels. The change in P^* is

$$\Delta P^* = \frac{\Delta a}{b + e} \tag{8-18}$$

$$= \frac{-20 \text{ bushels}}{2 \text{ bushels/dollar} + 3 \text{ bushels/dollar}}$$

$$= \frac{-20 \text{ bushels}}{5 \text{ bushels/dollar}}$$

$$= -\$4$$

and the change in Q^* is

$$\Delta Q^* = \frac{e\,\Delta a}{b + e} \tag{8-20}$$

$$= \frac{(3 \text{ bushels/dollar})(-20 \text{ bushels})}{2 \text{ bushels/dollar} + 3 \text{ bushels/dollar}}$$

$$= \frac{-60 \text{ bushels}^2/\text{dollar}}{5 \text{ bushels/dollar}}$$

$$= -12 \text{ bushels}$$

The results of the 20-bushel decrease in demand are a $4 fall in the equilibrium price and a 12-bushel decline in the equilibrium quantity.[3]

The effects of changes in supply

To find the effects of changes in supply on equilibrium price and equilibrium quantity we again use our equilibrium equations.

The effect on price The formula for P^* is

$$P^* = \frac{a - c}{b + e} \tag{8-13}$$

When supply changes by Δc, P^* changes by ΔP^*.

$$P^* + \Delta P^* = \frac{a - (c + \Delta c)}{b + e}$$

$$= \frac{a - c - \Delta c}{b + e}$$

From this equation we subtract equation 8-13 to obtain

$$\Delta P^* = \frac{-\Delta c}{b + e} \tag{8-22}$$

The effect of the change in supply is equal to a minus change in supply divided by the sum of the parameters b and e. Again $b + e$ is positive, but since the numerator of equation 8-22 is negative, $-\Delta c/(b + e)$ is also negative.

Dividing equation 8-22 by Δc, we have

$$\frac{\Delta P^*}{\Delta c} = \frac{-1}{b + e} \tag{8-23}$$

[3]We might also have found the effects of these changes in demand by putting the new values of a into equations 8-13 and 8-17 and solving for the new values of P^* and Q^*.

When Δc is positive, ΔP^* must be negative; and when Δc is negative, ΔP^* must be positive if $\Delta P^*/\Delta c$ is to be negative. An increase in supply brings about a decrease in P^*, and a decrease in supply results in an increase in P^*.

The effect on quantity For finding the effect of a change in supply upon the equilibrium quantity we shall provide only the equations.

$$Q^* = \frac{bc + ea}{b + e} \tag{8-17}$$

$$Q^* + \Delta Q^* = \frac{b(c + \Delta c) + ea}{d + b}$$

$$= \frac{bc + b\,\Delta c + ea}{d + b} \tag{8-24}$$

Subtracting 8-17 gives

$$\Delta Q^* = \frac{b\,\Delta c}{b + e} \tag{8-25}$$

$$\frac{\Delta Q^*}{\Delta c} = \frac{b}{b + e} \tag{8-26}$$

Equation 8-25 tells us that the change in Q^* is equal to the parameter b times the change in supply divided by the sum of the parameters b and e. Equation 8-26 says that because $b/(b + e)$ is positive, when supply increases, the equilibrium quantity will also increase and when supply decreases, the equilibrium quantity will also decrease.

Numerical examples Let us start with the same demand and supply equations we used previously.

$$D = 40 \text{ bushels} - 2\frac{\text{bushels}}{\text{dollar}}P$$

$$S = -10 \text{ bushels} + 3\frac{\text{bushels}}{\text{dollar}}P$$

Suppose supply increases by 5 bushels (from -10 to -5 bushels). The effect on P^* is

$$\Delta P^* = \frac{-\Delta c}{b + e} \tag{8-22}$$

$$= \frac{-5 \text{ bushels}}{2 \text{ bushels/dollar} + 3 \text{ bushels/dollar}}$$

$$= \frac{-5 \text{ bushels}}{5 \text{ bushels/dollar}}$$

$$= -\$1$$

The effect on Q^* is

$$\Delta Q^* = \frac{b\,\Delta c}{b + e} \tag{8-25}$$

$$= \frac{(2 \text{ bushels/dollar})(5 \text{ bushels})}{2 \text{ bushels/dollar} + 3 \text{ bushels/dollar}}$$

$$= \frac{10 \text{ bushels}^2/\text{dollars}}{5 \text{ bushels/dollar}}$$

$$= 2 \text{ bushels}$$

The effect of the 5-bushel increase in supply is a $1 reduction in the equilibrium price and a 2-bushel expansion in the equilibrium quantity.

If supply decreased by 10 bushels, the results would be

$$\Delta P^* = +\$2$$
$$\Delta Q^* = -4 \text{ bushels}$$

Using equations 8-22 and 8-25, the student should prove for himself that these would be the results of the 10-bushel decrease in supply.[4]

Simultaneous changes in demand and supply

It is quite possible for both the demand and supply functions to change at the same time. Just as a change in *either* demand *or* supply will affect P^* and Q^*, so a change in *both* demand *and* supply will have effects on P^* and Q^*.

The effect on price Let us suppose demand changes by Δa and supply changes by Δc. The equilibrium price will change by ΔP^*, or, using equation 8-13,

$$P^* + \Delta P^* = \frac{(a + \Delta a) - (c + \Delta c)}{b + e}$$
$$= \frac{a + \Delta a - c - \Delta c}{b + e}$$

and subtracting equation 8-13

$$\Delta P^* = \frac{\Delta a - \Delta c}{b + e} \qquad (8\text{-}27)$$

The change in equilibrium price is equal to the change in demand minus the change in supply divided by the sum of the parameters b and e.

From this last equation we discover that when demand and supply move in opposite directions, i.e., demand increases while supply decreases or demand decreases while supply increases, we can determine whether P^* will rise or fall. For if demand increases and supply decreases:

- Δa is positive and Δc is negative.
- $\Delta a - (-\Delta c) = \Delta a + \Delta c$.
- $\Delta a + \Delta c$ is positive.
- $(\Delta a - \Delta c)/(b + e)$ and, therefore ΔP^*, is positive.
- P^* will rise.

And, likewise, if demand decreases while supply increases:

- Δa is negative, and Δc is positive.
- $-\Delta a - \Delta c$ is negative.
- $\Delta a - \Delta c$ and ΔP^* are negative.
- P^* will fall.

The results when demand and supply change in the same direction, i.e., both increase or both decrease, are somewhat more complicated. Suppose demand

[4]The effects of the change in c might have been determined by inserting the new values of c into equations 8-13 and 8-17 and solving for the new P^* and Q^*.

and supply both increase:

- Δa and Δc are both positive.
- ΔP^* is positive if $\Delta a > \Delta c$.
- ΔP^* is negative if $\Delta c > \Delta a$.
- ΔP^* is zero if $\Delta c = \Delta a$.

And if demand and supply both decrease:

- Δa and Δc are both negative.
- ΔP^* is positive if $\Delta c > \Delta a$.
- ΔP^* is negative if $\Delta a > \Delta c$.
- ΔP^* is zero if $\Delta a = \Delta c$.

The effect on quantity If demand changes by Δa and supply changes by Δc, Q^* changes by ΔQ^*. Using equation 8-17

$$Q^* + \Delta Q^* = \frac{b(c + \Delta c) + e(a + \Delta a)}{b + e}$$

$$= \frac{bc + b\,\Delta c + ea + e\,\Delta a}{b + e}$$

Subtracting equation 8-17 from this last equation gives

$$\Delta Q^* = \frac{b\,\Delta c + e\,\Delta a}{b + e} \tag{8-28}$$

The change in the equilibrium quantity is equal to the quantity b times the change in supply plus e times the change in demand divided by the sum of the parameters b and e.

From equation 8-28 we can learn that if both demand and supply increase, i.e., if both Δa and Δc are positive, ΔQ^* will be positive: the equilibrium quantity will increase; and if both demand and supply decrease (Δa and Δc are negative), ΔQ^* will be negative: the equilibrium quantity will decrease.

But if demand increases and supply decreases (or if demand decreases and supply increases), the effect on Q^* may be positive, negative, or zero. For when demand increases and supply decreases:

- Δa is positive, and Δc is negative.
- ΔQ^* will increase if $e\,\Delta a > b\,\Delta c$.
- ΔQ^* will decrease if $e\,\Delta a < b\,\Delta c$.
- ΔQ^* will be zero if $e\,\Delta a = b\,\Delta c$.

And when demand decreases and supply increases:

- Δa is negative, and Δc is positive.
- ΔQ^* will increase if $b\,\Delta c > e\,\Delta a$.
- ΔQ^* will decrease if $b\,\Delta c < e\,\Delta a$.
- ΔQ^* will be zero if $b\,\Delta c = e\,\Delta a$.

Numerical examples Imagine that initially the demand and supply functions are

$$D = 100 \text{ tons} - 4\frac{\text{tons}}{\text{dollar}}P$$

$$S = -30 \text{ tons} + 6\frac{\text{tons}}{\text{dollar}}P$$

and now the demand *increases* by 10 tons and the supply *increases* by 20 tons.

$$\Delta P^* = \frac{\Delta a - \Delta c}{b + e} \tag{8-27}$$

$$= \frac{10 \text{ tons} - 20 \text{ tons}}{4 \text{ tons/dollar} + 6 \text{ tons/dollar}}$$

$$= \frac{-10 \text{ tons}}{10 \text{ tons/dollar}}$$

$$= -\$1$$

And

$$\Delta Q^* = \frac{b\,\Delta c + e\,\Delta a}{b + e} \tag{8-28}$$

$$= \frac{(4 \text{ tons/dollar})(20 \text{ tons}) + (6 \text{ tons/dollar})(10 \text{ tons})}{4 \text{ tons/dollar} + 6 \text{ tons/dollar}}$$

$$= \frac{80 \text{ tons}^2\text{/dollar} + 60 \text{ tons}^2\text{/dollar}}{10 \text{ tons/dollar}}$$

$$= \frac{140 \text{ tons}^2\text{/dollar}}{10 \text{ tons/dollar}}$$

$$= 14 \text{ tons}$$

Suppose demand had *increased* by 20 tons and supply had *decreased* by 30 tons. Using formulas 8-27 and 8-28, the student should be able to find that the change in P^* is $+\$5$ and that there is no change in Q^*.[5]

Exercise 8-2

1 By definition:

a A change in demand is a change in the parameter ___________

b A change in supply is a change in the parameter ___________

2

a When demand increases, Δa is ___________

b When supply decreases, Δc is ___________

3 Show that:

a $\Delta P^* = \dfrac{\Delta a}{b + e}$

b $\Delta P^* = \dfrac{-\Delta c}{b + e}$

[5]The effects of simultaneous changes in demand and supply can also be computed by placing the new values of a and c in equations 8-13 and 8-17 and then solving for P^* and Q^*.

c $\Delta Q^* = \dfrac{e\,\Delta a}{b + e}$

d $\Delta Q^* = \dfrac{b\,\Delta c}{b + e}$

4 Explain, using the equations in question 3, why:
a An increase in demand increases both P^* and Q^*.
b A decrease in supply increases P^* and decreases Q^*.

5 Suppose that

$$D = 100 \text{ bales} - 20\frac{\text{bales}}{\text{dollar}}P$$

$$S = -40 \text{ bales} + 30\frac{\text{bales}}{\text{dollar}}P$$

What would be the effect on P^* and Q^* of:
a A 40-bale increase in demand?
b A 100-bale decrease in demand?
c A 20-bale increase in supply?
d A 60-bale decrease in supply?

6 Show that:

a $\Delta P^* = \dfrac{\Delta a - \Delta c}{b + e}$

b $\Delta Q^* = \dfrac{e\,\Delta a + b\,\Delta c}{b + e}$

7 Using the demand and supply functions in question 5, what are the effects on P^* and Q^* when:
a Demand increases by 20 bales and supply increases by 40 bales?
b Demand increases by 50 bales and supply decreases by 20 bales?
c Demand decreases by 60 bales and supply decreases by 10 bales?
d Demand decreases by 80 bales and supply increases by 25 bales?

8 When will:
a An increase in both demand supply raise P^*?
b A decrease in both demand and supply raise P^*?
c An increase in demand and a decrease in supply lower Q^*?
d A decrease in demand and an increase in supply lower Q^*?

9 Show that:
a An increase in demand and a decrease in supply must increase P^*.
b A decrease in both demand and supply must decrease Q^*.

10 Explain when:
a Changes in both demand and supply will not affect P^*.
b Changes in both demand and supply will not affect Q^*.

MARGINAL REVENUE AND PRICE ELASTICITY

The purpose of Chapter 9 is the extension of the analysis of demand and supply begun in the last chapter. To do this we must introduce two new *economic* concepts, marginal revenue and price elasticity. Marginal revenue, which we examine in the first section of the chapter, is the useful companion of the demand function, and we shall utilize this concept when we examine product markets in Chapters 12 and 13. In the second section we look at the price elasticity of demand and supply. The important relationship between marginal revenue and the price elasticity of demand is examined in the final section of the chapter.

As we extend our understanding of demand and supply, we introduce two new *mathematical* concepts which we shall use extensively in the remaining chapters, namely, *limit* and *derivative*. This chapter is one in which we develop microeconomic tools. It does not contain any economic models. The construction of models will be undertaken in Chapters 12 and 13 after we have fashioned the necessary tools in this and the next two chapters.

MARGINAL REVENUE

In Chapter 8 we saw that demand was a function relating the quantity demanded D of a commodity during some period of time to the price P of the commodity during the same period of time. We assumed that the demand function was linear and decreasing and could be written

$$D = a - bP \tag{9-1}$$

Having written a decreasing and linear demand function such as equation 9-1, we saw later that we could also express the price of the commodity as a function of the quantity demanded. For if

$$D = a - bP \tag{9-1}$$

then

$$D - a = -bP$$

$$\frac{D - a}{b} = -P$$

and, multiplying through by -1,

$$P = \frac{a - D}{b} \tag{9-2}$$

We shall find this form of the demand function useful in developing an equation for total revenue.

Total revenue

The total revenue R of an individual seller of a commodity is defined as equal to the price P at which he sells his product times the number of units of the product he is able to sell at this price. The number of units he can sell at any price depends upon the demand for his product and is equal to the quantity demanded D by buyers at that price. Therefore we may write the following definitional equation:

$$R \equiv P \cdot D \tag{9-3}$$

This total-revenue equation has three variables, R, P, and D. Using equation 9-2, we can reduce it to an equation in which only two variables, R and D, appear. Starting with equation 9-3, we substitute the term $(a - D)/b$ (from equation 9-2) for P and have

$$R = \frac{a - D}{b} D$$

Our total-revenue equation is

$$R = \frac{aD - D^2}{b} \tag{9-4}$$

or

$$R = \frac{1}{b}(aD - D^2) \tag{9-5}$$

The total-revenue equation has only two variables, R and D. It contains the same two parameters as the demand equation, a and b. It is important to observe that the variable D appears in the equation both to the first power and to the second power. Because the highest power to which a variable appears in this equation is the second, this is a second-degree equation (or an equation of the second degree). It is often also referred to as a quadratic equation, but we shall use the term second-degree equation.

Numerical example If the demand equation is

$$D = 40 \text{ cases} - 3\frac{\text{cases}}{\text{dollar}}P$$

the total-revenue equation for this commodity is

$$R = \frac{1}{3 \text{ cases/dollar}}[40 \text{ cases } (D - D^2)]$$

The value of parameter a from the demand equation is 40 cases, and the value of b is 3 cases/dollar.

In Table 9-1 we have shown D (in column 2) at various prices (column 1) when D = 40 cases − 3 (cases/dollar)(P). R at each P and D has been computed by multiplying P by D and is given in column 3. In column 4 we have shown the computation of R using equation 9-5.

We should observe two things in this table: (1) R can be found equally well by multiplying P times D or by using equation 9-5; and (2) as P decreases (and D increases), R increases at first, reaches a maximum (when $P = \$6\frac{2}{3}$ and $D = 20$), and then decreases to zero. Put the other way around, as P increases (and D decreases), R at first increases, reaches a maximum, and decreases thereafter.

Graph of total revenue We have plotted the total-revenue equation

$$R = \frac{1}{3 \text{ cases/dollar}}[40 \text{ cases } (D - D^2)]$$

TABLE 9-1

(1) P	(2) D, cases	(3) R	(4) $\frac{1}{b}(aD - D^2) = R$
$\$13\frac{1}{3}$	0	\$ 0	$\frac{1}{3}[40(0) - 0] = \$ 0$
13	1	13	$\frac{1}{3}[40(1) - 1] = 13$
12	4	48	$\frac{1}{3}[40(4) - 16] = 48$
11	7	77	$\frac{1}{3}]40(7) - 49] = 77$
10	10	100	$\frac{1}{3}[40(10) - 100] = 100$
9	13	117	$\frac{1}{3}[40(13) - 169] = 117$
8	16	128	$\frac{1}{3}[40(16) - 256] = 128$
7	19	133	$\frac{1}{3}[40(19) - 361] = 133$
$6\frac{2}{3}$	20	$133\frac{1}{3}$	$\frac{1}{3}[40(20) - 400] = 133\frac{1}{3}$
6	22	132	$\frac{1}{3}[40(22) - 484] = 132$
5	25	125	$\frac{1}{3}[40(25) - 625] = 125$
4	28	118	$\frac{1}{3}[40(28) - 784] = 118$
3	31	93	$\frac{1}{3}[40(31) - 961] = 93$
2	34	68	$\frac{1}{3}[40(34) - 1{,}156] = 68$
1	37	37	$\frac{1}{3}[40(37) - 1{,}369] = 37$
0	40	0	$\frac{1}{3}[40(40) - 1{,}600] = 0$

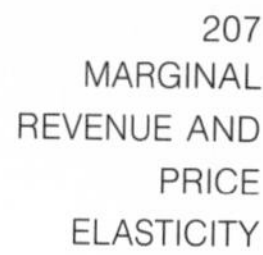

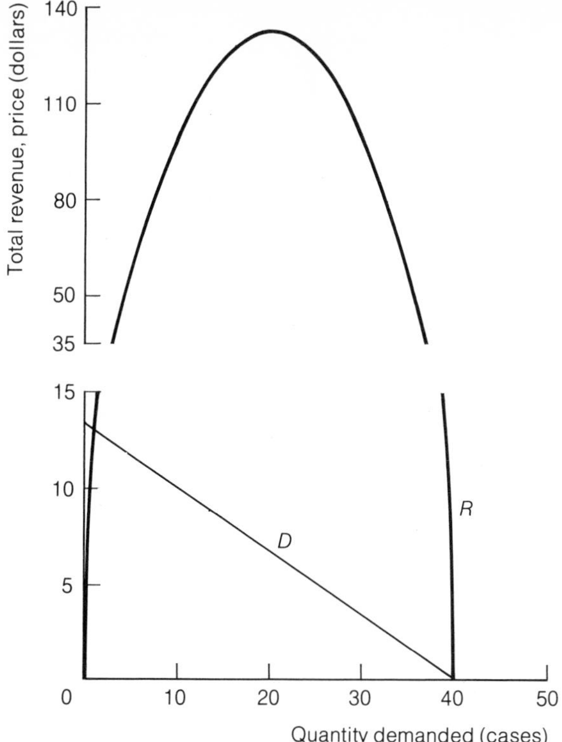

FIGURE 9-1

in Figure 9-1; i.e., we have plotted R when

$$R \equiv P \cdot D \tag{9-3}$$

and

$$P = \frac{40 \text{ cases} - D}{3 \text{ cases/dollar}}$$

For reference we have also plotted the demand function (the equation above), or $D = 40$ cases $- 3$ (cases/dollar)(P).

Again we observe that as D increases (because P decreases), R at first increases, reaches a maximum when D is 20 cases, and then decreases. Geometrically we can observe that:

- Up to 20 cases the total-revenue curve is positively sloped (because R increases as D increases).
- At 20 cases the total-revenue curve is flat and has a slope of zero.
- Past 20 cases the total-revenue curve is negatively sloped (because R decreases as D increases).

Marginal revenue

The ordinary definition of marginal revenue M is the change in the total revenue ΔR of a seller when he increases his sales of a product by a very small quantity.

In mathematical language,

$$M \equiv \frac{\Delta R}{\Delta D} \tag{9-6}$$

Marginal revenue is the change in total revenue divided by the change ΔD in the quantity demanded or sold.

A marginal-revenue function We have seen that when the demand function is decreasing and linear (equation 9-1), the total-revenue equation is

$$R = \frac{1}{b}(aD - D^2) \tag{9-5}$$

From this equation we can find an equation that tells us what marginal revenue will be. Using equation 9-5, when D changes by ΔD, R will change by ΔR.

$$R + \Delta R = \frac{1}{b}[a(D + \Delta D) - (D + \Delta D)^2]$$

$$= \frac{1}{b}(aD + a\,\Delta D - D^2 - 2D\,\Delta D - \Delta D^2)$$

If we subtract equation 9-5 from this last equation, we have

$$\Delta R = \frac{1}{b}(a\,\Delta D - 2D\,\Delta D - \Delta D^2)$$

Dividing through by ΔD, we find marginal revenue $\Delta R/\Delta D$ to be

$$\frac{\Delta R}{\Delta D} = \frac{1}{b}(a - 2D - \Delta D) \tag{9-7}$$

The change in total revenue per additional small amount sold is equal to 1 divided by the parameter b times the quantity the parameter a minus $2D$ minus the change in D.

A numerical example When the demand equation is $D = 40$ cases $- 3$ (cases/dollar)(P), the parameter a is 40 cases and b is 3 cases/dollar. If we wish to find the change in total revenue when the sellers sells *one additional unit* of his product, we use equation 9-7.

$$\frac{\Delta R}{\Delta D} = \frac{1}{3 \text{ cases/dollar}}(40 \text{ cases} - 2D - 1 \text{ case}) \tag{9-8}$$

Were the seller selling 10 cases to start (D), his marginal revenue would be

$$\frac{\Delta R}{\Delta D} = \frac{1}{3 \text{ cases/dollar}}[40 \text{ cases} - 2(10 \text{ cases}) - 1 \text{ case}]$$

$$= \frac{1}{3 \text{ cases/dollar}}(40 \text{ cases} - 20 \text{ cases} - 1 \text{ case})$$

$$= \frac{1}{3 \text{ cases/dollar}}(19 \text{ cases})$$

$$= \$6.33\tfrac{1}{3}$$

The change in total revenue when the seller increases his sales from 10 to 11 cases is $6.33⅓ per case.

We can also use equation 9-7 to find the change in total revenue *per one additional unit sold* when a seller increases his sales by more than one unit. Looking back to Table 9-1, we can see that if the seller lowers his price from \$12 to \$11, his sales will increase from 4 to 7 cases. This is an increase in sales of 3 cases. His total revenue will increase from \$48 to \$77, an increase of \$29 for the 3 cases. This is an increase of \$9.66⅔ *per case*. Using equation 9-7, we obtain the same marginal-revenue figure.

$$\frac{\Delta R}{\Delta D} = \frac{1}{3 \text{ cases/dollar}}[40 \text{ cases} - 2(4 \text{ cases}) - 3 \text{ cases}]$$

$$= \frac{1}{3 \text{ cases/dollar}}(40 \text{ cases} - 8 \text{ cases} - 3 \text{ cases})$$

$$= \frac{1}{3 \text{ cases/dollar}}(29 \text{ cases})$$

$$= \$9.66\tfrac{2}{3}$$

Exercise 9-1

1 Suppose

$$D = 100 \text{ cartons} - 20\frac{\text{cartons}}{\text{dollar}}P$$

Write the equation which expresses price as a function of the two parameters and quantity demanded. $P =$ ____________

2 Define:

a Total revenue: $R \equiv$ ____________

b Marginal revenue: $M =$ ____________

3 If $D = a - bP$, then:

a $R =$ ____________

b $\Delta R/\Delta D =$ ____________

4 Assume

$$D = 100 \text{ cartons} - 20\frac{\text{cartons}}{\text{dollar}}P$$

a The total-revenue function is $R =$ ____________

b The marginal-revenue function is $\Delta R/\Delta D =$ ____________

5 Using the equation and your answers to parts *a* and *b* in question 4:

a How much is P when $D = 80$ cartons? $P =$ \$____________

b How much is D when $P = \$2$? $D =$ ____________ cartons.

c How much is R when $D = 30$ cartons? $R =$ \$____________

d How much is R when $P = \$4$? $R =$ \$____________

e How much is $\Delta R/\Delta D$ if $D = 40$ cartons and $\Delta D = 1$? $\Delta R/\Delta D =$ \$ ____________

f How much is $\Delta R/\Delta D$ if $P = \$2$ and $\Delta D = 1$? $\Delta R/\Delta D =$ \$ ____________

6 Show that when $D = a - bP$:

a $R = \frac{1}{b}(aD - D^2)$

b $\frac{\Delta R}{\Delta D} = \frac{1}{b}(a - 2D - \Delta D)$

7 As P decreases and D increases, R at first (increases, decreases) __________, reaches a (maximum, minimum) __________, and then __________.

8 The total-revenue curve is at first (positive, negative) __________, reaches a slope of __________, and then becomes (positive, negative) __________.

The concept of a limit

If we look again at equation 9-7

$$\frac{\Delta R}{\Delta D} = \frac{1}{b}(a - 2D - \Delta D) \qquad (9\text{-}7)$$

we shall see that the smaller the change in D, the smaller the term ΔD on the right side of the equation, the *larger* the right side of the equation, and the larger the value of marginal revenue. As ΔD becomes smaller and smaller, i.e., as it approaches zero, the value of the right side of the equation and M become closer and closer to, i.e., approach, $(1/b)(a - 2D)$.

To see this happen, let us again suppose that $a = 40$ cases, $b = 3$ cases/dollar, and $D = 10$ cases. What happens to $\Delta R/\Delta D$, which is equal to $(1/b)(a - 2D - \Delta D)$, as we let ΔD become smaller and smaller? We can see in Table 9-2 that $\Delta R/\Delta D$ becomes larger and moves closer to \$6.66⅔, which is equal to $(1/b)(a - 2D)$.

What conclusions can we draw from this example of ΔD becoming smaller and smaller? As ΔD approaches zero, $\Delta R/\Delta D$ approaches some value beyond

TABLE 9-2

If ΔD is	$\frac{1}{b}(a - 2D - \Delta D)$ is	And $\frac{\Delta R}{\Delta D}$ is
1	$\frac{1}{3}(40 - 20 - 1) = \frac{1}{3}(19)$	\$6.3333
$\frac{1}{2}$	$\frac{1}{3}(40 - 20 - \frac{1}{2}) = \frac{1}{3}(19\frac{1}{2})$	6.5000
$\frac{1}{4}$	$\frac{1}{3}(40 - 20 - \frac{1}{4}) = \frac{1}{3}(19\frac{3}{4})$	6.5833
$\frac{1}{8}$	$\frac{1}{3}(40 - 20 - \frac{1}{8}) = \frac{1}{3}(19\frac{7}{8})$	6.6225
$\frac{1}{16}$	$\frac{1}{3}(40 - 20 - \frac{1}{16}) = \frac{1}{3}(19\frac{15}{16})$	6.64583
$\frac{1}{32}$	$\frac{1}{3}(40 - 20 - \frac{1}{32}) = \frac{1}{3}(19\frac{31}{32})$	6.65625
$\frac{1}{100}$	$\frac{1}{3}(40 - 20 - \frac{1}{100}) = \frac{1}{3}(19\frac{99}{100})$	6.6633
$\frac{1}{1,000}$	$\frac{1}{3}(40 - 20 - \frac{1}{1,000}) = \frac{1}{3}(19\frac{999}{1,000})$	6.66633
$\frac{1}{1,000,000}$	$\frac{1}{3}(40 - 20 - \frac{1}{1,000,000}) = \frac{1}{3}(19\frac{999,999}{1,000,000})$	6.66666633

which it will never go. The value that $\Delta R/\Delta D$ approaches as ΔD approaches zero is called the *limit* of $\Delta R/\Delta D$. We should observe that the limit of $\Delta R/\Delta D$ in the numerical example above is

$$\frac{1}{3 \text{ cases/dollar}}(40 \text{ cases} - 20 \text{ cases})$$

or \$6.66⅔. In more general terms, the limit of $\Delta R/\Delta D$ is $(1/b)(a - 2D)$.

The derivative

In mathematical language the limit which $\Delta R/\Delta D$ approaches as ΔD approaches zero is called the *derivative* of R with respect to D [or the derivative of the function, $R = f(D)$]. Instead of the symbol $\Delta R/\Delta D$ for the derivative, the symbol dR/dD is used. The replacement of Δ by d indicates that we are talking about the limit $\Delta R/\Delta D$ approaches as ΔD approaches zero. Mathematicians write

$$\frac{dR}{dD} = \text{limit of } \frac{\Delta R}{\Delta D} \text{ as } \Delta D \text{ approaches zero}$$

or, in mathematical shorthand,

$$\frac{dR}{dD} = \lim_{\Delta D \to 0} \frac{\Delta R}{\Delta D} \tag{9-9}$$

(where lim stands for limit and →0 means approaches zero).

We found the value $\Delta R/\Delta D$ and obtained equation 9-7 by:

- First finding the value of R when D was equal to $D + \Delta D$.
- Then finding the value of R when D was equal to D.
- Subtracting the latter from the former.
- And finally dividing by ΔD.

Because R is a function of D (equation 9-5), or

$$R = f(D)$$

in mathematical symbols we can say

$$\frac{dR}{dD} = \lim_{\Delta D \to 0} \frac{\Delta R}{\Delta D} = \lim_{\Delta D \to 0} \frac{f(D + \Delta D) - f(D)}{\Delta D} \tag{9-10}$$

This equation tells us *how* to find the derivative.

1 Find the value of R (which is a function of D) when D is equal to $D + \Delta D$.

2 Find the value of R when D is equal to D.

3 Subtract the value of R when $D = D$ from the value of R when $D = D + \Delta D$.

4 Divide the difference between the two values of R by ΔD.

5 Have the value of ΔD (wherever it appears on the right side of the equation) become so small that it can be treated *as if* it were zero.

The value obtained in this fashion is the derivative of R with respect to D, or the derivative of $R = f(D)$.

Illustration of the derivative-finding process To see how we found the derivative dR/dD to be $(1/b)(a - 2D)$ when $R = (1/b)(aD - D^2)$, we follow the steps listed in the section above.

1 We found the value of R when D was $D + \Delta D$ to be

$$R + \Delta R = \frac{1}{b}(aD + a\,\Delta D - D^2 - 2D\,\Delta D - \Delta D^2)$$

2 We know the value of R when D is equal to D to be

$$R = \frac{1}{b}(aD - D^2)$$

3 We subtracted the value of R when D was $D + \Delta D$ from the value of R when D was D and obtained

$$\Delta R = \frac{1}{b}(a\,\Delta D - 2D\,\Delta D - \Delta D^2)$$

4 We divided the equation above by ΔD to obtain

$$\frac{\Delta R}{\Delta D} = \frac{1}{b}(a - 2D - \Delta D)$$

5 We treated ΔD on the right side of the equation above as if it were zero and were left with

$$\frac{dR}{dD} = \frac{1}{b}(a - 2D) \tag{9-11}$$

which is the derivative of R with respect to D, or the limit which $\Delta R/\Delta D$ approaches as ΔD approaches zero.

Numerical example of finding the derivative To see how we found dR/dD to be

$$\frac{1}{3\text{ cases/dollars}}(40\text{ cases} - 20\text{ cases})$$

when

$$R = \frac{1}{3\text{ cases/dollars}}[40\text{ cases }(D - D^2)]$$

let us go through the five steps again.

1 When D was equal to $D + \Delta D$, R was equal to

$$\frac{1}{3\text{ cases/dollar}}[40\text{ cases }(D + \Delta D) - (D + \Delta D)^2]$$

2 When D was simply equal to D, R was equal to

$$\frac{1}{3\text{ cases/dollar}}[40\text{ cases }(D - D^2)]$$

3 Subtracting the value in step 1 from the value in step 2, we have

$$\frac{1}{3\text{ cases/dollar}}[40\text{ cases }(\Delta D - 2D\,\Delta D - \Delta D^2)]$$

4 Dividing through by ΔD:

$$\frac{1}{3 \text{ cases/dollar}}(40 \text{ cases} - 2D - \Delta D)$$

5 Treating ΔD as if it were zero:

$$\frac{1}{3 \text{ cases/dollars}}(40 \text{ cases} - 2D) = \frac{dR}{dD}$$

A simple technique for finding the derivative[1] If we compare equation 9-11 with equation 9-5, we discover a simple and quick method for finding dR/dD.

$$R = \frac{1}{b}(aD - D^2) = \frac{a}{b}D - \frac{1}{b}D^2 \qquad (9\text{-}5)$$

$$\frac{dR}{dD} = \frac{1}{b}(a - 2D) = \frac{a}{b} - \frac{2}{b}D \qquad (9\text{-}11)$$

We can find dR/dD without going through the five steps used above if we employ the following direct technique.

First, take each term on the right side of equation 9-5 separately. In each term:

- Multiply the *exponent* of D times the *coefficient* of D.
- Reduce the *exponent* of D by exactly 1.
- Multiply the product of the exponent of D and the coefficient of D by D with its exponent reduced by 1.

This will give us the derivative of each term.

If we do this for $(a/b)D$ in equation 9-5, we have:

- 1 (the exponent of D) times a/b (the coefficient of D), or 1 times a/b, which is equal to a/b.
- D (which is really D^1) when its exponent is reduced by 1 is D^0, and D^0 is equal to 1.
- Multiplying a/b by 1, we have a/b.

In this way we find the derivative of $(a/b)D$ to be a/b.

When we do this for the second term in equation 9-5, we have:

- 2 (the exponent of D) times $1/b$ (the coefficient of D^2) $= 2/b$.
- D^2 with its exponent reduced by 1 is D^1 or simply D.
- Multiplying $2/b$ by D gives us $(2/b)D$.

This gives us the derivative of the second term. The derivative of $(1/b)D^2$ is $(2/b)D$.

The second step is to add (taking account of any minus signs) the derivatives of each term obtained in the first step. Add a/b and $(2/b)D$, taking account of the minus sign that separated the two terms of which these are derivatives,

[1]The technique for finding a derivative described below can be employed to find the derivatives of polynomial functions commonly found in algebra, but it is not applicable to trigonometric or exponential functions.

to obtain

$$\frac{a}{b} - \frac{2}{b}D$$

or, simplifying,

$$\frac{1}{b}(a - 2D)$$

This is the value of dR/dD, and it is equal to the value we obtained by going through the five steps.

Generalization We can find the value of the derivative of a function such as

$$Y = f(X)$$

containing two variables by taking each term in the function separately and finding the derivative of each term. To find the derivative of a term multiply its exponent by its coefficient and reduce the exponent by 1. The algebraic sum of the derivatives of all the terms is equal to the derivative of the function.

Suppose, for example, that

$$Y = aX^2 + bX + c$$

and we wish to find dY/dX. To find the derivative of aX^2 we multiply the exponent (2) times the coefficient of X (a) and reduce the exponent by 1 (from 2 to 1) to obtain $2aX$. In the term bX, the exponent of X is 1. Multiplying 1 times b and reducing the exponent of X by 1, we have bX^0. Because the value of any number to the power of zero is equal to 1, bX^0 is b times 1, or simply b. The exponent of X in the third term is zero. Zero (the exponent) times c (the coefficient) is zero, and so the derivative of c is zero. When we sum the two derivatives that remain, we find that

$$\frac{dY}{dX} = 2aX + b$$

It is important to note two things: (1) The derivative of a second-degree equation is a first-degree equation. We may generalize and say that the derivative of an equation is an equation of one degree less and that the derivative of a term is a term which is one degree less. (2) The derivative of any constant term (such as c in the equation above) is zero.

A numerical example Let us go back to the total-revenue equation we used earlier

$$R = \frac{1}{3 \text{ cases/dollar}}[40 \text{ cases } (D - D^2)]$$

which, for the purpose of finding the derivative, can be written

$$R = \frac{40 \text{ cases}}{3 \text{ cases/dollar}}\left(D - \frac{1}{3 \text{ cases/dollar}}D^2\right)$$

We wish to find dR/dD, which is marginal revenue. To find the derivative of the first term, multiply the exponent of D, that is, 1, by the coefficient

$$\frac{40 \text{ cases}}{3 \text{ cases/dollar}}$$

and reduce the exponent of D by 1 to obtain

$$1 \times \frac{40 \text{ cases}}{3 \text{ cases/dollar}} D^0 \qquad \text{or} \qquad \frac{40 \text{ cases}}{3 \text{ cases/dollar}}$$

The derivative of the second term is 2 (the exponent of D^2) times 1/(3 cases/dollar) (the coefficient of D^2) times D^1 (D^2 with its exponent reduced by 1); or

$$2 \times \frac{1}{3 \text{ cases/dollar}} D^1$$

which is

$$\frac{2}{3 \text{ cases/dollar}} D$$

The algebraic sum of the two derivatives is

$$\frac{dR}{dD} = \frac{40 \text{ cases}}{3 \text{ cases/dollar}} - \frac{2}{3 \text{ cases/dollar}} D$$

or, more simply,

$$\frac{dR}{dD} = \frac{1}{3 \text{ cases/dollar}} (40 \text{ cases} - 2D)$$

Note that this is the same value for dR/dD we obtained by going through the five steps on pages 212–213.

The importance of the derivative The derivative is important because it has many uses in economic analysis. Not only are we interested in the derivative of the total revenue function, but later we shall need to know the derivatives of other economic functions. The derivatives will then be employed in developing a number of economic models.

It is fair to ask why we did not use the derivative in the macroeconomic analysis of earlier chapters. The answer is that all the functions we used in macroeconomics were first-degree (or linear) functions. When a function is of the first degree, for example,

$$Y = a + bX$$

there is no difference between the value of $\Delta Y/\Delta X$ and dY/dX. The derivative of the function above, using the technique we learned for finding the derivative, is equal to b. We saw many times in earlier chapters that $\Delta Y/\Delta X$ is also equal to b.

In short, we did not use derivatives *by that name* in macroeconomics because there was no need to use them as long as $\Delta Y/\Delta X$ and dY/dX were equal. When we employed a term such as $\Delta Y/\Delta X$ and the function was linear, we were really using a derivative but we did not call it by that name. It is only when we come to second- and third-degree equations that we need the derivative, because when equations of a degree greater than 1 are employed, $\Delta Y/\Delta X$ and dY/dX are *not* equal.

Four derivative-finding rules In future chapters we shall want to find the derivatives of many different terms and of many different functions. For finding these derivatives we need only four rules, which we shall apply again and again:

1 *The derivative of a constant is zero.* If

$$Y = k$$

where k is a constant, then

$$\frac{dY}{dX} = 0$$

For example, if $Y = 3$, then $dY/dX = 0$.

2 *The derivative of X^n is nX^{n-1}.* If

$$Y = X^n$$

$$\frac{dY}{dX} = nX^{n-1}$$

As examples:

- If $Y = X^3$, $dY/dX = 3X^2$.
- If $Y = X^2$, $dY/dX = 2X$.
- If $Y = X$, that is, $Y = X^1$, $dY/dX = X^0 = 1$.

3 *The derivative of kX^n is knX^{n-1}.* If

$$Y = kX^n$$

where k is a constant and k does not equal zero, then

$$\frac{dY}{dX} = knX^{n-1}$$

As examples:

- If $Y = 4X^3$, then $dY/dX = 4(3X^2) = 12X^2$.
- If $Y = 6X^2$, then $dY/dX = 6(2X^1) = 12X$.
- If $Y = 5X$, then $dY/dX = 5(1X^0) = 5$(since $X^0 = 1$).

4 *The derivative of a function whose terms are separated by plus or minus signs is the algebraic sum of the derivatives of the terms.* If

$$Y = 3 + X^2 + 4X^3$$

then

$$\frac{dY}{dX} = 0 + 2X + 12X^2$$
$$= 2X + 12X^2$$

If

$$Y = 5X + 6X^2$$

then

$$\frac{dY}{dX} = 5 + 12X$$

If

$$Y = 3 - 3X^2$$

then

$$\frac{dY}{dX} = 0 - 6X = -6X$$

If

$$Y = -2 + 4X - 5X^4$$

then

$$\frac{dY}{dX} = 0 + 4 - 20X^3$$
$$= 4 - 20X^3$$

Exercise 9-2

1 $\frac{\Delta R}{\Delta D} = \frac{1}{b}(a - 2D - \Delta D)$.

a As ΔD becomes smaller, $\Delta R/\Delta D$ becomes (larger, smaller) ____________

b As ΔD approaches zero, $\Delta R/\Delta D$ approaches a value equal to ____________

c The value which $\Delta R/\Delta D$ approaches as ΔD approaches zero is called the ____________ of $\Delta R/\Delta D$ or the ____________ of R with respect to D.

2 Suppose

$$\frac{\Delta R}{\Delta D} = \frac{1}{20 \text{ cartons/dollar}}(100 \text{ cartons} - 2D - \Delta D)$$

a The limit which $\Delta R/\Delta D$ approaches as ΔD approaches zero is equal to ____________

b The derivative of R with respect to D equals ____________

3 Complete the following definition of the derivative of R with respect to D:

dR/dD = the ____________ of $\Delta R/\Delta D$ as ____________ approaches ____________

4 Suppose C is a function of Y. To find dC/dY:

a Find the value of C when Y is equal to ____________

b Find the value of C when Y is equal to ____________

c Subtract ____________ from ____________

d Divide this difference by ____________

e Treat as zero ____________ where it appears on the right side of the equation.

5 Going through the five steps in question 4, find dC/dY for each of the following equations:

a $C = g + hY$
b $C = Z$
c $C = aY^3 - bY^2$
d $C = aY^2 + b$
e $C = aY^n$

6 Use the simple technique to find the derivative of Y with respect to $X(dY/dX)$ in each of the following equations:

a $Y = 3X^4$
b $Y = 30$
c $Y = -30 - 12X$
d $Y = 2X^3 - 15X^2$
e $Y = 4X^2 + 40$

7 If $C = a + bY$:

a $\Delta C/\Delta Y =$ ____________

b $dC/dY =$ ____________

c $\Delta C/\Delta Y$ and dC/dY are ____________

8 The derivative of a fourth-degree equation is a ____________ degree equation, and the derivative of a second-degree equation is a ________________

Marginal revenue as the derivative of the total-revenue function Instead of defining marginal revenue M as equal to $\Delta R/\Delta D$ we shall define marginal revenue as the derivative of the total-revenue function. Thus

$$M \equiv \frac{dR}{dD} \tag{9-12}$$

If our demand function is

$$D = a - bP \tag{9-1}$$

then, as we have seen, total revenue is

$$R = \frac{1}{b}(aD - D^2) \tag{9-5}$$

and

$$\frac{dR}{dD} = \frac{1}{b}(a - 2D) \tag{9-11}$$

In Figure 9-2 we have plotted the demand function, the total-revenue function, and the marginal-revenue function (assuming that $a = 40$ cases and $b = 3$ cases/dollar). From the plotting of these three functions we are able to observe the following relationships.

The degree of the marginal-revenue function The marginal-revenue function is an equation of the first degree. Looking back at equation 9-11,

$$\frac{dR}{dD} = \frac{a}{b} - \frac{2}{b}D \tag{9-11}$$

we see that the highest power to which any variable appears is 1. All first-degree (or linear) equations, when plotted, are straight lines. In short, when demand

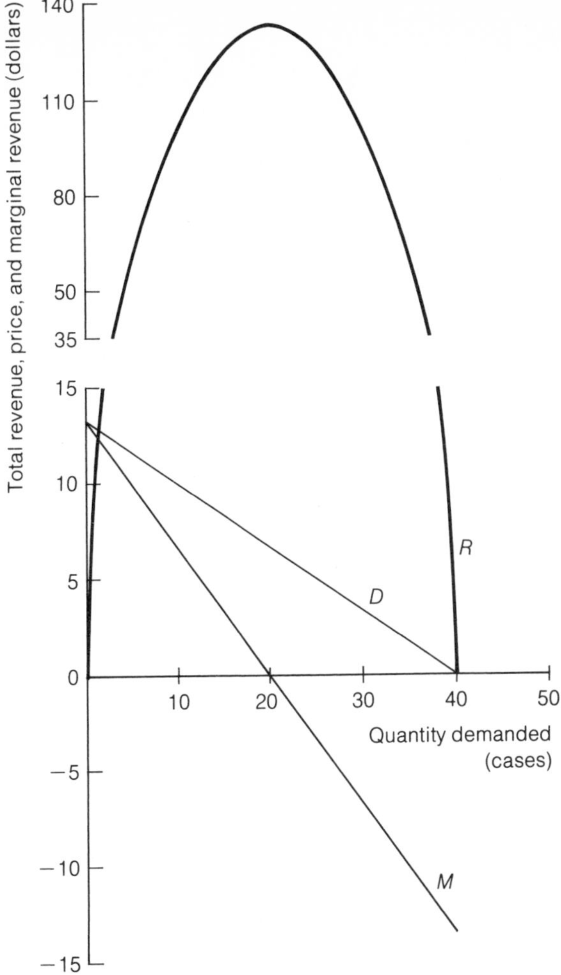

FIGURE 9-2

is a first-degree equation, the marginal-revenue equation is also of the first degree.

The sign of marginal revenue We can see on the graph that when *D* is small (less than 20 cases in this example), marginal revenue is positive and when *D* is larger (more than 20 cases), marginal revenue is a negative quantity. We can also see that there is a *D* (here 20 cases) at which marginal revenue is equal to zero.

To find the *D* at which *M* is equal to zero, let us allow dR/dD in equation 9-11 to be zero; and solve for *D*.

$$\frac{dR}{dD} = \frac{a}{b} - \frac{2}{b}D \qquad (9\text{-}11)$$

$$0 = \frac{a}{b} - \frac{2}{b}D$$

$$\frac{2}{b}D = \frac{a}{b}$$

Multiplying through by b,

$$2D = a$$
$$D = \tfrac{1}{2}a$$

The D at which marginal revenue is zero is equal to one-half the value of the parameter a. The parameter a, you will recall, is the quantity that would be demanded if the price of the commodity were zero. Therefore marginal revenue is zero when D is one-half the quantity that would be demanded if the price were zero. In our example, a is 40 cases; and marginal revenue is therefore zero when D is 20 cases.

Using another form of equation 9-11,

$$\frac{dR}{dD} = \frac{1}{b}(a - 2D) \qquad (9\text{-}11)$$

we can see that:

- If D is greater than $\tfrac{1}{2}a$, $2D$ is greater than a, $a - 2D$ is negative, and $(1/b)(a - 2D)$ and dR/dD are therefore negative.
- If D is less than $\tfrac{1}{2}a$, $2D$ is less than a, $a - 2D$ is positive, and $(1/b)(a - 2D)$ and dR/dD are therefore positive.

Marginal revenue and price At any D (with one exception) marginal revenue is less than the price at which the commodity sells. The only exception to this relationship is where D is equal to zero. For if

$$\frac{dR}{dD} = \frac{a}{b} - \frac{2}{b}D \qquad (9\text{-}11)$$

and

$$P = \frac{a - D}{b} \qquad (9\text{-}2)$$

we can find the D at which M and P are equal by letting the equations for these two variables be equal and solving for D.

$$\frac{dR}{dD} = P$$

$$\frac{a}{b} - \frac{2}{b}D = \frac{a - D}{b}$$

Multiplying through by b,

$$a - 2D = a - D$$
$$a - a = D$$
$$D = 0$$

This tells that only when D is zero are marginal revenue and P equal.

But if D is greater than zero, M is less than P. To see that this is true, we start again with equation 9-11.

$$\frac{dR}{dD} = \frac{a}{b} - \frac{2}{b}D \qquad (9\text{-}11)$$

For D we substitute equation 9-1 ($D = a - bP$).

$$\frac{dR}{dD} = \frac{a}{b} - \frac{2}{b}(a - bP)$$

$$= \frac{a}{b} - 2\frac{a}{b} + 2P$$

$$= -\frac{a}{b} + 2P \qquad (9\text{-}13)$$

The term a/b is nothing other than the price at which D is zero. We can show that a/b is the price at which D is zero in the following way. Starting with the demand function

$$D = a - bP \qquad (9\text{-}1)$$

set D equal to zero to obtain

$$0 = a - bP$$
$$-a = -bP$$
$$bP = a$$

$$P_0 = \frac{a}{b}$$

P_0, the price at which D is zero, is equal to the ratio of a to b.

Now if D is *greater than* zero, the price of the commodity must be *less than* a/b. This follows from the law of demand: to increase D, P must decrease. Thus if D is any quantity greater than zero, P must be less than a/b, the price at which D is zero. Going back now to equation 9-13,

$$\frac{dR}{dD} = -\frac{a}{b} + 2P \qquad (9\text{-}13)$$

if D is greater than zero:

- P is less than a/b.
- Or a/b is greater than P.
- The expression $-a/b + 2P$ is less than P.
- dR/dD is less than P.

In the numerical example in which a is 40 cases and b is 3 cases/dollar, the P at which D is zero is

$$\frac{40 \text{ cases}}{3 \text{ cases/dollar}}$$

or \$13.33⅓. Suppose P is \$10. In equation 9-13, $2P$ is \$20 and a/b is \$13.33⅓. M is therefore −\$13.33⅓ + \$20, or \$6.66⅔. This \$6.66⅔ marginal-revenue figure is less than the \$10 price.

Observe that if P were \$13.33⅓, the P at which D is zero, then

$$\frac{dR}{dD} = \frac{a}{b} + 2P \qquad (9\text{-}13)$$

$$= -\$13.33\tfrac{1}{3} + 2(\$13.33\tfrac{1}{3})$$

$$= -\$13.33\tfrac{1}{3} + \$26.66\tfrac{2}{3}$$

$$= \$13.33\tfrac{1}{3}$$

Where D is zero and only where D is zero are P and M equal.

Marginal revenue and total revenue We may observe in Figure 9-2 that where the total-revenue curve is positive (slopes up from left to right), marginal revenue is positive and where the total-revenue curve is negative (slopes downward), marginal revenue is negative. We should also see that where total revenue is a *maximum* (at 20 cases and a price of \$6.66⅔), marginal revenue is zero.

The reason for this relationship is fairly simple. Marginal revenue, as we have defined it, is the change in R divided by the change in D (as the change in D approaches zero). If the change in D is positive and R increases, then the ratio of the change in R to the change in D must also be positive: marginal revenue is positive. But if R decreases as D increases, the change in R is negative while the change in D is positive; and the ratio of the change in R to the change in D, marginal revenue, must be negative.

Where total revenue is a maximum, a *very* small change in D does not affect R: the change in R is zero. Thus the change in R divided by the change in D (where ΔD is positive *or* negative) is equal to zero because zero divided by any number is equal to zero.

The observation that M is zero where R is a maximum gives us a very powerful tool not only for finding where total revenue is a maximum but (later) for finding where the value of any other economic variable is a maximum. To find the maximum R we need only to know where M or dR/dD is equal to zero. If the marginal-revenue function is

$$\frac{dR}{dD} = \frac{1}{b}(a - 2D) \tag{9-11}$$

we may substitute zero for dR/dD to find the D at which R is a maximum.

$$0 = \frac{1}{b}(a - 2D)$$

$$-\frac{a}{b} = -\frac{2}{b}D$$

$$\frac{2}{b}D = \frac{a}{b}$$

$$2D = a$$

$$D = \tfrac{1}{2}a$$

This is exactly the same result we obtained earlier when we determined the D at which M was zero. But now, finding the D at which M is zero enables us to find the D at which R is a maximum.

Using the numerical example in which

$$\frac{dR}{dD} = \frac{1}{3\text{ cases/dollar}}(40\text{ cases} - 2D)$$

and substituting zero for dR/dD, we find

$$0 = \frac{1}{3\text{ cases/dollar}}(40\text{ cases} - 2D)$$

$$-13\tfrac{1}{3}\text{ cases}^2\text{/dollar} = \frac{2}{3\text{ cases/dollar}}D$$

$$D = 20\text{ cases}$$

What we have done is determined when R is a maximum by finding where dR/dD is equal to zero. Having found the D at which R is a maximum, we can find the maximum value of R by substituting the value of D when R is a maximum into the total-revenue equation. Our total-revenue function is

$$R = \frac{1}{b}(aD - D^2) \tag{9-5}$$

R is a maximum, we learned, when D is $\frac{1}{2}a$. Substituting $\frac{1}{2}a$ for D in equation 9-5, the maximum value of R is

$$\begin{aligned} R &= \frac{1}{b}a\left[\frac{a}{2} - \left(\frac{a}{2}\right)^2\right] \\ &= \frac{1}{b}\left(\frac{a^2}{2} - \frac{a^2}{4}\right) \\ &= \frac{1}{b}\left(\frac{a^2}{2} - \frac{1}{2}\frac{a^2}{2}\right) \\ &= \frac{1}{b}\frac{a^2}{2}(1 - \tfrac{1}{2}) \\ &= \frac{a^2}{2b}\frac{1}{2} \\ &= \frac{a^2}{4b} \end{aligned}$$

In our numerical example, the maximum value of R is

$$\begin{aligned} R &= \frac{(40 \text{ cases})^2}{4(3 \text{ cases/dollar})} \\ &= \frac{1{,}600 \text{ cases}}{12 \text{ cases/dollar}} \\ &= \$133.33\tfrac{1}{3} \end{aligned}$$

The P at which R is a maximum is found by substituting $\frac{1}{2}a$ for D in equation 9-2

$$P = \frac{a - D}{b} \tag{9-2}$$

$$\begin{aligned} &= \frac{a - a/2}{b} \\ &= \frac{a/2}{b} \\ &= \frac{a}{2b} \end{aligned}$$

The P at which R is a maximum is equal to the parameter a divided by 2 times the parameter b. In our example, the P at which R is a maximum is

$$\begin{aligned} P &= \frac{40 \text{ cases}}{2(3 \text{ cases/dollar})} \\ &= \$6.66\tfrac{2}{3} \end{aligned}$$

We should observe in Table 9-1 that when P is $\$6.66\frac{2}{3}$, D is 20 cases and R is $\$133.33\frac{1}{3}$. This line in the table shows the P and D at which R is a maximum and the maximum value of R.

Before concluding this section on the relation of marginal revenue to total revenue we should note for those who like geometry that the slope of the R curve is equal to M. The slope of the R curve at any point on that curve is equal to the slope of a tangent drawn through that point. The slope of the tangent is equal to the vertical displacement (the change in R) divided by the horizontal displacement (the change in D). If we are dealing with a point on the curve, the changes in R and D are very small, and so the slope of the curve is equal to dR/dD, which, as we know, is marginal revenue. Marginal revenue at any D is equal to the slope of the total-revenue curve at that D.

Exercise 9-3

1 Instead of defining marginal revenue as $\Delta R/\Delta D$, we define marginal revenue as the limit $\Delta R/\Delta D$ approaches as ΔD approaches zero. Marginal revenue:

a In symbols is equal to __________

b Is the derivative of the __________ function.

2 If $D = a - bP$, $R = (1/b)(aD - D^2)$, and $dR/dD =$ __________

a The marginal-revenue function is a function of the __________ degree.

b When graphed, marginal revenue is a __________

c Marginal revenue is equal to zero when D is equal to __________

d When D is:

(1) Greater than __________, marginal revenue is __________

(2) Less than __________, marginal revenue is __________

3 Assuming $D = a - bP$, show that:

a $D = \frac{1}{2}a$ when dR/dD is zero.

b When P and dR/dD are equal, D is zero.

c When D is greater than zero, dR/dD is less than P.

4 Suppose

$$D = 100 \text{ cartons} - 20 \frac{\text{cartons}}{\text{dollar}} P$$

a $dR/dD =$ __________

b D is zero when $P =$ \$__________

c P is zero when $D =$ __________ cartons.

d R is a maximum when $dR/dD =$ \$__________

e dR/dD is zero when $D =$ __________ cartons and $P =$ \$__________

5 The slope of the total-revenue curve at any D is equal to __________ at that D.

a Where R increases as D increases, dR/dD is __________

b Where R decreases as D increases, dR/dD is __________

c Where R is a maximum, dR/dD is __________

6 When:

a $D = 0$, P __________ dR/dD

b $D > 0$, P __________ dR/dD

7 Assume

$$D = 80 \text{ tons} - 10\frac{\text{tons}}{\text{dollar}}P$$

a dR/dD is positive when D is __________

b dR/dD is negative when D is __________

c dR/dD is zero when D is __________

PRICE ELASTICITY

In microeconomic analysis (and in macroeconomic analysis, too) economists are often concerned with the relationship between the *relative* (or percentage) changes in the values of two variables that are functionally related to each other. If Y is a function of X,

$$Y = f(X)$$

the ratio of the relative (percentage) change in Y (when X changes) to the relative change in X is defined as the elasticity of Y with respect to X, or

Elasticity of Y with respect to X

$$= \frac{\text{relative change in } Y}{\text{relative change in } X}$$

$$= \frac{\text{percentage change in } Y}{\text{percentage change in } X}$$

Of particular importance in microeconomics are the price elasticity of demand and the price elasticity of supply. In this section we first examine the price elasticity of demand in detail and then briefly examine the price elasticity of supply.

The price elasticity of demand

The price elasticity of demand E_d—or, for simplicity, the elasticity of demand—is usually defined at the ratio of the relative change in quantity demanded (when price changes) to the relative change in price. The relative (or percentage) change in quantity demand is the change in quantity demanded divided by the original quantity demanded, or $\Delta D/D$. Similarly, the relative (or percentage) change in price is $\Delta P/P$. The usual definition of the elasticity of demand is therefore

$$E_d = \frac{\Delta D/D}{\Delta P/P} \qquad (9\text{-}14)$$

Equation 9-14 can be rewritten in the more useful forms

$$E_d = \frac{\Delta D}{D}\frac{P}{\Delta P}$$

and

$$E_d = \frac{\Delta D}{\Delta P}\frac{P}{D}$$

If we now let the change in P approach zero, we may redefine the price elasticity of demand as the limit which

$$\frac{\Delta D}{\Delta P}\frac{P}{D}$$

approaches as ΔP approaches zero, or

$$E_d = \lim_{\Delta P \to 0} \frac{\Delta D}{\Delta P}\frac{P}{D} = \frac{dD}{dP}\frac{P}{D} \tag{9-15}$$

Degrees of elasticity This last form of the elasticity-of-demand equation tells us that the elasticity of demand depends upon two factors. If we have a demand equation in which D is a function of P $[D = f(P)]$, then dD/dP is the derivative of D with respect to P. The first factor, therefore, in equation 9-15 is the derivative of quantity demanded with respect to price. The second factor is the ratio of P to D, or the ratio of the price to the quantity demanded at which we wish to know the elasticity of demand.

If our demand equation were

$$D = a - bP \tag{9-1}$$

the derivative of D with respect to P would be equal to $-b$. To find E_d at any price we would find D at that price from equation 9-1 and multiply $-b$ times the ratio of the P to D at that price. For example, if

$$D = 40 \text{ cases} - 3\frac{\text{cases}}{\text{dollar}}P$$

$$\frac{dD}{dP} = -3\frac{\text{cases}}{\text{dollar}}$$

Wishing to know the elasticity of demand when price is \$5, we find that at this price

$$D = 40 \text{ cases} - 3\frac{\text{cases}}{\text{dollar}}(\$5)$$

$$= 25 \text{ cases}$$

The elasticity of demand at \$5 is

$$E_d = \left(-3\frac{\text{cases}}{\text{dollar}}\right)\frac{\$5}{25 \text{ cases}}$$

$$= -\tfrac{3}{5}$$

The value we obtain for E_d we call the *coefficient* of the elasticity of demand. In the example above, $-\tfrac{3}{5}$ is the coefficient.

To take another price. Suppose P is \$10. D would be 10 cases, and E_d would be

$$E_d = \left(-3\frac{\text{cases}}{\text{dollar}}\right)\frac{\$10}{10 \text{ cases}}$$

$$= -3$$

Still another example. If P were $\$6.66\frac{2}{3}$, D would be 20 cases. E_d would be

$$E_d = \left(-3\,\frac{\text{cases}}{\text{dollar}}\right)\frac{\$6.66\frac{2}{3}}{20\text{ cases}}$$
$$= -1$$

From these three numerical examples we discover four things: (1) The sign of the coefficient of the elasticity of demand is negative. This negative coefficient merely reflects the inverse relation we assume to exist between price and quantity demanded. Because this coefficient is always negative when the relation between price and quantity demand is inverse, we shall consider only the absolute value of the coefficient; i.e., we shall ignore its negative value. (2) The coefficient is a pure number. It is not cases or dollars or any other physical or monetary unit. (3) The coefficient may be greater than 1 (the second example), less than 1 (the first example), or equal to 1 (the third example). Let us look at each of these three possible values of E_d separately.

1 If E_d is greater than unity, demand is said to be *elastic*. Because

$$E_d = \frac{dD/D}{dP/P}$$

a coefficient larger than 1 means the relative change dD/D in quantity demanded is larger than the relative change dP/P in price. At the \$10 price in the examples above, demand is elastic because $E_d = 3$.

2 When E_d is less than unity, demand is defined as *inelastic*. The relative change in D is smaller than the relative change in P. When price was \$5 in the examples above, demand was inelastic because E_d was $\frac{3}{5}$.

3 Demand is *unitary elastic* when E_d is equal to unity; and the relative changes in D and in P are equal. Demand was unitary elastic at a price of $\$6.66\frac{2}{3}$ in the numerical examples above.

Finally (4) we see that with the *same* demand function, demand is elastic at some prices, inelastic at other prices, and unitary elastic at still another price. It would appear that demand is inelastic at the lower prices, elastic at the higher prices, and unitary elastic at a price in between. Where

$$D = 40\text{ cases} - 3\,\frac{\text{cases}}{\text{dollar}}\,P$$

demand is elastic at prices above $\$6.66\frac{2}{3}$, inelastic at prices below $\$6.66\frac{2}{3}$, and unitary elastic at the price of $\$6.66\frac{2}{3}$. We shall return to this topic later in the chapter.

Two special cases In our analysis we have assumed D to be a decreasing function of P, but the law of demand has two exceptions that require our attention.

Perfectly inelastic demand The first case is the one in which D does not change as P changes. Geometrically such a demand function would be a vertical line like that in Figure 9-3. Mathematically the demand function would be

$$D = k$$

where k is a constant number (of physical units of the commodity). For example,

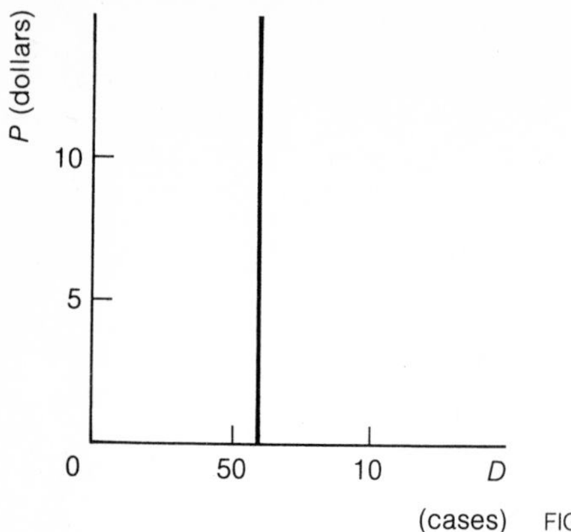

FIGURE 9-3

we might have

$$D = 60 \text{ cases}$$

This equation tells us that the quantity demanded is a fixed amount and that changes in the price of the commodity do not alter the quantity demanded.

When D does not change as P changes, E_d is equal to zero. Applying equation 9-15,

$$E_d = \frac{dD}{dP}\frac{P}{D} \tag{9-15}$$

and recalling that the derivative of any constant is equal to zero, when we substitute zero for dD/dP, the coefficient of the elasticity of demand turns out to be equal to zero. Because zero is less than unity, demand is inelastic; and because zero is the smallest absolute value a number can have, this kind of demand function is called *perfectly inelastic demand.* It should be noted that E_d is zero at all prices and does not vary with the price.

Perfectly elastic demand A demand function which, when plotted, looks like the curve in Figure 9-4 is the second special case. This horizontal demand curve

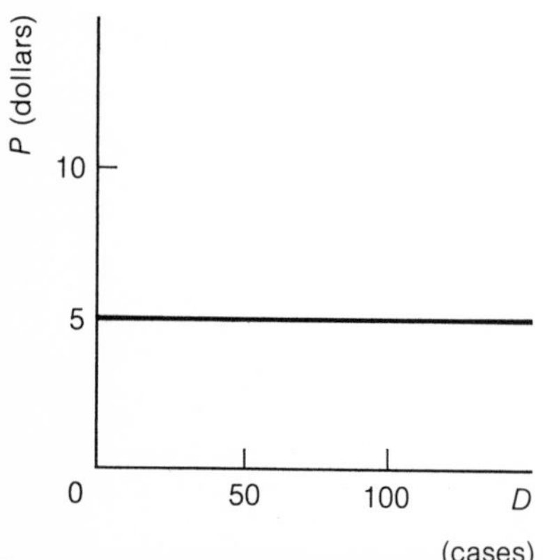

FIGURE 9-4

says that quantity demanded will change without any change in price taking place. Mathematically we can express this function as

$$P = K$$

where K is a constant number (of dollars per unit). As an example of such a demand function we might have

$$P = \$5$$

This equation tells us that P and D are *not* inversely related to each other, that P is constant, and that D may increase without P falling and decrease without P rising.

Employing the formula for the elasticity of demand

$$E_d = \frac{\Delta D/D}{\Delta P/P} \qquad (9\text{-}14)$$

to measure the elasticity of demand, we find the denominator, $\Delta P/P$, to be zero: no change in P is required to bring about a change in D. Mathematically, division by zero is not possible. We can say, however, that E_d becomes exceedingly or indefinitely great. E_d, in short, has no finite limit; or E_d approaches *infinity* (an indefinite number which is indefinitely larger than all ordinary numbers).

Because infinity is greater than 1, this kind of demand function is elastic; and because infinity is the largest number greater than 1 we can imagine, we call this kind of demand function *perfectly* (or infinitely) *elastic*. It should be noted that demand is perfectly elastic at every D along the demand curve. We shall have more to say about perfectly elastic demand later in this chapter, and we shall employ a perfectly elastic demand function in Chapter 13.

The price elasticity of supply

Much of what we have said about the price elasticity of demand can be applied to the price elasticity of supply—or, for short, the elasticity of supply—if we substitute "supply" for "demand," "quantity supplied" for "quantity demanded," and "relative change in quantity supplied" for "relative change in quantity demanded."

Tentatively we may define the elasticity of supply E_s as the ratio of the relative change in quantity supplied $\Delta S/S$ to the relative change in price $\Delta P/P$, or

$$E_s = \frac{\Delta S/S}{\Delta P/P} \qquad (9\text{-}16)$$

This equation may be rewritten in the more convenient form

$$E_s = \frac{\Delta S}{S}\frac{P}{\Delta P}$$

and so

$$E_s = \frac{\Delta S}{\Delta P}\frac{P}{S}$$

Being concerned only with the elasticity of supply when the change in price is very small, we may redefine E_s as the limit which

$$\frac{\Delta S}{\Delta P}\frac{P}{S}$$

approaches as the change in price approaches zero. In mathematical language

$$E_s = \lim_{\Delta P \to 0} \frac{\Delta S}{\Delta P}\frac{P}{S} = \frac{dS}{dP}\frac{P}{S} \qquad (9\text{-}17)$$

Like the elasticity of demand, the coefficient of the elasticity of supply may be greater than, less than, or equal to 1. Unlike the elasticity of demand, the coefficient of the elasticity of supply is positive and reflects the assumption that the relation between price and quantity supplied is a direct one.

- If E_s is greater than 1, supply is *elastic;* and the relative change dS/S in quantity supplied is greater than the relative change dP/P in price.
- If E_s is less than 1, supply is inelastic; and the relative change in quantity supplied is less than the relative change in price.
- If E_s is equal to 1, supply is *unitary elastic;* and the relative changes in price and quantity supplied are equal.

If the supply function is linear and increasing and takes the form

$$S = c + eP$$

we recognize, applying the technique for finding the derivative of a function we learned earlier in the chapter, that dS/dP is equal to e. Using equation 9-17,

$$E_s = \frac{dS}{dP}\frac{P}{S} \qquad (9\text{-}17)$$

we can see that the elasticity of supply is equal to the derivative of the supply function times the ratio of the price (at which we wish to know elasticity) to the quantity supplied at that price.[2]

If the supply function were

$$S = -10 \text{ cases} + 4\frac{\text{cases}}{\text{dollar}}P$$

the derivation of the supply function would be

$$\frac{dS}{dP} = 4\frac{\text{cases}}{\text{dollar}}$$

If we wish to find the coefficient of the elasticity of supply, i.e., the value of E_s, when the price is $5, using the supply function above shows that the quantity

[2]The curious student may be interested in the relation between the value of the parameter c in the supply function and the magnitude of E_s. If

$$E_s = \frac{dS}{dP}\frac{P}{S}$$

(equation 9-17), we may substitute e for dS/dP and $c + eP$ (from the equation for the supply function) for S to obtain

$$E_s = \frac{eP}{c + eP}$$

Using this equation, we can see that if $c = 0$, $E_s = 1$ (since the numerator and denominator are equal); if $c > 0$, E_s is <1 (since the denominator is greater than the numerator); and if $c < 0$, $E_s > 1$ (since the denominator is less than the numerator).

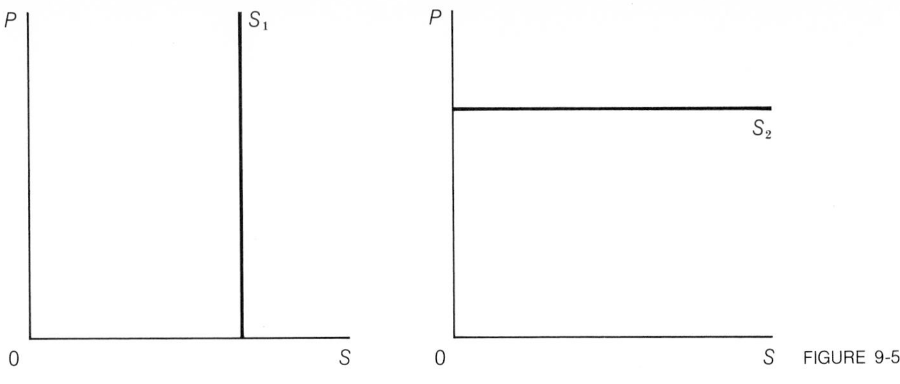

FIGURE 9-5

supplied is 10 cases. The elasticity of supply is therefore

$$E_s = 4\frac{\text{cases}}{\text{dollar}}\frac{\$5}{10\text{ cases}}$$
$$= 2$$

Note again that E_s is positive and a pure number. In this example supply is elastic at $5 because E_s is greater than 1.

Again like demand, supply may be perfectly inelastic (when $E_s = 0$) or perfectly elastic (when E_s becomes indefinitely large as dP/P approaches zero). In Figure 9-5, S_1 is a perfectly inelastic supply curve. When supply is perfectly inelastic, $S = k$ (where k is a fixed quantity of physical units of the commodity). If supply is perfectly elastic, the supply function is $P = K$ (where K is a fixed price). Such a perfectly elastic supply function is curve S_2 in Figure 9-5.

Our examination of the elasticity of supply has been intentionally brief because the greater part of the analysis of the price elasticity of demand applies to the analysis of the price elasticity of supply and because in this and the next few chapters we are more interested in demand than in supply.

Exercise 9-4

1 Define the price elasticity of demand:

a In words: ______

b In symbols: ______

2 If $E_d = (dD/D)/(dP/P)$, it also equals ______

3 If

$$D = 100\text{ cartons} - 20\frac{\text{cartons}}{\text{dollar}}P$$

a $\frac{dD}{dP} =$ ______

b $E_d =$ ______

c When D is equal to:

(1) 50 cartons, E_d = ____________

(2) 60 cartons, E_d = ____________

(3) 40 cartons, E_d = ____________

4 The sign of E_d is ____________, and E_d is a ____________ number.

5 When:

a E_d is greater than 1, demand is said to be ____________.

b E_d is less than 1, demand is said to be ____________

c E_d is equal to 1, demand is said to be ____________

6 Suppose demand is perfectly inelastic.

a The demand function may be written as D = ____________

b The demand curve is ____________ line.

c E_d = ____________

7 When demand is perfectly elastic:

a The demand function may be written as P = ____________

b The demand curve is ____________ line.

c E_d = ____

8 E_s = ____________ / ____________ or ____________ · ____________

a When supply is:

(1) Elastic, E_s is ____________

(2) Inelastic, E_s is ____________

(3) Unitary elastic, E_s is ____________

b E_s is (positive, negative) ____________ and a ____________ number.

c When supply is:

(1) Perfectly inelastic, E_s = ____________ and S = ____________

(2) Perfectly elastic, E_s = ____________ and P = ____________

9 Assume

$$S = -70 \text{ cartons} + 30 \frac{\text{cartons}}{\text{dollar}} P$$

a dS/dP = ____________

b E_s = ____________

c When $P = \$10$, E_s = ____________

MARGINAL REVENUE AND THE PRICE ELASTICITY OF DEMAND

In the first section we found that marginal revenue is the derivative of the total-revenue function, or

$$M \equiv \frac{dR}{dD} \tag{9-12}$$

In the second we found that the elasticity of demand is equal to the ratio of the relative change in quantity demanded to the relative change in price (as the change in price approaches zero) and

$$E_d = \frac{dD}{dP}\frac{P}{D} \qquad (9\text{-}15)$$

Now we wish to find the relationship that exists between marginal revenue and the elasticity of demand.

The relation of marginal revenue to the elasticity of demand

The relation between marginal revenue and the price elasticity of demand is expressed by

$$M = P\left(1 - \frac{1}{E_d}\right) \qquad (9\text{-}18)$$

which tells us that marginal revenue is equal to the price at which the commodity sells times the quantity 1 minus the reciprocal of the coefficient of the price elasticity of demand at that price. This equation has a number of useful applications, which we shall examine a little later. First, however, we need to demonstrate that M does, in fact, equal $P(1 - 1/E_d)$.

The derivative of total revenue To prove that equation 9-18 is really an equation we must return to equation 9-3, which defines total revenue as

$$R = P \cdot D \qquad (9\text{-}3)$$

to find another way of expressing the derivative of the total-revenue function. We shall again follow the five steps we employed earlier for finding the derivative of a function. We know that if D changes by ΔD, the change in D was due to a change P equal to ΔP and that as a result R will change by ΔR. Therefore, applying equation 9-3, we write

$$R + \Delta R = (P + \Delta P)(D + \Delta D)$$

Since P and D are inversely related and D becomes larger only when P becomes smaller, we can rewrite this last equation as

$$R + \Delta R = (P - \Delta P)(D + \Delta D)$$

and multiply the two parts of the right side of the equation to obtain

$$R + \Delta R = PD + P\,\Delta D - \Delta P\,D - \Delta P\,\Delta D \qquad (19\text{-}19)$$

The second step is to find the value of R when D is equal to D. This is given by equation 9-3: $R = P \cdot D$. Subtracting equation 9-3 from equation 9-19 is the third step.

$$\Delta R = P\,\Delta D - \Delta P\,D - \Delta P\,\Delta D$$

The fourth step is to divide both sides of the equation by ΔD.

$$\frac{\Delta R}{\Delta D} = P\frac{\Delta D}{\Delta D} - \frac{\Delta P}{\Delta D}D - \Delta P\frac{\Delta D}{\Delta D}$$

Because $\Delta D/\Delta D$ is equal to 1, we can rewrite this as

$$\frac{\Delta R}{\Delta D} = P - \frac{\Delta P}{\Delta D}D - \Delta P$$

Finally, as ΔD approaches zero so does ΔP,[3] and we treat ΔP in the equation above as it it were zero and rewrite the equation as

$$\frac{dR}{dD} = P - \frac{dP}{dD}D \qquad (9\text{-}20)$$

This last equation tells us that marginal revenue (dR/dD as ΔD approaches zero) is equal the price at which the commodity sells minus the derivative of price with respect to quantity demanded times the quantity demanded.

Proof of the relationship Knowing the relationship expressed in equation 9-20, we can now show that $dR/dD = P(1 - 1/E_d)$. Equation 9-20 can be rewritten

$$\frac{dR}{dD} = P\left(1 - \frac{dP}{dD}\frac{D}{P}\right)$$

The term

$$\frac{dP}{dD}\frac{D}{P}$$

we recognize from equation 9-15 as the *reciprocal* of the price elasticity of demand E_d. For this term we substitute $1/E_d$ and write

$$M = \frac{dR}{dD} = P\left(1 - \frac{1}{E_d}\right) \qquad (9\text{-}18)$$

This is the relationship between marginal revenue and the price elasticity of demand we started out to prove: marginal revenue equals price times the quantity 1 minus the reciprocal of the price elasticity of demand.

The uses of the relationship

With equation 9-18 we can now discover three additional relationships.

Perfectly elastic demand When the demand for a commodity takes the form

$$P = K$$

we say that demand is perfectly elastic and that the coefficient of the price elasticity of demand E_d approaches infinity as ΔP approaches zero. Looking at equation 9-18, we can see that as the absolute value of E_d increases, the value of $1/E_d$ decreases; that as E_d approaches infinity, $1/E_d$ approaches zero. As $1/E_d$ approaches zero, the term $1 - 1/E_d$ approaches 1. At the limit, if $1/E_d$ is zero, $1 - 1/E_d$ is equal to 1.

If $1 - 1/E_d$ is 1, then M equals P times 1, or M equals P. In short, when the demand for a commodity is perfectly elastic, the price at which the commodity sells and the marginal revenue from the sale of an additional small quantity of the commodity are equal.

[3] If $D = a - bP$, $\Delta D = -b\,\Delta P$, and $\Delta P = \Delta D/-b$.

Another way to see that this is true is to take a perfectly elastic demand for the commodity

$$P = K$$

and to note that with this demand function, total revenue is

$$R = K \cdot D$$

If we find the derivative of R with respect to D, that is, marginal revenue, we have, following the technique for finding the derivative,

$$\frac{dR}{dD} = K$$

This says that marginal revenue is equal to the constant price.

If, for example,

$$P = \$5$$

then

$$R = \$5 \cdot D$$

and

$$\frac{dR}{dD} = \$5$$

Less than perfectly elastic demand When demand is less than perfectly elastic, the coefficient of price elasticity is a number the value of which is not indefinitely large. This means that E_d has an absolute value greater than zero but less than infinity. When E_d is greater than zero, $1/E_d$ is also greater than zero. If $1/E_d$ is greater than zero, $1 - 1/E_d$ must be less than 1 (because 1 minus any number greater than zero is less than 1). This being the case, and employing equation 9-18, marginal revenue has to be less than price. Marginal revenue is less than price because marginal revenue is equal to price times a number less than 1; and price times a number less than 1 is less than price. In short, when demand is less than perfectly elastic, marginal revenue is less than the price of the commodity. This is a proposition we demonstrated in a different fashion on pages 220–221.

As an example, assume the price of the commodity is \$6 and at this price E_d is (still ignoring the minus sign) equal to 3. Applying equation 9-18,

$$\begin{aligned}\frac{dR}{dD} &= \$6(1 - \tfrac{1}{3})\\ &= \$6(\tfrac{2}{3})\\ &= \$4\end{aligned}$$

This \$4 marginal revenue is less than the \$6 price. Even if E_d were as large as 1,000,000 or as small as 1/1,000,000, M would be smaller than P.

Marginal revenue and the coefficient of the elasticity demand We saw earlier that E_d might be greater than, less than, or equal to 1. If E_d is greater than 1, then $1/E_d$ is less than 1; and $1 - 1/E_d$ is less than 1, too, but greater than zero. Price times a number greater than zero means, using equation 9-18, that

TABLE 9-3

If E_d is	Then $\frac{1}{E_d}$ is	$1 - \frac{1}{E_d}$ is	And $MR = P\left(1 - \frac{1}{E_d}\right)$ is
3	$\frac{1}{3}$	$\frac{2}{3}$	$\$10(\frac{2}{3}) = \$6\frac{2}{3}$
$\frac{1}{4}$	4	-3	$10(-3) = -30$
1	1	0	$10(0) = 0$

marginal revenue is also greater than zero. In short, where demand is elastic, marginal revenue has a positive magnitude.

But if E_d is less than 1, $1/E_d$ is greater than 1; and $1 - 1/E_d$ is a negative number. Price times a negative number means that marginal revenue is also negative. Where demand is inelastic, marginal revenue is negative. Finally, if E_d were equal to 1, $1/E_d$ would also be equal to 1, $1 - 1/E_d$ would equal zero, and price times zero would result in a marginal revenue equal to zero. When demand is of unitary elasticity, marginal revenue is equal to zero. In short, where demand is:

- Elastic ($E_d > 1$), marginal revenue is positive.
- Inelastic ($E_d < 1$), marginal revenue is negative.
- Unitarily elastic ($E_d = 1$), marginal revenue is zero.

Looking back to Figure 9-2, we can now observe that demand is elastic at quantities less than 20 cases and as a result marginal revenue is positive; that demand is inelastic at quantities greater than 20 cases and as a result marginal revenue is negative; and that demand is of unitary elasticity and marginal revenue is equal to zero at 20 cases.

The relationship between P and E_d is illustrated in Table 9-3. It is assumed in all three cases that the price of the commodity is $10.

Exercise 9-5

1 Show that:

a $\dfrac{dR}{dD} = P - \dfrac{dP}{dD}D$

b $\dfrac{dR}{dD} = P\left(1 - \dfrac{1}{E_d}\right)$

2 When demand is perfectly elastic and ΔP approaches zero:

a E_d approaches __________

b $1/E_d$ approaches __________

c $1 - 1/E_d$ approaches __________

d dR/dD approaches __________

3 When demand is less than perfectly elastic:

a E_d is less than __________

b $1/E_d$ is greater than ____________

c $1 - 1/E_d$ is less than ____________

d dR/dD is less than ____________

4 Suppose the demand function is $P = \$12$.

a $dR/dD = \$$____________

b The value of E_d is ____________

5 Assume $P = \$12$ and E_d is 4. dR/dD is equal to $____________ and is ____________ price.

6 When:

a E_d is greater than 1, demand is ____________ and dR/dD is ____________

b E_d is less than 1, demand is ____________ and dR/dD is ____________

c E_d is equal to 1, demand is ____________, and dR/dD is ____________

7 Suppose

$$D = 100 \text{ cartons} - 20 \frac{\text{cartons}}{\text{dollar}} P$$

a Demand is inelastic and dR/dD negative when D is ____________ than ____________ cartons.

b Demand is elastic and dR/dD positive when D is ____________ than ____________ cartons.

c Demand is unitary elastic and dR/dD zero when D is ____________ to ____________ cartons.

8 When demand is:

a Perfectly elastic, dR/dD ____________ P.

b Less than perfectly elastic, dR/dD ____________ P.

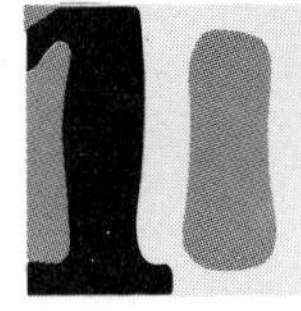

CONSUMER DEMAND

The law of demand is the generalization that the relationship between the price and the quantity demanded of a commodity is an inverse one. The commodity to which the law refers may be either a product demanded by consumers or a resource demanded by business firms. In this chapter we are concerned with the individual consumer and why he tends to buy more of a good or service as its price falls and less of it as its price rises. We are, in short, interested in consumer demand.

To explain this inverse relation between the price of a product and the quantity demanded of it by a consumer it is necessary to introduce a new concept and a new technique. The new concept is the indifference curve, and the new technique is the method which uses indifference curves to explain consumer demand. Indifference curves are employed in the first section of this chapter to explain consumer behavior and to find consumer equilibrium. Then in the second section the theory of consumer behavior is employed to discover how a consumer reacts to a change in the price of a consumer good or service and to a change in his income.

The technique, or method, we employ in this chapter differs from that used in previous chapters. We continue to use mathematics, but the mathematics we employ is geometry, and little attention is paid to algebra or arithmetic.

THE EQUILIBRIUM OF THE CONSUMER

The amount of a good or service an individual consumer will purchase depends upon a number of economic variables. We assume that the quantity D_X he demands of commodity X is a function of the price P_X of commodity X, the prices of other commodities P_Y, P_Z, . . . , the amount of income I the consumer has to spend on the various commodities, his preferences or tastes T, his wealth (the quantity of goods and financial assets, including money, he already possesses), and his expectations of future prices and income. To simplify the analysis, we assume that a consumer's wealth and expectations are fixed and do not change. In mathematical language

$$D_X = f_X(P_X, P_Y, P_Z, \ldots; I; T) \tag{10-1}$$

The symbol f_X is a functional notation. f means "depends on." The subscript X tells us that we are talking about the variables upon which the demand for commodity X depends.

The quantity demanded of any other commodity depends upon the *same* set of variables. The quantity the consumer will demand of commodity Y is a function of the price of Y, the prices of other commodities, his income, and his tastes; or

$$D_Y = f_Y(P_X, P_Y, P_Z, \ldots; I; T) \tag{10-2}$$

f_Y is the functional notation that tells us we are now talking about the demand function for commodity Y.

In order to simplify the analysis still further without reducing its usefulness, we shall make two additional assumptions. First, we assume that the commodities a consumer might purchase are *perfectly divisible*. This means that he may buy the commodity in as large or as small a quantity as he wishes. If the commodity is cigarettes, he may buy a case, a carton, a package, a single cigarette, or any fraction of a single cigarette. The second assumption is that there are only two commodities, X and Y, a consumer may purchase with his income and only two prices to affect the amount of each commodity he purchases. Employing this latter assumption,

$$D_X = f_X(P_X, P_Y, I, T) \tag{10-3}$$

and

$$D_Y = f_Y(P_X, P_Y, I, T) \tag{10-4}$$

Commodity X is the commodity upon which we shall focus our attention. In examining the consumer's demand for a commodity we shall explain his demand for X. We shall also be interested, however, in what happens to the quantity of Y demanded when the price of X changes.

The four variables that determine the amounts of X and Y the consumer buys can be divided into two groups. The first group consists of a single variable, the consumer's tastes. The second group consists of his income and the prices of the two commodities. The income of the consumer and the prices of the two commodities are the consumer's *budget restraint*. The tastes of the consumer are his *indifference curves*. The consumer's indifference curves and budget restraint together determine the quantities of X and Y he will purchase. We examine indifference curves in the first section and the budget restraint in the section following it; we use the two together to determine his purchases in the section following that.

Indifference curves

An indifference curve is a curve that shows various combinations of X and Y. The consumer has no preference for any combination of X and Y on an indifference curve over any other combinations of X and Y *on the same indifference curve*. In short, all combinations of X and Y on an indifference curve are combinations among which he is indifferent. Put another way, all the combinations of X and Y on an indifference curve give the consumer the same satisfaction, pleasure, or utility.

The single indifference curve In Figure 10-1 we have drawn an indifference curve. Notice that we measure *physical units* of commodity X along one axis and *physical units* of the commodity Y along the other axis. While the graph does not show it, there is a time element to every indifference curve. All the combinations of X and Y along the curve are quantities of X and Y *per unit of time*. On the graphs in this chapter we have not taken the trouble to add "per unit of time" in labeling the axes, but it should not be forgotten that the consumption of X and Y has a time dimension.

We have labeled this indifference curve U_{30}. The 30 is the *index* of the utility the combinations of X and Y along this indifference curve give the consumer. The number 30 is *not* a measure of the utility he receives. All the number 30 indicates is that this indifference curve gives the consumer more utility than

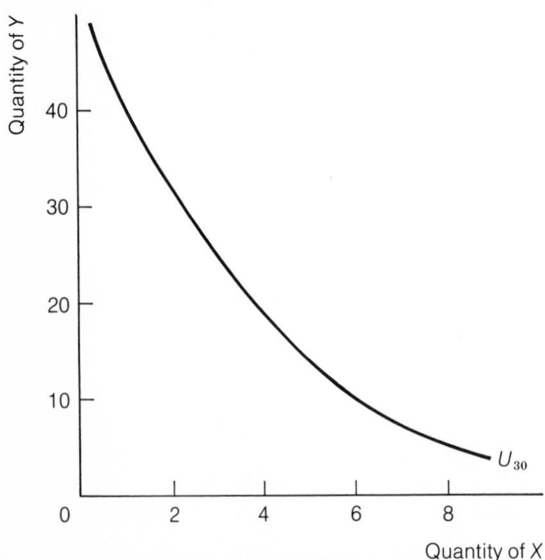

FIGURE 10-1

TABLE 10-1

Quantity of X	Quantity of Y
1	40
2	32
3	25
4	19
5	14
6	10
7	7
8	5

indifference curves with lower indexes and less utility than curves with higher indexes. It does not tell us the *amount* of utility he obtains from the different combinations of X and Y on the indifference curve. The amount of utility he obtains from the combinations on an indifference curve is the same, but it is not known how much it is. And, as it turns out, we do not really need to know the amount of utility associated with any indifference curve to explain consumer demand.

Some of the combinations of X and Y that give a consumer the same utility can be put in a table like Table 10-1. We have not included all possible combinations of X and Y giving the consumer the same utility because the number of such combinations is indefinitely large, but each of the eight combinations in the table affords the consumer the same utility. He finds that any combination has just as much utility as any of the seven other combinations.

We can express the notion of an indifference curve in the form of an equation if we first write

$$U = f(X,Y) \tag{10-5}$$

This equation says that the amount of utility U a consumer receives from the consumption of X and Y depends upon the quantities of X and Y, that is, the combination of X and Y, he consumes (X,Y). If we change this equation slightly to

$$\bar{U} = f(X,Y) \tag{10-6}$$

where $\bar{U}$ is a fixed amount of utility, and then plot all the combinations of X and Y that give the consumer this fixed amount of utility, we have an indifference curve. Because of the mathematical complexity of such an equation, we shall not use any numerical examples of this indifference function. We stick to geometry and curves.

Looking back to the graph of an indifference curve in Figure 10-1, we may observe two things about the curve. It has a negative slope, and this slope decreases as we move from left to right along the curve. These two characteristics of the indifference curve are the geometric counterparts of the two basic assumptions we make about the nature of every individual indifference curve.

The negative slope of the indifference curve The slope of the indifference curve in Figure 10-1 is plainly negative: as X increases, Y decreases; and as

Y increases, X decreases. We can also see this inverse relationship in Table 10-1. The greater the amount of X in the combination, the smaller the amount of Y; and the greater the quantity of Y, the smaller the quantity of X.

The slope of a curve *between two points,* we know, is equal to the ratio of the vertical to the horizontal displacement. Measuring Y vertically and X horizontally, the slope of an indifference curve between two points would be equal to $\Delta Y/\Delta X$. But because we are concerned with the slope of an indifference curve *at a point* (and not between two points) on a curve, we are concerned with the limit which $\Delta Y/\Delta X$ approaches as ΔX approaches zero.

We define the *marginal rate of substitution of X for Y* ($\text{MRS}_{X:Y}$) as the slope of an indifference curve at a point. We may say, therefore, that the $\text{MRS}_{X:Y}$ is the limit which $\Delta Y/\Delta X$ approaches as ΔX approaches zero and call this limit dY/dX. In short,

$$\text{MRS}_{X:Y} \equiv \lim_{\Delta X \to 0} \frac{\Delta Y}{\Delta X} \equiv \frac{-dY}{dX} \tag{10-7}$$

The first assumption made about every indifference curve is that its slope is negative, or that

$$\frac{dY}{dX} < 0 \tag{10-8}$$

The reason for making this assumption is fairly simple. All combinations of X and Y along an indifference curve must give the consumer the same utility. If X were to increase by dX and Y were to remain unchanged, the consumer would obtain more utility from his consumption of X and Y. To keep his utility constant when X increases it is necessary to decrease Y by some amount equal to dY. When X changes by dX, Y must change by $-dY$ if the consumer's utility is to remain unchanged. The ratio $-dY/dX$, the marginal rate of substitution of X for Y, is therefore negative.

The convexity of the indifference curve The second thing we see when we look at the indifference curve in Figure 10-1 is that it is *convex* to the origin. It bends in toward the intersection of the X and Y axes (the origin or zero point of the graph). The curve is plainly not a straight line, and it is not concave to the origin (bending away from the origin).[1]

What we see is that as X increases (and Y decreases) the slope of the curve decreases. When X is small and Y is large, the slope of the curve is almost vertical; but when X is large and Y is small, the curve is almost horizontal. Because the slope of the indifference curve is the marginal rate of substitution of X for Y, as X increases (and Y decreases), the marginal rate of substitution of X for Y decreases.

At point A on the indifference curve in Figure 10-2, X is 3, and the slope of

[1] A curve concave to the origin would look like this:

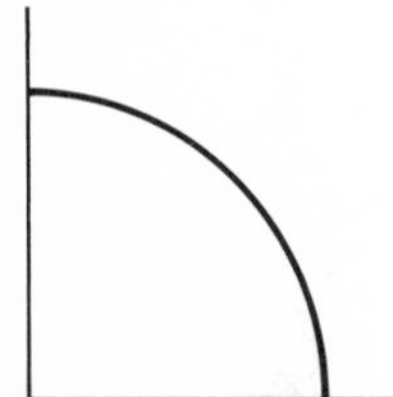

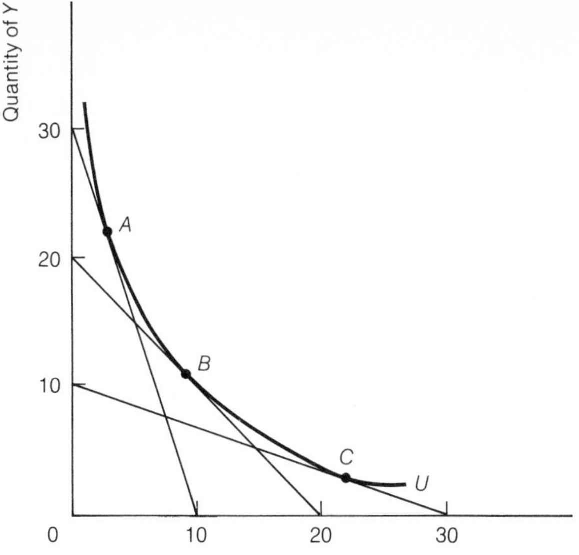

FIGURE 10-2

the curve is equal to $-30/10$, or -3. At point *B*, where *X* is 9, the slope of the curve is $-20/20$, or -1. And the slope of the curve at point *C*, where *X* is 22, is equal to $-10/30$, or $-\frac{1}{3}$. We can see that as *X* increases, the negative slope of the curve and the marginal rate of substitution of *X* for *Y* decrease in value.

To say that the *negative* value of the marginal rate of substitution decreases as *X* increases is really to say that the marginal rate of substitution *in*creases as *X* increases. The MRS increased from -3 to -1 as *X* increased from 3 to 9; and when *X* increased from 9 to 22, the MRS increased from -1 to $-\frac{1}{3}$. In mathematical terms we are saying that the marginal rate of substitution of *X* for *Y*, or dY/dX, is directly related to *X*: when *X* increases, dY/dX also increases. Said another way, when ΔX is positive the change in dY/dX is also positive (and when ΔX is negative, the change in dY/dX is negative).

This means that the ratio of a small change in dY/dX [or $\Delta(dY/dX)$] to the small change in *X* (or ΔX) is positive. This we can write as

$$\frac{\Delta(dY/dX)}{\Delta X} > 0$$

When we are concerned with the limit this ratio approaches as ΔX approaches zero, we write

$$\frac{d(dY/dX)}{dX} > 0$$

or (using the special notation mathematicians use for this)

$$\frac{d^2Y}{dX^2} > 0$$

All this last inequality really says is that the limit

$$\frac{\Delta(dY/dX)}{\Delta X}$$

approaches as ΔX approaches zero is positive. When X increases by some very small amount dx, the algebraic value of dY/dX also increases.

It is customary in economics to ignore the minus sign in front of the value of the MRS and the slope of the indifference curve and to think only of the absolute value of dY/dX. When we do this, it is permissible to say that the slope of the indifference curve and the MRS decrease as X increases. But if we do not ignore the minus sign, we must say that dY/dX increases as X increases.

An indifference map Figure 10-3 shows a set or family of indifference curves, called an *indifference map.* We note that each of the three indifference curves has a negative slope whose algebraic value increases (or whose absolute value decreases) as X increases and Y decreases.

The indifference map of an individual consumer is the method we employ to express the tastes of the consumer. The tastes of the consumer *are* his indifference map. Besides the two characteristics of the individual indifference curve discussed above, two characteristics of an indifference map require explanation.

The level of utility For each possible level of utility a consumer might obtain from the consumption of X and Y there is an indifference curve. And every combination of X and Y he might consume lies on some indifference curve. The farther to the right of the Y axis (or the farther above the X axis) an indifference curve lies, the greater the amount of utility associated with that indifference curve. In Figure 10-3 the utility of U_{31} is greater than the utility of U_{30}; and the

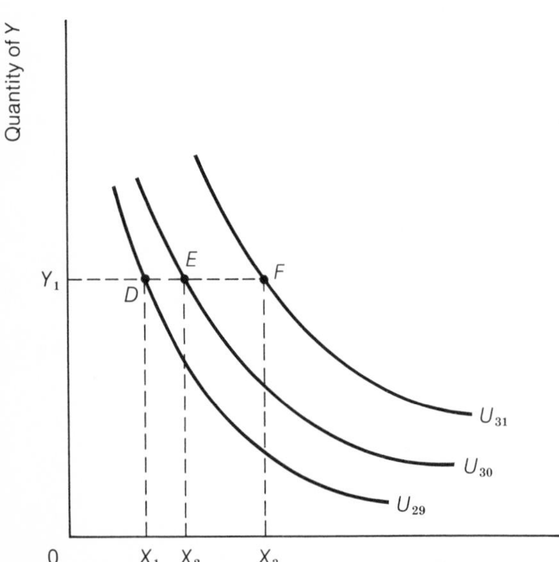

FIGURE 10-3

utility of U_{30} is greater than the utility of U_{29}. (It should be recalled that the subscripts 29, 30, and 31 are not the amounts of utility associated with the three curves. They are indexes used to show which indifference curve has the greater amount of utility: the larger the index, the greater the utility of the curve.)

It is fairly simple to show that U_{31} has more utility than U_{30}. Both combination F on U_{31} and combination E on U_{30} contain Y_1 of Y. Combination F has more X than combination E, however. The consumer will prefer combination F to combination E because it has more X and the same amount of Y. Combination F, because it is preferred to combination E, has more utility to the consumer than combination E. Recall that all combinations on U_{31} have the same utility as combination F and that all combinations on U_{30} have the same utility as combination E. If combination F is preferred to, and has more utility than, combination E, U_{31} is preferred to, and has more utility than, U_{30}. By the same kind of reasoning it can be shown that U_{30} is preferred to, and has more utility than, U_{29}.

Nonintersecting curves The second characteristic of an indifference map is that no two indifference curves touch or intersect each other. To see why two indifference curves may not intersect, look at the two intersecting indifference curves in Figure 10-4. Consider the combination of X and Y represented by the point at which U_a and U_b cross. This combination lies on two different indifference curves. But each indifference curve represents a different level of utility. This means X_1 of X and Y_1 of Y yield the consumer two different amounts of utility.

To allow indifference curves to cross would be to allow two different quantities of utility to be attained from the consumption of the same combination of commodities. But this is not plausible. Every combination of commodities gives the consumer one and only one amount of utility.

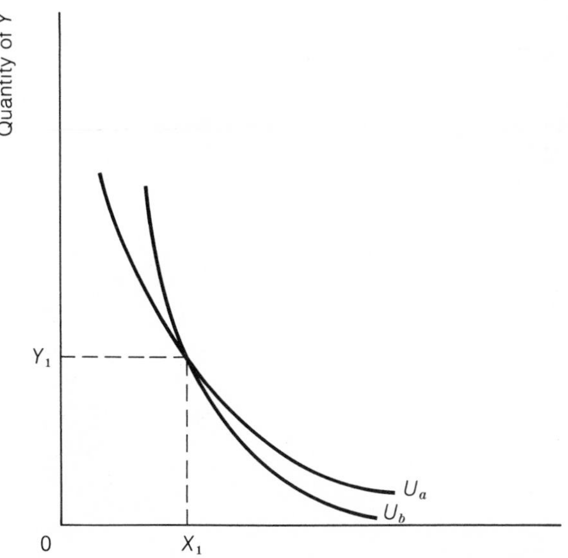

FIGURE 10-4

Summary The four important characteristics of indifference curves are:

1 The marginal rate of substitution of X for Y or the slope of an indifference curve dY/dX is negative.

2 The marginal rate of substitution of Y for X decreases absolutely (and increases algebraically) as X increases.

3 The farther up or to the right an indifference curve lies, the greater its utility.

4 Indifference curves do not intersect.

The budget restraint

The tastes or indifference map of a consumer is one of the two groups of variables that determine the quantities of X and Y he will purchase. The other group of variables determines the quantities of X and Y he is *able* to purchase. How much a consumer is able to buy depends upon the size of his income I, the price P_X he has to pay for X, and the price P_Y he has to pay for Y.

We assume that in any period of time a consumer has a given income. It is also assumed that the prices of X and Y are given or fixed and do not vary with the quantities of X and Y he actually purchases. The fact that a consumer's purchases are restrained by the size of his income and the prices of commodities is called the *budget restraint*.

To take an example of the budget restraint, suppose a consumer has an income of $10, the price of X is $2, and the price of Y is $1. If he spent all his income on X, he could purchase 5 units of X. This we determine by dividing his income ($10) by the price of X ($2). The maximum amount of any commodity he is able to purchase equals his income divided by the price of that commodity. The maximum quantity of Y he can purchase, the amount of Y he could purchase if he spent all his income on Y, is equal to $10 divided by $1 (the price of Y) or 10 units of Y. Of course, a consumer need not spend all his income on either X or Y. He can spend some on each. Some of the different combinations of X and Y he can purchase are given in Table 10-2. Not all the combinations he is able to purchase are included. Assuming he can buy fractional parts of X

TABLE 10-2

Quantity of X	Quantity of Y
0	10
½	9
1	8
1½	7
2	6
2½	5
3	4
3½	3
4	2
4½	1
5	0

and Y, the number of possible combinations he is able to buy is indefinitely larger.

We should note two things in this budget table: (1) The more X he buys, the less Y he can buy; and the more Y he buys, the less X he can buy. (2) To acquire an additional unit of Y he must give up $\frac{1}{2}$ unit of X, and to acquire an additional X he must give up 2 units of Y. That is, giving up $\frac{1}{2}$ unit of X enables him to acquire one more Y; and giving up one Y makes it possible for him to consume another $\frac{1}{2}$ unit of X.

The budget equation Instead of expressing the combinations of X and Y the consumer is able to purchase in a table, we can indicate the consumer's budget restraint in an equation. An equation has an advantage over a table because it shows *all* the possible combinations a consumer can purchase. Such an equation is called the *budget equation* and is

$$(P_X)(X) + (P_Y)(Y) \equiv I \qquad (10\text{-}9)$$

The price of X times the quantity of X purchased is the amount the consumer spends on X; and the price of Y multiplied by the quantity of Y purchased is the amount he spends on Y. The budget equation simply tells us that the amounts spent on the two commodities must equal his income; or the consumer's income must equal the total amount spent on X and Y. With the prices of X and Y and the consumer's income given, the consumer may decide for himself how much X and Y to buy. But the quantity he purchases of X times its price plus the quantity of Y he decided to purchase multiplied by its price must equal his income.

If a consumer's income is \$10 and the prices of X and Y are \$2 and \$1, respectively, then the budget equation of the consumer will be

$$(\$2)(X) + (\$1)(Y) = \$10 \qquad (10\text{-}10)$$

The budget line Let us plot the consumer's budget equation (10-10) on a graph. The curve we obtain appears in Figure 10-5. (This curve is also a graph of the combinations of X and Y in Table 10-2.) The curve we have plotted is called the *budget line* (or, sometimes, the line of attainable combinations or the opportunity line). We should notice that the axes of the graph are the same as used in plotting an indifference curve. The quantity of X is plotted on the horizontal axis, and the quantity of Y is plotted on the vertical axis. The income of the consumer and the prices of the two commodities are not directly plotted on this graph.

There are two important characteristics of the budget line to observe. It is a straight line, and it has a negative slope. Let us look at each of these two characteristics separately.

The linearity of the budget line If we go back to the budget equation

$$(P_X)(X) + (P_Y)(Y) \equiv I \qquad (10\text{-}9)$$

rewrite it as

$$(P_Y)(Y) = I - (P_X)(X)$$

and then divide through by P_Y, we obtain

$$Y = \frac{I}{P_Y} - \frac{P_X}{P_Y}X \qquad (10\text{-}11)$$

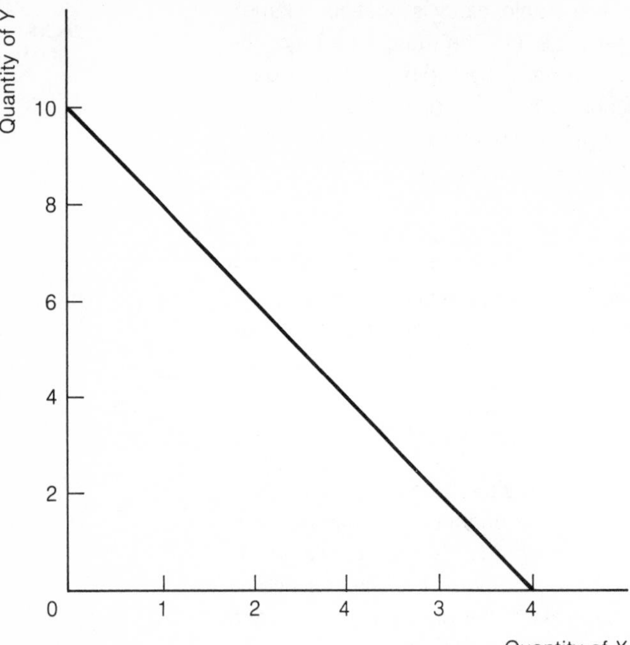

FIGURE 10-5

Equation 10-11 is a first-degree equation because the exponents of the two variables, X and Y, are both 1. We already know that when a first-degree equation is plotted, the resulting curve is a straight line. The general form of a first-degree, or linear, equation is

$$Y = a + bX \tag{10-12}$$

In equation 10-12, I/P_Y takes the place of the parameter a, and P_X/P_Y takes the place of the parameter b.

Equation 10-11 tells us that the amount of Y a consumer can purchase is equal to the maximum amount of Y he is able to purchase (I/P_Y) less the ratio of the price of X to the price of Y (P_X/P_Y) times the quantity of X he purchases. In our numerical example, the consumer's budget equation would be written

$$Y = \frac{\$10}{\$1} - \frac{\$2}{\$1}X$$

or

$$Y = 5 \text{ units of } Y - 2X$$

What makes the budget line linear is the assumption that the prices of X and Y are fixed. If they are fixed, then P_X/P_Y is constant and P_X/P_Y is the slope of the budget line.

The negative slope of the budget line In equation 10-11 we recognize P_X/P_Y is the *slope* of the budget line. We can see that P_X/P_Y is preceded by a minus sign. Assuming that both P_X and P_Y are positive, i.e., that the prices of both

X and Y are greater than zero, then $-P_X/P_Y$ indicates that the slope of the budget line is negative.

We can devise another method of showing that the slope of the budget line is equal to $-P_X/P_Y$. We already know that the maximum quantity of X the consumer can purchase is equal to I/P_X. If he buys I/P_X of X, he must purchase zero units of Y. Plotting zero Y and I/P_X of X in Figure 10-6 gives us point A on the X axis. Likewise, if the consumer purchases zero X, he can purchase at most I/P_y of Y. When we plot this point in Figure 10-6, we have point B on the Y axis.

To measure the slope of a straight line we need to know the ratio of the vertical to the horizontal displacement. In Figure 10-6, if Y were to decrease from I/P_Y to zero, the vertical displacement of Y or ΔY would be $-I/P_Y$. Were Y to decrease by I/P_Y, X would increase from zero to I/P_X. The horizontal displacement, or ΔX, would be I/P_X. The slope of the budget line is $\Delta Y/\Delta X$. ΔY is $-I/P_Y$, and ΔX is I/P_X. We have, therefore,

$$\text{Slope of budget line} = \frac{\Delta Y}{\Delta X} = \frac{-I/P_Y}{I/P_X}$$

or

$$\frac{\Delta Y}{\Delta X} = \frac{-I}{P_Y}\frac{P_X}{I}$$

and

$$\frac{\Delta Y}{\Delta X} = \frac{-P_X}{P_Y}$$

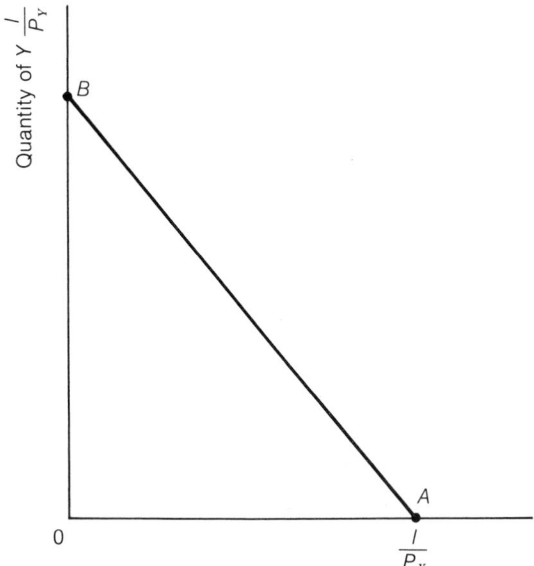

FIGURE 10-6

In our numerical example, where $P_X = \$2$, $P_Y = \$1$, and $I = \$10$, ΔY is -10 and ΔX is 5. $\Delta Y/\Delta X$, or the slope of the budget line, is therefore $-10/5$, or -2. But we could have found the slope of the budget line if we had computed $-P_X/P_Y$ because $-\$2/\$1$ is also equal to -2.

Consumer equilibrium

To find out how much X and Y a consumer will purchase in any time period we need to know his tastes, or indifference map, and his budget restraint or budget line for that time period. It is also necessary to know the aim or goal of the consumer. We assume that the goal of the consumer is to purchase the combination of X and Y that brings him the maximum amount of utility: his aim is the maximization of utility. In terms of indifference curves, this means that his goal is to purchase a combination of X and Y that puts him on the highest indifference curve his income and the prices of X and Y permit him to reach. When he purchases this combination, the consumer is said to be in equilibrium. Consumer equilibrium is found where the consumer is on the highest indifference curve he is able to reach.

The analysis of equilibrium In Figure 10-7 we have placed both the consumer's budget line and three of the many indifference curves that make up his indifference map. All the combinations of X and Y along the budget line are combinations which his income and the prices of X and Y make it *possible* for him to purchase. The combination along his budget line that he will choose to purchase is the one which puts him on the highest indifference curve.

The combination that puts him on the highest indifference curve is combination C. Combination C is on his budget line, but so are combinations A and B.

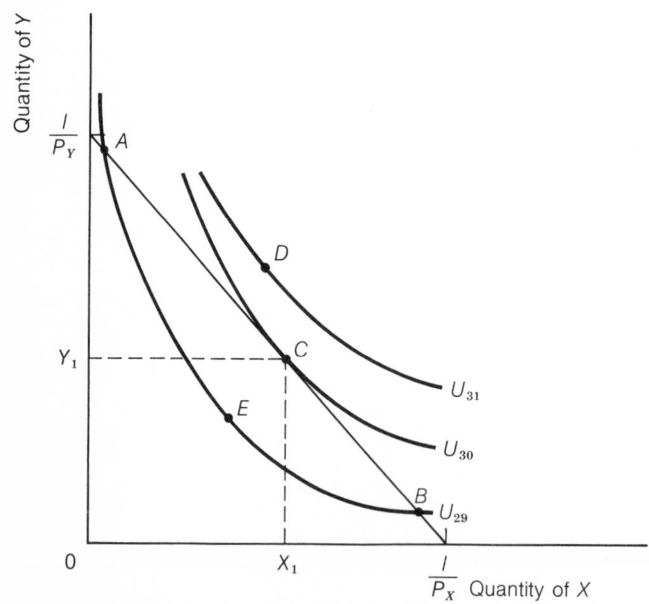

FIGURE 10-7

Combination C, however, is on a higher indifference curve than either combination A or B. Notice that combination D is on a higher indifference curve than combination C, but combination D is not on his budget line. It is a combination that his income and the prices of X and Y do not permit him to buy. Our consumer is in equilibrium only when he purchases combination C: X_1 of commodity X and Y_1 of commodity Y.

If we look more closely at combination C, we can see that at this point the *slope* of the indifference curve and the *slope* of the budget line are the same. Both the indifference curve and the budget line pass through point C, and the budget line and the indifference curve touch each other only at this point. In the language of geometry, the budget line and the indifference curve are *tangent* to each other at point C.

The slope of the indifference curve is the marginal rate of substitution of X for Y and is equal to $-dY/dX$. The slope of the budget line is equal to $-P_X/P_Y$. If the consumer is in equilibrium where the slope of the indifference curve is equal to the slope of the budget line, he is in equilibrium when

$$-\frac{dY}{dX} = -\frac{P_X}{P_Y} \qquad (10\text{-}13)$$

At point C the slope of U_{30} and $-P_X/P_Y$ are equal. It is not, however, sufficient to say that the consumer is in equilibrium when $-dY/dX = -P_X/P_Y$. If it were, combinations D and E would also be equilibrium combinations because the slope of U_{29} at E and the slope of U_{31} at D are both equal to $-P_X/P_Y$. To be in equilibrium the consumer must also buy a combination that lies on his budget line. The quantities of X and Y he purchases must also satisfy his budget equation, or

$$(P_X)(X) + (P_Y)(Y) \equiv I \qquad (10\text{-}9)$$

Equations 10-9 and 10-13 tell us when the consumer is in equilibrium and maximizing the utility he obtains. Both equations must be satisfied for the consumer to be in equilibrium. At points A and B, for example, equation 10-9 is satisfied because these points lie on his budget line. And at points D and E equation 10-13 is satisfied because the slopes of the budget line and the indifference curve are equal at these points. But at point C both equations are satisfied: the consumer is not only on his budget line, but the slopes of the budget line and the indifference curve are also equal. Only at point C, where both equations are satisfied, is the consumer in equilibrium. Only when he buys a combination on his budget line *and* a combination at which the slope of the budget line is equal to the slope of the indifference curve is the consumer maximizing his utility and in equilibrium.

Exercise 10-1

1 Using the simplifying assumptions we make in this chapter:

a $D_X = f_X$ (__________, __________, __________, __________)

b $D_Y = f_Y$ (__________, __________, __________, __________)

c The budget restraint is determined by the three exogenous variables __________, __________, and __________

d The tastes of a consumer are his __________

2 Define an indifference curve. __________

____

3 The slope of an indifference curve is equal to __________ and is called the __________

a The slope of an indifference curve is (positive, negative, neither) __________

____

b The absolute value of the slope of an indifference curve (increases, decreases, remains constant) __________

c An indifference curve is (linear, convex to the origin, concave to the origin)

____

4 In mathematical language:

a The equation for an indifference curve may be written: __________

b $\frac{dY}{dX}$ __________ 0

c $\frac{d^2Y}{dX^2}$ __________ 0

5 Indifference curves do not __________, and the (farther from, closer to) __________ the X and Y axes an indifference curve is, the smaller the utility associated with that indifference curve.

6 In mathematical terms, a consumer's budget equation is __________

a The maximum quantity of X he can purchase is __________

b The maximum quantity of Y he can purchase is __________

c The slope of the budget line is equal to __________

d If the consumer purchased a quantity of X equal to g, he would have to purchase an amount of Y equal to __________

7 Show that the slope of the budget line is negative and is equal to $-P_X/P_Y$.

8 Suppose a consumer has an income of \$50, that the price of X is \$3, and the price of Y is \$4.

a The maximum quantity of X he can purchase is __________ units

b The maximum quantity of Y he can purchase is __________ units

c The slope of the budget line is equal to __________

d If the consumer purchased 4 units of X, he would have to purchase __________ units of Y; and if he purchased 6 units of Y, he would have to purchase __________ units of X.

9 When the consumer is in equilibrium, the utility he is able to achieve is a __________ and two conditions or equations are satisfied. These two equations are:

a __________ = __________

b __________ = __________

10 Below are a consumer's indifference map and budget line.

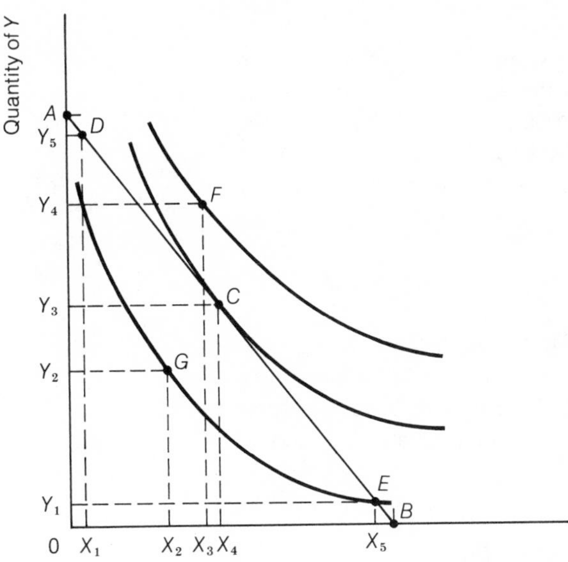

FIGURE 10-A

a What is:

(1) Point *A*? ______________________________

(2) Point *B*? ______________________________

b Which point is the equilibrium combination of *X* and *Y*? __________

c Why are combinations *D* and *E* not equilibrium combinations of *X* and *Y*?

____

d Why are combinations *F* and *G* not equilibrium combinations of *X* and *Y*?

____

e How much *X* and how much *Y* does the consumer purchase to maximize the utility he obtains from his income? ______________________________

CONSUMER BEHAVIOR

Probably the most important reason for having a theory which explains consumer equilibrium is that the theory enables us to understand how a consumer will behave in the marketplace: how he will react to a change in the price of one of the commodities or a change in his income. In finding the combination of X and Y that brings the individual consumer the maximum utility we assumed that his income and the prices of X and Y were parameters. If we change one of these parameters, the combination of X and Y that maximizes his utility will also change. The quantity of X, the quantity of Y, or both will change. An income or price change, in short, will move the consumer from one equilibrium to another equilibrium combination.

In this section we want to do three things: (1) We want to learn how changes in the price of X may affect the quantities of X the consumer buys and show why the law of demand for a consumer tends to be an inverse relation. (2) We want to discover how changes in the price of X affect the quantities of Y he purchases. (3) We want to know how changes in his income affect the quantity of X he consumes.

Consumer demand

Consumer demand is the relation between the price of a product and the quantity of that product the consumer purchases. We can see in Figure 10-8 the effects of a change in the price of X upon the quantity of X a consumer buys. The price of Y and the income of the consumer are assumed to be equal to P_{Y_1} and I_1, respectively, and to remain constant.

When the price of X is equal to P_{X_1}, the budget line of the consumer is the

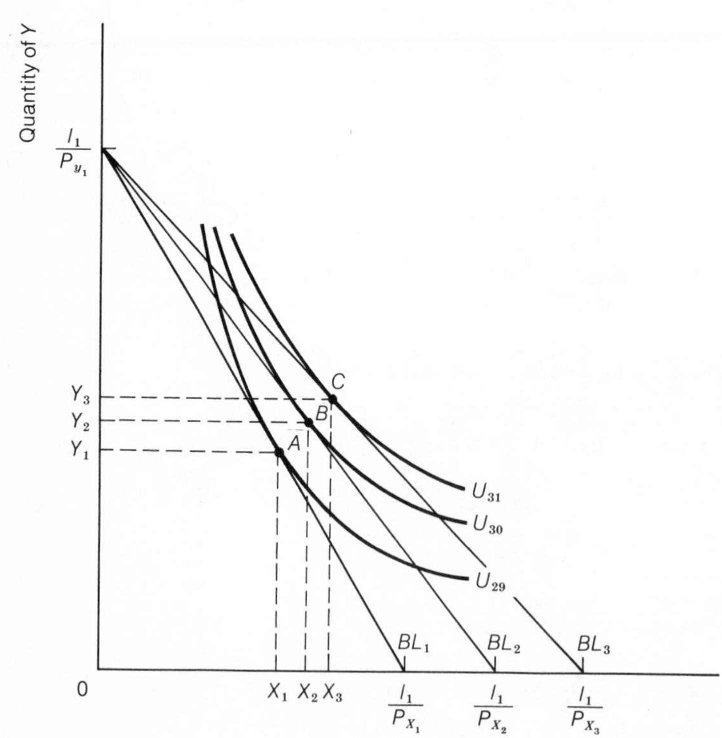

FIGURE 10-8

one labeled BL_1. It connects I_1/P_{Y_1} on the Y axis with I_1/P_{X_1} on the X axis. The slope of this budget line is equal to $-P_{X_1}/P_{Y_1}$. BL_1 is tangent U_{29} at point A. At point A, on the budget line, the slope of the budget line is equal to the slope of U_{29}. The consumer is in equilibrium and purchases X_1 of X and Y_1 of Y.

Now let us allow the price of X to *decrease* from P_{X_1} to P_{X_2} and keep the price of Y and the income of the consumer unchanged. The *maximum* quantity of X the consumer is able to purchase increases from I_1/P_{X_1} to I_1/P_{X_2}. (If his income were \$10 and the price of X fell from \$2 to \$1.50, the maximum quantity of X he could buy would rise from 5 units, which is \$10/\$2, to 7½ units of X, which is \$10/\$1.50.) His new budget line is BL_2, which connects I_1/P_{Y_1} with I_1/P_{X_2}. Notice that the point at which this new budget line touches the Y axis has not changed because a change in the price of X, the price of Y and income remaining constant, does not alter the maximum quantity of Y the consumer can purchase. Notice also that the slope of the budget line (ignoring the minus sign) has decreased from P_{X_1}/P_{Y_1} to P_{X_2}/P_{Y_1}. With a decrease in the price of X, the numerator in the ratio P_X/P_Y decreases, and the value of this ratio, which is equal to the slope of the budget line, therefore decreases too. For example, if the price of X decreases from \$2 to \$1.50 while the price of Y remains constant at \$1, the absolute value of the slope of the budget line decreases from 2 to 1.5.

This change in the budget line changes the equilibrium position of the consumer from point A (on BL_1 and U_{29}) to point B on BL_2 and U_{30}. The important thing to observe is that this decrease in the price of X has altered the quantities of X and Y the consumer purchases: the quantity of X has increased from X_1 to X_2, and the quantity of Y has increased from Y_1 to Y_2.

If the price of X were to decrease still further from P_{X_2} to P_{X_3}:

- The budget line would shift from BL_2 to BL_3.
- The absolute value of the slope of the budget line would decrease from P_{X_2}/P_{Y_1} to P_{X_3}/P_{Y_1}.
- The consumer equilibrium would change from point B on U_{30} to point C on U_{31}.
- The quantity of X the consumer purchases would increase from X_2 to X_3 (and the quantity of Y from Y_2 to Y_3).

What we have seen in Figure 10-8 is that decreases in the price of X increase the quantity of X the consumer buys. Decreases in the price of X also affect the quantity of Y purchased and increase the utility the consumer receives. If we turned the analysis around, we would find that *in*creases in the price of X would *de*crease the quantities of X bought, alter the quantities of Y, and decrease the consumer's levels of utility.

The law of consumer demand If we plotted what we learned about the relation between the price of X and the quantity of X demanded by the consumer on a graph, we would have a *demand curve*. Putting the relation between P_X and X in a table would give us a *demand schedule*. The expression of this relationship in the form of an equation is the *demand function*. Doing any or all of these, we would find that the relationship between the price of X and the quantity of X purchased by the consumer is an inverse one. And this is all the law of consumer demand says: quantity demanded is inversely related to the price of the product.

Exceptions to the law of consumer demand Does the consumer always increase his purchases of X as the price of X falls? Are there exceptions to this law? In Figure 10-9 we see one of the two exceptions. As the price of X falls from P_{X_1} to P_{X_2} to P_{X_3}, the quantity of X the consumer purchases remains constant at X_1. This is the case, discussed in Chapter 9, of the consumer's demand for X being perfectly inelastic. And if we were to plot the quantity he demands at each price, the quantity would be the same at all prices and the demand curve would be vertical.

The second exception to the law of consumer demand is seen in Figure 10-10. When the price of X falls from P_{X_1} to P_{X_2}, the consumer *decreases* his purchase of X from X_1 to X_2; and when the price of X falls still further from P_{X_2} to P_{X_3}, he decreases his purchases of X further from X_2 to X_3. The relation between the price of X and the quantity of X demanded by the consumer is a direct one. If we plotted the consumer's demand for X on a graph, we would find that the demand curve slopes upward, rather than downward like the usual demand curve.

So there are exceptions to the law of consumer demand. The law is not really a law at all. But it requires an unusual set of circumstances (which we will not discuss) for the quantity of X demanded either to remain constant or to decrease as the price of X falls. Quantity demanded increasing as price decreases is the usual case. And the law of consumer demand is therefore simply a statement of the usual relationship between price and quantity demanded. It is a

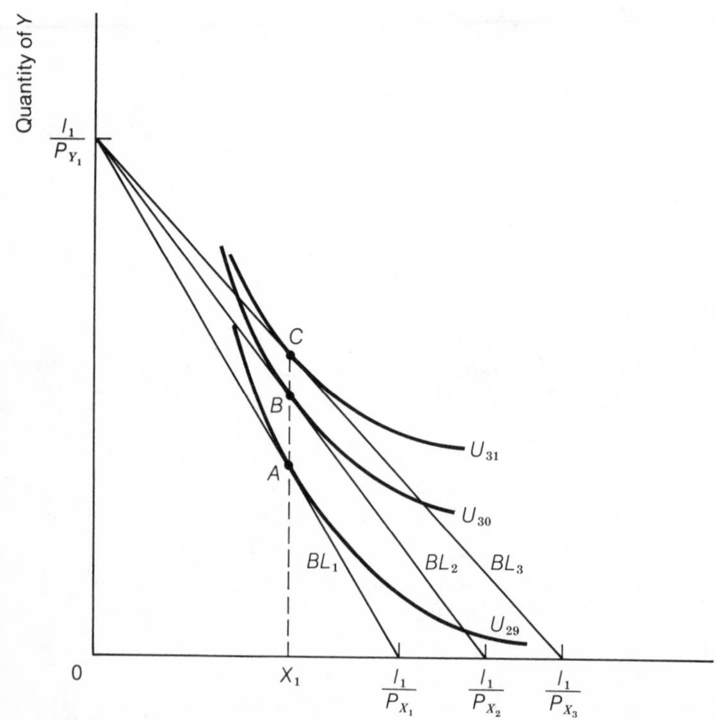

FIGURE 10-9

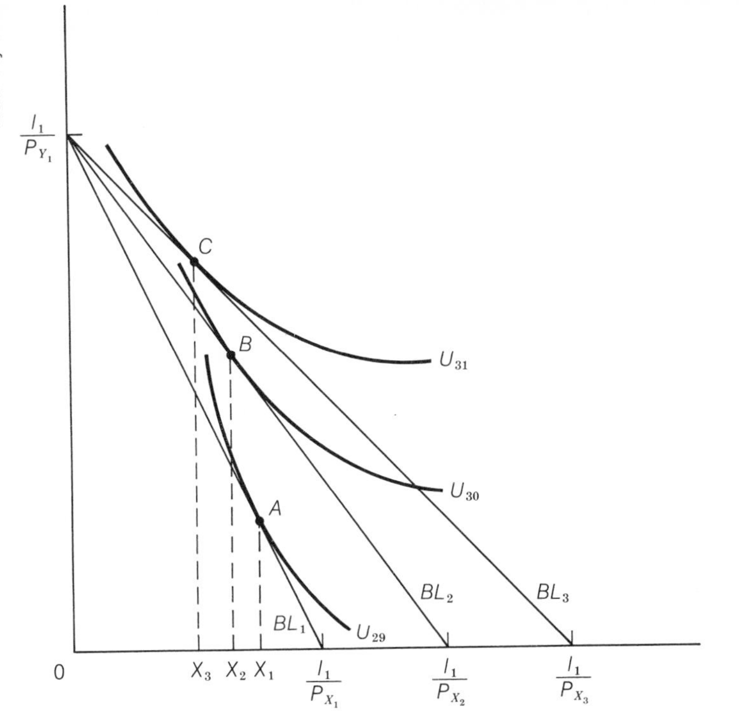

FIGURE 10-10

statement of the most frequent relationship rather than a statement of an invariant relationship.

Complements and substitutes

If we look back at Figure 10-8, we shall see that when the price of X decreases, both the quantity of X and the quantity of Y demanded by the consumer increase. X and Y, in this case, are complementary goods. When a decrease in the price of one good results in an increased demand for the other good, the two goods are defined as *complements*. In short, commodities are complements when there is an inverse relation between the price of one and the demand for the other.

In the language of mathematicians, when the ratio of the change in the quantity of Y demanded to the change in the price of X is negative, X and Y are complements; or X and Y are complements when

$$\frac{\Delta D_Y}{\Delta P_X} < 0$$

As ΔP_X approaches zero, the limit $\Delta D_Y/\Delta P_X$ approaches is dD_Y/dP_X. The mathematical definition of complements is a pair of goods such that

$$\frac{dD_Y}{dP_X} < 0 \qquad (10\text{-}14)$$

Figure 10-11 shows a pair of goods that are *substitutes*: as the price of X decreases the quantity of Y demanded by the consumer also decreases. There is a direct relation between the price of X and the demand for Y. The ratio of the change in the quantity of Y to the change in the price of X when goods are substitutes is positive, or

$$\frac{\Delta D_Y}{\Delta P_X} > 0$$

The limit $\Delta D_Y / \Delta P_X$ approaches as ΔP_X approaches zero will also be positive. The definition of substitutes is a pair of goods such that

$$\frac{dD_Y}{dP_X} > 0 \tag{10-15}$$

A pair of goods need not be either complements or substitutes. When

$$\frac{dD_Y}{dP_X} = 0 \tag{10-16}$$

X and Y are *independent* goods. A change in the price of X does not change the demand for Y. Such a pair of goods is shown in Figure 10-12, in which as the price of X decreases, the quantity of Y consumed remains constant at Y_1.

The theory of consumer behavior does not tell us whether a particular pair of goods are complements, substitutes, or independent. It does tell us that each

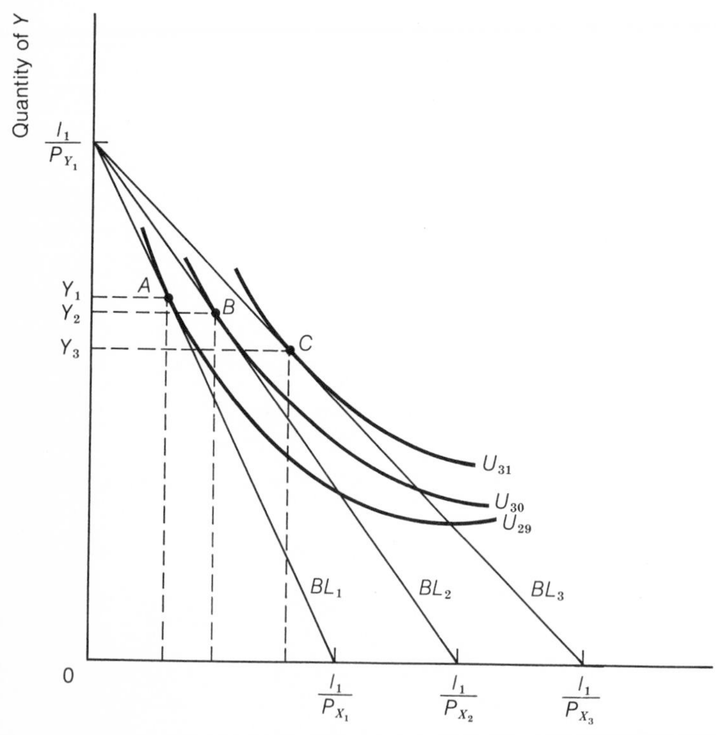

FIGURE 10-11

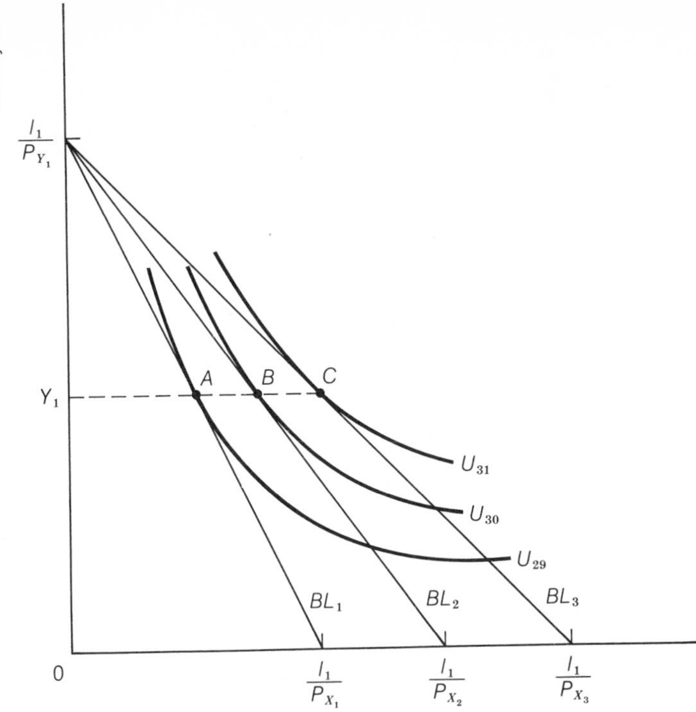

FIGURE 10-12

of these three relations is possible and that:

- If $dD_Y/dP_X < 0$, the goods are defined as complements.
- If $dD_Y/dP_X > 0$, the goods are defined as substitutes.
- If $dD_Y/dP_X = 0$, the goods are defined as independent.

Changes in income: normal and inferior goods

When the income of a consumer changes, the equilibrium combination of *X* and *Y* he consumes will also change. In Figure 10-13 we show an increase in the income of the consumer, the prices of *X* and *Y* remaining constant. The movement of the budget line from BL_1 to BL_2 reflects this increase in income. Notice that the increase in income has not changed the slope of the budget line: BL_2 is parallel to BL_1.

The unchanged slope of the budget line reflects the assumption that the prices of *X* and *Y* are constant. Since the slope of the budget line is equal to $-P_X/P_Y$, when P_X and P_Y do not change, $-P_X/P_Y$ does not change.

The distance the budget line moves to the right (or upward) depends upon the size of the increase in income. Recall that I/P_X is the maximum quantity of *X* the consumer can buy and the point at which the budget line crosses the *X* axis. If income changes from I to $I + \Delta I$, the point at which the budget line intersects the *X* axis changes from I/P_X to $(I + \Delta I)/P_X$. Subtracting I/P_X from

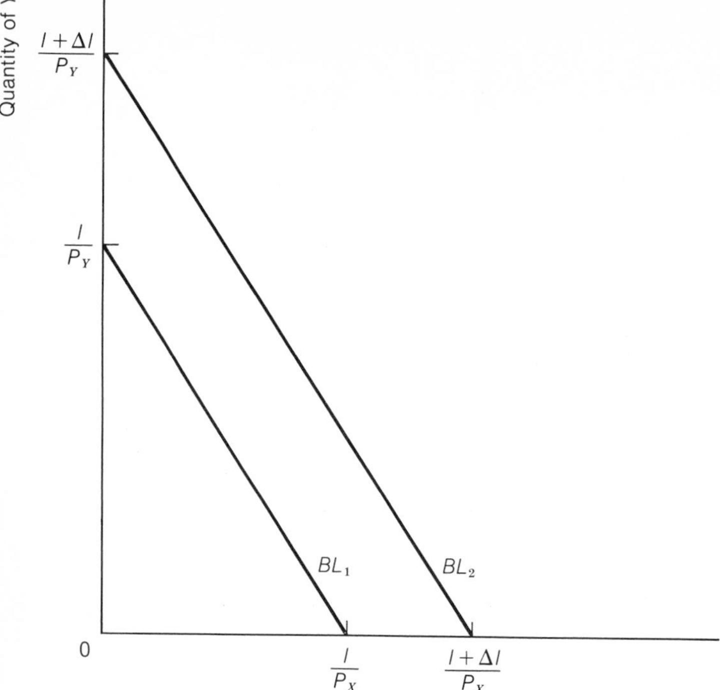

FIGURE 10-13

$(I + \Delta I)/P_X$, we find that the change in the maximum amount of X the consumer can purchase is equal to $\Delta I/P_X$, the change in his income divided by the price of X. If his income increases, the maximum amount of X he can buy also increases; and if his income decreases, the maximum amount of X he can purchase decreases.

For example, if a consumer's income increased from \$10 to \$15, the price of X remaining constant at \$2, the maximum amount of X he could purchase would increase from 5 units of X (= \$10/\$2) to $7\frac{1}{2}$ units of X (= \$15/\$2). The increase in the maximum quantity of X is $2\frac{1}{2}$ units. We could have obtained the same result and found that the increase in his income (\$5) divided by the price of X (\$2) is $2\frac{1}{2}$ units of X.

Similarly, I/P_Y is the maximum quantity of Y the consumer can purchase and the quantity of Y at which the budget line crosses the Y axis. When I changes by ΔI, the maximum amount of Y he can purchase changes by $\Delta I/P_Y$. If income increases from \$10 to \$15, the price of Y remaining \$1, the point at which the budget line crosses the Y axis moves from \$10/\$1, or 10 units of Y, to \$15/\$1, or 15 units of Y: it moves upward by 5 units of Y (= \$5/\$1).

In summary, when I increases, the budget line:

- Moves to the right by an amount equal to the increase in I divided by P_X.
- Moves upward by an amount equal to the increase in I divided by P_Y.

A normal good In Figure 10-14 we see that when his income increases from I_1 to I_2 and his budget line moves from BL_1 to BL_2, the consumer increases his consumption of X from X_1 to X_2. X is here a *normal* (or superior) good because an increase in income brought about an increase in the quantity of X consumed. A normal good is defined as a good such that the relationship between income and consumption is direct. The ratio of the change in his consumption of the good (the prices of all goods remaining constant) to the change in income is positive, or

$$\frac{\Delta D_X}{\Delta I} > 0$$

If we let ΔI approach zero, our definition of a normal good is one such that

$$\frac{dD_X}{dI} > 0 \qquad (10\text{-}17)$$

We might note in Figure 10-14 that Y is also a normal good because the increase in I results in the consumer's increasing his consumption of Y.

An inferior good When income increases, a consumer does not always increase his consumption of a good. In Figure 10-15 we see that when his income increases from I_1 to I_2, his consumption of X *de*creases from X_1 to X_2. (His consumption of Y increases, and it is a normal good.)

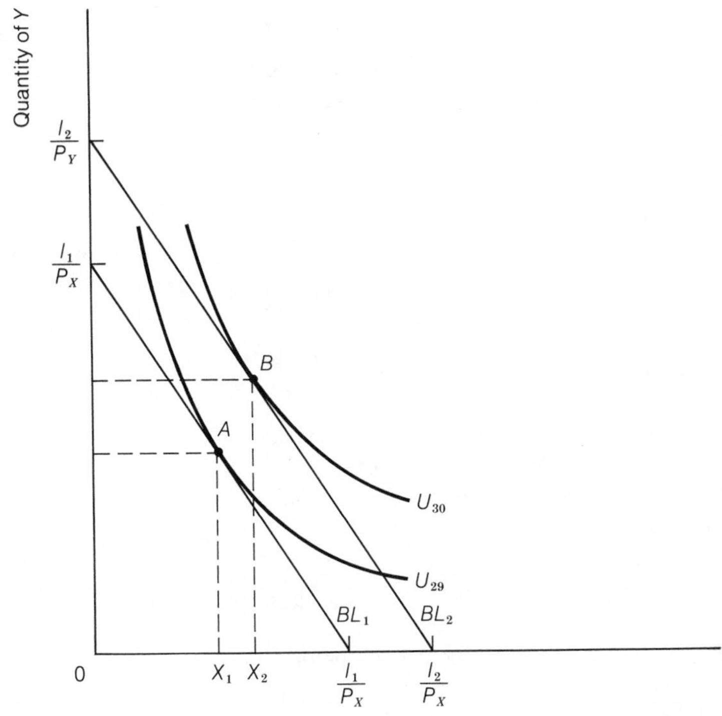

FIGURE 10-14

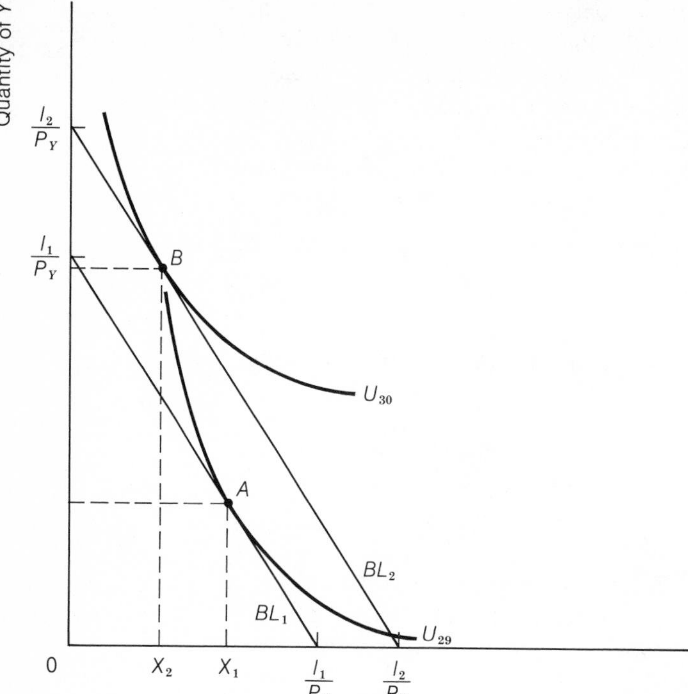

FIGURE 10-15

When increased income results in decreased consumption of a good, the good is defined as an *inferior* good. The relation between income and consumption is inverse, and the ratio of the change in consumption to the change in income is negative.

$$\frac{\Delta D_X}{\Delta I} < 0$$

and letting ΔI approach zero, our definition of an inferior good is one such that

$$\frac{dD_X}{dI} < 0 \tag{10-18}$$

A third possibility It is quite possible that when a consumer's income increases, he will not change his consumption of X. In this case, shown in Figure 10-16, the good is neither normal nor inferior. The ratio of the change in the consumption of X to the change in income is zero, and

$$\frac{dD_X}{dI} = 0 \tag{10-19}$$

Summary We cannot tell from the theory of consumer behavior whether a particular good is normal, inferior, or neither. The theory does tell us, however, that a good may be any of the three and that:

- If $dD_X/dI > 0$, the good is defined as normal.

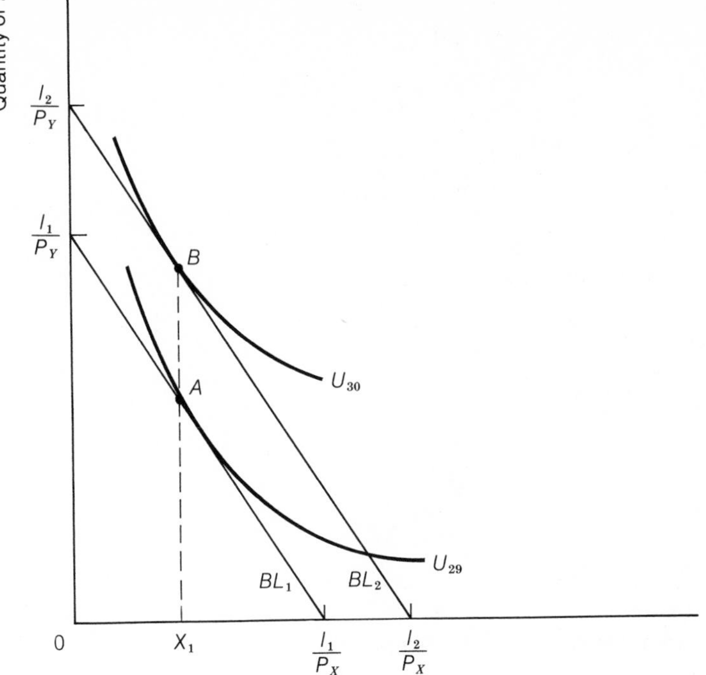

FIGURE 10-16

- If $dD_X/dI < 0$, the good is defined as inferior.
- If $dD_X/dI = 0$, the good is neither normal nor inferior.

Exercise 10-2

1 Below are a consumer's indifference map and three budget lines.

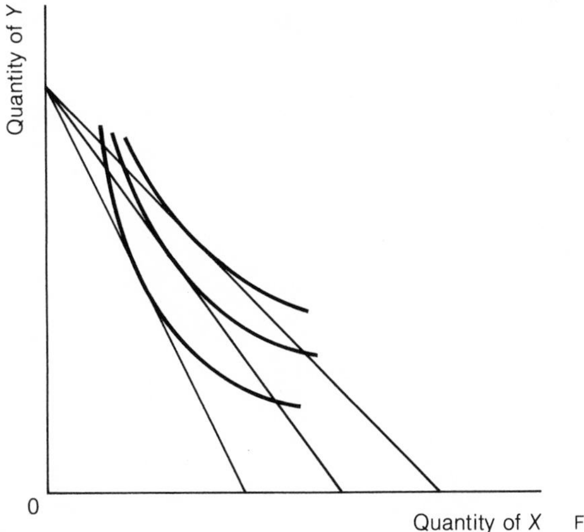

FIGURE 10-B

a When these three budget lines were drawn, it was assumed that __________ and __________ were constant and that __________ varied.

b The graph shows that as __________ decreases, the quantity of *X* consumed (increases, decreases, remains constant) __________

c The graph also shows that *Y* is a(n) (normal good, inferior good, substitute for *X*, a complement of *X*) __________

d The consumer's demand for *X* (does, does not) __________ conform to the law of demand.

2 Define in mathematical symbols:

a Complementary goods: __________

b Substitute goods: __________

c Independent goods: __________

3 In mathematical symbols, define:

a A normal good: __________

b An inferior good: __________

4 Below are a consumer's indifference map and three budget lines.

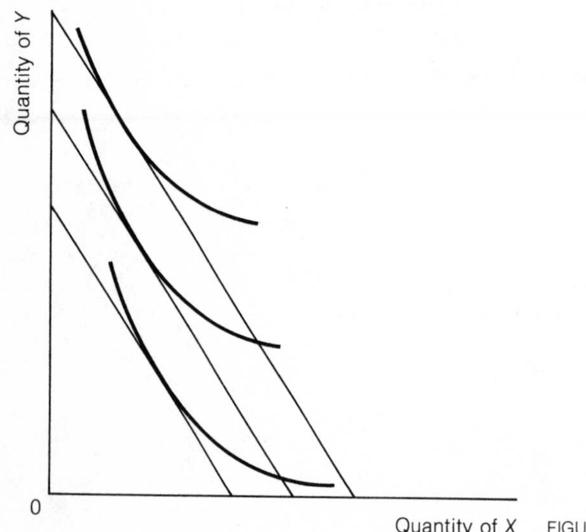

FIGURE 10-C

a When these three budget lines were drawn, it was assumed that __________ and __________ were constant and that __________ varied.

b The graph shows that as __________ decreases, the quantity of *X* consumed (increases, decreases, remains constant) __________ *c* *X* is a(n) ___________ good.

d *Y* is a(n) ___________ good.

5 A consumer's indifference map and three budget lines are shown on the graph below.

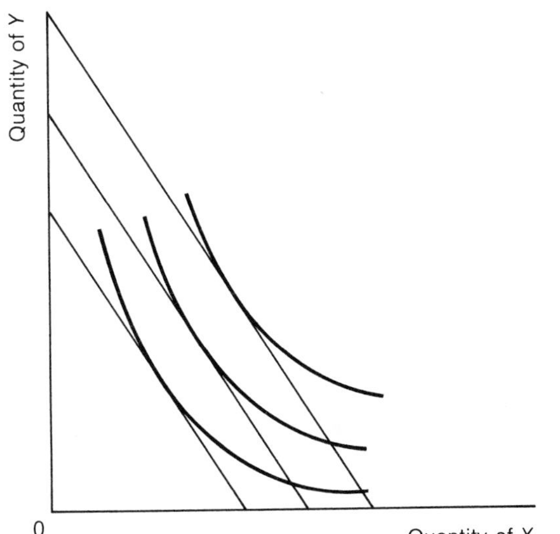

FIGURE 10-D

a This graph shows that as ___________ decreases, the quantity of *X* consumed ___________ and the quantity of *Y* consumed ___________

b *X* is a(n) ___________ good.

c *Y* is a(n) ___________ good.

6 Still another indifference map and set of budget lines are shown below.

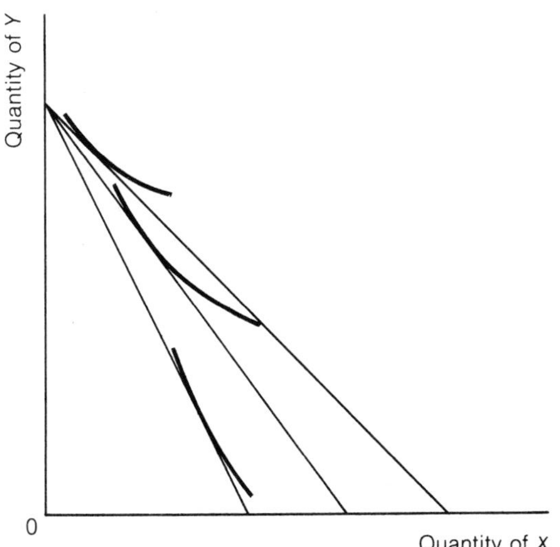

FIGURE 10-E

a The parameter that varies in this graph is ___________

b The graph shows that as ___________ increases, the quantity of *X* consumed ___________

c We can also see that *Y* is a(n) ___________

d The consumer's demand for *X* (does, does not) ___________ conform to the law of demand.

7

a When the price of *X* decreases, the consumer's level of utility (increases, decreases, remains constant) ___________

b When the price of *Y* increases, the consumer's utility ___________

c When the consumer's income increases, his utility ___________

8 If the quantity of *X* the individual consumes remains constant as the price of *X* falls, the consumer's demand for *X* is ___________

9 When the income of the consumer alone changes:

a The change in the maximum quantity of *X* he can purchase is equal to ___________/___________

b The change in the maximum quantity of *Y* he can purchase is equal to ___________/___________

10 When the price of *Y* alone increases, the absolute value of the slope of the budget line (increases, decreases, remains constant) ___________
When the income of the consumer alone changes, the absolute value of the slope of the budget line ___________

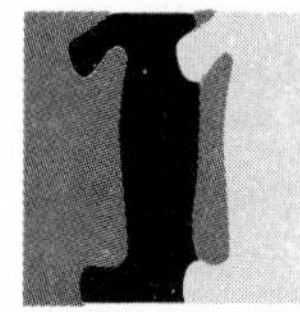

THE COSTS OF PRODUCTION

The output and the price of any product depend partly upon the demand for that product. Demand alone, however, does not determine how much of a good or service will be produced and the price at which it will sell. The amount of competition among firms producing a product and the cost of producing it also affect output and price. In this chapter we are concerned only with the costs of producing a product. In particular we wish to find out how the costs of production change when the quantity of the product a firm produces changes. We construct no particular competitive models in this chapter and are concerned solely with the assumed relationships between the level of production and the costs of producing a product. When we understand how cost varies with production, we can use our knowledge of demand and costs to explain (in Chapters 12 and 13) how much of a product will be produced and what its price will be.

This chapter is divided into three major sections. In the first we explain the terms and definitions we employ. How costs vary with production in the short run is examined in the second section. The third section examines the behavior of costs in the long run.

TERMS AND DEFINITIONS

The amount of a product a firm is able to produce depends upon the quantities of resources it employs, the amounts of other products it produces, and the techniques, methods, or technology it utilizes to produce these products.

For simplicity we shall make three assumptions: (1) we assume that the firm produces only one product, product X. (2) We assume that there are only two resources or inputs needed to produce X: input K and input L. (3) We assume that the firm always utilizes the most efficient method or technology available to it to produce X. This means that if there are two or more methods a firm can employ to produce some quantity of X, it will choose the least expensive method.

Having made these three assumptions, we can write

$$X = f(K,L) \tag{11-1}$$

This equation, called the *production function,* tells us that the quantity of X a firm is able to produce in any period of time depends *in some way* upon the quantities of K and L it employs in that time. That is, the quantities of K and L the firm uses determine the amount of X the firm produces. The production function, we should note, is the physical or technical relationship between quantities of inputs and the resulting quantity of output.

At this stage we are not interested in the precise nature of the relationship between the quantities of inputs employed and the amount of product produced. It is sufficient for us to observe that this relationship is generally an increasing one: as one input or both increase, the output or production of the item will usually increase.

Understanding that there is a relationship between X on the one hand and K and L on the other hand, however, will facilitate an understanding of the distinctions between short and long run and between fixed and variable costs. We turn, therefore, to the definitions of these terms. From there we go on to look at the meaning of average and marginal cost.

Time periods: short run and long run

Looking back at equation 11-1,

$$X = f(K,L) \tag{11-1}$$

we see that if K and L do not change, X will not change either. A period of time so short that it is impossible for the firm to vary the quantities of K and L it employs and therefore to vary its production X is defined as the *very short run*. (The very short run is also called the market period or immediate run.) We may define an input that the firm is unable to vary as a *fixed input* and an input which the firm is able to vary as a *variable input*. Our definition of the very short run then is a period of time in which all the inputs employed by the firm are fixed and none of its inputs is variable or a period of time in which the firm's output is fixed, i.e., cannot be changed or varied. When we use a bar over a symbol to indicate that it is fixed, the production function of the firm in the very short run is

$$\bar{X} = f(\bar{K},\bar{L}) \tag{11-2}$$

The short run The short run is defined as a period of time that is long enough to enable the firm to vary some but not all of the inputs it employs. At least one of the inputs it employs is fixed, and at least one of the inputs is variable.

When there are only two inputs, K and L, one of them is fixed and one is variable. Let us make K the fixed input and L the variable one. Then we can write the firm's production function in the short run as

$$X = f(\bar{K},L) \tag{11-3}$$

Even though K is fixed, the output of X is variable because L is variable. Unless the production function is a very special kind of function, the output of the firm in the short run is variable. This is indicated in equation 11-3 by the absence of a bar over X. In short, our definition of the short run is a period of time in which some but not all inputs are fixed, some but not all inputs are variable, and output is variable.

The long run The production function of the firm in the long run is

$$X = f(K,L) \tag{11-1}$$

The absence of a bar over any of the three variables indicates that the long run is a period of time in which all the inputs employed by the firm are variable and none is fixed and the output of X is variable.

Summary We are particularly interested in two of these periods, the short run and the long run. Our interest in time periods is based on the fact that the way in which the costs of producing X vary with the level of production depends upon the time period we examine. The costs of producing X in the short run are different from the costs of producing X in the long run. In the next two major sections of this chapter we shall look at the way costs vary with output in the short run and in the long run, respectively. But before we look at the relation of costs to output, we need to examine the distinction between fixed and variable costs and to define average and marginal cost.

Costs: fixed and variable

The cost of producing any given quantity of X depends upon the quantities of K and L the firm employs to produce that quantity of X and upon the prices the firm must pay for each unit of K and L it employs. We can define the cost C of producing X as

$$C \equiv K \cdot P_K + L \cdot P_L \tag{11-4}$$

P_K and P_L are the prices (per unit) of K and L, respectively. In our discussion of costs we shall assume that the prices of K and L are constants or parameters: they do not change during the time period and do not vary if the firm varies the quantities of K and L it utilizes.

In equation 11-4 we can see that the cost to the firm of employing input K is equal to the number of units of K it employs multiplied by the price of K. The cost of K is defined as $K \cdot P_K$. Likewise, the cost to the firm of input L is equal to the number of units of L it employs times the price of L. The cost of L is defined as $L \cdot P_L$. The total cost of employing both inputs is equal to the cost of K plus the cost of L. With the prices of K and L parameters, the cost of producing X varies only if the firm varies the quantities of K and of L it employs. Only if the firm varies its output by varying the quantities of K and L it uses do the costs of the firm change.

In the *very* short run we know that both K and L are fixed inputs: the firm cannot vary the amounts of them it employs and cannot vary its output. The cost equation of the firm in the very short run is thus

$$\bar{C} = \bar{K} \cdot \bar{P}_K + \bar{L} \cdot \bar{P}_L \tag{11-5}$$

where a bar over a variable once again indicates that it is fixed. We can see that the cost of K is fixed because both the quantity the firm employs and its price are fixed; that the cost of L is also fixed because the quantity of L and the price of L are fixed; and that, therefore, the cost of producing X is also fixed.

We define a *fixed cost* as the cost of a fixed input. It is clear, then, that because all inputs are fixed in the very short run, all the firm's costs in the very short run are fixed. We can therefore say the very short run is a period of time in which all inputs and the firm's output are fixed.

The short run is the time period in which some inputs are fixed and some are variable. The firm's production function is

$$X = f(\bar{K}, L) \tag{11-3}$$

Input K is fixed, and input L is variable. When we write the firm's cost function in the short run, we have

$$C = \bar{K} \cdot \bar{P}_K + L \cdot \bar{P}_L \tag{11-6}$$

The cost of K is a fixed cost because a fixed cost is the cost of a fixed input. But the cost of L is not a fixed cost because L is not fixed. L is a variable input. The cost of L is a variable cost because we define a *variable cost* as the cost of a variable input.

The short run, therefore, is not only a period in which some inputs are fixed and some are variable and in which output is variable; it is also a period in which some of the firm's costs are fixed and some are variable. We may note that if the firm is to vary its production of X in the short run, it must vary the amount of the variable input it employs and that when it changes the amount of the variable input, it also changes the cost to the firm of that input. In short, variable costs are those costs which change when the firm changes its output, and fixed costs are those costs which do not change when a firm changes its output. Our redefinition of the short run is a period in which some of the firm's costs are fixed and some are variable.

In the long run the firm's production function is

$$X = f(K, L) \tag{11-1}$$

All the inputs the firm employs are variable, and its output is variable. The long-run cost equation of the firm is therefore

$$C = K \cdot \bar{P}_K + L \cdot \bar{P}_L \tag{11-7}$$

We see that the firm has no fixed costs because fixed costs are the costs of fixed inputs and these are not fixed inputs. The cost of K and the cost of L are variable; and the cost of K plus the cost of L is variable. The long run, then, is also a period of time in which all the firm's costs are variable and in which none of its costs are fixed.

In summary:

- Fixed costs are the costs of fixed inputs and costs which do not change when the firm changes its output.

- Variable costs are the costs of variable inputs and costs which do change when the firm changes its level of production.
- Costs in the short run are partly fixed and partly variable.
- All costs in the long run are variable.

In equation form the costs C of the firm in the short run are

$$C \equiv F + V \tag{11-8}$$

where F means fixed cost and V means variable cost. In the long run, however, the costs of the firm are

$$C \equiv V \tag{11-9}$$

(The costs of the firm in the very short run are $C \equiv F$.)

With the distinction between fixed and variable costs and the definitions of short and long run established, we can go on to define total, average, and marginal cost.

Total, average, and marginal cost

The costs we examined above were all total costs: the total payments made (either explicitly or implicitly) to owners of resources to assure the continued use of these inputs by the firm. For example, if the firm employs 10 units of K at a price of \$3 per unit and 20 units of L at a price of \$4 per unit, its total cost C is

$$\begin{aligned} C &= 10K\frac{\$3}{K} + 20L\frac{\$4}{L} \\ &= \$30 + \$80 \\ &= \$110 \end{aligned}$$

Notice that the price of an input is expressed in terms of dollars per unit of the input. The price of K is \$3 per unit of K, and the price of L is \$4 per unit of L.

If K is the fixed input and L the variable one (as in the short run), the firm's total fixed cost is \$30, its total variable cost is \$80, and its total cost is \$110. If both K and L are fixed inputs (as in the very short run), the firm has no variable costs. Its total cost and its total fixed cost are both \$110. But if K and L are both variable inputs (as in the long run), the firm has no fixed costs; its total variable cost and its total cost both equal \$110.

Business firms and economists are interested in the total costs of producing a product, but they are also interested in the average cost and the marginal cost of producing that product. Both terms require definition.

Average costs In the numerical example above, suppose the firm which spent \$110 on inputs K and L was able to produce 10 units of product X. The total cost of producing X is \$110 when the firm produces $10X$. The average (or per unit) cost of X is equal to the total cost of producing X divided by the number of units of X produced by the firm. If we use the symbol A_c for average cost, we define *average cost* as

$$A_c \equiv \frac{C}{X} \tag{11-10}$$

Producing 10 units of X at a total cost of \$110 means that

$$A_C = \frac{\$110}{10}$$

$$= \$11$$

If some of the \$110 is fixed cost and some is variable cost, we can compute both the average fixed cost and the average variable cost. Suppose the firm's total fixed cost is \$30 and its total variable cost is \$80. The average (or per unit) fixed cost is equal to the total fixed cost of producing X divided by the number of units of X produced. Letting A_F stand for average fixed cost, we define *average fixed cost* as

$$A_F \equiv \frac{F}{X} \qquad (11\text{-}11)$$

If the firm produces $10X$ and has a total fixed cost of \$30, then

$$A_F = \frac{\$30}{10}$$

$$= \$3$$

Similarly, *average* (or per unit) *variable cost* A_V is equal to total variable cost divided by the number of units of X produced, or

$$A_V \equiv \frac{V}{X} \qquad (11\text{-}12)$$

And if total variable cost is \$80 when the firm produces $10X$,

$$A_V = \frac{\$80}{10}$$

$$= \$8$$

We should note that total cost is the sum of total fixed cost and total variable cost, or

$$C \equiv F + V \qquad (11\text{-}8)$$

and that average total cost is

$$A_C \equiv \frac{C}{X} \qquad (11\text{-}10)$$

For C in equation 11-10 we may substitute $F + V$ and find

$$A_C \equiv \frac{F + V}{X}$$

or

$$A_C \equiv \frac{F}{X} + \frac{V}{X} \qquad (11\text{-}13)$$

Equation 11-13 tells us that average total cost is equal to the sum of average fixed cost (F/X) and average variable cost (V/X). We can say that

$$A_C \equiv A_F + A_V \qquad (11\text{-}14)$$

We know that in the very short run, total variable costs are zero and all costs are fixed. This means that V/X in equation 11-13 is equal to zero. It follows that if V/X is zero, in the very short run

$$A_C = \frac{F}{X} + 0$$

or average total cost is equal to average fixed cost. But in the long run total fixed cost is zero, and so F/X is also zero. Therefore

$$A_C = 0 + \frac{V}{X}$$

Average cost in the long run is equal to average variable cost.

In summary, we may find average total, average fixed, and average variable cost at any level of output by dividing total cost, total fixed cost, and total variable cost, respectively, by the level of output. And just as total fixed cost plus total variable cost equals total cost, so average fixed cost plus average variable cost equals average total cost.

Marginal cost A firm is able to change its level of production only by changing the quantity of variable inputs it employs. But when a firm changes the quantity of variable inputs, it also changes its total costs. Tentatively, we may define marginal cost as the amount by which a firm's total costs change when it changes its output by 1 unit, or the ratio of the change in total costs to the change in output. In mathematical language marginal cost C_M is

$$C_M \equiv \frac{\Delta C}{\Delta M} \tag{11-15}$$

Because a firm must increase the quantity of variable inputs and thereby increase its total costs if it is to increase its production of X, and because decreasing the quantity of variable inputs decreases its total costs and its production, marginal cost is a positive amount.

$$C_M > 0$$

Suppose, for example, a firm is incurring costs of \$110 to produce 10 units of X. When it increases its total costs to \$120, its production of X increases to 12. The change in total cost is +\$10, and the change in the production of X is +2. Its marginal cost is then

$$C_M = \frac{\Delta C}{\Delta M} = \frac{+\$10}{+2} = \$5$$

The additional cost per additional unit of X is \$5. If the firm decreased its production of X from 10 to 9 and its total costs fell from \$110 to \$100, we would find that

$$C_M = \frac{-\$10}{-1} = +\$10$$

Because we shall be concerned with the ratio of the change in total cost to the change in output when the change in output approaches zero, we redefine marginal cost as the limit $\Delta C/\Delta X$ approaches as ΔX approaches zero. This, we

$$C_M \equiv \frac{dC}{dX} \equiv \lim_{\Delta X \to 0} \frac{\Delta C}{\Delta X} \tag{11-16}$$

Later in this chapter we shall see how we can find the marginal-cost function or equation when we know the total-cost function for a product. We shall utilize the technique we learned in Chapter 9 to find the derivative of the total-cost function, which is the marginal-cost function.

Exercise 11-1

1 Suppose a firm employs two inputs, N and R, to produce product Y.

a Express mathematically the firm's production function. ____________

b Using a bar to indicate fixed quantities, write the firm's production function in:

(1) The very short run: ____________

(2) The long run: ____________

c If R is the fixed input, what is the firm's production function in the short run? ____________

2

a In the very short run a firm's inputs are all ____________, and its output is ____________

b In the long run a firm's inputs are all ____________, and its output is ____________

c In the short run a firm's inputs are ____________, and its output is ____________

3 For the firm employing inputs N and R to produce Y, the cost function is $C =$ ____________

Assuming the prices of the two inputs are exogenous variables and that R is the fixed input, write the firm's cost function in:

a The very short run: $C =$ ____________

b The short run: $C =$ ____________

c The long run: $C =$ ____________

4 We define a firm's:

a Fixed costs as the cost of ____________ inputs and costs which (do, do not) ____________ change when the firm changes its output.

b Variable costs as the cost of ____________ inputs and costs which ____________ change when the firm changes its output.

c Fixed costs plus its variable costs as its ____________

5 In:

a The very short run a firm's output is (fixed, variable) ____________, and all its costs are ____________

b The long run a firm's output is ____________, and all its costs are ____________ *c* The short run a firm's output is ___________, and its costs are ___________

6 Using the symbols *F* and *V*, the firm's costs in equation form in:

a The very short run are $C =$ ___________

b The short run are $C =$ ___________

c The long run are $C =$ ___________

7 Define in symbols each of the following:

a $A_F =$ ___________ / ___________

b $A_V =$ ___________ / ___________

c $A_C =$ ___________ / ___________ = ___________ / ___________

\+ ___________ / ___________

8 In:

a The very short run $A_C =$ ___________ / ___________ or ___________

b The long run $A_C =$ ___________ / ___________ or ___________

c The short run $A_C =$ ___________ / ___________ + ___________ / ___________ or ___________ + ___________

9 Suppose that a firm employs 6 units of *N* and 5 units of *R* to produce 20 units of *Y*, that the price of *N* is $5 per unit and the price of *R* is $8 per unit, and that *R* is the fixed input.

a The firm's:

(1) Total fixed cost is $___________

(2) Total variable cost is $___________

(3) Total cost is $___________

b The firm's:

(1) Average fixed cost is $___________

(2) Average variable cost is $___________

(3) Average total cost is $___________

c Now assume that the firm employs 1 unit more of *N* and that as a result its production of *Y* increases by 3 units.

(1) The increase in its variable cost is $___________

(2) The increase in its total cost is $___________

(3) The marginal cost of each of the 3 additional units of *Y* is equal to ___________ / ___________ or $___________

10 Marginal cost is defined as the limit which ___________ approaches as ___________ approaches zero; and in symbols it is C_M or ___________

COSTS IN THE SHORT RUN

We defined in the first section of this chapter the different kinds of costs of producing a product: fixed and variable, average and total, and marginal cost. This section is concerned with how each of these different costs changes or varies when the firm changes its output in the short run. (The next section is concerned with how cost varies when the firm varies its output in the long run.) What we are interested in is the functional relationship between each of the different kinds of costs on the one hand and the level of production on the other.

The relationships between cost and output we examine are relationships which economists assume to exist between cost and output. Whether these relationships exist in fact is a question we shall not examine. In the order in which we take them up, the relations we shall examine are those between fixed cost and output, variable cost and output, total cost and output, and marginal cost and output.

Fixed costs

In the short run, one of the inputs a firm employs is fixed and one is variable. This means that one of its costs, the cost of the fixed input, is fixed and that one of its costs, the cost of the variable input, is variable. Its total cost C in the short run is the sum of its fixed cost F and its variable cost V or

$$C \equiv F + V \tag{11-8}$$

As we know, a fixed cost is the cost which does not change when the firm changes its production of X. It is fixed because it is the cost of an input which the firm cannot vary in the short run. The fixed-cost *function* we may write as

$$F = \bar{F} \tag{11-17}$$

where $\bar{F}$ is a fixed number of dollars. For example, we might have

$$F = \$100 \tag{11-18}$$

for the fixed-cost function. It is assumed that F is greater than zero. We should note in equation 11-17 that the variable X does not appear. The absence of X from the fixed-cost function means that fixed cost does not depend in any way upon the amount of product X produced by the firm. F does not change when X changes.

If we plot a firm's fixed cost and its output of X on a graph, the *fixed-cost curve* will look like the curve labeled F in Figure 11-1. Note that the curve is

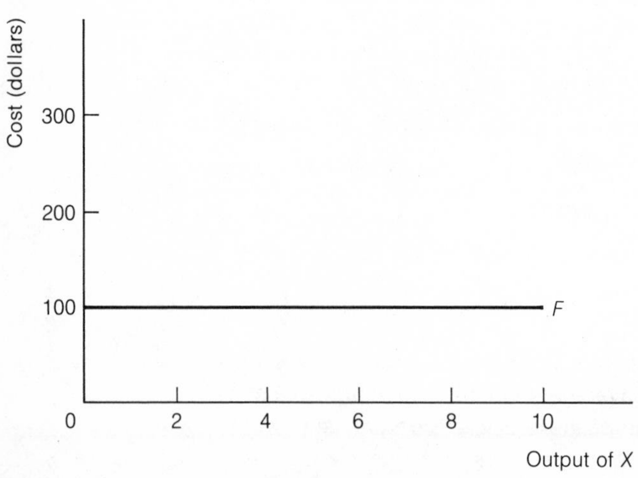

FIGURE 11-1

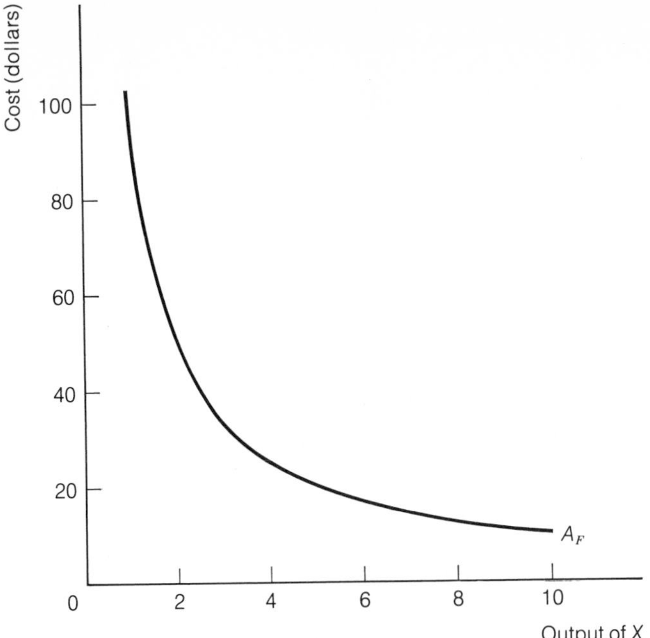

FIGURE 11-2

a horizontal line. The fixed-cost curve has a slope of zero. It tells us that fixed cost neither increases nor decreases as X varies.

Average fixed cost A_F at any level of production we have defined as

$$A_F \equiv \frac{F}{X} \tag{11-11}$$

It should be observed that while a firm's fixed costs do not change when the firm changes its output, its *average* fixed costs do vary when output varies. With F constant in equation 11-11, as X increases, A_F must decrease. For example, if $F = \$100$ *and* $X = 1$, then A_F is equal to \$100/1, or \$100. When X is 2, A_F is \$100/2, or \$50. When X is 3, A_F is \$100/3, or \$33.33; etc.

When we plot average fixed cost and the output of X on a graph, we obtain the *average-fixed-cost curve,* which looks like the one labeled A_F in Figure 11-2. Notice that as X increases, A_F decreases but that A_F never becomes zero. As X increases, A_F approaches zero; and the greater the output of X, the smaller the average fixed cost of X.

In summary, $F = \overline{F}$ is the fixed-cost function, and fixed cost does not depend on X. $A_F = F/X$ is the average-fixed-cost function, and A_F does depend on X. With F fixed or constant, A_F and X are inversely related to each other.

Variable cost

Variable cost is a cost which changes as the firm changes its production of X. It is variable because it is the cost of the input which the firm must change if it is to change its output in the short run.

The variable-cost function We shall assume that variable cost is an increasing and nonlinear function of X and that

$$V = aX^3 - bX^2 + cX \qquad (11\text{-}19)$$

We can see at once that the assumed relationship between V and X takes the form of a third-degree equation because the greatest exponent of any variable in the equation is 3.

There are certain assumptions we make about the nature of the variable-cost function. Notice that the term bX^2 is preceeded by a minus sign. This is the first assumption. In addition, we assume that 3 times a times c is greater than b squared, or

$$3ac > b^2$$

We made these two assumptions for two reasons: (1) We want variable cost to change in a very specific way as the output of the firm changes. (2) We do not want to obtain any values for average variable cost or marginal cost that are economic nonsense. We do not want to find that average variable cost or marginal cost is zero or even less than zero.

We can see if we look at equation 10-19 that there is no term on the right side of the equation that does not contain X. This means that if X is zero, V must also be zero because each of the three terms on the right side will be zero. This is one of our assumptions about the nature of the variable-cost function: when output is zero, the firm's variable cost is also zero. (If there were a term on the right side that did not contain X, a term such as $+Z$, we would find that when X is zero, V equals $+Z$.)

Our numerical example of the variable cost function is

$$V = X^3 - 12X^2 + 108X \qquad (11\text{-}20)$$

Notice that the parameters a, b, and c are 1, 12, and 108, respectively. Each is greater than zero. We have also made $3ac$ greater than b^2. The value of $3ac$ is 3(1)(108), or 324; and 324 is greater than the value of b^2, which is $(12)^2$, or 144.

In Figure 11-3 we have plotted equation 11-20. What do we see when we look at this figure? First, when X is zero, V is zero. Second, V is an increasing function of X: as X increases, so does V. Third, the *variable-cost curve* (labeled V) is not a straight line. As we move from left to right, the slope of the curve is not constant. The slope of V at first decreases and then increases as X increases.

Why we have made these specific assumptions about the relation of V to X will be explained later when we discuss marginal cost.

The average-variable-cost function The average variable cost A_V of producing X at any level of production we defined earlier as

$$A_V \equiv \frac{V}{X} \qquad (11\text{-}12)$$

If we substitute the right side of equation 11-19 for V in the equation above, we have

$$A_V = \frac{aX^3 - bX^2 + cX}{X}$$

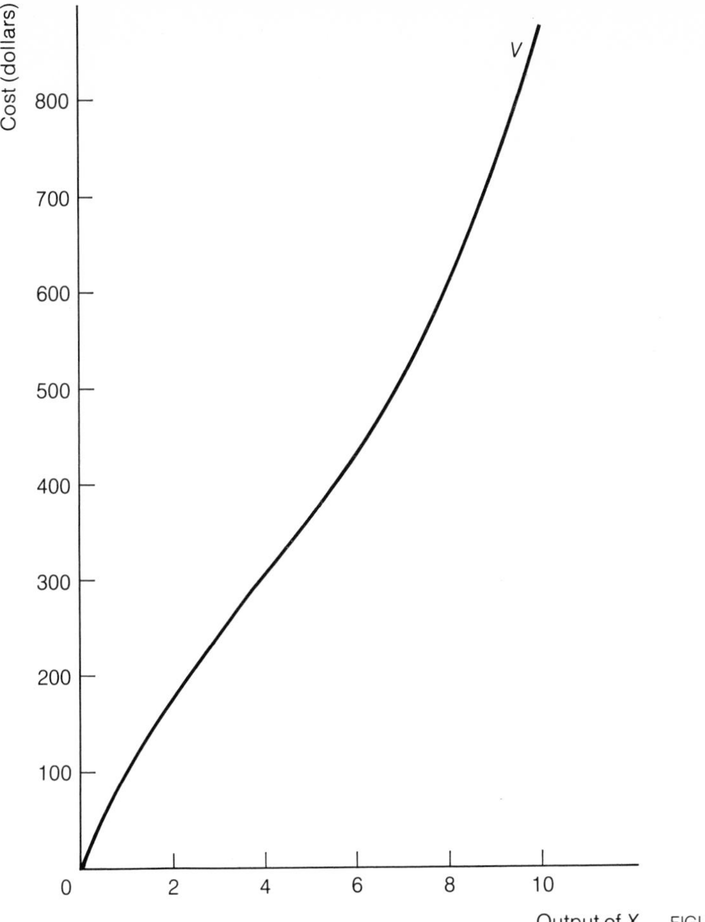

FIGURE 11-3

or

$$A_V = aX^2 - bX + c \tag{11-21}$$

Equation 11-21 is the average-variable-cost function. From it we can find average variable cost at every level of production. The average-variable-cost function, we can see, is a second-degree equation. Recalling that we have assumed that $3ac$ is greater than b^2, what kind of function is the average-variable-cost function?

We can see this best if we plot a numerical example of average variable cost. If the variable-cost function is

$$V = X^3 - 12X^2 + 108X \tag{11-20}$$

and we substitute $X^3 - 12X^2 + 108X$ for V in equation 11-12, we find

$$A_V = \frac{X^3 - 12X^2 + 108X}{X}$$

and the variable-cost function is

$$A_V = X^2 - 12X + 108 \tag{11-22}$$

When we plot A_V and X on a graph, as in Figure 11-4, we obtain a curve like the one labeled A_V. We can see that this *average-variable-cost curve* is U-shaped: as X increases, A_V at first decreases, reaches a minimum, and then increases. In our example, A_V is a minimum when X is equal to 6. Between 0 and 6 units of X, average variable cost decreases as X increases; but when X is greater than 6, average variable cost increases as X increases.

Again we might ask why average variable cost behaves in this fashion. The answer is that A_V varies this way because we have assumed that the variable-cost function is a third-degree equation, that the sign preceeding bX^2 is negative, and that $3ac$ is greater than b^2. The explanation of why we have made this specific assumption we defer until we discuss marginal cost.

Total cost

In the short run a firm's total cost is

$$C \equiv F + V \tag{11-8}$$

Now if

$$F = \bar{F} \tag{11-17}$$

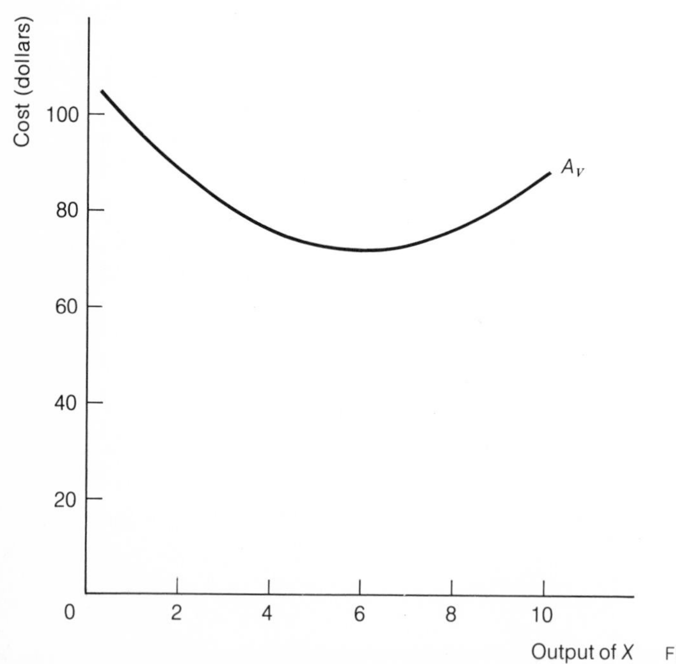

FIGURE 11-4

and

$$V = aX^3 - bX^2 + cX \tag{11-19}$$

we can find the *total-cost function* by adding the fixed- and variable-cost functions

$$C = F + (aX^3 - bX^2 + cX)$$

or

$$C = aX^3 - bX^2 + cX + \bar{F} \tag{11-23}$$

Equation 11-23 is the total-cost function. It tells us the total cost of producing X at every level of X. We can see that (unlike the variable-cost function) when X is zero, C is *not* zero. For if X is zero, then C is equal to $\bar{F}$. In short, when output is zero, its total cost is equal to $\bar{F}$, its fixed cost. Like the variable-cost function, the total-cost function is a third-degree equation. But the latter function has a term in it which does not contain X: the term $\bar{F}$. And the term $\bar{F}$ is nothing more than the firm's fixed cost.

In our numerical example,

$$F = \$100 \tag{11-18}$$

and

$$V = X^3 - 12X^2 + 108X \tag{11-20}$$

Our total-cost function is therefore

$$C = \$100 + X^3 - 12X^2 + 108X$$

or

$$C = X^3 - 12X^2 + 108X + \$100 \tag{11-24}$$

In Figure 11-5 we have plotted equation 11-4 along with the fixed-cost function (equation 11-17) and the variable-cost function (equation 11-20). We can observe in Figure 11-5 that the total-cost curve has the same general shape as the variable-cost curve. Both C and V increase as X increases, and the slopes of both C and V decrease at first and then increase as X increases. The vertical (or cost) distance between the C and V curves is constant because this distance is simply the fixed cost, which is constant. It should also be observed that while V is zero when X is zero, C is not zero when X is zero. When X is zero, C is equal to the firm's fixed costs.

Average total cost Our definition of average total cost is

$$A_c \equiv \frac{C}{X} \tag{11-10}$$

Substituting the total-cost function (equation 11-23) for C in equation 11-10, we find that

$$A_c = \frac{aX^3 - bX^2 + cX + \bar{F}}{X} = aX^2 - bX + c + \bar{F}/X \tag{11-25}$$

Equation 11-25 is the *average-total-cost function*. We should recognize that

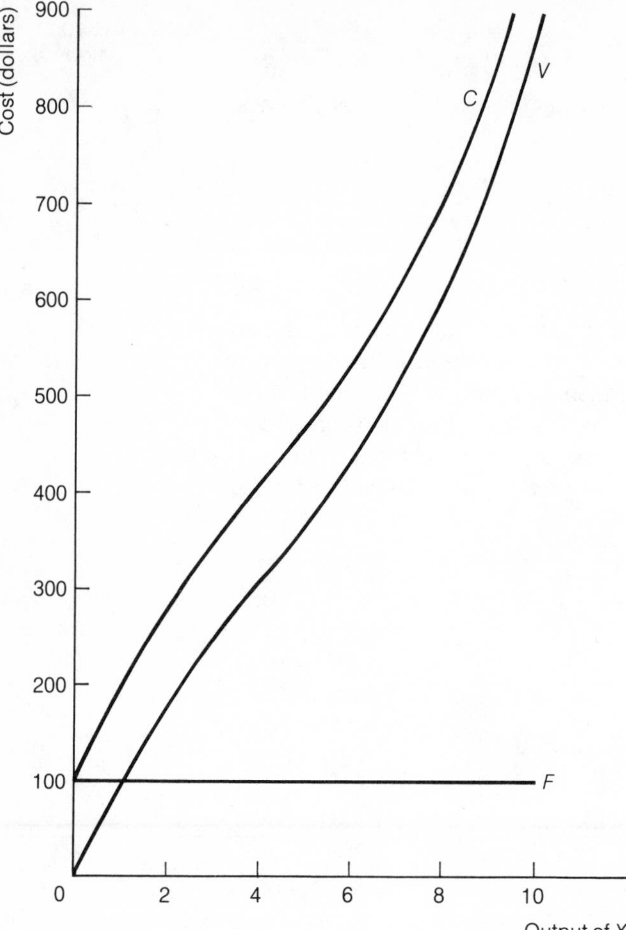

FIGURE 11-5

$aX^2 - bX + c$ is the average variable cost (equation 11-21) and that $\bar{F}/X$ is the average fixed cost (equation 11-11). This simply tells us that average total cost is equal to average variable cost plus average fixed cost. We can also see that equation 11-25 is a second-degree equation, like the average-variable-cost function.

Using our earlier numerical examples, in which F was \$100, V was equal to $X^3 - 12X^2 + 108X$, and C was $X^3 - 12X^2 + 108X + \$100$, we find that

$$A_c = \frac{X^3 - 12X^2 + 108X + \$100}{X}$$

or

$$A_c = X^2 - 12X + 108 + \frac{\$100}{X} \tag{11-26}$$

Again we recognize that $\$100/X$ is average fixed cost and that $X^2 - 12X + 108$ is average variable cost.

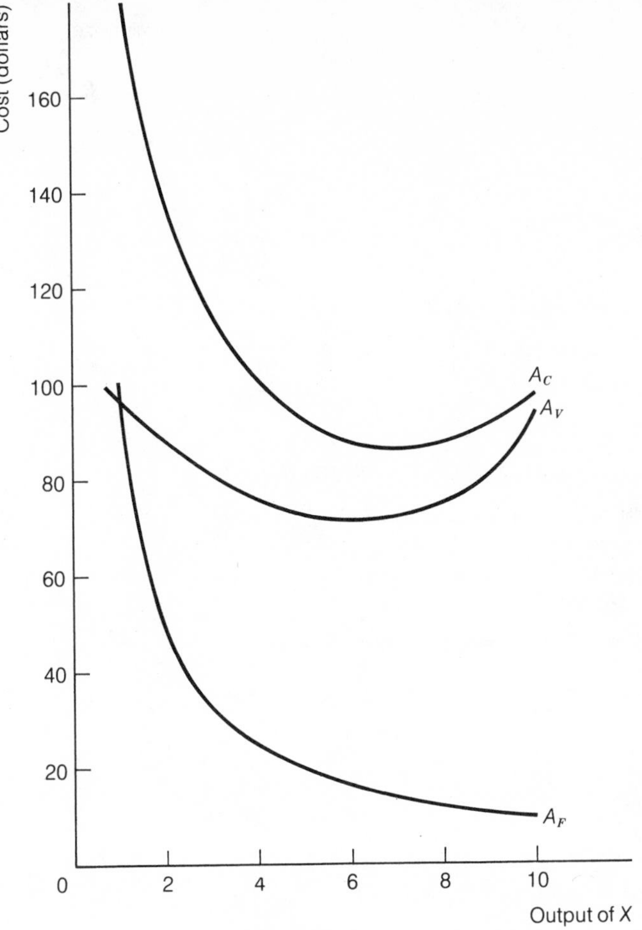

FIGURE 11-6

The average-total-cost curve In Figure 11-6 we have plotted equation 11-26, the average-total-cost function, along with equations 11-21 (the average-variable-cost function) and 11-11 (the average-fixed-cost function). We can see that A_C has the same general shape as A_V. A_C decreases at first as X increases, reaches a minimum, and then increases. In our example, A_C is a minimum when X is about 7.015. Note that A_C is a minimum at an output greater than the output at which A_V is a minimum, an output of 6. Said the other way around, A_V reaches a minimum before A_C reaches its minimum. We also observe in Figure 11-6 that as X increases, the vertical (or cost) distance between A_C and A_V decreases. This vertical distance between A_C and A_V is simply the average fixed cost; and we already know that A_F decreases as X increases.

Exercise 11-2

1 In the short run a firm's:

a $C \equiv$ __________ + __________

b $A_C \equiv$ __________ + __________

2 If $F = \bar{F}$ and $V = aX^3 - bX^2 + cX$, then:

a $C =$ ____________

b $A_F =$ ____________

c $A_V =$ ____________

d $A_C =$ ____________

3 When the variable-cost function is $V = aX^3 - bX^2 + cX$, it is assumed that $3ac$ is ____________ than b^2.

4 As the production of X increases:

a A_F (increases, decreases, remains constant) ____________

b A_V at first ____________ and then ____________

c A_C ____________ at first and then ____________. The output at which A_C is a minimum is (greater than, less than, equal to) ____________ the output at which A_V is a minimum.

5 Assume $F = \$300$ and $V = X^3 - 15X^2 + 200X$.

a $3ac$ is equal to ____________ and is greater than b^2, which is equal to ____________

b $C =$ ____________

c $A_F =$ ____________

d $A_V =$ ____________

e $A_C =$ ____________

6 Using the functions in question 5, when X is 5:

a $F = \$$____________

b $V = \$$____________

c $C = \$$____________

d $A_F = \$$____________

e $A_V = \$$____________

f $A_C = \$$____________

7 Plot the average-fixed, average-variable, and average-total-cost functions from question 5 on the graph on the next page.

a At approximately what output is average variable cost a minimum? ____________

b At approximately what output is average total cost a minimum? ____________

8 When the output of X is zero, in symbols:

a V is equal to ____________

b C is equal to ____________

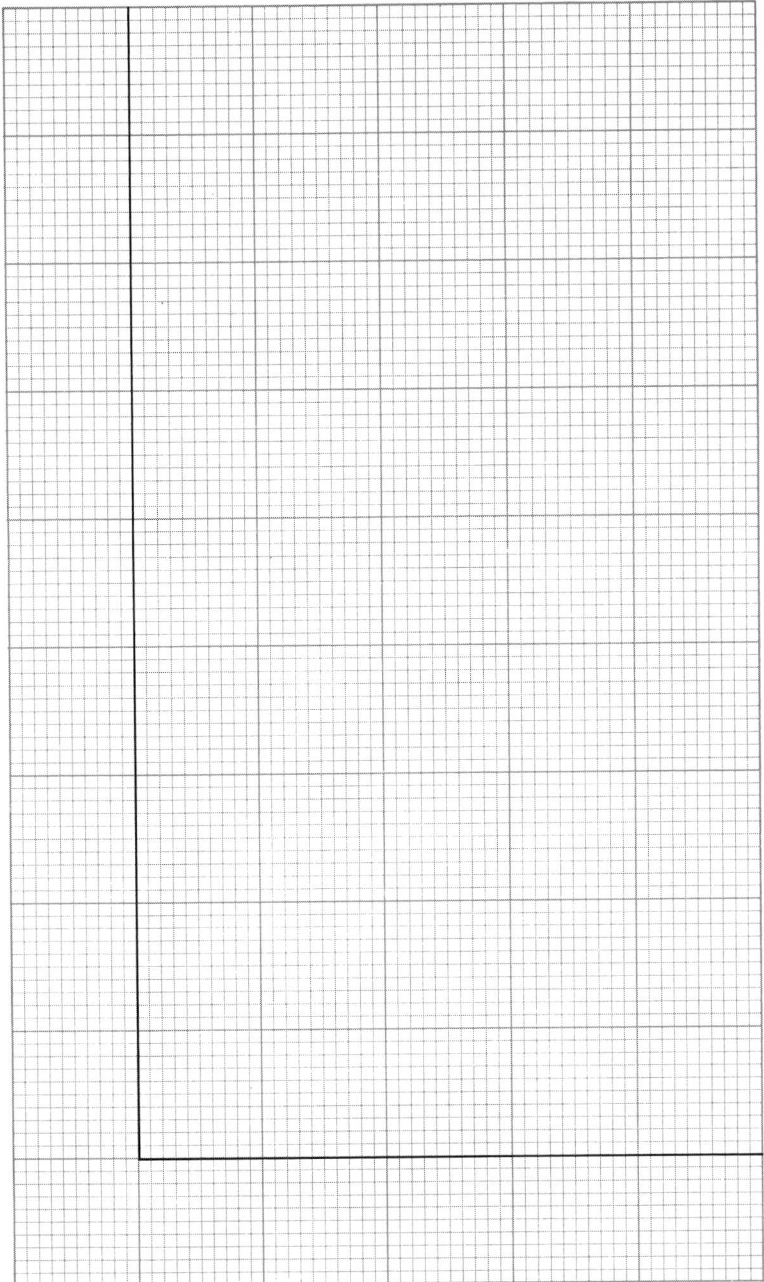

Marginal cost

In equation 11-16 we defined marginal cost C_M as the limit $\Delta C/\Delta X$ approaches as ΔX approaches zero and used the notation dC/dX for marginal cost. We now wish to do two things: (1) find the marginal-cost function or equation and (2) explain why marginal cost in the short run varies as it does with the output of the firm.

The marginal-cost function Starting with equation 11-23, the total-cost function,

$$C = aX^3 - bX^2 + cX + \bar{F} \qquad (11\text{-}23)$$

we can find dC/dX by using the technique for determining the derivative of a function we learned in Chapter 9. Employing this simple technique for derivative finding, we take each term on the right side of equation 11-23 separately and find its derivative. In each term we multiply the exponent of X times the coefficient of X and reduce the exponent of X by 1. The derivative of:

- aX^3 is $3aX^2$.
- $-bX^2$ is $-2bX$.
- cX is cX^0 or simply c (X^0 is equal to 1).
- $\bar{F}$ (which is really $\bar{F}X^0$) is $0X^{-1}$ or 0.

Then we add the derivatives of each term to find the derivative of the total-cost function. Adding, we find that

$$\frac{dC}{dX} = 3aX^2 - 2bX + c \qquad (11\text{-}27)$$

This is the *marginal-cost function*. It tells at every level of the production of X what the change in total cost per unit change in output is as the change in output approaches zero.

If the total-cost function is $C = X^3 - 12X^2 + 108X + \$100$ (equation 11-24), then the derivative of:

- X^3 is $3X^2$
- $-12X^2$ is $-24X$
- $108X$ is 108
- \$100 is zero

and, adding, marginal cost is

$$\frac{dC}{dX} = 3X^2 - 24X + 108 \qquad (11\text{-}28)$$

The marginal-cost function, we see, is a second-degree equation. When we plot equation 11-28 in Figure 11-7, we find that the marginal-cost curve is U-shaped. As X increases, marginal cost at first decreases, reaches a minimum (where X is 4 and marginal cost is \$60 in our example), and then increases.

It is important to note that we could also have determined the marginal-cost function by finding the derivative of the total-*variable*-cost function. The total-variable-cost function is $V = aX^3 - bX^2 + cX$ (equation 11-19). Its derivative, dV/dX, using the same derivative-finding technique, is $3aX^2 - 2bX + c$. This is precisely the same value we found for marginal cost in equation 11-27. In our numerical example $V = X^3 - 12X^2 + 108X$, and dV/dX is $3X^2 - 24X + 108$, the value of the marginal-cost function in equation 11-28.

This result—that marginal cost is the derivative of both the total-cost and the

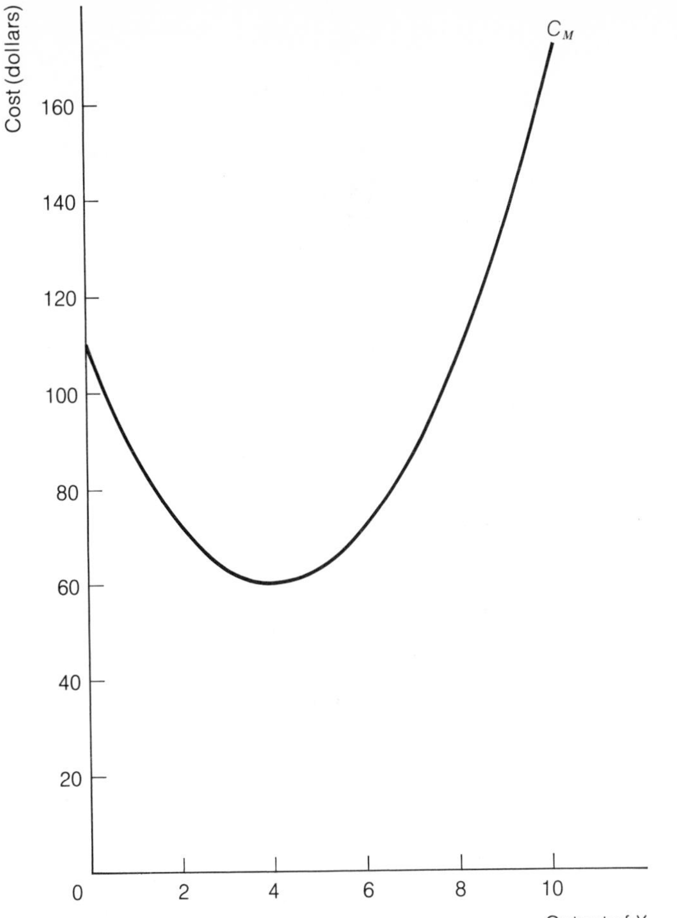

FIGURE 11-7

total-variable-cost functions—is not too surprising. We know that $C \equiv F + V$. If C changes by a very small amount equal to dC (which we assume is identical or at least almost identical to ΔC), this change in C will equal the change in F (or dF, which is approximately equal to ΔF) plus the change in V (or dV, which we treat as equal to ΔV).[1] Therefore,

$$dC = dF + dV$$

But in the short run F is constant and does not change. The change in F is zero, and so

$$dC = 0 + dV$$

and

$$dC = dV$$

[1]Such terms as dC, dF, and dV are called *differentials* in mathematics. While they are not really the same thing as ΔC, ΔF, and ΔV, they are approximately equal to ΔC, ΔF, and ΔV when the changes in C, F, and V are very small.

If we now divide both sides of the equation above by dX (a very small change in X), we have

$$\frac{dC}{dX} = \frac{dV}{dX}$$

This tells us that in the short run the derivative of the total-cost function and the derivative of the total-variable-cost function are equal. In short, marginal cost is the derivative of both the total-cost and total-variable-cost functions.

Marginal cost and the production function in the short run We now turn to the question of *why* marginal cost decreases, reaches a minimum, and then increases as the output of the firm increases. When we have an answer to this question, we shall have an answer to the question of why variable cost and total cost vary with output in the manner described above.

The output of X is a function of the quantities of inputs K and L employed by the firm. In the short run, one of the inputs (K) is fixed, and the other (L) is variable. This means that changes in X occur only as a result of changes in the variable input L. With L the variable input, the only cost changes that can occur in the short run are the changes in cost that result from changes in the quantity of L employed. Assuming that the price of L is constant, the firm's cost equation in the short run is

$$C = \bar{K} \cdot \bar{P}_K + L \cdot \bar{P}_L \qquad (11\text{-}6)$$

The derivative of this function with respect to L (the limit which the ratio of ΔC to ΔL approaches as ΔL approaches zero) is dC/dL. We can find this derivative as we have found the derivatives of other functions. The derivative of the term $\bar{K} \cdot \bar{P}_K$, in which the variable L does not appear, is zero; and the derivative of the term $\bar{L} \cdot \bar{P}_L$ (which can be written as $\bar{P}_L L^1$) is $\bar{P}_L L^0$ or $\bar{P}_L$. dC/dL is therefore equal to zero plus $\bar{P}_L$; and we can write

$$\frac{dC}{dL} = \bar{P}_L \qquad (11\text{-}29)$$

We find that dC/dL is constant and equal to the price (per unit) of L.

The assumed relationship between X and L in the short run is a third-degree equation of the type

$$X = aL^2 - bL^3 \qquad (11\text{-}30)$$

The sign preceeding bL^3 is minus. It is also assumed that the parameter a is greater than the parameter b. As an example of this relationship between L and X we might have

$$X = 12L^2 - L^3 \qquad (11\text{-}31)$$

If we plot L on the horizontal axis and X on the vertical axis, as in Figure 11-8, we obtain a curve like the one labeled X. (In plotting this curve we have assumed that a is 12 and b is 1.) Notice that this relationship between L and X is direct until L reaches approximately 8 and that thereafter it is inverse. We should also observe where the slope is positive; the slope at first increases, reaches a maximum (where L is approximately 4), and then decreases.

What interests us is the relationship between changes in L and the resulting

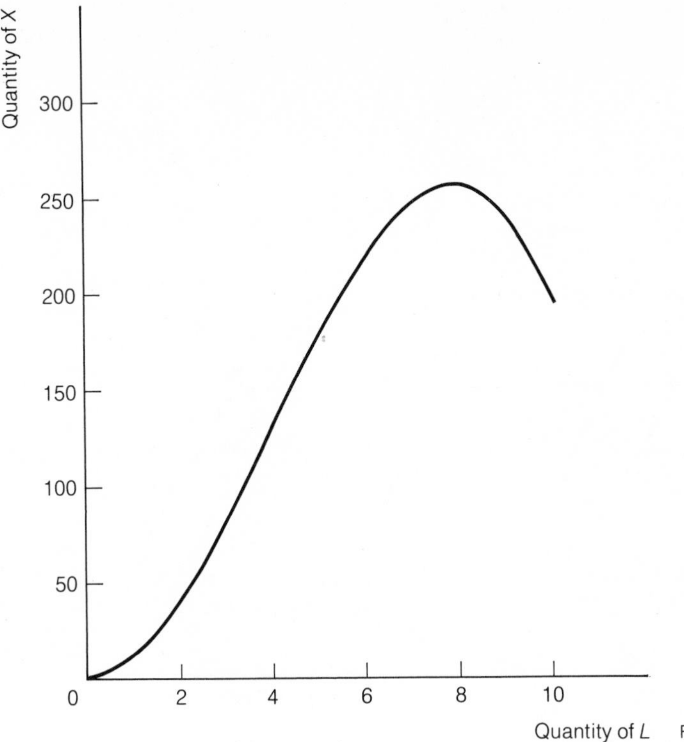

FIGURE 11-8

changes in X. More specifically, we are interested in the *ratio* of the change in X to the change in L as the change in L approaches zero. We are, in short, interested in dX/dL, the derivative of equation 11-31.

If $X = aL^2 - bL^3$, then employing the technique for finding the derivative of a function gives

$$\frac{dX}{dL} = 2aL - 3bL^2 \tag{11-32}$$

and if $X = 12L^2 - L^3$,

$$\frac{dX}{dL} = 24L - 3L^2$$

In Figure 11-9 we have plotted equation 11-32 with dX/dL on the vertical axis and L on the horizontal axis. The derivative of X with respect to the variable input L, or dX/dL, is called the *marginal product* (or the marginal physical product) of L. Notice that the marginal product of L at first increases, reaches a maximum (where L is equal to 4), and then decreases (becoming zero where $L = 8$ and less than zero where $L > 8$).

This behavior of dX/dL is called the *law of diminishing returns* (or the law of variable proportions). The law of diminishing returns is the assumption that, with some input fixed, as the quantity of the variable input increases, the marginal product of the variable input (while it may at first increase) will eventually

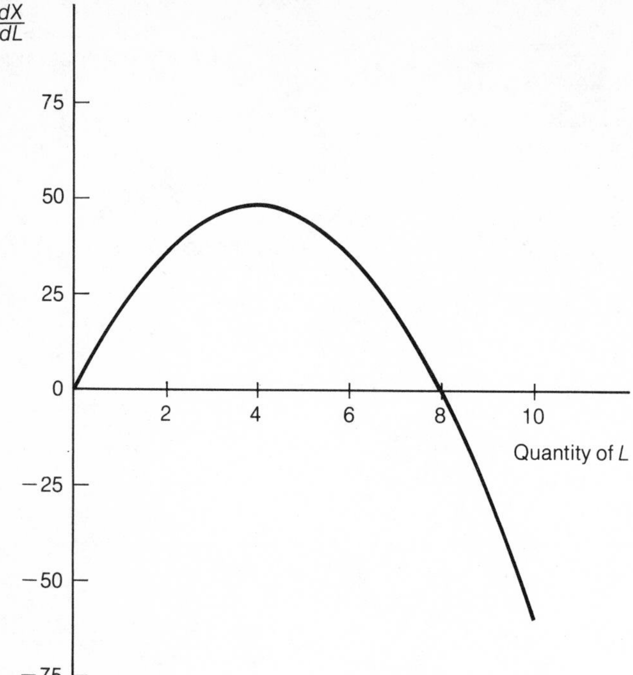

FIGURE 11-9

decrease. Now let us take dC/dL and divide it by the marginal product of L, dX/dL.

$$\frac{dC/dL}{dX/dL} = \frac{dC}{dL}\frac{dL}{dX}$$

$$\frac{dC/dL}{dX/dL} = \frac{dC}{dX} \tag{11-33}$$

The term dC/dX we recognize as the *marginal cost* of the product X. What we have discovered is that the marginal cost of X is equal to dC/dL divided by the marginal product of L. Using this knowledge we can (from equation 11-29) substitute $\bar{P}_L$ for dC/dL.

$$\frac{dC}{dX} = \frac{dC/dL}{dX/dL} \tag{11-33}$$

$$\frac{dC}{dX} = \frac{\bar{P}_L}{dX/dL} \tag{11-34}$$

The marginal cost of X is equal to the fixed price of the variable input L divided by the marginal product of input L. This is an important equation because, knowing how the marginal product of L behaves, we can determine how the marginal cost of X must behave.

We already know the following:

- As the firm increases its use of L, its output of X increases until L reaches some value (such as 8 in Figure 11-8).

- As L increases in this range, the marginal product of L at first increases and then decreases.
- The marginal cost of X equals the fixed price of input L divided by the marginal product of L.

From these three propositions we can draw two conclusions: (1) When the marginal product of L increases as X increases, the marginal cost of X (dC/dX) must decrease. This is true because the value of any fraction decreases if its denominator (dX/dL) increases while its numerator ($\bar{P}_L$) remains constant. (2) When the marginal product of L decreases as X increases, the marginal cost of X must increase. The value of the fraction dC/dX increases because the denominator dX/dL decreases and its numerator $\bar{P}_L$ is fixed. In short, marginal cost at first decreases and then increases because the marginal product of the variable input at first increases and then decreases. Where marginal product is increasing, marginal cost is decreasing; and where marginal product is decreasing, marginal cost is increasing. We can also note (without proving it) that when dX/dL reaches its *maximum*, dC/dX reaches its *minimum*.

We now know why marginal cost is assumed to behave as it does: because marginal product is assumed to increase and then to decrease. We can now explain why we assumed that the total-variable-cost function is an equation like 11-19. We must have an equation like 11-19 if its derivative, which is marginal cost, is to decrease at first and then decrease. And if we have a variable-cost function like equation 11-19, the total-cost function will be similar to equation 11-23; and its derivative (which is also marginal cost) will decrease and then increase as X increases.

As soon as we have total-variable-cost and total-cost functions like equations 11-19 and 11-23, respectively, the average-variable-cost and average-cost functions must be equations similar to equations 11-21 and 11-25, respectively. The behavior, in short, of C_V, C, A_V, and A_C is all due to the behavior of C_M; and the behavior of C_M is the direct result of the assumed behavior of marginal product.

The relation of marginal to average cost

If we look at Figure 11-10, in which we have plotted equations 11-22, 11-26, 11-28 and average fixed cost when fixed cost is $100, we see that:

- Where average variable cost is a minimum, average variable and marginal cost are equal.
- Where average total cost is a minimum, average total and marginal cost are equal.

We now want to do two things: (1) We want to find the output at which average variable cost is a minimum, determine the minimum average variable cost, and show that at this output average variable and marginal cost are equal. (2) We want to find the approximate output at which average total cost is a minimum, determine the approximate value of minimum average total cost, and demonstrate that average total cost and marginal cost approach equality as average total cost approaches its minimum value.

Average variable and marginal cost The average-variable-cost function is

$$A_V = aX^2 - bX + c \qquad (11\text{-}21)$$

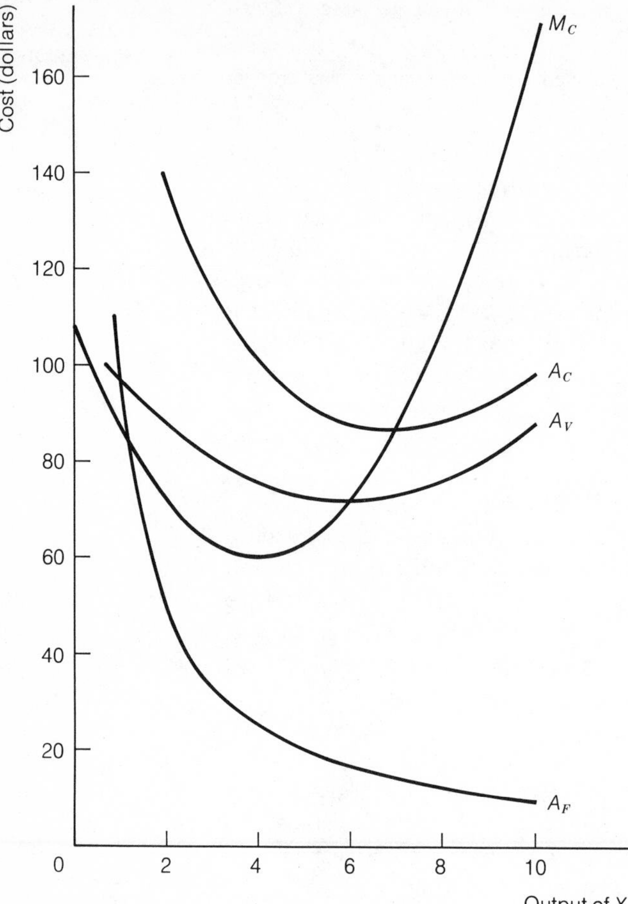

FIGURE 11-10

Looking at Figure 11-10, we see that when A_V is a minimum, the slope of the average-variable-cost curve is equal to zero. Since the slope of the average-variable-cost curve is the derivative of the average-variable-cost function, we want to find the output at which the derivative of equation 11-21 is equal to zero. The derivative of equation 11-21, using the derivative-finding technique we learned in Chapter 9, is

$$\frac{dA_V}{dX} = 2aX - b \qquad (11\text{-}35)$$

Notice that we found the derivative of each term on the right side of equation 11-21 by multiplying the exponent of each X by its coefficient and reducing the exponent of X by 1. We then added the derivatives of each term to find the derivative of the function. The derivative of:

- aX^2 is $2aX^1$, or simply $2aX$.
- $-bX$ is $-bX^0$ or (because $X^0 = 1$) $-b$.
- c (which is really cX^0) is $c \cdot 0 \cdot X^{-1}$, or 0.

The derivative of the function is therefore $2aX - b$.

Knowing the derivative of the average-variable-cost function, we can find the output at which A_V is minimum by setting the derivative equal to zero and solving for X.

$$2aX - b = 0$$
$$2aX = b$$
$$X = \frac{b}{2a} \tag{11-36}$$

Average variable cost is a minimum when X is equal to the parameter b divided by 2 times the parameter a.

To find the value of A_V when it is a minimum, we substitute $b/2a$ for X in equation 11-21.

$$A_V = aX^2 - bX + c \tag{11-21}$$
$$= a\left(\frac{b}{2a}\right)^2 - b\frac{b}{2a} + c$$
$$= a\frac{b^2}{4a^2} - \frac{b^2}{2a} + c$$
$$= \frac{b^2}{4a} - \frac{2b^2}{4a} + c$$
$$= -\frac{b^2}{4a} + c \tag{11-37}$$

The minimum average variable cost is $-b^2/4a + c$.

To show that average variable and marginal cost are equal when A_V is a minimum, we substitute $b/2a$ for X in the marginal-cost function (equation 11-27). When X is $b/2a$, marginal cost is

$$\frac{dC}{dX} = 3aX^2 - 2bX + c \tag{11-27}$$
$$= 3a\left(\frac{b}{2a}\right)^2 - 2b\frac{b}{2a} + c$$
$$= 3a\frac{b^2}{4a^2} - \frac{2b^2}{2a} + c$$
$$= 3\frac{b^2}{4a} - 4\frac{b^2}{4a} + c$$
$$= -\frac{b^2}{4a} + c \tag{11-38}$$

What we see is that when X is $b/2a$, A_V has a minimum value of $-b^2/4a + c$ and C_M (when X is $b/2a$) is also equal to $-b^2/4a + c$. A_V and C_M are equal when A_V is a minimum.

Using our numerical example, in which

$$A_V = X^2 - 12X + 108 \tag{11-22}$$

and

$$\frac{dC}{dX} = 3X^2 - 24X + 108 \tag{11-28}$$

the derivative of the average variable cost function is

$$\frac{dA_C}{dX} = 2X - 12 \tag{11-39}$$

which is equal to zero when A_V is a minimum. Therefore

$$2X - 12 = 0$$
$$2X = 12$$
$$X = 6$$

A_V is a minimum when X is 6. When X is 6, A_V (using equation 11-22) is

$$\begin{aligned} A_V &= 6^2 - 12(6) + 108 \\ &= 36 - 72 + 108 \\ &= 72 \end{aligned}$$

The minimum A_V is \$72 and is reached when X equals 6. When X is 6 (using equation 11-28), marginal cost is

$$\begin{aligned} \frac{dC}{dX} &= 3(6^2) - 24(6) + 108 \\ &= 108 - 144 + 108 \\ &= 72 \end{aligned}$$

A_V and C_M are both \$72 when X is 6, and 6 is the output at which A_V is a minimum. In short, when A_V is a minimum at an output of 6, both A_V and C_M are \$72.

Average total and marginal cost With the mathematical tools at our disposal we cannot determine the precise output at which A_C is a minimum, but we can show that the minimum A_C occurs at an output greater than the output (of $b/2a$) at which A_V is a minimum, find the approximate minimum A_C, and demonstrate that C_M approaches A_C as A_C approaches its minimum value.

For A_C to be a minimum, the slope of the average-cost function must be zero; or, mathematically, the derivative of the average-cost function (dA_C/dX) must be zero. The average-cost function may be written

$$A_C = A_F + A_V \tag{11-14}$$

and its derivative is equal to the sum of the derivatives of the average-variable-cost and the average-fixed-cost functions, or

$$\frac{dA_C}{dX} = \frac{dA_F}{dX} + \frac{dA_V}{dX}$$

If dA_C/dX is equal to zero, then

$$0 = \frac{dA_F}{dX} + \frac{dA_V}{dX}$$

or

$$-\frac{dA_F}{dX} = \frac{dA_V}{dX} \tag{11-40}$$

Equation 11-40 tells us that average cost is a minimum where the derivative of the average-fixed-cost function has the same *value* as the derivative of the average-variable-cost function. In terms of Figure 11-10, we find the minimum A_C where the negative slope of the average-fixed-cost curve has the same value as the positive slope of the average-variable-cost curve.

The derivative of the average-fixed-cost function, $A_F = F/X = FX^{-1}$ (equation 11-11), is

$$\frac{dA_F}{dX} = -FX^{-2} = -\frac{F}{X^2} \tag{11-41}$$

This last equation tells us that the derivative of the average-fixed-cost function is negative no matter what the value of X (as long as X is positive): the slope of the average-fixed-cost curve is always negative.

To satisfy equation 11-40, then, the slope of the average-fixed-cost curve must be positive. This occurs at outputs greater than the output at which A_V is a minimum, at outputs greater than $b/2a$. For at outputs less than $b/2a$, the slope of the average-variable-cost curve (which is dA_V/dX) is negative; and at an output of $b/2a$, the slope of the average-variable-cost curve and dA_V/dX are zero. The slope of A_V and dA_V/dX is positive only if X is greater than $b/2a$. Equation 11-40 is satisfied only if X is greater than $b/2a$. In short, average cost is a minimum at an output greater than $b/2a$.

In our numerical example

$$A_V = X^2 - 12X + 108 \tag{11-22}$$

$$A_F = \frac{100}{X}$$

$$A_C = X^2 - 12X + 108 + \frac{100}{X} \tag{11-26}$$

$$\frac{dC}{dX} = 3X^2 - 24X + 108 \tag{11-28}$$

We found that A_V reached a minimum of \$72 when X is 6. When X is 6, average total cost is

$$\begin{aligned} A_C &= 6^2 - 12(6) + 108 + 100/6 \\ &= \$88.67 \end{aligned}$$

and C_M is also equal to \$88.67.

If X is larger by 1 and equals 7, then

$$\begin{aligned} A_C &= 7^2 - 12(7) + 108 + 100/7 \\ &= \$87.29 \end{aligned}$$

But marginal cost is

$$\begin{aligned} \frac{dC}{dX} &= 3(7^2) - 24(7) + 108 \\ &= \$87 \end{aligned}$$

Marginal cost is still less than average cost when X is 7. From Figure 11-10 we can see that if C_M is less than A_C, A_C has not yet reached its minimum value.

When we let X equal 8, we find that A_C is

$$\begin{aligned} A_C &= 8^2 - 12(8) + 108 + 100/8 \\ &= \$88.51 \end{aligned}$$

TABLE 11-1

When X is	A_C is	and C_M is
7	\$87.2857	\$87.0000
7.01	87.2854	87.1803
7.015	87.2854	87.2707
7.02	87.2854	87.3612
7.03	87.2857	87.5427
7.05	87.2869	87.9075
7.1	87.2945	88.8300
7.25	87.3556	91.6875
7.50	87.5833	96.7500
8.00	88.5060	108.0000

and C_M is

$$\frac{dC}{dX} = 3(8^2) - 24(8) + 108$$

$$= \$108$$

Marginal cost is now greater than average cost; and from Figure 11-10 we can see that average cost is beyond its minimum, and so the minimum average cost occurs at an output between 7 and 8 units of X.

The average cost and marginal costs at various levels of output between 7 and 8 are found in Table 11-1. We can see that A_C and C_M are very close to being equal when X is 7.015. The minimum average cost is approximately \$87.29 and is found where X is just a little less than 7.015 units of X. By the process of successive approximation we can determine the approximate value of X at which A_C and C_M are equal and at which A_C is a minimum and the value of A_C when it is a minimum.

Exercise 11-3

1 Suppose $C = aX^3 - bX^2 = cX + F$.

a The derivative of this function is equal to __________

b The derivative of this function is called __________ and in symbols is __________/__________

c This derivative is the limit __________/__________ approaches as __________ approaches zero.

2 Assume $C = X^3 - 15X^2 + 200X + 300$.

a Marginal cost is dC/dX and equals __________

b Marginal cost is a minimum where the derivative of the marginal-cost function is equal to zero.

(1) The derivative of the marginal-cost function is equal to __________

(2) Marginal cost is a minimum, therefore, when $X =$ __________

c The variable-cost function is $V =$ ____________

d The derivative of the variable-cost function is dV/dX and is equal to ____________

e The derivative of the total-cost function is ____________ the derivative of the variable-cost function.

3 If $dC = dF + dV$:

a Then $dC/dX =$ $\frac{\_\_\_\_\_\_}{\_\_\_\_\_\_} + \frac{\_\_\_\_\_\_}{\_\_\_\_\_\_}$

b dF/dX is always equal to ____________

c dC/dX is therefore equal to $\frac{\_\_\_\_\_\_}{\_\_\_\_\_\_}$

4 The firm's cost equation in the short run is $C = \bar{K} \cdot \bar{P}_K + L \cdot \bar{P}_L$.

a The derivative of this function with respect to L is $\frac{\_\_\_\_\_\_}{\_\_\_\_\_\_}$

b This derivative has a value equal to ____________

5 If the relation between the output of X and the variable input of L is $X = aL^2 - bL^3$:

a The derivative of this function is dX/dL and is called the ____________ of L.

b This derivative has a value equal to ____________

c As L increases, this derivative (increases, decreases) ____________ at first and then ____________

6

a What does $\frac{dC/dL}{dX/dL}$ equal? ____________, which, in words, is ____________

b What does dC/dX equal if dC/dL equals $\bar{P}_L$? ____________ ÷ ____________ / ____________

c What happens to dC/dX if dX/dL increases at first and then decreases? ____________

7 Show that if $V = aX^3 - bX^2 + cX$:

a A_V is a minimum where $X = b/2a$.

b When A_V is a minimum, $A_V = -b^2/4a + c$.

c $C_M = A_V$ where A_V is a minimum.

8 Assume $V = X^3 - 15X^2 + 100X$.

a At what output is A_V a minimum? ____________

b What is the minimum A_V? ____________

c When A_V is a minimum, what is the value of C_M? ____________

9 Demonstrate that the output at which A_C is a minimum is greater than the output at which A_V is a minimum.

10 If $C = X^3 - 15X^2 + 200X + 300$:

a At approximately what output is A_C a minimum? ____________

b What is the approximate minimum value of A_C? ____________

c What is the approximate value of C_M when A_C is a minimum? ____________

COSTS IN THE LONG RUN

We have defined the long run as the time period in which all inputs, all costs, and the firm's output are variable. In the long run there are no fixed inputs and therefore no fixed costs. The only costs that concern us in the long run are thus total, average total, and marginal cost.

In this section we examine the assumed functional relationships between total cost, average cost, and marginal cost on the one hand and the level of output on the other. We want to know how each of these three costs is assumed to vary as the firm's output varies.

Total cost

It is assumed by economists that total cost in the long run C_L is an increasing and nonlinear function of X and that

$$C_L = eX^3 - fX^2 + gX \tag{11-42}$$

This equation is the *long-run total-cost function*. It is identical *in form* to the equation describing the relationship between total variable cost V and the production of X in the short run (equation 11-19). We see that it is a third-degree equation and the term containing X^2 is preceded by a minus sign.

As a numerical example of the long-run total-cost function we might have

$$C_L = 4X^3 - 40X^2 + 200X \tag{11-43}$$

Notice we have made $3eg$ greater than f^2 in this example. $3eg$ is equal to 3(4)(200), or 2,400, while f^2 is $(40)^2$, or 1,600.

If we plot this example of the long-run total-cost function in Figure 11-11, we obtain the *long-run total-cost curve*. It is similar to the total-variable-cost curve we plotted earlier in Figure 11-3. We again see that if X is zero, total cost is also zero, that total cost is an increasing function of X, and that the long-run cost curve is not a straight line. As X increases, the slope of the total-cost curve decreases at first and then increases. (In our example, the slope of the total-cost curve decreases until X is approximately 3.3 and then increases.)

Average cost

Average cost in the long run is equal to long-run total cost divided by output, or

$$A_L = \frac{C_L}{X} \tag{11-44}$$

Substituting equation 11-42 for C_L, we find

$$A_L = \frac{eX^3 - fX^2 + gX}{X}$$

or

$$A_L = eX^2 - fX + g \tag{11-45}$$

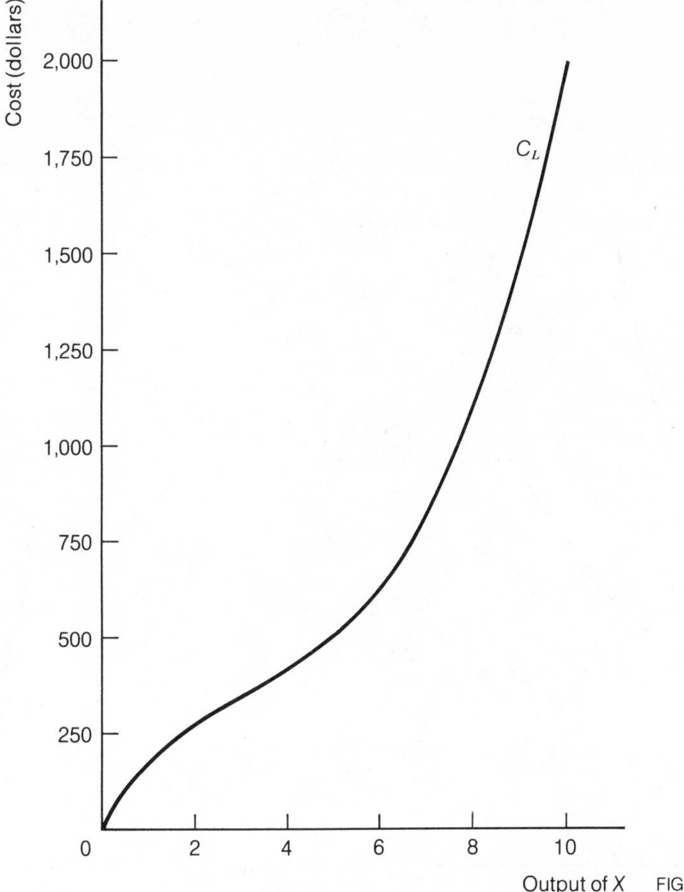

FIGURE 11-11

This is the *average-cost function*. The average-cost function, like the average-variable-cost function (equation 11-21), is a second-degree equation. If the total-cost function is $C_L = 4X^3 - 40X^2 + 200X$ (equation 11-43), then

$$A_L = \frac{4X^3 - 40X^2 + 200X}{X}$$

or

$$A_L = 4X^2 - 40X + 200 \tag{11-46}$$

The *average-cost curve* is U-shaped. As X increases, average cost decreases, reaches a minimum (of \$100 when X is equal to 5 in our example), and then increases.

Marginal cost

Long-run marginal cost C_{LM} is the limit the ratio of the change in total cost to the change in output approaches as the change in output approaches zero, or

$$C_{LM} = \lim_{\Delta X \to 0} \frac{\Delta C_L}{\Delta X} = \frac{dC_L}{dX} \tag{11-47}$$

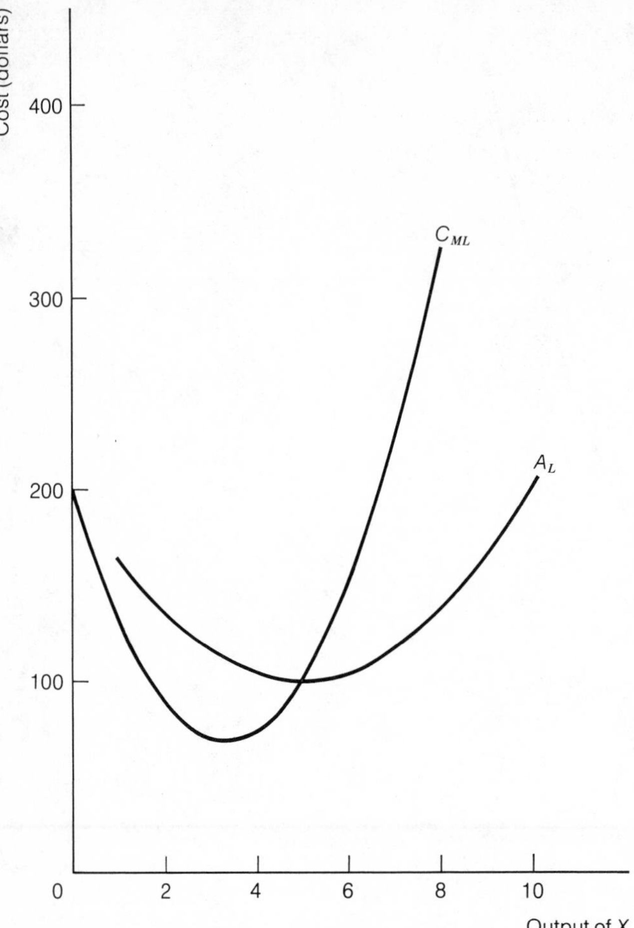

FIGURE 11-12

The marginal-cost function Marginal cost dC_L/dX is the derivative of the total-cost function. If the total-cost function is

$$C_L = eX^3 - fX^2 + gX \tag{11-42}$$

then, employing the derivative-finding technique,

$$\frac{dC_L}{dX} = 3eX^2 - 2fX + g \tag{11-48}$$

In our numerical example where $C_L = 4X^3 - 40X^2 + 200X$ we find that marginal cost is

$$\frac{dC_L}{dX} = 12X^2 - 80X + 200 \tag{11-49}$$

The *marginal-cost function,* like the marginal-cost function in the short run, is a second-degree equation. In Figure 11-12 we have plotted the *long-run marginal-cost curve* (labeled C_{LM}), assuming again that e is 4, f is 40, and g

is 200. We see in this graph that as X increases, marginal cost decreases, reaches a minimum (when X is approximately 3.3 in our example), and then increases.

The relation of marginal to average cost We should observe in Figure 11-12 that marginal cost and average cost are equal when average cost is a minimum. Recalling our technique for finding the output at which average cost is a minimum, we first find the derivation of the average cost function; i.e., we find dA_L/dX. If

$$A_L = eX^2 - fX + g \qquad (11\text{-}45)$$

then

$$\frac{dA_L}{dX} = 2eX - f$$

A_L is a minimum when dA_L/dX is equal to zero. If we set $2eX - f$ equal to zero, we find

$$2eX - f = 0$$
$$2eX = f$$
$$X = \frac{f}{2e}$$

A_L is a minimum where X is equal to $f/2e$. In our numerical example in which e is 4 and f is 40, A_L reaches its minimum value where

$$\begin{aligned} X &= \frac{f}{2e} \\ &= {}^{40}/_{8} \\ &= 5 \end{aligned}$$

We can find the value of the minimum A_L if we substitute $f/2e$ for X in the average-cost function (equation 11-45).

$$\begin{aligned} A_L &= eX^2 - fX + g && (11\text{-}45) \\ &= e\left(\frac{f}{2e}\right)^2 - f\frac{f}{2e} + g \\ &= e\frac{f^2}{4e^2} - \frac{f^2}{2e} + g \\ &= \frac{f^2}{4e} - \frac{2f^2}{4e} + g \\ &= -\frac{f^2}{4e} + g && (11\text{-}50) \end{aligned}$$

In the numerical example, the minimum A_L is

$$\begin{aligned} A_L &= -\frac{(40)^2}{16} + 200 \\ &= -\frac{1{,}600}{16} + 200 \\ &= -100 + 200 \\ &= \$100 \end{aligned}$$

Obtaining the same result in another way, we might have substituted 5, the value of X when A_L is a minimum, into equation 11-46 and found

$$\begin{aligned} A_L &= 4(5^2) - 40(5) + 200 \\ &= 100 - 200 + 200 \\ &= \$100 \end{aligned}$$

The value of marginal cost when average cost is a minimum we find is equal to average cost. For when average cost is a minimum, X is equal to $f/2e$. Substituting $f/2e$ for X in the marginal-cost function (equation 11-48), we find

$$\begin{aligned} \frac{dC_L}{dX} &= 3e\left(\frac{f}{2e}\right)^2 - 2f\frac{f}{2e} + g \\ &= 3e\frac{f^2}{4e^2} - \frac{2f^2}{2e} + g \\ &= \frac{3f^2}{4e} - \frac{4f^2}{4e} + g \\ &= -\frac{f^2}{4e} + g \end{aligned}$$

This is precisely the value we found for the minimum average cost in equation 11-49. In short, at the output at which average cost is a minimum, marginal cost and average cost are equal. We can see this in our numerical example where the minimum average cost of $100 was found where X was 4. If X is 4, then (from equation 11-49), marginal cost is

$$\begin{aligned} \frac{dC_L}{dX} &= 12(5^2) - 80(5) + 200 \\ &= 300 - 400 + 200 \\ &= \$100 \end{aligned}$$

Again, where average cost is a minimum, average and marginal cost are equal; or average and marginal cost are equal where average cost is a minimum.

We can also see in Figure 11-12 that:

- At outputs less than the output at which average cost is a minimum, marginal cost is less than average cost.
- At outputs greater than the output at which average cost is a minimum, marginal cost is greater than average cost.

Economies and diseconomies of scale We need not examine in detail why long-run marginal and average costs decrease and then increase. Economists often assume that they do behave in this way and attribute this behavior to the economies and diseconomies of scale. By economies of scale they mean that long-run average cost decreases as the output of the firm expands in the long run. And by diseconomies of scale they mean that long-run average cost increases. Economists generally assume that every firm in the long run initially finds that there are economies as they expand their output but that every firm eventually encounters diseconomies. In short, the behavior of long-run average and marginal costs we examined above is nothing more than an assumption. We shall not ask whether this assumption is warranted by the facts. In economic theory it is merely assumed that long-run average and marginal cost behave in the fashion described above, and this assumption is called the *economies and diseconomies of scale.*

Exercise 11-4

1 The long-run cost function is $C_L =$ ______

a This is a ______ degree equation.

b It is assumed that $3eg$ is ______ f^2.

2 The long-run:

a Average-cost function is $A_L =$ ______

b Marginal-cost function is $C_{LM} =$ ______

3 Show that:

a The minimum long-run average cost is equal to $-f^2/4e + g$.

b The minimum long-run average cost occurs when $X = f/2e$.

c When long-run average cost is a minimum, long-run average and marginal cost are equal.

4 Assume $C_L = 6X^3 - 25X^2 + 40X$.

a The average-cost function is $A_L =$ ______

b $dC_L/dX =$ ______

c A_L is a minimum:

(1) When $X =$ ______

(2) And is equal to ______

d When A_L is a minimum, it is also equal to ______

e Long-run marginal cost is a minimum where the derivative of the marginal-cost function is equal to zero.

(1) The derivative of the marginal-cost function is equal to ______

(2) Marginal cost is a minimum when X (in decimal form) is equal to approximately ______

(3) The minimum marginal cost is about ______

5 As X increases in the long run:

a Marginal cost at first ______ and then ______

b Average cost at first ______ and then ______

c Increasing long-run average cost is referred to as ______ of ______; and decreasing long-run average cost is called ______ of ______

6 When average cost is:

a Decreasing, marginal cost is ______ than average cost.

b Increasing, marginal cost is ______ than average cost.

PURE MONOPOLY

We now have at our disposal the basic tools we need to explain the output that will be produced and the price that will be charged by purely competitive industries and pure monopolists in both the short and long runs. These basic tools are the short- and long-run behavior of costs (Chapter 11) and the functional relationships between price, total revenue, marginal revenue, and the quantity demanded of a product (Chapters 8 and 9).

To determine the production and the price of purely competitive industries and of pure monopolies we require, however, one more ingredient. We need to know the goal or aim of the firm or, at least, what economists assume this goal to be. In the first section of this chapter, therefore, we examine the assumption of profit maximization to determine exactly what this assumption implies.

While it is usual in economics textbooks to examine pure competition before studying pure monopoly, the study of monopoly is mathematically easier than the study of competition. Monopoly analysis is less complex than the analysis of competition. For this reason alone we look first at monopoly in this chapter and then, in Chapter 13, go on to pure competition.

The second section of this chapter develops two models for monopoly, one for the short run and one for the long run. In each model we use five equations and two inequalities to find the equilibrium price, output, revenue, cost, and profit. The five equations will not be new to the student. One comes from Chapter 11, two from Chapter 9, and two from the first section of this chapter. The two inequalities also come from the first section of this chapter.

PROFIT MAXIMIZATION

The assumed goal of every firm is the greatest possible economic profit. We define the economic profit (or, for simplicity, the profit) π of the firm as equal to its total revenue R less its total costs C. That is,

$$\pi \equiv R - C \tag{12-1}$$

The profit of a firm is positive if revenue exceeds costs, negative if cost exceeds revenue, and zero if cost and revenue are equal. When a firm has a negative profit, we often speak of its *loss*.

The question we must now answer is what output the firm must produce to achieve a maximum profit.

Marginal cost and marginal revenue

The revenue a firm obtains from the production and sale of product X depends upon the demand for X and the quantity of X the firm sells. We shall assume that the demand function for X is given. With demand given, the firm's revenue is a function of the amount of X it sells; and we can write

$$R = f_R(X)$$

where f_R is a functional notation meaning revenue function. In a similar way, the cost of producing X depends upon the quantity of X the firm produces. Cost is a function of output, or

$$C = f_C(X)$$

f_C is the notation that indicates the cost function.

If both R and C are functions of X, a firm's profit is also a function of the quantity of X the firm produces and sells. We can say, substituting into equation 12-1, that

$$\pi = f_R(X) - f_C(X)$$

or

$$\pi = f_\pi(X)$$

The functional notation meaning profit function is f_π.

The total-profit function In very general terms, as the firm increases its output of X, profit at first increases, reaches a maximum, and then decreases. Figure 12-1 indicates the general relationship between π and X. Notice that π is negative at outputs between 0 and X_1 and at outputs greater than X_3. Between X_1 and X_3 profit is positive. At X_2 profit is a maximum.

Profit behaves in this fashion because of the behavior of total revenue and total cost. The total cost of the firm increases with output in the manner indicated by curve C in Figure 12-2.[1] Total revenue also varies with output. If demand is less than perfectly elastic, the firm's revenue curve is the one labeled R in Figure 11-2*a*; and if demand is perfectly elastic, the firm's revenue curve is the

[1] See pages 275 to 302 for review.

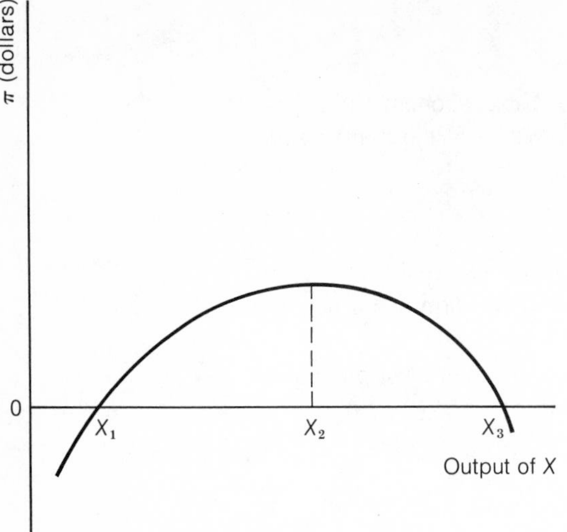

FIGURE 12-1

one labeled R in Figure 12-2*b*.[2] In both cases we see that profit, the amount by which R exceeds C, is at first negative, becomes positive, reaches a maximum (at X_2), decreases, and again becomes negative as X increases.

It is quite possible that the firm's maximum profit is zero. We show in Figure 12-3*a* a total-profit curve for this situation. In Figure 11-3*b* we have a total-profit curve for a firm whose maximum profit is negative. Even if maximum profit is zero or negative, the profit curve has the same general shape as the one shown

[2]See pages 205 to 207 and 234 to 236 for review.

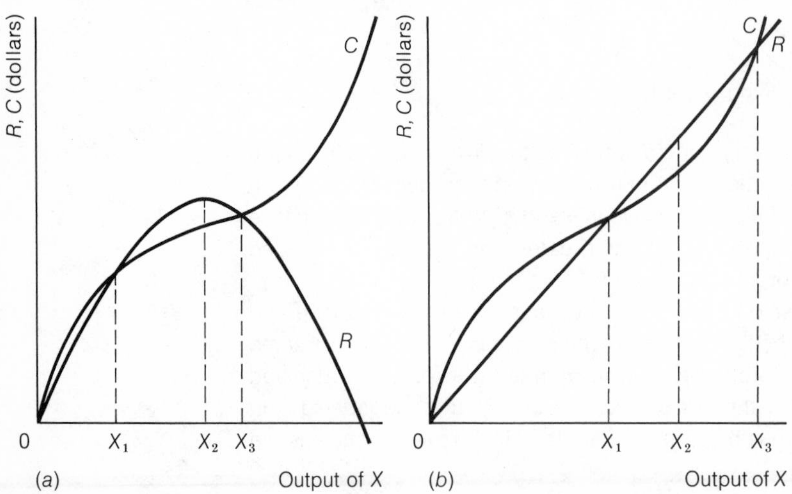

FIGURE 12-2

in Figure 12-1: as X increases, profit increases, reaches a maximum, and then decreases. Regardless of whether maximum profit is positive, zero, or negative there is some level of output at which profit is a maximum.

Marginal profit Looking at Figures 12-1 and 12-3, we can see that where profit is a maximum (at output X_2) the *slope* of the profit curve is equal to *zero*. The slope of the profit curve between any two outputs, if we measure profit vertically and output horizontally, is equal to $\Delta\pi/\Delta X$. We call this ratio marginal profit, the change in profit that occurs (when the firm changes its output) to the change in output. If we let the change in output approach zero, marginal profit is the limit $\Delta\pi/\Delta X$ approaches. Our definition of marginal profit then, substituting $d\pi$ for $\Delta\pi$ and dX for ΔX, is

$$\frac{d\pi}{dX} = \lim_{\Delta X \to 0} \frac{\Delta\pi}{\Delta X} \tag{12-2}$$

If total profit is to be a maximum, marginal profit must be equal to zero. Put another way, for the firm to maximize profit it is necessary that the firm produce the output at which

$$\frac{d\pi}{dX} = 0 \tag{12-3}$$

The equality of marginal cost and marginal revenue Let us go back now to equation 12-1.

$$\pi \equiv R - C \tag{12-1}$$

If π changes by a very small amount equal to $d\pi$, it is because R has changed by a very small amount equal to dR and C has changed by a very small amount equal to dC. (We are here assuming that $d\pi = \Delta\pi$, $dR = \Delta R$, and $dC = \Delta C$.) We can therefore write

$$d\pi \equiv dR - dC \tag{12-4}$$

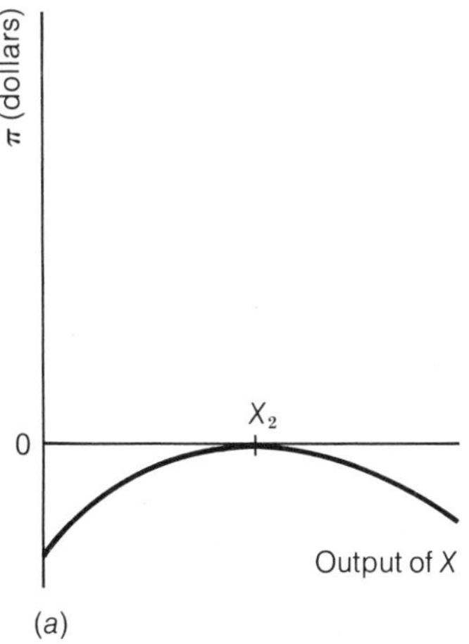

(a)

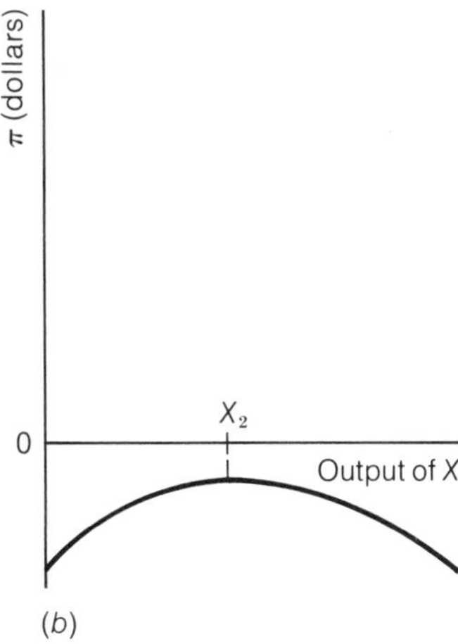

(b)

FIGURE 12-3

A firm's revenue changes when it changes its output of X; and the change in revenue is equal to the change in output of X multiplied by the marginal revenue from the sale of X, or

$$dR = dX\frac{dR}{dX}$$

Similarly, the change in the firm's costs is equal to the change in the quantity of X produced multiplied by the marginal cost of X, or

$$dC = dX\frac{dC}{dX}$$

Substituting $dX(dR/dX)$ for dR and $dX(dC/dX)$ for dC, respectively, in equation 12-4 gives us

$$d\pi = dX\frac{dR}{dX} - dX\frac{dC}{dX}$$

Dividing both sides of this equation by dX gives

$$\frac{d\pi}{dX} = \frac{dR}{dX} - \frac{dC}{dX} \qquad (12\text{-}5)$$

Equation 12-5 tells us that marginal profit is equal to marginal revenue minus marginal cost.

For profit to be a maximum, we know that marginal profit must be equal to zero. Recalling equation 12-3,

$$\frac{d\pi}{dX} = 0 \qquad (12\text{-}3)$$

we may substitute into equation 12-3 the right side of equation 12-5 for $d\pi/dX$ and find that

$$\frac{dR}{dX} - \frac{dC}{dX} = 0 \qquad (12\text{-}6)$$

For profit to be a maximum, the firm must produce the output at which marginal revenue less marginal cost is equal to zero. This equation we may rewrite as

$$\frac{dR}{dX} = \frac{dC}{dX} \qquad (12\text{-}7)$$

This is a basic or fundamental equation we use throughout this and the next chapter. It tells us that *if a firm is going to produce any quantity at all, and if it is to maximize its profit, it must produce the output at which marginal revenue and marginal cost are equal.*

To maximize profit

Suppose the profit curve, instead of looking like the curves in Figures 12-1 and 12-3, looked like the curve in Figure 12-4. At output X_2 the firm's profit is a *minimum* rather than a maximum. The slope of the profit curve at X_2 is, however, equal to zero, and so at X_2 marginal profit is equal to zero and marginal revenue is equal to marginal cost. In short, $dR/dX = dC/dX$ at X_2, but profit is a minimum and not a maximum.

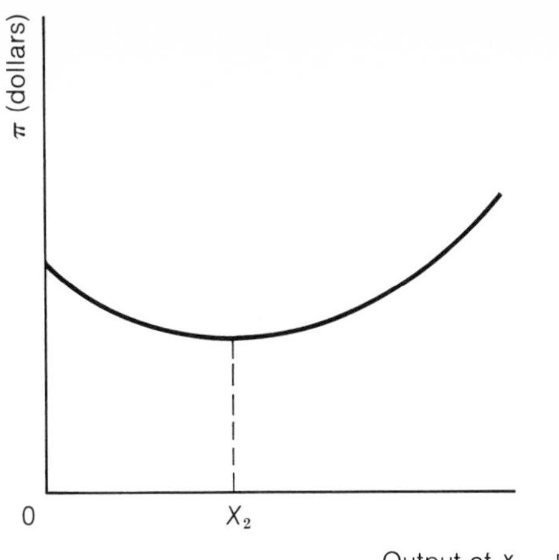

FIGURE 12-4

When a firm produces an output at which $dR/dX = dC/dX$, profit therefore is *either* a maximum *or* a minimum.[3] It is not enough to say that a firm maximizes profit when it produces an output at which marginal revenue and marginal cost are equal. Something more must be said to distinguish maximum from minimum profit. We have to add a second condition to ensure that profit is in fact a maximum rather than a minimum.

The second condition If the profit curve looks like the one in Figure 12-1, we can see that the slope of the curve is *negative* at any output greater than X_2, the output at which marginal profit ($d\pi/dX$) is zero. If the firm were producing X_2 and increased its output by a very small amount equal to dX, the slope of the curve would change from zero to a negative value. The *change* in the slope would be negative because a change from zero to less than zero is a negative

[3]Strictly speaking, this statement is not quite true. If we had a profit curve that looked like the one below, $d\pi/dX$ would equal zero and dR/dX would equal dC/dX at an output of X_1. At X_1 profit would be neither a maximum nor a minimum. In this case the second condition (see below) for profit maximization would not be satisfied, and the second condition for profit minimization likewise would not be satisfied.

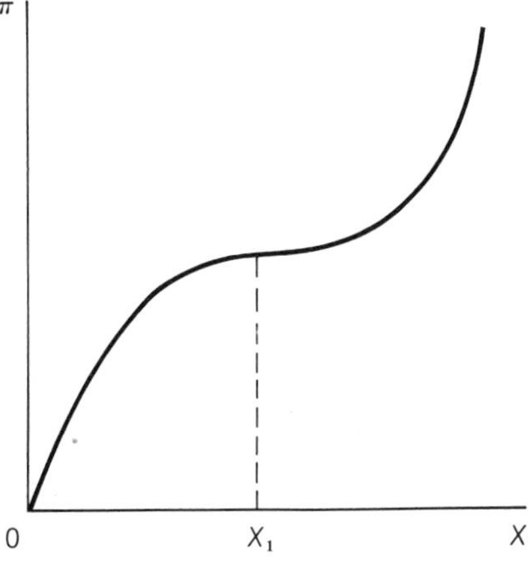

change. We can write then

$$d\frac{d\pi}{dX} < 0$$

This means that the small change d in the slope $d\pi/dX$ is negative. If we divide this change in slope by the positive change dX in X that brought about the change in slope, we have

$$\frac{d(d\pi/dX)}{dX}$$

Because the numerator is negative when the denominator is positive, we can say that

$$\frac{d(d\pi/dX)}{dX} < 0$$

Mathematicians write the left side of this inequality as $d^2\pi/dX^2$. Using this term, we can say that for profit to be a maximum, two conditions must be satisfied:

$$\frac{d\pi}{dX} = 0 \qquad (12\text{-}3)$$

and

$$\frac{d^2\pi}{dX^2} < 0 \qquad (12\text{-}8)$$

The change in the slope of the profit curve divided by the positive change in output must be negative if profit is to be a maximum.[4]

Marginal cost and marginal revenue again We can express the second condition for profit maximization in a way that involves marginal cost and marginal revenue. Starting with equation 12-5,

$$\frac{d\pi}{dX} = \frac{dR}{dX} - \frac{dC}{dX} \qquad (12\text{-}5)$$

if we change $d\pi/dX$ by a very small amount equal to $d(d\pi/dX)$, then dR/dX and dC/dX will also change by very small amounts equal to $d(dR/dX)$ and $d(dC/dX)$ respectively; or

$$d\frac{d\pi}{dX} = d\frac{dR}{dX} - d\frac{dC}{dX} \qquad (12\text{-}9)$$

Next we divide equation 12-9 by dX, a very small change in X, and obtain

$$\frac{d(d\pi/dX)}{dX} = \frac{d(dR/dX)}{dX} - \frac{d(dC/dX)}{dX}$$

Using the notation mathematicians employ,

$$\frac{d^2\pi}{dX^2} = \frac{d^2R}{dX^2} - \frac{d^2C}{dX^2} \qquad (12\text{-}10)$$

The ratio of the change in marginal profit to the change in X is equal to the ratio

[4] It seems reasonable and it can be shown (though we omit it here) that when $d^2\pi/dX^2$ is greater than zero, profit is a minimum at the output at which $d\pi/dX$ is equal to zero. At output X_1, in footnote 3, $d^2\pi/dX^2$ is neither less than nor greater than zero.

of the change in marginal revenue to the change in X minus the ratio of the change in marginal cost to the change in X (as the change in X approaches zero).

For profit to be a maximum it is necessary that

$$\frac{d^2\pi}{dX^2} < 0 \tag{12-8}$$

If the left side of equation 12-10 is negative, it means that d^2C/dX^2 is greater than d^2R/dX^2. As an example, suppose $d^2\pi/dX^2$ is negative and equal to -10. Then the right side of equation 12-10 must also be equal to -10. The right side can be negative only if d^2C/dX^2 exceeds d^2R/dX^2 by 10. Thus, we might have

$$-10 = 20 - 30$$

For the firm's profit to be a maximum (rather than a minimum), it is therefore necessary when the firm produces the output at which $dR/dX = dC/dX$ that

$$\frac{d^2C}{dX^2} > \frac{d^2R}{dX^2} \tag{12-11}$$

In geometric terms, this means that at the output at which marginal cost equals marginal revenue, profit is a maximum if the *slope* of the marginal-cost curve (d^2C/dX^2) is greater than the slope of the marginal-revenue curve (d^2R/dX^2).

To produce or not to produce

We have seen that if a firm is to produce an output that maximizes its profit, it must produce an output which satisfies both equation 12-7 and inequality 12-11. But every firm always has an alternative to producing. That alternative is not producing: it may choose to produce an output of zero.

What we must now determine is when a firm will choose to produce an output of zero and when it will produce an output that satisfies 12-7 and 12-11.

The short run In the short run a firm finds that some of its costs are fixed F and some are variable V, or

$$C \equiv F + V$$

Should a firm decide to produce an output of zero, it would have zero revenue and zero variable costs; and its profit at zero output π_0 would be

$$\begin{aligned} \pi_0 &= R - (F + V) \\ &= 0 - (F + 0) \\ &= 0 - F \\ &= -F \end{aligned} \tag{12-12}$$

Its profit would be negative and equal to its fixed costs if it produced no output. It would have a loss equal to fixed costs.

When will a firm decide to produce no output? When the loss it suffers producing no output is smaller than the loss it suffers producing the output that satisfies 12-7 and 12-11. Put another way, it will produce the output that satisfies 12-7 and 12-11 if its profit when it produces that output π_X is greater than (or at least, equal to) its profit when it produces no output, or when

$$\pi_X \geqq \pi_0 \tag{12-13}$$

When the firm produces, its profit π_X equals its revenue less the sum of its fixed and variable costs, or

$$\pi_X \equiv R - (F + V)$$

We already know that when it produces no output, its profit is

$$\pi_0 = -F \qquad (12\text{-}12)$$

Substituting into inequality 12-13, a firm will produce if

$$R - F - V \geqq -F$$

When we add F to both sides of this inequality, we have

$$R - V \geqq 0$$

which says that the firm will produce if its revenue less its variable costs is greater than or equal to zero or, adding V to both sides, if

$$R \geqq V \qquad (12\text{-}14)$$

A firm will produce (rather than not produce at all) if at its most profitable output its total revenue exceeds or is equal to its *variable* costs.

Dividing both sides of 12-14 by X, the output of the firm, we have

$$\frac{R}{X} \geqq \frac{V}{X} \qquad (12\text{-}15)$$

From Chapter 9 we recognize R/X as the price at which the firms sells its product, and from Chapter 11 we recognize V/X as average variable cost. The firm, in other words, will produce where both 12-7 and 12-11 are satisfied only if the price at which it can sell its product exceeds or is equal to the average variable cost of producing it.

The long run A firm's costs in the long run are all variable; it has no fixed costs. Should it decide to produce no output, its revenue is zero and its costs are also zero; its profit at zero output is

$$\begin{aligned}\pi_0 &= R - C \\ &= 0 - 0 \\ &= 0\end{aligned}$$

Its profit at zero output in the long run is equal to zero.

For the firm to produce at all, its profit at its most profitable output π_X must exceed or at least equal its profit if it produces no output, or

$$\pi_X \geqq \pi_0 \qquad (12\text{-}13)$$

When the firm produces, in the long run its profit equals its revenue minus its cost. When it does not produce, its profit is zero. Substituting in 12-13,

$$R - C \geqq 0$$

Moving C to the right side gives

$$R \geqq C \qquad (12\text{-}16)$$

Its revenue must exceed or equal its cost at its most profitable output if the firm is to produce at all. If C exceeds R when the firm produces its most profitable output, the firm will choose to produce no output. If we divide 12-16 by X, we have

$$\frac{R}{X} \geqq \frac{C}{X} \tag{12-17}$$

Price must equal or exceed average cost in the long run if the firm is to produce rather than not produce.

Summary

The assumed goal of all firms is the maximization of profit. The output which maximizes profit is the output at which

- $\frac{dC}{dX} = \frac{dR}{dX}$ or $\frac{d\pi}{dX} = 0$
- $\frac{d^2C}{dX^2} > \frac{d^2R}{dX^2}$ or $\frac{d^2\pi}{dX^2} > 0$

if at this output

- $R \geqq V$ $\left(\text{or } P \geqq \frac{V}{X}\right)$ in the short run
- $R \geqq C$ $\left(\text{or } P \geqq \frac{C}{X}\right)$ in the long run

Should $R < V$ in the short run or $C < R$ in the long run, the firm's most profitable output is zero.

Exercise 12-1

1 Define economic profit. $\pi \equiv$ ____________

2 Because both revenue and cost are functions of output, a firm's profit is also a function of ____________

3 As the output of X increases, a firm's profit at first ____________, reaches a ____________, and then ____________

4 When profit is a maximum:

a The slope of the profit curve is equal to ____________

b Marginal profit, which (in symbols) is ____________ / ____________, is equal to ____________

5 Show that when marginal profit is equal to zero, marginal cost is equal to marginal revenue.

6 For profit to be a maximum at the output at which $dR/dX = dC/dX$, it is necessary that the slope of the profit curve be ____________ at any greater output. This means that:

a The change in the slope of the profit curve or, in symbols, $d($____________$)$ is ____________ *b* Dividing through by dX, $\frac{d\left(\frac{\quad}{\quad}\right)}{\quad}$ is ______

c Or, as mathematicians write it, ______ is ______

7 Show that if $d^2\pi/dX^2$ is less than zero, d^2C/dX^2 is greater than d^2R/dX^2.

8 In the short run a firm will:

a Produce if $R \geqq$ ______ or if ______ $\geqq$ ______

b Not produce if ______ or if ______

9 In the long run a firm will:

a Produce if $R \geqq$ ______ or if ______ $\geqq$ ______

b Not produce if ______ or if ______

10 Show that to maximize profits a firm will produce in the:
a Short run only if $R \geqq V$.
b Long run only if $R \geqq C$.

TWO MONOPOLY MODELS

The output a monopolist produces and the price he charges depend upon the demand for his product, the costs of producing it, and the aim or goal of the monopolist. Having examined demand, costs, and profit maximization, we can now construct a short-run and a long-run monopoly model. These two models are basically the same. Each consists of five equations and two inequalities, from which we can determine the equilibrium output, price, revenue, cost, and profit of the monopolist. For the short-run model, however, we use the short-run cost equation, and for the long-run model we use the long-run cost equation. This is the only major difference between the two models.

Monopoly in the short run

The five equations of the short-run model are

$$C = aX^3 - bX^2 + cX + \bar{F} \tag{12-18}$$

$$P = \frac{A - X}{B} \tag{12-19}$$

$$R \equiv X \cdot P \tag{12-20}$$

$$\pi \equiv R - C \tag{12-1}$$

$$\frac{dC}{dX} = \frac{dR}{dX} \tag{12-7}$$

The first of these equations is the short-run cost function and is the same as equation 11-23. Equation 12-19 is the demand equation and is the same as equation 9-2. In equation 12-19 we have substituted X for D because the quantity demanded D at any price is identical with the quantity X the monopolist will produce at that price. The parameters a and b in equation 9-2 have been replaced by A and B since we are using a and b as parameters in the cost equation. (The demand function can also be written $X = A - B \cdot P$, but equation 12-19 is the more useful form for developing the monopoly model.)

Equations 12-20 and 12-1 are the definitional equations for total revenue and total profit, respectively, and 12-20 is the same as equation 9-3. Equation 12-7 is the equilibrium equation and tells us that the monopolist will produce that output at which marginal cost and marginal revenue are equal.

To these five equations we must add two inequalities,

$$\frac{d^2C}{dX^2} > \frac{d^2R}{dX^2} \tag{12-11}$$

$$R \geqq V \tag{12-14}$$

The first ensures that profit is a maximum rather than a minimum, and the second tells us that revenue must equal or exceed total variable cost if the firm is to produce at all.

Our model has five equations. The first two are behavioral; the next two are definitional; and the last is the equilibrium equation. It also has five variables: X, C, P, R, and π. The model, therefore, should have at least one solution for the values of the five variables. The two inequalities will assure us that it has only one set of equilibrium values for the variables.

Equilibrium To find the equilibrium output of the monopolist we must first find the equations for dC/dX and dR/dX. From equation 12-18, the total cost equation, we determine marginal cost by the derivative-finding technique.

$$\frac{dC}{dX} = 3aX^2 - 2bX + c \tag{12-21}$$

Substituting $(A - X)/B$ (from the demand equation) for P in the revenue equation, we find that

$$R = X\frac{A - X}{B}$$

or

$$R = \frac{A}{B}X - \frac{X^2}{B} \tag{12-22}$$

Now we can determine marginal revenue by finding the derivative of equation 12-22.

$$\frac{dR}{dX} = \frac{A}{B} - \frac{2}{B}X \tag{12-23}$$

We now substitute the right sides of equations 12-21 and 12-23 for dC/dX and dR/dX, respectively, in equation 12-7 and have

$$3aX^2 - 2bX + c = \frac{A}{B} - \frac{2}{B}X \tag{12-24}$$

This is a second-degree equation containing only one variable, X, the output of the firm. We can rewrite this equation as

$$(3a)X^2 + \left(\frac{2}{B} - 2b\right)X + \left(c - \frac{A}{B}\right) = 0 \tag{12-25}$$

In any college algebra book[5] we find that when we have a second-degree, or quadratic, equation the value of the unknown variable is

$$X = \frac{-\beta \pm \sqrt{\beta^2 - 4\alpha\gamma}}{2\alpha} \qquad (12\text{-}26)$$

where α is the coefficient of X^2, β is the coefficient of X, and γ is the constant term. In equation 12-25

- $\alpha = 3a$
- $\beta = \frac{2}{B} - 2b$
- $\gamma = c - \frac{A}{B}$

If we substitute these values into equation 12-26, we find

$$X = \frac{-(2/B - 2b) \pm \sqrt{(2/B - 2b)^2 - 4(3a)(c - A/B)}}{2(3a)} \qquad (12\text{-}27)$$

If we solve this equation for X, we obtain either no real solutions or two real solutions. (We obtain imaginary solutions when the term under the radical sign is negative because we cannot find the square root of a negative number.) When the values of X both turn out to be negative, we have no real solution because a firm cannot produce a negative output. We may, however, obtain two solutions for X, one equal to

$$\frac{2/B - 2b \textit{ plus } \sqrt{(2/B - 2b)^2 - 4(3a)(c - A/B)}}{2(3a)}$$

and the other equal to

$$\frac{2/B - 2b \textit{ minus } \sqrt{(2/B - 2b)^2 - 4(3a)(c - A/B)}}{2(3a)}$$

If both solutions are positive, one of them will be the profit *minimizing* output because it does not satisfy inequality 12-11. The other solution will be the profit *maximizing* output because it does satisfy inequality 12-11. If the output that maximizes profit also satisfies inequality 12-14, we have found the equilibrium output of the monopolist.[6]

Once we have determined the equilibrium value of X, we can insert this X into equation 12-18 to determine total cost and into 12-19 to determine price. Knowing X and P, we can find total revenue from equation 12-20; and then, knowing C and R, we can find profit from equation 12-1. We can also, if we

[5]See pages 27 to 29 for a review of the formula used to find the solutions to a second-degree equation.

[6]Mathematically speaking, the maximum and the minimum profits we have been talking about are *local* (or relative) maximums and minimums. If we have a function such as $y = f(x)$, we *define* the local maximum of the variable y as a value of y such that at slightly greater *and* slightly smaller values for x, y is smaller (and the local minimum of the variable y is *defined* as a value for y such that at slightly larger *and* smaller values for x, y is greater). If the function relating x and y is the one graphed below, the local minimum and the local maximum values for y are found when x is x_2 and x_3. We can see, however, that y is greater than its local maximum when x is less than x_1; that y is less than its local maximum when x is less than x_1; and that y is less than its local minimum when x is greater than x_4. These values of y which are greater than or less than the local maximum and minimum, respectively, are not local maximums or minimums because they do not satisfy the definitions of these two terms. The value of y when x is less than x_1 is not a local maximum because when x decreases, *y increases;* and the value of y when x is greater than x_4 is not a local minimum because when x

wish, find average cost by dividing C by X and average profit by dividing π by X.

This may also seem unduly complicated, but when we employ numbers instead of letters for the parameters, the computation of the equilibrium values is much easier.

Numerical examples To see how we can use this model to determine X, P, C, R, and π, we take three different numerical examples. In the first example the firm will produce zero output, in the second it will produce at a loss, and in the third it will produce at a profit.

Case 1: zero output in the short run Assume that

$$C = X^3 - 9.25X^2 + 29X + 10$$

$$P = \frac{20 - X}{4}$$

Marginal cost is then

$$\frac{dC}{dX} = 3X^2 - 18.5X + 29$$

and marginal revenue is

$$\frac{dR}{dX} = \frac{20}{4} - \frac{2}{4}X$$

Setting marginal cost equal to marginal revenue, we have

$$3X^2 - 18.5X + 29 = {}^{20}\!/_4 - {}^{2}\!/_4X$$

or

$$3X^2 + ({}^{2}\!/_4 - 18.5)X + (29 - {}^{20}\!/_4) = 0$$
$$3X^2 + (-18)X + 24 = 0$$

Employing equation 12-26,

$$\alpha = 3$$
$$\beta = -18$$
$$\gamma = 24$$

---

increases, *y decreases*. Most but not all of the functions we employ in this book are such that there are no values for a variable that are greater than or less than their local maximum and minimum, respectively.

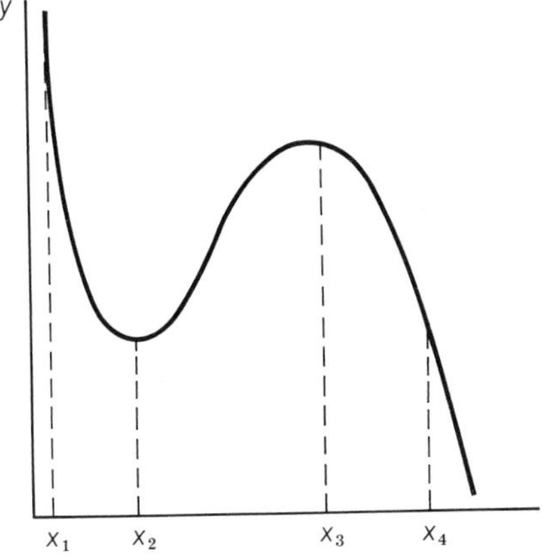

and

$$X = \frac{-(-18) \pm \sqrt{(-18)^2 - 4(3)(24)}}{2(3)}$$

$$= \frac{18 \pm \sqrt{324 - 288}}{6}$$

$$= \frac{18 \pm \sqrt{36}}{6}$$

$$= \frac{18 \pm 6}{6}$$

$$X_1 = {}^{24}\!/_6 = 4 \qquad X_2 = {}^{12}\!/_6 = 2$$

Marginal cost and marginal revenue are equal when X is 2 and when X is 4. But when X is 2, taking the derivative of the marginal-cost function,

$$\frac{d^2C}{dX^2} = 6(2) - 18.5$$

$$= 12 - 18.5 = -6.5$$

The derivative of the marginal-revenue function is

$$\frac{d^2R}{dX^2} = -{}^2\!/_4X$$

$$= -{}^2\!/_4(2)$$

$$= -1$$

We see that when X is 2, d^2C/dX^2 is *less than* d^2R/dX^2. Profit is therefore not a maximum but a minimum when X is 2. When X is 4, however,

$$\frac{d^2C}{dX^2} = 6X - 18.5$$

$$= 6(4) - 18.5$$

$$= 24 - 18.5 = 5.5$$

and

$$\frac{d^2R}{dX^2} = -{}^2\!/_4X$$

$$= -{}^2\!/_4(4) = -2$$

d^2C/dX^2 is *greater than* d^2R/dX^2, and profit is therefore a maximum.

Will the firm produce an output of 4? No. V is greater than R when X is 4. To sell 4 units of X the firm would charge a price equal to

$$P = \frac{20 - X}{4}$$

$$= \frac{20 - 4}{4}$$

$$= {}^{16}\!/_4$$

$$= \$4$$

Its revenue would be

$$R = X \cdot P$$
$$= 4 \cdot 4$$
$$= \$16$$

and V is

$$\begin{aligned} V &= X^3 - 9.25X^2 + 29X \\ &= 4^3 - 9.25(4)^2 + 29(4) \\ &= 64 - 148 + 116 \\ &= \$32 \end{aligned}$$

Total variable cost exceeds total revenue. The firm finds that if it produces 4 units of X, its *loss* will equal its revenue ($16) less its total variable cost ($32) and its total fixed cost ($10). Its loss will be $26. If it produces no output, its loss is equal to its total fixed cost of only $10. For this reason the firm will not produce the 4 units but will close its doors and produce no output.

We have in this case the pure monopolist who in the short run will produce no output because even at its most profitable output its loss exceeds what its loss would be if it shut down and produced no output. It minimizes its loss by not producing at all.

Case 2: production at a loss in the short run Let us examine a case in which the monopolist produces in the short run but finds that at its most profitable output it must suffer a loss. Suppose that

$$C = X^3 - 19.75X^2 + 101X + 55$$

$$P = \frac{44 - X}{4}$$

Then

$$\frac{dC}{dX} = 3X^2 - 39.5X + 101$$

$$\frac{dR}{dX} = 11 - \tfrac{2}{4}X$$

Setting marginal cost equal to marginal revenue,

$$\begin{aligned} 3X^2 - 39.5X + 101 &= 11 - \tfrac{2}{4}X \\ 3X^2 + (\tfrac{2}{4} - 39.5)X + 90 &= 0 \\ 3X^2 + (-39)X + 90 &= 0 \end{aligned}$$

Solving for X, where

$$\begin{aligned} \alpha &= 3 \\ \beta &= -39 \\ \gamma &= 90 \end{aligned}$$

gives

$$\begin{aligned} X &= \frac{-(-39) \pm \sqrt{(39)^2 - 4(3)(90)}}{2(3)} \\ &= \frac{39 \pm \sqrt{1{,}521 - 1{,}080}}{6} \\ &= \frac{39 \pm \sqrt{441}}{6} \\ &= \frac{39 \pm 21}{6} \end{aligned}$$

$$X_1 = \frac{39 + 21}{6}; \qquad X_2 = \frac{39 - 21}{6}$$

$$= \tfrac{60}{6} \qquad\qquad = \tfrac{18}{6}$$

$$= 10 \qquad\qquad = 3$$

There are two outputs at which marginal cost and marginal revenue are equal, an output of 3 and an output of 10. At one of these outputs, however, profit is a maximum, and at the other profit is a minimum. When X is 3,

$$\begin{aligned}\frac{d^2C}{dX^2} &= 6X - 39.5\\ &= 6(3) - 39.5\\ &= 18 - 39.5 = -21.5\end{aligned}$$

and

$$\begin{aligned}\frac{d^2R}{dX^2} &= -\tfrac{2}{4}\\ &= -\tfrac{1}{2}\end{aligned}$$

The second condition for profit maximization is not satisfied when X is 3 because d^2C/dX^2 is *less than* d^2R/dX^2. When X is 10, however,

$$\begin{aligned}\frac{d^2C}{dX^2} &= 6X - 39.5\\ &= 6(10) - 39.5\\ &= 60 - 39.5 = 20.5\end{aligned}$$

and

$$\begin{aligned}\frac{d^2R}{dX^2} &= -\tfrac{2}{4}\\ &= -\tfrac{1}{2}\end{aligned}$$

The second condition *is* satisfied because d^2C/dX^2 is greater than d^2R/dX^2.

The price the firm would charge to sell $10X$ is

$$\begin{aligned}P &= \frac{44 - X}{4}\\ &= \frac{44 - 10}{4}\\ &= \tfrac{34}{4}\\ &= \$8.50\end{aligned}$$

The firm's profit when X is 10 is $-\$5$ because

$$\begin{aligned}V &= X^3 - 19.75X^2 + 101X\\ &= 10^3 - 19.75(10)^2 + 101(10)\\ &= 1{,}000 - 1{,}975 + 1{,}010\\ &= \$35\end{aligned}$$

and

$$\begin{aligned}R &\equiv X \cdot P\\ &\equiv 10(\$8.50)\\ &= \$85\end{aligned}$$

Its R (\$85) exceeds V (\$35) by \$50, and it will produce rather than close down. For with a total fixed cost of \$55, its loss if it produces 10 units of X is equal to its R (\$85) less V (\$35) and F (\$55), or $-\$5$. If it produced no output, its loss would equal its $\bar{F}$ of \$55; its profit would be −\$55. A \$5 loss is less than a \$55 loss. Therefore in the short run it will produce 10X even though it suffers a loss.

Case 3: profit in the short run In the third case the monopolist has a profit in the short run. Assume

$$C = X^3 - 19.75X^2 + 101X + 10$$

$$P = \frac{44 - X}{4}$$

Just as in case 2,

$$\frac{dC}{dX} = 3X^2 - 19.75X + 101$$

$$\frac{dR}{dX} = 11 - \tfrac{2}{4}X$$

Because marginal cost and marginal revenue are exactly the same functions we had in case 2, marginal cost and marginal revenue are again equal where X is 3 and X is 10. Again, however, profit is a maximum when X is 10 and a minimum when X is 3. The firm's price is again \$8.50, its revenue is again \$85, and its total variable cost is again \$35. But since its total fixed cost in this case is only \$10, its profit is

$$\begin{aligned}\pi &= \$85 - (\$35 + \$10)\\ &= \$40\end{aligned}$$

In this third case the monopolist has a profit in the short run.

Summary The short-run monopoly model contains a total-cost, demand, total-revenue, total-profit, and equilibrium equation and two inequalities which determine when profit is a maximum (rather than a minimum) and whether the firm will produce a positive output (rather than no output at all). There are an equal number of variables: output, price, total cost, total revenue, and total profit. Setting the marginal-cost equation equal to the marginal-revenue equation, we can find two values for X at which marginal cost and marginal revenue are equal. One of these is the output at which profit is a minimum. At the other X profit is a maximum. If this output is one at which total revenue is greater than total variable cost, the firm will produce this output. It may receive a positive profit or a negative profit, but the negative profit will be less than its total fixed cost. We can determine the price the firm will charge, its total cost, total revenue, and total profit by inserting the equilibrium value of X into the other four equations that make up the model.

Exercise 12-2

1 The equations of the short-run monopoly model are:

a $C =$ ____________

b $P =$ ____________

c $R \equiv$ ____________

d $\pi \equiv$ ____________

e ____________ = ____________

2 The two inequalities of the short-run monopoly model are:

a ____________ $>$ ____________

b ____________ $\geqq$ ____________

3 What is the algebraic formula for finding the values of X in the second-degree equation $\alpha X^2 + \beta X + \gamma c = 0$? $X =$ ____________

4 If:

$$C = aX^3 - bX^2 + cX + F$$

$$P = \frac{A - X}{B}$$

a What is the marginal-cost function?

$dC/dX =$ ____________

b What is the marginal-revenue function?

$dR/dX =$ ____________

c The equilibrium output of the firm is found when

(1) ____________ $=$ ____________

(2) Or ____________ $= 0$

d Using the formula in question 3, the equilibrium output of the firm is found when $X =$ ____________

5 When we employ the equation in part *d* of question 4 to find the equilibrium X, we obtain two solutions. If both solutions are positive, the firm will produce the output at which ____________ $>$ ____________ provided that ____________ $\geqq$ ____________

6 Having found the equilibrium value of X, we can find:

a The price the firm will charge by putting X into the equation $P =$ ____________

b The total costs of the firm by putting X into the equation $C =$ ____________

c The total revenue of the firm by putting P and X into the equation ____________ $\equiv$ ____________

d The total profit of the firm by putting R and C into the equation ____________ $\equiv$ ____________

e The average cost of the firm by ____________

f The average profit of the firm by ____________

7 Assume

$$C = X^3 - 22.75X^2 + 175X + 50$$

$$P = \frac{100 - X}{4}$$

In the short run:

a What output will the firm produce? ____________

b Its total revenue will be ____________

c Its total cost will be ____________

d Its total profit will be ____________

8 Suppose
$C = X^3 - 23X^2 + 175X + 100$

$$P = \frac{67 - X}{1}$$

In the short run:

a The firm will produce an output of ____________

b Charge a price of $____________

c Have total revenue of $____________

d Have total costs of $____________

e Have a profit of $____________

9 Assume
$C = X^3 - 23X^2 + 175X + 200$

$$P = \frac{67 - X}{1}$$

In the short run:

a What output will the firm produce? ____________

b What price will it charge? $____________

c What total revenue will it receive? $____________

d What will be its total costs? $____________

e What profit will it have? $____________

10 On the graphs:

a Plot from question 7 the firm's demand, marginal-revenue, average-total-cost, average-variable-cost, and marginal-cost functions.

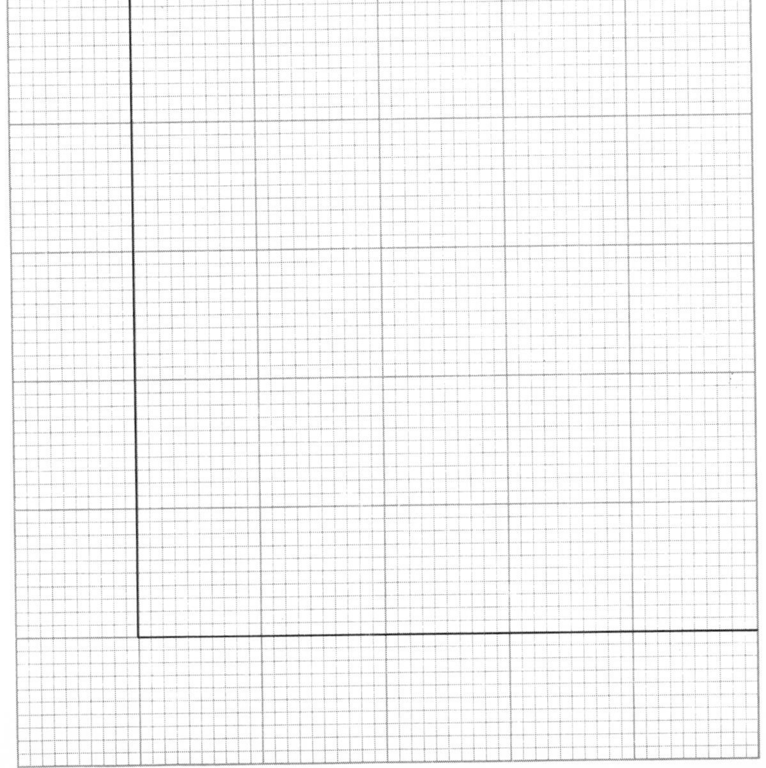

b Plot from questions 8 and 9 the firm's demand, marginal-revenue, average-variable-cost, and marginal-cost functions. Also plot from question 8 the firm's average-total-cost function and from question 9 the firm's average-total-cost function.

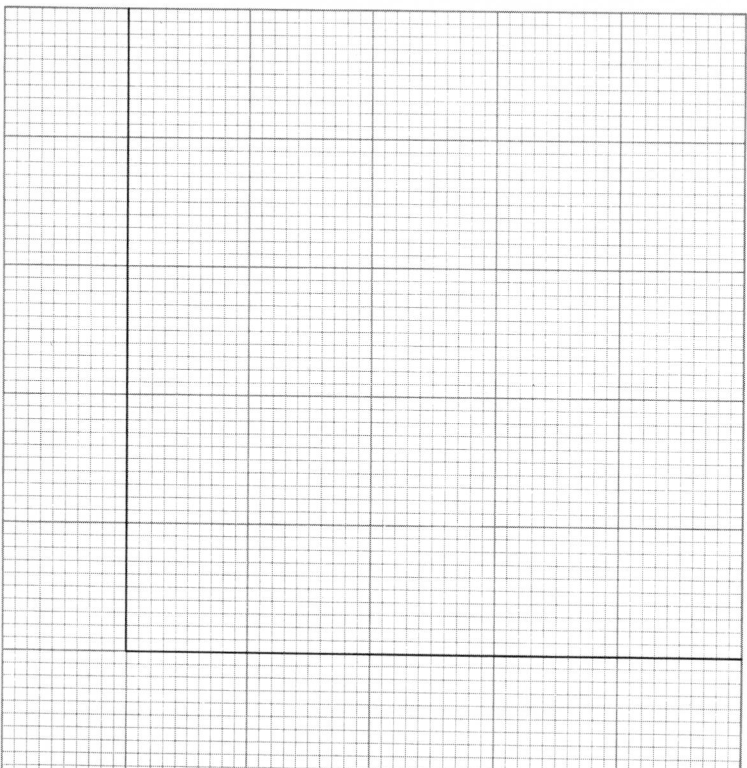

Monopoly in the long run

The monopoly model for the long run also contains five equations and two inequalities. We can determine from this model the monopolist's output, price, total cost, total revenue, and total profit in the long run. Adding two more equations, we can find his average cost and average profit.

The equations of the model are

$$C = eX^3 - fX^2 + gX \qquad (12\text{-}28)$$

$$P = \frac{A - X}{B} \qquad (12\text{-}29)$$

$$R \equiv X \cdot P \qquad (12\text{-}20)$$

$$\pi \equiv R - C \qquad (12\text{-}1)$$

$$\frac{dC}{dX} = \frac{dR}{dX} \qquad (12\text{-}7)$$

All but the first equation are the same equations employed in the short-run model. The first equation is the long-run cost function of the firm; and it does not contain a constant term because there are no fixed costs in the long run. The firm's marginal costs (dC/dX) in equation 12-7 are the firm's long-run marginal costs instead of the short-run marginal costs employed in the earlier model.

In addition to the five equations there are two inequalities.

$$\frac{d^2C}{dX^2} > \frac{d^2R}{dX^2} \tag{12-11}$$

$$R \geqq C \tag{12-16}$$

Inequality 12-11 is essentially the same inequality used in the short-run model and enables us to distinguish the maximum from the minimum profit.[7] The costs in d^2C/dX^2 are, of course, now the long-run costs of the firm. The second inequality tells us that total revenue must exceed or equal total cost in the long run if the firm is to produce at all. If $C > R$, the firm will produce no output because it can thereby reduce its loss to zero.

This model contains the same variables as the short-run model: X, C, P, R, and π. Since there are an equal number of equations and variables, the model should have a solution for each of the five variables. Of the five equations, two are again functional, two are definitional, and one is an equilibrium equation.

Equilibrium We employ exactly the same method used in the short-run model to find the equilibrium X. From equation 12-28 we find

$$\frac{dC}{dX} = 3eX^2 - fX + g \tag{12-30}$$

and from equation 12-19

$$\frac{dR}{dX} = \frac{A}{B} - \frac{2}{B}X \tag{12-23}$$

Substituting into equation 12-7 we find

$$3eX^2 - fX + g = \frac{A}{B} - \frac{2}{B}X \tag{12-31}$$

or

$$(3e)X^2 + \left(\frac{2}{B} - 2f\right)X + \left(g - \frac{A}{B}\right) = 0 \tag{12-32}$$

Once again we let $\alpha = 3e$; $\beta = 2/B - 2f$; and $\gamma = g - A/B$. We then have an equation of the form $\alpha X^2 + \beta X + \gamma = 0$. We can solve this equation by employing the equation for the solution of a second-degree equation.

$$X = \frac{-\beta \pm \sqrt{\beta^2 - 4\alpha\gamma}}{2\alpha} \tag{12-26}$$

and

$$X = \frac{-(2/B - 2f) \pm \sqrt{(2/B - 2f)^2 - 4(3e)(g - A/B)}}{2(3e)} \tag{12-33}$$

The solution of this equation gives us two values for X. If both solutions are

[7] The maximum and the minimum profit are again the local maximum and the local minimum. See footnote 6, pages 316–317.

positive, the firm will produce the output which satisfies 12-11 provided it also satisfies 12-16. If these two conditions are not satisfied, the firm will produce no long-run output. By substituting the equilibrium value of X into equations 12-28, 12-19, 12-20, and 12-1 we can determine the firm's long-run total cost, price, total revenue, and profit. If we wish, we can also determine average cost and average profit.

Numerical examples For examples we need only two cases, one in which the firm produces no output in the long run because at its maximum-profit output total cost is greater than total revenue and one in which the firm produces and has a profit in the long run.

Case 1: zero long-run output Assume that

$$C = X^3 - 28.75X^2 + 260X$$

$$P = \frac{200 - X}{4}$$

Marginal cost is

$$\frac{dC}{dX} = 3X^2 - 57.5X + 260$$

and marginal revenue is

$$\frac{dR}{dX} = \frac{200}{4} - \frac{2}{4}X$$

Setting marginal cost equal to marginal revenue,

$$3X^2 - 57.5X + 260 = {}^{200}\!/_{4} - {}^{2}\!/_{4}X$$

or

$$3X^2 - 57X + 210 = 0$$

This equation we can solve by using the formula of equation 12-26. Skipping the arithmetic this time, we find that marginal cost and marginal revenue are equal when X is 5 and X is 14. At an output of 5, however, d^2C/dX^2 is -27.5 and d^2R/dX^2 is $-\frac{1}{2}$. These values do not satisfy the inequality of 12-11. Profit is here a minimum rather than a maximum. When the output of the firm is 14, d^2C/dX^2 is 26.5 and d^2R/dX^2 is $-\frac{1}{2}$. Here profit is a maximum because 12-11 is satisfied.

When the firm produces $14X$, its C is \$606.25 and its R is \$593.75. Its costs exceed its revenue by \$12.50, and it has a loss of \$12.50. Inequality 12-16 is not satisfied, and so the firm will produce no output in the long run. Its revenue, costs, and profit will all be zero.

Case 2: positive output and profit in the long run Assume now that

$$C = X^3 - 24.5X^2 + 200X$$

$$P = \frac{224 - X}{4}$$

$$\frac{dC}{dX} = 3X^2 - 49X + 200$$

and

$$\frac{dR}{dX} = \frac{224}{4} - \frac{2}{4}X$$

Setting marginal cost equal to marginal revenue,

$$3X^2 - 49X + 200 = {}^{224}\!/_4 - {}^{2}\!/_4X$$
$$3X^2 - 48.5X + 144 = 0$$

Solving for X, using equation 12-26, X_1 is 4 and X_2 is 12. When X is 4, however, d^2C/dX^2 is less than d^2R/dX^2 and profit is a minimum. An output of 12 maximizes profit because at an output of 12 d^2C/dX^2 is greater than d^2R/dX^2. When X is 12, moreover, the firm will set a price equal to

$$P = \frac{224 - 12}{4}$$
$$= \$53$$

and its total revenue is 12($53), or $636. Its total cost at an output of 12 is

$$\begin{aligned} C &= X^3 - 24.5X^2 + 200X \\ &= 12^3 - 24.5(12^2) + 200(12) \\ &= 1{,}728 - 3{,}528 + 2{,}400 \\ &= \$600 \end{aligned}$$

Total revenue ($636) exceeds total cost ($600); since inequality 12-11 is satisfied, the firm will produce an output of 12 units of X in the long run. The firm has a profit equal to

$$\begin{aligned} \pi &= R - C \\ &= \$636 - \$600 \\ &= \$36 \end{aligned}$$

Its average cost is $600 divided by 12, or $50 per unit of X, and its average profit is $36 divided by 12, or $3 per unit.

This firm, in short, will produce 12 units, charge a price of $53, have total revenue of $636, total cost of $600, and a total profit of $36.

Exercise 12-3

1 The five equations and two inequalities of the long-run monopoly model are:

a $C =$ ____________

b ____________ $=$ ____________

c ____________ $\equiv$ ____________ $\cdot$ ____________

d ____________ $\equiv$ ____________ $-$ ____________

e ____________ $=$ ____________

f ____________ ____________

g ____________ ____________

2 Assume that:

$$C = X^3 - 38.5X^2 + 1{,}100X$$

$$P = \frac{92 - X}{0.1}$$

In the long run:

a What output will the firm produce? ____________

b What price will it charge? $____________

c What total revenue will it receive? $____________

d What total costs will it have? $____________

e What total profit will it receive? $____________

3 Suppose that

$$C = X^3 - 15\tfrac{1}{3}X^2 - 80X$$

$$P = \frac{51 - X}{3}$$

In the long run the firm will:

a Produce an output of ____________

b Have total revenue of $____________

c Have total costs of $____________

d Receive a total profit of $____________

PURE COMPETITION

We saw in the last chapter that demand and the costs of production determine the output and price of the pure monopolist seeking the maximum economic profit. In this chapter we examine a purely competitive industry and its short- and long-run output and price. As in pure monopoly, the output and price of a purely competitive industry depend upon the demand for the product, the costs of producing it, and the profit-maximization goal of the firm. But because the structures of pure monopoly and pure competition differ, the way in which demand and costs interact to determine price and output also differs; however, we shall be able to use much of what we learned about the pure monopolist and apply it to the purely competitive firm.

In the first section we look at two characteristics of pure competition that distinguish it from pure monopoly and explain two of the simplifying assumptions we employ in our analysis of pure competition. The second and third sections examine the purely competitive industry in the short and long run, respectively. In both these sections we develop models for the individual firm and for the industry that determine their outputs. These models also explain the price of the product and the firm's total cost, total revenue, and total profit.

CHARACTERISTICS AND ASSUMPTIONS

An industry which is composed of a large number of relatively small firms producing an identical product and which firms may enter or leave in the long run is called a *purely competitive industry*. At least two important consequences of this definition require additional explanation.

The number of firms and economic profit

The short run we defined earlier as a period of time in which some of a firm's inputs and costs are fixed and some are variable. When we consider an industry composed of a number of firms, we must expand this definition. We say that the short run is also a period of time in which the number of firms in the industry is fixed. The short run is a period that is not long enough to enable new firms to enter or old firms to leave the industry. In mathematical language,

$$N = \bar{N} \qquad (13\text{-}1)$$

where N stands for the number of firms in the industry and the bar indicates that it is constant or fixed.

In the long run, as we know from our study of costs, all the inputs employed by a firm and all its costs are variable. In addition, the long run is a period in which the number of firms in an industry is variable. The long run is a period of time that is long enough to enable new firms to come into the industry or old firms to leave the industry.

We shall assume that firms leave an industry when their long-run economic profits are negative. If a firm would suffer an economic loss by remaining, it leaves the industry. New firms enter an industry when the firms already in the industry are receiving positive economic profits. When profits are neither positive nor negative, firms do not enter or leave the industry. Firms, in short, leave when profits are negative, enter when profits are positive, and do neither when profits are zero. For the industry to be in long-run equilibrium there must be no motive for firms either to enter or to leave the industry. We find, therefore, that when there is long-run equilibrium,

$$\pi = 0 \qquad (13\text{-}2)$$

Demand

Each purely competitive firm is relatively small. There are a large number of such firms, and each firm produces the same product as the other firms in the industry. The consequence of these characteristics of a purely competitive firm is that the firm has no control over the price at which sells its product. It produces such a small amount of the product, relative to the total output of the product, that increasing or decreasing its production has no significant effect on the total supply of the product. And if increasing or decreasing its output has no effect on total supply, it cannot affect or influence the price at which the product sells.

Mathematically we can write

$$P = \bar{P} \qquad (13\text{-}3)$$

where P is the price at which the firm can sell its product and the bar indicates that as far as an individual firm is concerned, P is an exogeneous variable. This equation is the same as the first equation on page 228. There we made two observations about this kind of demand equation. First, if price is fixed and constant, the demand for the product is perfectly elastic and the demand curve is a horizontal line.[1] Second, and more important, the price of the product and the

[1] For a review, see pages 234 to 235.

marginal revenue from the sale of an additional unit of the product are equal;[2] or

$$\frac{dR}{dx} = \bar{P} \tag{13-4}$$

This does not mean that the demand for the total output *of the industry* is perfectly elastic. All it means is that the demand for the output *of each individual firm* is perfectly elastic. We shall continue to assume that the market demand for the product is less than perfectly elastic. Market demand, we assume, is a decreasing and linear function, or

$$P = \frac{A - D}{B} \tag{13-5}$$

where P is price, D is the total quantity demanded of the product, and A and B are parameters.

Two special assumptions

To ensure that our analysis does not become too complex we shall make two assumptions that do not distort reality too much. First, we assume that all firms have identical cost functions. In the short run each firm's cost function is

$$C = ax^3 - bx^2 - cx + \bar{F} \tag{13-6}$$

and in the long run each firm's cost function is

$$C = ex^3 - fx^2 + gx \tag{13-7}$$

Total cost is C; x is the output of an individual firm; and a, b, c, e, f, g, and $\bar{F}$ are parameters.

Second, we assume that the industry is a constant-cost industry. This means that the entry or exit of firms in the long run does not change the cost functions of firms in the industry. The values of the parameters e, f, and g in equation 13-7 are not altered by the expansion or contraction of the industry's output.

Exercise 13-1

1 In the short run the number of firms in a purely competitive industry is ____________. Mathematically, $N =$ ____________.

2 In the long run firms:

a Enter a purely competitive industry when ____________ are (positive, negative, zero) ____________

b Leave a purely competitive industry when ____________ are (positive, negative, zero) ____________

c Neither enter nor leave when ____________ are ____________

3 The demand function for the product of the individual purely competitive firm is ____________ elastic. Mathematically this means that:

[2]See pages 228 to 229 for a review.

a $P =$ __________

b $dR/dX =$ __________

4 We assume in this chapter that all firms in a purely competitive industry have __________ cost functions.

5 We also assume that the purely competitive industry is a __________-cost industry. This means that the __________ or __________ of firms does not change the (short-run, long-run) __________ cost __________ of firms in the industry.

6 In this chapter we assume that the market demand for the product produced by a purely competitive industry is __________ perfectly elastic and that:

a $D =$ __________

b Or $P =$ __________

THE SHORT RUN

Demand and supply determine both the short- and long-run output of a purely competitive industry and the price of the product produced by that industry. We assume a given demand for the industry's product. The industry's supply of the product, however, is the sum of the supply functions of each of the individual firms in the industry. For this reason we look first at the firm to determine its supply function. Then we add the supply functions of the individual firms to determine the industry's supply function. Finally we combine the industry supply function with the industry demand function to find the price of the product and the total output of the industry in the short run.

The firm's supply function

Like our model for the pure monopolist, the model for the purely competitive firm in the short run consists of five equations and two inequalities. The five equations are

$$C = ax^3 - bx^2 + cx + \bar{F} \qquad (13\text{-}6)$$
$$P = \bar{P} \qquad (13\text{-}3)$$
$$R \equiv x \cdot P \qquad (13\text{-}8)$$
$$\pi \equiv R - C \qquad (13\text{-}9)$$
$$\frac{dC}{dx} = \frac{dR}{dx} \qquad (13\text{-}10)$$

We have replaced X with x in the first, third, and fifth equations. The small x will indicate the output of the *individual* firm while the large X will indicate the total output of the industry.

Equation 13-6 is the short-run cost function of the firm. The definitions of revenue and profit are provided by equations 13-8 and 13-9. Equation 13-10 is the equilibrium equation. The equation $P = \bar{P}$ tells us that the individual firm is not able to influence the price of the product and that as far as the firm is concerned, price is a parameter.

The two inequalities are

$$\frac{d^2C}{dx^2} > \frac{d^2R}{dx^2} \tag{13-11}$$

$$R \geqq V \tag{13-12}$$

To ensure that profit is a maximum (rather than a minimum) when marginal cost and marginal revenue are equal, 13-11 tells us that the derivative of the marginal-cost function must exceed the derivative of the marginal-revenue function. And for profit to be a maximum at this output (rather than at an output of zero) expression 13-12 says that total revenue must exceed or equal total variable cost.

With the exception of equation 13-3, the five equations and two inequalities of this model are the same as the equations and inequalities in the model for pure monopoly in the short run. There are, however, in the short-run model for the purely competitive firm only four *endogeneous* variables: x, R, C, and π. The price of the product is an exogenous variable to the firm. The five equations and two inequalities are sufficient to determine the values of the five variables.

Equilibrium output of the firm To determine the equilibrium output of the firm we first find the marginal-cost function from the total-cost function. With the total-cost function expressed by equation 13-6, the marginal-cost function is

$$\frac{dC}{dx} = 3ax^2 - 2bx + c \tag{13-13}$$

Then we recall that when price is a parameter, marginal revenue and price are equal, or

$$\frac{dR}{dx} = \bar{P} \tag{13-4}$$

Now we substitute the right sides of equations 13-13 and 13-4 into the equilibrium equation, equation 13-10.

$$3ax^2 - 2bx + c = \bar{P} \tag{13-14}$$

or

$$3ax^2 - 2bx + c - \bar{P} = 0$$

which can be written

$$3ax^2 + (-2b)x + (c - \bar{P}) = 0 \tag{13-15}$$

Equation 13-15 is a second-degree, or quadratic, equation containing one variable. It can be solved by using equation 12-26 for the solution to a second-degree equation

$$x = \frac{-\beta \pm \sqrt{\beta^2 - 4\alpha\gamma}}{2\alpha} \tag{13-16}$$

where α is the coefficient of x^2, β is the coefficient of x, and γ is the constant term. Substituting from equation 13-15 into equation 13-16,

$$x = \frac{-(-2b) \pm \sqrt{(-2b)^2 - 4(3a)(c - \bar{P})}}{2(3a)}$$

or

$$x = \frac{2b \pm \sqrt{4b^2 - 12a(c - \bar{P})}}{6a} \qquad (13\text{-}17)$$

Such an equation has two solutions. One solution is

$$x = \frac{2b - \sqrt{4b^2 - 12a(c - \bar{P})}}{6a}$$

This solution, however, is the output at which profit is a minimum, because at this output, inequality 13-11 is not satisfied. At this output $d^2C/dx^2 < d^2R/dx^2$.

The other solution to equation 13-17 is

$$x = \frac{2b + \sqrt{4b^2 - 12a(c - \bar{P})}}{6a} \qquad (13\text{-}18)$$

This is the output at which profit is a maximum.[3] At this output, inequality 13-11 is satisfied: $d^2C/dx^2 > d^2R/dx^2$.

Equation 13-18 is the supply function of the individual purely competitive firm. The quantity x the firm will supply is a function of the market price P of the product. It contains three parameters from the firm's total cost function, a, b, and c. To equation 13-18 we must add one restriction. We know that the firm in the short run will produce the profit maximizing output only if

$$R \geqq V \qquad (13\text{-}12)$$

If we divide both sides of this inequality by x, the output of the firm, we have

$$\frac{R}{x} \geqq \frac{V}{x} \qquad (13\text{-}19)$$

The left side of this inequality is the market price of the product. (If $R \equiv X \cdot P$, then $R/x \equiv P$.) The right side is the average variable cost A_V of producing the product. The firm will produce the profit-maximizing output indicated by equation 13-18 only if at that output

$$P \geqq A_V \qquad (13\text{-}20)$$

Price must exceed or equal average variable cost in the short run, or the firm will not produce at all.

From our study of costs in Chapter 11 we already know that average variable cost is a minimum when x is equal to $b/2a$ and that when x is $b/2a$, average variable cost is equal[4] to $c - b^2/4a$. Thus if $c - b^2/4a$ is the minimum value A_V reaches, we can substitute it for A_V in the inequality. The price of the product, if the firm is to produce at all in the short run, must exceed or equal the minimum average variable cost, or

$$P \geqq c - \frac{b^2}{4a} \qquad (13\text{-}21)$$

In summary, the supply function of the purely competitive firm in the short run is

$$x = \frac{2b + \sqrt{4b^2 - 12a(c - \bar{P})}}{6a} \qquad (13\text{-}18)$$

[3] The maximum and minimum profits are the local maximum and the local minimum. See footnote 6 in Chapter 12, pages 316 to 317.

[4] See pages 291 to 293.

where

$$P \geqq c - \frac{b^2}{4a} \qquad (13\text{-}21)$$

If P is less than $c - b^2/4a$, the firm will not produce the output indicated by equation 13-18 but will produce an output of zero.

We should note in equation 13-18 that x is an increasing function of P. Given the values of the cost parameters (a, b, and c), the greater the price of the product, the greater the value of the term under the radical sign and the greater, therefore, is x, the quantity supplied by the firm.

Numerical example Let us assume that the firm's total-cost function is

$$C = 0.1x^3 - 1.5x^2 + 25x + 10$$

Its marginal-cost function is then

$$\frac{dC}{dx} = 0.3x^2 - 3x + 25$$

Setting marginal cost equal to marginal revenue or price,

$$0.3x^2 - 3x + 25 = P$$

or

$$0.3x^2 - 3x + 25 - P = 0$$

which can be written

$$0.3x^2 + (-3)x + (25 - P) = 0$$

Using equation 13-18 to find x,

$$\begin{aligned} x &= \frac{-(-3) + \sqrt{(-3)^2 - 4(0.3)(25 - P)}}{2(0.3)} \\ &= \frac{3 + \sqrt{9 - 1.2(25 - P)}}{0.6} \\ &= 5 + \frac{\sqrt{9 - 30 + 1.2P}}{0.6} \\ &= 5 + \frac{\sqrt{1.2P - 21}}{0.6} \qquad (13\text{-}22) \end{aligned}$$

Equation 13-22 is the firm's supply function. But it is subject to the restriction imposed by inequality 13-21. In our numerical example the minimum average variable cost is

$$\begin{aligned} c - \frac{b^2}{4a} &= 25 - \frac{(1.5)^2}{4(0.1)} \\ &= 25 - \frac{2.25}{0.4} \\ &= 25 - 5.625 \\ &= 19.375 \end{aligned}$$

The firm will supply the quantities indicated by equation 13-22 provided that the price of the product is at least \$19.375. If price is less than \$19.375, the firm will supply none of the product in the short run. [The output at which average variable cost is a minimum and equal to \$19.375 is $b/2a = 1.5/2(0.1) = 1.5/0.2 = 7.5$.]

Three cases We can now employ the firm's supply function to determine the quantity of its product it will offer for sale at various prices. In the first case the price is high enough for the firm to produce at a profit; in the second case the price is lower and the firm produces at a loss; and in the third case the price is so low that the firm produces no output.

Case 1: production at a profit Assume that $P = \$25$. Employing the firm's supply function, equation 13-22,

$$\begin{aligned} x &= 5 + \frac{\sqrt{1.2(25) - 21}}{0.6} \\ &= 5 + \frac{\sqrt{30 - 21}}{0.6} \\ &= 5 + \frac{\sqrt{9}}{0.6} \\ &= 5 + \frac{3}{0.6} \\ &= 5 + 5 \\ &= 10 \end{aligned}$$

The firm will produce 10 units of the product when its price is \$25. Note that the price is greater than the minimum average variable cost of \$19.375.

When x is 10, the firm's total revenue is

$$\begin{aligned} R &\equiv x \cdot P \qquad (13\text{-}8) \\ &= 10(\$25) \\ &= \$250 \end{aligned}$$

Its total cost is

$$\begin{aligned} C &= 0.1x^3 - 1.5x^2 + 25x + 10 \\ &= 0.1(10^3) - 1.5(10^2) + 25(10) + 10 \\ &= 100 - 150 + 250 + 10 \\ &= \$210 \end{aligned}$$

And its profit is

$$\begin{aligned} \pi &= R - C \\ &= \$250 - \$210 \\ &= \$40 \end{aligned}$$

Case 2: production at a loss Assume in this case that $P = \$20.20$. Because price is greater than the minimum average variable cost (\$19.375), the firm will produce in the short run. Employing equation 13-22 to find its output,

$$\begin{aligned} x &= 5 + \frac{\sqrt{1.2(20.20) - 21}}{0.6} \\ &= 5 + \frac{\sqrt{24.24 - 21}}{0.6} \\ &= 5 + \frac{\sqrt{3.24}}{0.6} \\ &= 5 + \frac{1.8}{0.6} \\ &= 5 + 3 \\ &= 8 \end{aligned}$$

When the price is \$20.20, the firm will produce 8 units of the product.

The firm's revenue is

$$R = 8(\$20.20) = \$161.60$$

Its total cost is

$$\begin{aligned} C &= 0.1(8^3) - 1.5(8^2) + 25(8) + 10 \\ &= 0.1(512) - 1.5(64) + 200 + 10 \\ &= 51.20 - 96 + 200 + 10 \\ &= \$165.20 \end{aligned}$$

It has a profit, therefore, equal to

$$\begin{aligned} \pi &= \$161.60 - \$165.20 \\ &= -\$6.40 \end{aligned}$$

The firm suffers a loss of \$6.40 in the short run. But because this loss is smaller than its total fixed costs of \$10 (the loss of the firm would suffer if it produced no output), it produces in order to minimize its loss.

Case 3: zero production The assumed price in this case is $P = \$18.70$. This price is less than the minimum average variable cost of \$19.375, and so the firm will produce zero output. To see that it will not produce, let us find its profit-maximizing output and then see that the loss it would suffer if it produced this output is greater than its loss if it produces no output.

Again employing equation 13-22 to find the profit-maximizing output,

$$\begin{aligned} x &= 5 + \frac{\sqrt{1.2(18.70) - 21}}{0.6} \\ &= 5 + \frac{\sqrt{22.44 - 21}}{0.6} \\ &= 5 + \frac{\sqrt{1.44}}{0.6} \\ &= 5 + \frac{1.2}{0.6} \\ &= 5 + 2 \\ &= 7 \end{aligned}$$

If the firm produced 7 units when the price is \$18.70, its total revenue would be

$$\begin{aligned} R &= 7(\$18.70) \\ &= \$130.90 \end{aligned}$$

its total cost would be

$$\begin{aligned} C &= 0.1(7^3) - 1.5(7^2) + 25(7) + 10 \\ &= 34.30 - 73.50 + 175 + 10 \\ &= \$219.30 \end{aligned}$$

and its total profit would be

$$\begin{aligned} \pi &= \$130.90 - \$219.30 \\ &= -\$78.40 \end{aligned}$$

It would suffer a loss of \$78.40 if it produced 7 units of the product. But if it produced no output, its loss would be only \$10, the amount of its total fixed costs. It can reduce its loss from \$78.40 to \$10 if it produces an output of zero in the short run.

The supply curve and the supply schedule In Figure 13-1 we have plotted the firm's average-cost function ($A_c = 0.1x^2 - 1.5x + 25 + 10/x$), average-variable-cost function ($A_v = 0.1x^2 - 1.5x + 25$), and marginal-cost function ($dC/dx = 0.3x^2 - 3x + 25$). We have also plotted the three marginal-revenue functions ($dR/dx = P =$ \$25, = \$20.20, and = \$18.70) used in the three cases above.

The graph shows that when price and marginal revenue are \$25, the marginal-cost and marginal-revenue curves intersect at outputs of 0 and 10; 10 units is the profit-maximizing output because at 10 units the slope of the marginal-cost curve (which is d^2C/dx^2) is greater than the slope of the marginal-revenue curve (which is d^2R/dx^2); and price is greater than average variable cost. At 0 units, the slope of the marginal-cost curve is less than the slope of the marginal-revenue curve.

At a price and marginal revenue of \$20.20 the marginal-revenue and marginal-cost curves cross at 2 and 8 units of output. The profit-maximizing output is 8 because price is greater than average variable cost and the slope of the

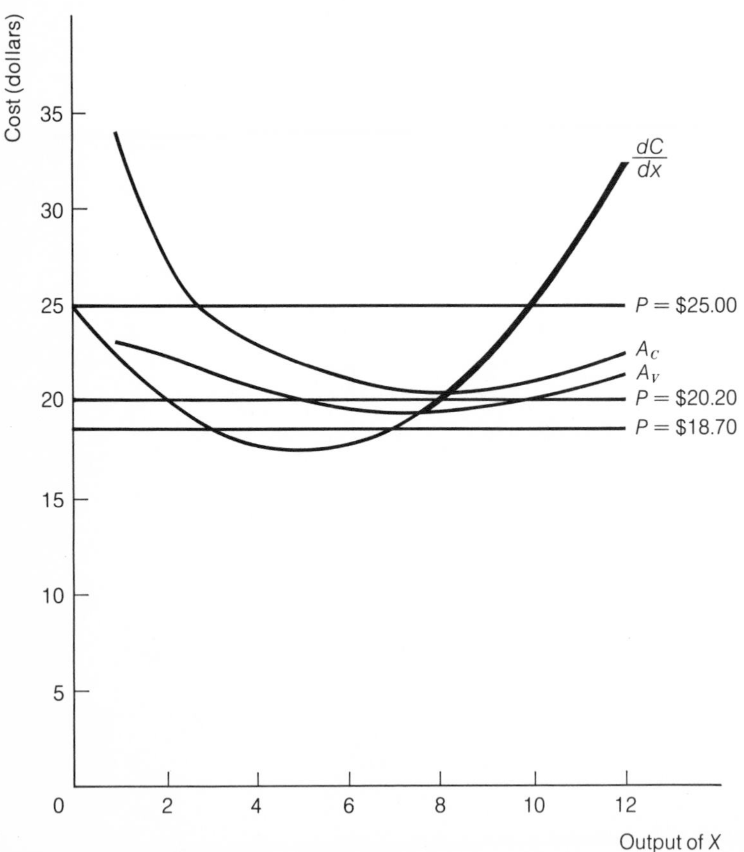

FIGURE 13-1

TABLE 13-1 THE FIRM'S SHORT-RUN SUPPLY SCHEDULE

Price	Quantity Supplied
$18.70	0
19.375	7.5
20.20	8
22.30	9
25.00	10
28.30	11
32.20	12

marginal-cost curve is greater than the slope of the marginal-revenue curve. When the price is $18.70, $4\frac{2}{3}$ and 7 are the outputs at which marginal cost and marginal revenue intersect. The slope of the marginal-cost curve is greater than the slope of the marginal-revenue curve at 7 units, but price is less than average variable cost. The firm will therefore not produce the 7 units but will produce zero output.

The marginal-cost curve where marginal cost is greater than or equal to the minimum average variable cost has been darkened to show that it is the purely competitive firm's short-run supply curve. It should be noted that it is the rising portion of the marginal-cost curve above the average-variable curve, or, more simply, that part of the marginal-cost curve above average variable cost.

Table 13-1 shows the firm's short-run supply schedule. It shows the quantity the firm will offer at the three prices we assumed in the three cases above. It also shows (by employing equation 13-22) the quantities the firm would supply at several other prices. Note that when price is equal to the minimum average variable cost ($19.375), the quantity offered is the output ($7\frac{1}{2}$) at which average variable cost is a minimum. It should also be observed again that price and quantity supplied are directly related to each other.

The industry: supply, equilibrium price, and output

In the short run the number of firms in a purely competitive industry is constant because the short run is not long enough to enable new firms to enter or old firms to leave the industry.

$$N = \bar{N} \tag{13-1}$$

Each of these firms, we assume for simplicity, has exactly the same cost function. As a result each firm will have the same supply function:

$$x = \frac{2b + \sqrt{4b^2 - 12a(c - P)}}{6a} \tag{13-8}$$

where

$$P \geqq c - \frac{b^2}{4a} \tag{13-21}$$

The supply function for the industry is the total quantity that will be offered for sale or supplied S by all firms in the industry as a function of the price of the product. The industry supply function is equal to the number of firms in the industry multiplied by the supply function of the firm.

$$S = \bar{N}\frac{2b + \sqrt{4b^2 - 12a(c - P)}}{6a} \qquad (13\text{-}23)$$

where

$$P \geqq c - \frac{b^2}{4a} \qquad (13\text{-}21)$$

The model We shall assume that the market demand for the product produced by the industry is a linear and decreasing function.

$$D = A - BP \qquad (13\text{-}24)$$

D is the total quantity demanded, P is the price of the product, and A and B are parameters.

Our model for the purely competitive industry in the short run consists of three equations and one inequality.

$$S = \bar{N}\frac{2b + \sqrt{4b^2 - 12a(c - P)}}{6a} \qquad (13\text{-}23)$$

$$D = A - BP \qquad (13\text{-}24)$$

$$S = D \qquad (13\text{-}25)$$

$$P \geqq c - \frac{b^2}{4a} \qquad (13\text{-}21)$$

Equations 13-23 and 13-24 are the supply and demand functions, respectively. Equation 13-25 is the equilibrium equation and tells us that price of the product will be the price at which the quantity supplied and the quantity demanded are equal. Inequality 13-21 says that the price of the product must exceed or equal the minimum average variable cost of producing it. If a price that satisfies the three equations is less than $c - b^2/4a$, the product will not be supplied at that price and that price, therefore, cannot be an equilibrium price.

To find the equilibrium price we substitute the right sides of equations 13-23 and 13-24 for S and D, respectively, in equation 13-25.

$$\bar{N}\frac{2b + \sqrt{4b^2 - 12a(c - P)}}{6a} = A - BP \qquad (13\text{-}26)$$

This is a solution equation for the variable, P, and can be solved. We shall not solve the equation, however, because the algebra is extremely complicated and the solution of a second-degree equation is required. Solving a second-degree equation, we know, yields two solutions. When we solve equation 13-26, therefore, we obtain two solutions. But at least one of these solutions will give us a price that is *greater than* or equal to the price *at which the quantity demanded D is zero*. Since $D = A - BP$, then the price at which D is zero is

$$0 = A - BP$$

$$-A = -BP$$

$$P = \frac{A}{B}$$

We can eliminate one of the prices we obtain when we solve equation 13-26 by eliminating the one that shows price to be greater than or equal to A/B.

If the other solution satisfies inequality 13-21, we have found the equilibrium price of the product. We can then find the equilibrium output of the product by substituting the equilibrium price either into equation 13-23 or into equation 13-24 and solving for D or S. If this other solution does not satisfy inequality 13-21, there is no equilibrium price or output for the product. The absence of an equilibrium price and output means that the demand for the product is so small relative to the cost of producing it (or the cost of producing it is so great relative to the demand) that there is no price that will result in both a positive quantity demanded and a positive quantity supplied.

Numerical example To see that we can find both the equilibrium price and output of a purely competitive industry in the short run, let us suppose that the number of firms in the industry in the short run is

$$N = 100$$

and that the market demand for the product is

$$D = 2{,}000 - 40P$$

The supply function of the single firm, using our earlier numerical example, is

$$x = 5 + \frac{\sqrt{1.2P - 21}}{0.6}$$

This means that the market supply function is

$$S = 100\left(5 + \frac{\sqrt{1.2P - 21}}{0.6}\right)$$

When we set the supply function equal to the demand function, we have

$$100\left(5 + \frac{\sqrt{1.2P - 21}}{0.6}\right) = 2{,}000 - 40P$$

or

$$500 + \frac{100\sqrt{1.2P - 21}}{0.6} = 2{,}000 - 40P$$

Subtracting 500 from both sides of the equation leaves

$$\frac{100\sqrt{1.2P - 21}}{0.6} = 1{,}500 - 40P$$

Multiplying through by 0.6, we have

$$100\sqrt{1.2P - 21} = 900 - 24P$$

and dividing through by 100 leaves

$$\sqrt{1.2P - 21} = 9 - 0.24P$$

We now square both sides of this equation and obtain

$$\begin{aligned} 1.2P - 21 &= (9 - 0.24P)^2 \\ &= 81 - 4.32P + 0.0576P^2 \end{aligned}$$

Moving all terms to the left side, gives

$$0.0576P^2 - 5.52P + 102 = 0$$

This last equation we recognize as a second-degree equation which can be solved by using the formula for the solution to a quadratic equation,

$$P = \frac{-\beta \pm \sqrt{\beta^2 - 4\alpha\gamma}}{2\alpha} \qquad (13\text{-}16)$$

where α is 0.0576, β is -5.52, and γ is 102. We find that

$$\begin{aligned} P &= \frac{-(-5.52) \pm \sqrt{(-5.52)^2 - 4(0.0576)(102)}}{2(0.0576)} \\ &= \frac{5.52 \pm \sqrt{30.4704 - 23.5008}}{0.1152} \\ &= \frac{5.52 \pm \sqrt{6.9796}}{0.1152} \\ &= \frac{5.52 \pm 2.64}{0.1152} \end{aligned}$$

$$\begin{aligned} P_1 &= \frac{5.52 + 2.64}{0.1152} & P_2 &= \frac{5.52 - 2.64}{0.1152} \\ &= \frac{8.16}{0.1152} & &= \frac{2.88}{0.1152} \\ &= \$70.83\tfrac{1}{3} & &= \$25 \end{aligned}$$

The equilibrium market price is either $70.83⅓ or $25. Which is it? The price of $70.83⅓ is greater than the price at which the quantity demanded is zero. Quantity demanded is zero when

$$\begin{aligned} 0 &= 2{,}000 - 40P \\ -2{,}000 &= -40P \\ P &= \$50 \end{aligned}$$

Because $70.83⅓ is greater than $50, we eliminate it as a possible equilibrium price. The equilibrium price is $25.

Just to be sure that $25 is, in fact, the equilibrium price we must check to see whether $25 is greater than or equal to the minimum average variable cost. We determined earlier that the minimum average variable cost is $19.375. Since $25 is greater than $19.375, $25 is the short-run equilibrium price.

The equilibrium quantity we find by substituting $25 into the market-demand or market-supply equation. The quantity demanded is

$$\begin{aligned} D &= 2{,}000 - 40(\$25) \\ &= 2{,}000 - 1{,}000 \\ &= 1{,}000 \end{aligned}$$

and the quantity supplied is

$$\begin{aligned} S &= 100\left(5 + \frac{\sqrt{1.2(\$25) - 21}}{0.6}\right) \\ &= 100\left(5 + \frac{\sqrt{30 - 21}}{0.6}\right) \\ &= 100\left(5 + \frac{\sqrt{9}}{0.6}\right) \\ &= 100(5 + 3/0.6) \\ &= 100(5 + 5) \\ &= 1{,}000 \end{aligned}$$

The equilibrium output or quantity of the industry is 1,000 units.

Exercise 13-2

1 The short-run model for the purely competitive firm consists of five equations and two inequalities.

a The five equations are:

(1) ____________ $= ax^3 - bx^2 + cx + F$

(2) $P =$ ____________

(3) $R \equiv$ ____________ $\cdot$ ____________

(4) $\pi \equiv$ ____________

(5) ____________ = ____________

b The two inequalities are:

(1) ____________ $>$ ____________

(2) ____________ $\geqq$ ____________

c This model has a total of ____________ variables, of which ____________ are (is) exogeneous and ____________ are (is) endogeneous.

2 Using the equations and inequalities of question 1, show that the supply function of the firm is

$$x = \frac{2b + \sqrt{4b^2 - 12a(c - P)}}{6a}$$

where

$$P \geqq A_V$$

3 Why will the firm not produce an output equal to

$$x = \frac{2b - \sqrt{4b^2 - 12a(c - P)}}{6a}$$

4 The output of the firm at which average variable cost is a minimum is, using the sumbols in equation (1) of question 1, equal to ____________

a At this output average variable cost = ____________

b If price is below the minimum average variable cost, the firm in the short run will produce an output equal to ____________

5 Suppose a purely competitive firm has the short-run cost function

$$C = 0.2x^3 - 5x^2 + 45x + 25$$

a The firm's marginal cost function is $dC/dx =$ ____________

b The minimum average variable cost is equal to ____________ and is incurred when the firm produces an output of ____________

c $dR/dx =$ ____________

d Setting marginal cost equal to marginal revenue:

(1) ____________ = ____________

(2) Or ____________ + ____________ + ____________ = 0

e Using the equation for the solution to a second-degree equation,

$x =$ ____________

f The firm's short-run supply function is

$x =$ ____________

where

$P \geqq$ ____________

6 Given the cost function in question 5, when:

a The price of the product is \$16.40:

(1) The firm will produce ____________ units of the product.

(2) The firm will have a total revenue of ____________, total cost of ____________, and a profit of ____________

b The price of the product is \$30.00:

(1) The firm will produce ____________ units of the product.

(2) The firm will have a total revenue of ____________, total cost of ____________, and a profit of ____________

c The price of the product is \$11.40:

(1) The firm will produce ____________ units of the product.

(2) The firm will have a total revenue of ____________, total cost of ____________, and a profit of ____________

7 The model for the purely competitive industry in the short run is:

a $S =$ ____________ $\dfrac{2b + \sqrt{4b^2 - 12(c - \bar{P})}}{6a}$

b ____________ $= A - BP$

c ____________ $=$ ____________

d ____________ $\geqq c - \dfrac{b^2}{4a}$

8 Using the model in question 7:

a What is the second-degree equation that must be solved to determine the equilibrium market price of the product? ____________

b This second-degree equation has two solutions, but we can eliminate the solution which shows the equilibrium price to be greater than or equal to ____________

9 Assume that all the firms in a purely competitive industry have the same short-run cost function as the firm in question 5 and that the number of firms in the industry is 80.

a The industry's short-run supply function is

$S =$ ____________

where

$P \geqq$ ____________

b If the market demand for the product is $D = 2{,}250 - 50P$:

(1) The price at which the quantity demanded is zero is ____________

(2) The market price of the product will be ____________
[*Hint:* $(24.336)^2 = 592.24086$, $4(0.36)(366.12) = 527.2128$, and $\sqrt{65.028096} = 8.064$.]

(3) The total output of the industry is ____________

(4) Each firm in the industry will produce ____________ units and have total revenue of ____________, total cost of ____________, and a profit of ____________

THE LONG RUN

The price and the output of the product produced by a purely competitive industry in the long run depends, as it did in the short run, upon demand and supply. We shall again assume a given linear demand for the product. The industry's supply of the product is the sum of the long-run supplies of all the firms in the industry. The number of firms in the long run, however, is not constant. Firms enter the industry if profits are being received by firms already in the industry, and firms leave the industry if they are suffering losses. The industry is in long-run equilibrium only when there are neither profits nor losses. We look first in this section at the individual firm and its long-run supply function. Then we look at the industry to find the long-run price and output of the industry.

The firm

The five equations and the two inequalities of our long-run model of the purely competitive firm are

$$C = ex^3 - fx^2 + gx \qquad (13\text{-}7)$$
$$P = \bar{P} \qquad (13\text{-}3)$$
$$R \equiv x \cdot P \qquad (13\text{-}8)$$
$$\pi \equiv R - C \qquad (13\text{-}9)$$
$$\frac{dC}{dx} = \frac{dR}{dx} \qquad (13\text{-}10)$$
$$\frac{d^2C}{dx^2} > \frac{d^2R}{dx^2} \qquad (13\text{-}11)$$
$$R \geqq C \qquad (13\text{-}27)$$

We have replaced the short-run cost function (13-6) with the long-run cost function (13-7), and we have replaced the second inequality (13-12) with inequality 13-27. The costs in all equations are now long-run rather than short-run costs.

The firm's supply function Our method for finding the long-run supply function of the firm is the same one we used to find the firm's short-run supply function. First we find the marginal-cost and marginal-revenue functions.

$$\frac{dC}{dx} = 3ex^2 - 2fx + g$$

$$\frac{dR}{dx} = P$$

Setting marginal cost equal to marginal revenue,

$$3ex^2 - 2fx + g = P$$
$$3ex^2 - 2fx + g - P = 0$$

$$3ex^2 + (-2f)x + (g - P) = 0 \qquad (13\text{-}28)$$

This quadratic equation is solved by using the general equation for the solution of a quadratic equation:

$$x = \frac{-\beta \pm \sqrt{\beta^2 - 4\alpha\gamma}}{2\alpha} \qquad (13\text{-}16)$$

Substituting from equation 13-28 into equation 13-16,

$$x = \frac{-(-2f) \pm \sqrt{(-2f)^2 - 4(3e)(g - P)}}{2(3a)}$$

But, as in the short run, only one of the solutions to this equation satisfies inequality 13-11. This is

$$x = \frac{2f + \sqrt{4f^2 - 12e(g - P)}}{6a} \qquad (13\text{-}18a)$$

To equation 13-18*a* we must add the restriction imposed by inequality 13-27, that total revenue exceed or equal total cost, or

$$R \geqq C \qquad (13\text{-}27)$$

Dividing through by x,

$$\frac{R}{x} \geqq \frac{C}{x}$$

Price (R/x) must exceed or equal average cost (C/x). But from our study of costs in Chapter 11 we know that the minimum average cost (in the long run) is $g - f^2/4e$. Therefore for C/x in the inequality above we may substitute $g - f^2/4e$ and write

$$P \geqq g - \frac{f^2}{4e} \qquad (13\text{-}29)$$

Price must exceed or equal the minimum average cost, $g - f^2/4e$, in the long run.

Equation 13-18*a*, subject to the restriction of inequality 13-29, is the firm's long-run supply function.

Numerical example If the firm's long-run cost function is

$$C = 0.1x^3 - 2x^2 + 15x$$

marginal cost is

$$\frac{dC}{dx} = 0.3x^2 - 4x + 15$$

and marginal revenue is

$$\frac{dR}{dx} = P$$

When marginal cost and marginal revenue are equal,

$$0.3x^2 - 4x + 15 = P$$
$$0.3x^2 - 4x + 15 - P = 0$$

which can be written

$$0.3x^2 + (-4)x + (15 - P) = 0$$

This quadratic is solved by employing equation 13-18.

$$x = \frac{4 + \sqrt{4^2 - 4(0.3)(15 - P)}}{0.6}$$

$$= \frac{4 + \sqrt{16 - 1.2(15 - P)}}{0.6}$$

$$= \frac{4 + \sqrt{16 - 18 + 1.2P}}{0.6}$$

$$= \frac{4 + \sqrt{1.2P - 2}}{0.6} \qquad (13\text{-}30)$$

The value of $g - f^2/4e$ in our example is

$$15 - \frac{2^2}{(4)(0.1)} = 15 - \frac{4}{0.4}$$

$$= 15 - 10$$

$$= 5$$

The minimum average cost is \$5. The firm's supply function is equation 13-30 where price is greater than or equal to \$5. If price is less than \$5, the firm will supply no output in the long run.

Three cases In the long run the firm may produce at a profit, or it may have a profit of zero. If its profits would be negative, it would not produce at all. The three cases that follow illustrate each of these three possibilities.

Case 1: production at a profit Assume that the market price of the product is

$$P = \$7.30$$

Inserting \$7.30 for P in equation 13-30, the output of the firm is

$$x = \frac{4 + \sqrt{1.2(7.30) - 2}}{0.6}$$

$$= \frac{4 + \sqrt{8.76 - 2}}{0.6}$$

$$= \frac{4 + \sqrt{6.76}}{0.6}$$

$$= \frac{4 + 2.6}{0.6}$$

$$= \frac{6.6}{0.6}$$

$$= 11$$

Because the assumed price is greater than the minimum average cost, the firm will produce. Its output will be 11 units. At this price and output its total revenue is

$$\begin{aligned} R &= 11(\$7.30) \\ &= \$80.30 \end{aligned}$$

Its total cost is

$$\begin{aligned} C &= 0.1(11^3) - 2(11^2) + 15(11) \\ &= 133.10 - 242 + 165 \\ &= \$56.10 \end{aligned}$$

And its profit therefore is

$$\begin{aligned} \pi &= \$80.30 - \$56.10 \\ &= \$24.10 \end{aligned}$$

Case 2: zero output Suppose this time that

$$P = \$3.30$$

This price is less than the minimum average cost of \$5, and so the firm will produce no output in the long run. To verify this, let us determine its profit if it produced the profit-maximizing output. Substituting \$3.30 for P in equation 13-18*a*, its maximum-profit output is

$$\begin{aligned} x &= \frac{4 + \sqrt{1.2(3.30) - 2}}{0.6} \\ &= \frac{4 + \sqrt{3.96 - 2}}{0.6} \\ &= \frac{4 + \sqrt{1.96}}{0.6} \\ &= \frac{4 + 1.4}{0.6} \\ &= \frac{5.4}{0.6} \\ &= 9 \end{aligned}$$

If the firm produced at all, it would produce 9 units. But when it produces 9 units, its total revenue is

$$\begin{aligned} R &= 9(\$3.30) \\ &= \$29.70 \end{aligned}$$

its total cost is

$$\begin{aligned} C &= 0.1(9^3) - 2(9^2) + 15(9) \\ &= 72.90 - 162 + 135 \\ &= \$45.90 \end{aligned}$$

and its profit is

$$\begin{aligned} \pi &= \$29.70 - \$45.60 \\ &= -\$16.20 \end{aligned}$$

Producing 9 units, it would have a *loss* of \$16.20. If it produced no output, its profit would be zero. A zero profit is larger than a $-$\$16.20 profit. The firm therefore maximizes its profit by producing no output in the long run.

Case 3: zero profit Assume that price is

$$P = \$5$$

Using equation 13-18*a*,

$$x = \frac{4 + \sqrt{1.2(5) - 2}}{0.6}$$

$$= \frac{4 + \sqrt{6 - 2}}{0.6}$$

$$= \frac{4 + \sqrt{4}}{0.6}$$

$$= \frac{4 + 2}{0.6}$$

$$= \frac{6}{0.6}$$

$$= 10$$

At an output of 10 and a price of \$5, total revenue is \$50. Total cost is

$$\begin{aligned} C &= 0.1(10^3) - 2(10^2) + 15(10) \\ &= 100 - 200 + 150 \\ &= 50 \end{aligned}$$

Total revenue and total cost are equal, and so profit is zero. The firm will produce in the long run, however, because its profit when it produces is as large as its profit when it does not produce at all.

The supply curve and the supply schedule In Figure 13-2 are plotted the firm's long-run marginal-cost function ($dC/dx = 0.3x^2 - 4x + 15$) and its long-run average-cost function ($A_c = 0.1x^2 - 2x + 15$). Also shown are the three marginal-revenue functions and prices assumed in the three cases above. We have darkened in the firm's long-run supply curve, i.e., its long-run marginal-cost curve where marginal cost is greater than or equal to the minimum average cost.

We should observe both here and in equation 13-18 that the quantity the firm will supply is an increasing function of the price of the product: the greater the price (provided it is greater than or equal to minimum average cost) the larger the output the firm will supply. This can also be seen in the long-run supply schedule of the firm in Table 13-2.

The industry

In the long run the number of firms in the industry may vary. The entry of new firms increases the number of firms, and the exit of old firms decreases it. N is now an endogeneous variable rather than exogeneous (as it was in the short run). Firms enter when there are profits and leave when there are losses. There will be neither entry nor exit when profits are zero. For the industry to be in long-run equilibrium it is necessary that

$$\pi = 0 \tag{13-2}$$

The profits of a firm are zero when

$$R - C = 0$$

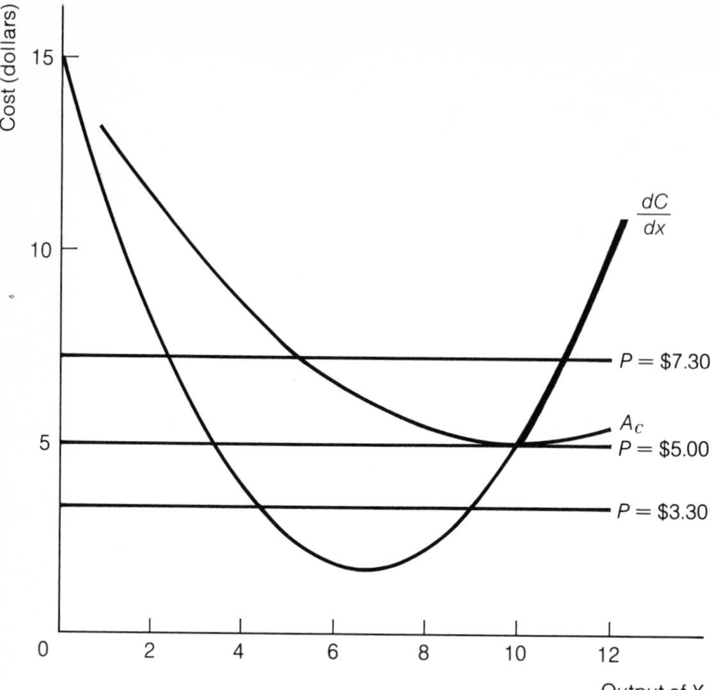

FIGURE 13-2

or, dividing through by x, when

$$\frac{R}{x} - \frac{C}{x} = 0$$

R/x is, of course, the price of the product, and C/x is average cost. Therefore, for the industry to be in long-run equilibrium it is necessary that

$$P = A_c \tag{13-31}$$

While it is necessary if the industry is to be in long-run equilibrium for the price of the product and the average cost of producing it to be equal, it is also necessary for all firms in the industry to be in equilibrium. This means that each

TABLE 13-2 THE FIRM'S LONG-RUN SUPPLY SCHEDULE

Price	Quantity Supplied
$ 3.30	0
5.00	10
7.30	11
10.20	12
13.20	13
17.80	14
22.50	15

firm must produce an output at which

$$\frac{dC}{dx} = \frac{dR}{dx} \tag{13-10}$$

Since to the individual firm marginal revenue and price are the same, the individual firm is in equilibrium when

$$\frac{dC}{dx} = \bar{P} \tag{13-4}$$

For there to be equilibrium in the industry, then, *two* conditions must be satisfied: (1) price and average cost must be equal, and (2) marginal cost and price must be equal. Both equations 13-31 and 13-4 must be satisfied if there is to be long-run equilibrium in a purely competitive industry. Combining equations 13-31 and 13-4, there is long-run equilibrium if

$$\frac{dC}{dx} = A_L = P \tag{13-32}$$

Long-run equilibrium is achieved when marginal cost, average cost, and the price of the product are equal.

From our study of costs in Chapter 11[5] we know that average cost and marginal cost are equal when average cost is a minimum. Therefore, for the purely competitive industry to be in long-run equilibrium each firm must produce where average cost is a minimum, and the price of the product must be equal to average cost. In short, the industry is in equilibrium where minimum long-run average cost is equal to price.

If the long-run cost function of the firm is

$$C = ex^3 - fx^2 + gx \tag{13-7}$$

we know from our previous analysis of costs that the minimum long-run average cost is achieved when the firm produces an output equal to $f/2e$. At this output average cost is equal to $g - f^2/4e$.

The model In our model we have four equations and four variables. The four equations are

$$P = g - \frac{f^2}{4d} \tag{13-33}$$

$$S = N\frac{f}{2e} \tag{13-34}$$

$$D = A - BP \tag{13-24}$$

$$S = D \tag{13-25}$$

Equation 13-33 says that the price of the product must equal the minimum long-run average cost. The quantity supplied of the product, equation 13-34 says, is equal to the number of firms in the industry multiplied by the output of each firm, the output at which long-run average cost is a minimum. The assumed linear demand for the product is given by equation 13-24. The equilibrium equation is 13-25. The four variables in the model are P, S, N, and D. There are five parameters in the model: three (e, f, and g) from the individual firm's cost function and two (A and B) from the market demand function.

[5] See pages 301 to 302.

To find the equilibrium values of the four variables we first substitute $N(f/2e)$ for S; and $A - BP$ for D in equation 13-25.

$$N\frac{f}{2e} = A - BP \tag{13-35}$$

Then we substitute $g - f^2/4e$ for P in equation 13-35 to obtain

$$N\frac{f}{2e} = A - B\left(g - \frac{f^2}{4e}\right) \tag{13-36}$$

Equation 13-36 contains only the variable N and can be solved to find the value of N. The solution equation for N is

$$\begin{aligned} N &= \left[A - B\left(g - \frac{f^2}{4e}\right)\right]\frac{2e}{f} \\ &= \frac{2e}{f}A - \frac{2e}{f}Bg + \frac{2e}{f}\frac{f^2}{4e}B \\ &= \frac{2eA}{f} - \frac{2eBg}{f} + \frac{fB}{2} \\ &= \frac{2e}{f}(A - Bg) + \frac{fB}{2} \end{aligned} \tag{13-37}$$

We find the price of the product directly from equation 13-33 to be $g - f^2/4e$. This price we substitute into equation 13-24 to find the quantity of the product demanded.

$$D = A - B\left(g - \frac{f^2}{4e}\right)$$

Finally we find the total output of the industry from equation 13-34 by substituting $(2e/f)(A - Bg) + fB/2$ for N.

$$\begin{aligned} S &= \left[\frac{2e}{f}(A - Bg) + \frac{fB}{2}\right]\frac{f}{2e} \\ &= (A - Bg) + \frac{fB}{2}\frac{f}{2e} \\ &= A - Bg + \frac{Bf^2}{4e} \end{aligned}$$

The total quantity supplied and the total quantity demanded are equal since

$$S = D$$

$$\begin{aligned} A - Bg + \frac{Bf^2}{4e} &= A - B\left(g - \frac{f^2}{4e}\right) \\ &= A - Bg + \frac{Bf^2}{4e} \end{aligned}$$

Numerical example Suppose

$$C = 0.1x^3 - 2x^2 + 15x$$

The parameters are $e = 0.1$, $f = 2$, and $g = 15$. If the demand function is

$$D = 20{,}000 - 2{,}000P$$

the parameter $A = 20{,}000$ and the parameter $B = 2{,}000$.

To find the number of firms in the industry we first substitute the values of the parameters into equation 13-35.

$$N\frac{2}{0.2} = 20{,}000 - 2{,}000P$$

For P we substitute from equation 13-33

$$N\frac{2}{0.2} = 20{,}000 - 2{,}000\left(15 - \frac{2^2}{0.4}\right)$$

and solve for N

$$\begin{aligned} N(10) &= 20{,}000 - 2{,}000\left(15 - \frac{4}{0.4}\right) \\ &= 20{,}000 - 2{,}000(5) \\ &= 20{,}000 - 10{,}000 \\ &= 10{,}000 \\ N &= 1{,}000 \end{aligned}$$

The number of firms in the long run is 1,000.

The price of the product, using equation 13-33, is

$$\begin{aligned} P &= 15 - \frac{2^2}{0.4} \\ &= 15 - 4/14 \\ &= 15 - 10 \\ &= \$5 \end{aligned}$$

The quantity demanded at this price is given by equation 13-24,

$$\begin{aligned} D &= 20{,}000 - 2{,}000(\$5) \\ &= 20{,}000 - 10{,}000 \\ &= 10{,}000 \end{aligned}$$

And the quantity supplied, using equation 13-24, is

$$\begin{aligned} S &= 1{,}000\frac{2}{0.2} \\ &= 1{,}000(10) \\ &= 10{,}000 \end{aligned}$$

The long-run price of the product is \$5. 1,000 firms produce an output of 10,000 units, and the quantity demanded of the product at the \$5 price is also 10,000. With 1,000 firms producing 10,000 units, each firm supplies 10 units.

Exercise 13-3

1 The long-run model for the purely competitive firm is:

a $C =$ __________

b $P =$ __________

c $R \equiv$ __________

d $\pi \equiv$ __________

e __________ $=$ __________

f ______ > ______

g ______ $\geqq$ ______

2 Employing the equations of question 1, the firm's supply function is

$x =$ ______

where

$P \geqq$ ______

3 Assume the firm's long-run cost function is $C = 0.4x^3 - 3x^2 + 30$. The firm's long-run supply function is

$x =$ ______

where

$P \geqq$ ______

4 Given the supply function in question 3, when the price of the product is:

a \$24.375, the firm will:

(1) Produce ______ units of the product.

(2) Have total revenue of ______, total cost of ______, and profit of ______

b \$22.80, the firm will:

(1) Produce ______ units of the product.

(2) Have total revenue of ______, total cost of ______, and profit of ______

c \$25.20, the firm will:

(1) Produce ______ units of the product.

(2) Have total revenue of ______, total cost of ______, and profit of ______

5 For a purely competitive industry to be in long-run equilibrium:

a It is necessary that $\pi = 0$. This means that:

(1) ______ = ______

(2) ______ / ______ = ______ / ______

(3) ______ = ______ cost.

b It is also necessary that each firm produce an output that maximizes its profit. This means it produces where:

(1) ______ = ______

(2) Or where ______ = ______ provided P is greater than or equal to ______

c Putting the conditions of parts *a* and *b* together, the purely competitive industry is in long-run equilibrium when

______ = ______ = ______

d dC/dx and A_L are equal only when long-run average cost is a minimum. We can say, therefore, that the purely competitive industry is in long-run equilibrium when ______ = the ______ long-run ______ cost.

6 The model for the purely competitive industry in the long run is:

a $P =$ __________

b $S =$ __________

c $D =$ __________

d __________ = __________

7 Using the model in question 6:

a The number of firms in the industry is

$N =$ __________

b The price of the product is $P =$ __________

c The total output of the industry is equal to __________

8 Assume that the long-run cost function of each firm is $C = 0.4x^3 - 3x^2 + 30$ and that the market demand function is $D = 390 - 8P$. When the industry is in long-run equilibrium:

a The number of firms in the industry is $N =$ __________

b The total output of the industry is __________

c The price of the product is $P =$ __________

d Each firm:

(1) Produces __________ units.

(2) Has total revenue of __________, total cost of __________, and a profit of __________

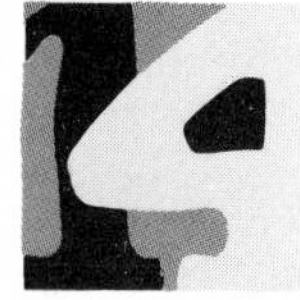

MARGINAL REVENUE PRODUCT AND MARGINAL RESOURCE COST

Firms produce products which they sell for a price. But firms do more than produce products. To produce their products they employ inputs for which they must pay a price. Our purpose in this chapter and the next is to explain what determines the quantity of an input an individual firm will employ and the price the firm must pay for that input.

This chapter introduces the new tools we need to explain the price and employment of an input. In the first section we look at marginal revenue product and the marginal-revenue-product function of a perfectly competitive seller and of a monopolist. In the second section we turn our attention to marginal resource cost and the marginal-resource-cost function of a perfectly competitive input user and of a monopsonist.

In the next chapter we shall look in more detail at the individual firm, the quantity of an input it will employ, and the price it will pay for that input. We shall use the marginal-revenue-product and marginal-resource-cost tools to analyze perfectly competitive employers of inputs and monopsonists in the short and long runs.

To explain the price and the employment of inputs we introduce a new mathematical concept, the *partial derivative*. This new concept, an extension of the simple derivative employed in earlier chapters, is needed to understand the relationship between two variables when three or more variables are functionally related to each other. If the student has understood the simple derivative and how to find it, he will have little trouble understanding the partial derivative and how to find it.

The firm (we shall assume in this and the next chapter) produces one product X from two inputs K and L. The firm's production function is

$$X = f(K,L) \tag{14-1}$$

We continue to assume that the goal of the firm is the maximization of its economic profit π. Profit, as before, is defined as equal to the firm's revenue R less its costs C.

$$\pi \equiv R - C \tag{14-2}$$

A firm's revenue equals the quantity of X it produces multiplied by the price P_X at which it sells its product.

$$R \equiv X \cdot P_X \tag{14-3}$$

With only two inputs, the firm's costs equal the quantity of input K employed multiplied by the price P_K it pays for K plus the quantity of L employed multiplied by the price P_L it pays for L. Its cost function is

$$C \equiv K \cdot P_K + L \cdot P_L \tag{14-4}$$

Given these assumptions and definitions, what quantity of the two inputs, K and L, will the firm employ, and what will be the prices of these inputs? Before we answer these questions in the next chapter, we need the marginal-revenue-product and marginal-resource-cost tools.

MARGINAL REVENUE PRODUCT

When the firm changes the quantity of one of the inputs it employs, the quantity of the other input remaining constant, the output of the firm changes. Suppose that input L is the one which is changed and K is the one that remains constant. If we change L by dL (some very small amount), the firm's output will change by dX (also a very small amount). The change in X will equal the change in L multiplied by the *marginal product*[1] of L, dX/dL. And so we may write

$$dX = dL \frac{dX}{dL} \tag{14-5}$$

Similarly, if the firm holds L constant and varies K, the output of the firm will vary. When K changes by dK, X changes by dX. Both dK and dX are very small amounts. The change in X will equal the change in K multiplied by the marginal product of K, dX/dK. The change in X is

$$dX = dK \frac{dX}{dK} \tag{14-6}$$

Changes in the firm's output result in a change in the revenue the firm receives from the sale of its product. The change dR in the firm's revenue is

$$dR = dX \frac{dR}{dX} \tag{14-7}$$

where dR/dX is the *marginal revenue*[2] from the sale of X. For dX in equation

[1] To review the meaning of marginal product, see page 289.
[2] To review marginal revenue, see pages 218 to 224.

14-7 we may substitute the right side of equation 14-5 to obtain

$$dR = \left(dL \frac{dX}{dL}\right) \frac{dR}{dX} \tag{14-8}$$

Dividing equation 14-8 through by dL, we have

$$\frac{dR}{dL} = \frac{dX}{dL} \frac{dR}{dX} \tag{14-9}$$

dR/dL is defined as the *marginal revenue product of the input L*. It is the limit which $\Delta R/\Delta L$ approaches as ΔL approaches zero, or

$$\frac{dR}{dL} = \lim_{\Delta L \to 0} \frac{\Delta R}{\Delta L} \tag{14-10}$$

The important thing to note in equation 14-9 is that *the marginal revenue product of input L is equal to the marginal product of L* (dX/dL) *multiplied by the marginal revenue from the sale of X* (dR/dX).

To find the marginal revenue product of input K we substitute the right side of equation 14-6 for dX in equation 14-7 and obtain

$$dR = \left(dK \frac{dX}{dK}\right) \frac{dR}{dX} \tag{14-11}$$

Dividing through by dK, we get

$$\frac{dR}{dK} = \frac{dX}{dK} \frac{dR}{dX} \tag{14-12}$$

Equation 14-12 tells us that the *marginal revenue product of the input K* is equal to the marginal product of K (dX/dK) multiplied by the marginal revenue (dR/dX) from the sale of X. The marginal revenue product of K is the limit $\Delta R/\Delta K$ approaches as ΔK approaches zero.

$$\frac{dR}{dK} = \lim_{\Delta K \to 0} \frac{\Delta R}{\Delta K} \tag{14-13}$$

The partial derivative

Because the revenue of the firm changes when the firm changes the employment of L *or* the employment of K *or* the employment of both K and L, we can say that the firm's revenue is a function of both K and L. R is a function of both K and L because the firm's output X is a function of both L and K; and R depends upon X.

Whenever one variable (such as R or X) is a function of two or more variables, mathematicians use a different symbol for the derivative. Instead of using dR/dL and dR/dK, they write $\partial R/\partial L$ and $\partial R/\partial K$, respectively. This notation is called a *partial* derivative rather than a simple or plain derivative. The use of ∂ instead of d indicates that the change in R may be a result of a change in L, a change in K, or a change in both L and K. And because X is also a function of both L and K (and because X may therefore change as a result of a change in L, a change in K, or a change in both L and K), we shall also replace dX/dL and dX/dK with $\partial X/\partial L$ and $\partial X/\partial K$, respectively.

Using these new symbols, we can replace equations 14-9 and 14-11 with

$$\frac{\partial R}{\partial L} = \frac{\partial X}{\partial L}\frac{dR}{dX} \qquad (14\text{-}14)$$

$$\frac{\partial R}{\partial K} = \frac{\partial X}{\partial L}\frac{dR}{dX} \qquad (14\text{-}15)$$

Equation 14-14 really says the same thing as equation 14-9. In our discussion of 14-9 we assumed that K was constant. Now when we write $\partial R/\partial L$ the use of the symbol ∂ means that we are assuming K constant. Likewise, equation 14-15 says the same thing as equation 14-11, but the use of the symbol ∂ tells us mathematically, instead of in words, that L is assumed to be constant. Notice that we have *not* replaced dR/dX with $\partial R/\partial X$ because we have assumed that the firm produces only one product. Its revenue, therefore, depends only on the single output variable, X.

To generalize, suppose that the value of a variable Z depends upon the values of two other variables U and V, or

$$Z = f(U,V)$$

There are two partial derivatives, $\partial Z/\partial U$ and $\partial Z/\partial V$. $\partial Z/\partial U$ is the limit which $\Delta Z/\Delta U$ approaches as ΔU approaches zero, *V remaining constant*. Similarly, $\partial Z/\partial V$ is the limit which $\Delta Z/\Delta V$ approaches as ΔV approaches zero, *U remaining constant*. To find the two partial derivatives is as simple as finding a simple derivative.

- To determine $\partial Z/\partial U$, assume V is constant and find $\partial Z/\partial U$ in exactly the same way that you would find dZ/dU.
- To determine $\partial Z/\partial V$, assume U is constant and find $\partial Z/\partial V$ in exactly the same way that you would find dZ/dV.

Suppose that

$$Z = a + bU + cV$$

and that a, b, and c are parameters. To find $\partial Z/\partial U$, assume that V is constant. Employing the technique we used in earlier chapters to find the simple derivative, we see that $\partial Z/\partial U$ is equal to b. To find $\partial Z/\partial V$, assume U is constant and employ the technique for finding the simple derivative. $\partial Z/\partial V$ is equal to c.

Assume that

$$Z = 100 + 3U^2 + 5V^3$$

Holding V constant, the derivative of Z with respect to U, or $\partial Z/\partial U$, is equal to $6U$. Holding U constant, the derivative of Z with respect to V, or $\partial Z/\partial V$, is equal to $15V^2$.

The production function We shall assume that the production function is

$$X = L^a \cdot K^{1-a} \qquad (14\text{-}16)$$

This production function contains a single parameter a. It is assumed that the parameter a is greater than zero and less than one.

$$1 > a > 0$$

The sum of the two exponents in this function is equal to 1 because $a + (1 - a)$ is equal to $a + 1 - a$, which is equal to 1. Since the sum of the exponents of the variables on the right (and the left) side is equal to 1, this is a first-degree equation. An example of such a function might be

$$X = L^{0.75} \cdot K^{1-0.75}$$

which can be rewritten as

$$X = L^{0.75} \cdot K^{0.25} \qquad (14\text{-}17)$$

We shall use equation 14-17 as our example of the production throughout the remainder of this chapter and in the next.[3]

A production function such as equation 14-16 has four characteristics that should be noted: (1) It is a relatively simple production function and easy to work with. (2) It requires that some quantity of *both* K and L be employed before any quantity of X can be produced: if either K or L is zero, X is also zero. (3) If a firm has this kind of production function, it will encounter neither economies nor diseconomies of scale: the returns to scale will be constant.[4] This means that if the firm increased (or decreased) both K and L by the same percentage, its output would also increase (or decrease) by that same percentage. The firm's average cost in the long run would be constant. (4) As the firm increases its employment of one input, holding the other input constant, the marginal product of the variable input will decrease. To see that this is a necessary result of a production function such as equation 14-16, let us look at the marginal product of K and of L.[5]

The marginal products The marginal product of input L is the partial derivative of X with respect to L, or $\partial X/\partial L$. To find $\partial X/\partial L$ we assume K^{1-a} is a constant in equation 14-16 and employ the same technique that we employed to find the simple derivative. This means that we first decrease the exponent of L by 1 (from a to $a - 1$) and then multiply L^{a-1} by a by K^{1-a}. The result is

$$\frac{\partial X}{\partial L} = aK^{1-a} \cdot L^{a-1}$$

The right side of this equation can be rewritten to obtain

$$\frac{\partial X}{\partial L} = aK^{1-a} \cdot L^{-(1-a)}$$

Since $L^{-(1-a)}$ is equal to $1/(L^{1-a})$,

$$\frac{\partial X}{\partial L} = a\frac{K^{1-a}}{L^{1-a}}$$

[3]The production function expressed by equation 14-16 and illustrated in equation 14-17 is usually referred to as a Cobb-Douglas production function. It is also one of the many varieties of production functions that are linear and homogenous.

[4]For the meaning of economies and diseconomies of scale, see pages 302 to 303.

[5]This kind of production function is somewhat different from the production function we assumed to exist when we examined a firm's costs in the short and long run in Chapter 11. In the short run there is no range of employment for the variable input in which marginal product is increasing and no range in which it is negative. But since the firm always produces an output at which marginal cost is increasing, it is always producing where marginal product is decreasing. It never produces where marginal product is increasing. The absence of a range of employment for the variable input in which marginal product is increasing or negative is not important because the profit-seeking firm will never produce in these ranges anyway.

and

$$\frac{\partial X}{\partial L} = a\left(\frac{K}{L}\right)^{1-a} \tag{14-18}$$

The marginal product of input L is equal to the parameter a times the ratio of K to L raised to the $(1 - a)$th power.

If K is constant, the ratio of K to L will decrease when L increases. As the ratio K/L decreases as L increases, K/L to the $(1 - a)$th power must also decrease. With the parameter a constant, $a(K/L)^{1-a}$ decreases when L increases. The marginal product of L $(\partial X/\partial L)$, in short, is an inverse function of the quantity of input L employed: as L increases, the marginal product of L decreases.

Let us look at a numerical example. Assuming that the production function is

$$X = L^{0.75} \cdot K^{0.25} \tag{14-17}$$

and K is equal to 60, the marginal product of L, employing equation 14-18, is

$$\frac{\partial X}{\partial L} = 0.75\left(\frac{60}{L}\right)^{0.25} \tag{14-19}$$

Table 14-1 shows the values of X, $60/L$, and $0.75(60/L)^{0.25}$ (or $\partial X/\partial L$) at different values for L. We should note that as L increases, so does X but that as L increases, the marginal product of L decreases. We can also observe in the table that the decreases in the marginal product of L decrease (or become smaller) as L increases.

On the graph in Figure 14-1*a* L is plotted on the horizontal axis and X on the vertical axis, assuming $X = L^{0.75} \cdot 60^{0.25}$. Notice again that as L increases, K remaining constant, total output increases. The slope of this total-output curve, however, decreases as L and X increase. The slope of the total-output curve is equal to the marginal product of the variable input L. The decreasing slope of the total-output curve indicates that the marginal product of L is decreasing as L increases. In Figure 14-1*b* L is again plotted on the horizontal axis. On the

TABLE 14-1 THE MARGINAL PRODUCT OF A VARIABLE INPUT

L	X	$\frac{60}{L}$	$0.75\left(\frac{60}{L}\right)^{0.25} = \frac{\partial X}{\partial L}$
0	0		
1	2.78	60	2.09
2	4.68	30	1.76
3	6.13	20	1.59
4	7.87	15	1.48
5	9.30	12	1.40
6	10.67	10	1.33
7	11.98	$8\frac{4}{7}$	1.28
8	13.24	$7\frac{1}{2}$	1.24
9	14.46	$6\frac{2}{3}$	1.21
10	15.69	6	1.17

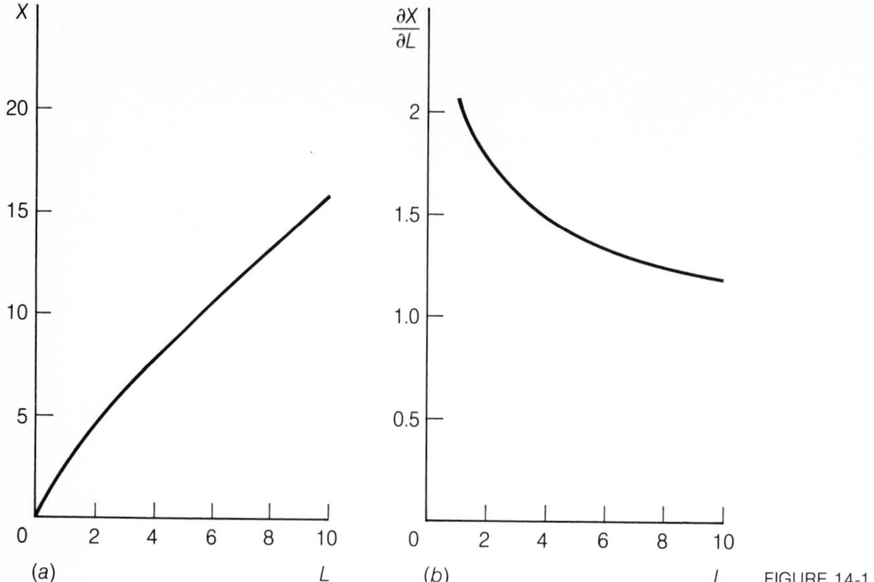

FIGURE 14-1

vertical axis is plotted the marginal product of L [$\partial X/\partial L = 0.75(60/L)^{0.25}$]. Here again we see that the marginal product diminishes as L increases, but we should also observe that the slope of the marginal-product curve decreases as L increases: the decreases in the marginal product become smaller as L continues to increase.

We can find the marginal product of the input K ($\partial X/\partial K$) in the same way we found the marginal product of L. Starting with the production function,

$$X = L^a \cdot K^{1-a} \tag{14-16}$$

we assume L^a is a constant and find the derivative: we decrease the exponent of K by 1 (from $1 - a$ to $-a$) and then multiply K^{-a} by $1 - a$ (the original exponent of K) by L^a.

$$\frac{\partial X}{\partial K} = (1 - a)L^a \cdot K^{-a}$$

This can be rewritten as

$$\frac{\partial X}{\partial K} = (1 - a)\frac{L^a}{K^a}$$

$$\frac{\partial X}{\partial K} = (1 - a)\left(\frac{L}{K}\right)^a \tag{14-20}$$

The marginal product of K is equal to 1 minus the parameter a times the ratio of L to K raised to the ath power.

If the production function is

$$X = L^{0.75} \cdot K^{0.25} \tag{14-17}$$

then, employing equation 14-20, the marginal product of K would be

$$\frac{\partial X}{\partial K} = 0.25 \left(\frac{L}{K}\right)^{0.75}$$

Notice that as K increases (L remaining constant), the ratio of L to K will decrease, the ratio L/K to the power of a (0.75 in the numerical example) will also decrease, and that therefore $1 - a$ (0.25 in the example) times $(L/K)^a$ will decrease too. In brief, the marginal product of K is inversely related to the quantity of K employed by the firm.

We shall not bother to show in a table and on graphs the values of X and $\partial X/\partial K$ as K varies. But before going on it is worth pointing out that the marginal product of L is an increasing function of K and that the marginal product of K is directly related to L. Looking at the equation for the marginal product of L,

$$\frac{\partial X}{\partial L} = a \left(\frac{K}{L}\right)^{1-a} \tag{14-18}$$

we see that the greater the constant value of K, the greater the ratio of K to L (at any given L) and the greater, therefore, the marginal product of L at that given L. Similarly, in the equation for the marginal product of K,

$$\frac{\partial X}{\partial K} = (1 - a) \left(\frac{L}{K}\right)^{a} \tag{14-20}$$

at any given K, the greater the value of L the greater the L/K and the greater the marginal product of K at the given L. Inputs such as these are called *complementary* inputs because an increase in either one increases the marginal product of the other. If an increase in one decreased the marginal product of the other, the two inputs would be *substitute* inputs. It is possible that an increase in one input would leave the marginal product of the other input unaffected. In this case the two inputs would be neither complements nor substitutes but *independent*.

In the analysis that follows we shall assume that input L is the variable input and K is fixed. We shall look only at the marginal revenue product and marginal product of L. But everything we say about input L might also be said about input K, and we could develop numerical examples not only for L but also for K. It would serve no useful purpose, however, to go through the same work twice: once for L and once for K. In what follows, the student may substitute K for L, $\partial X/\partial K$ for $\partial X/\partial L$, and $\partial R/\partial K$ for $\partial R/\partial L$ wherever they appear.

Marginal revenue product: the perfectly competitive seller

When a firm sells its product in a perfectly competitive market, we know (from our work in Chapters 9 and 13) that the demand for his output is perfectly elastic. This means that the price P_X at which the firm sells X is a constant $\bar{P}_X$, or that

$$P_X = \bar{P}_X \tag{14-21}$$

We also know that when demand is perfectly elastic, the marginal revenue from the sale of X is equal to the constant price of X, or that

$$\frac{dR}{dX} = \bar{P}_X \tag{14-22}$$

The marginal revenue of the perfectly competitive seller, then, is a constant and equal to the price at which the firm sells its product.

Employing equation 14-14,

$$\frac{\partial R}{\partial L} = \frac{\partial X}{\partial L} \frac{dR}{dX} \tag{14-14}$$

and substituting (from equation 14-22) $\bar{P}_X$ for dR/dX, we can say that the marginal revenue product of input L is

$$\frac{\partial R}{\partial L} = \frac{\partial X}{\partial L} \bar{P}_X \tag{14-23}$$

The marginal revenue product of input L, *when the firm sells X in a perfectly competitive market,* is equal to the marginal product of L multiplied by the constant price at which the firm is able to sell X.

When the firm's marginal-product function for input L is

$$\frac{\partial X}{\partial L} = a\left(\frac{K}{L}\right)^{1-a} \tag{14-18}$$

its marginal-revenue-product function, employing equation 14-23 and substituting $a(K/L)^{1-a}$ for $\partial X/\partial L$, is

$$\frac{\partial R}{\partial L} = a\left(\frac{K}{L}\right)^{1-a} \cdot \bar{P}_X \tag{14-24}$$

To take a numerical example, suppose that

$$\frac{\partial X}{\partial L} = 0.75\left(\frac{60}{L}\right)^{0.25} \tag{14-19}$$

If the price of X and the marginal revenue from the sale of X is \$2, using equation 14-23,

$$\frac{\partial R}{\partial L} = 0.75\left(\frac{60}{L}\right)^{0.25} (\$2)$$

or

$$\frac{\partial R}{\partial L} = \$1.50\left(\frac{60}{L}\right)^{0.25} \tag{14-25}$$

In Table 14-2 we show the marginal product of L (taken from Table 14-1), marginal revenue, and the marginal revenue product of L for values of L ranging from 1 to 10.

In Figure 14-2 the firm's marginal-revenue-product function is plotted. Marginal revenue product is plotted on the vertical axis and the employment of L on the horizontal axis. We should observe that $\partial R/\partial L$ behaves in the same fashion as marginal product. $\partial R/\partial L$ decreases as L increases, and the decreases in $\partial R/\partial L$ become smaller as L becomes larger.

TABLE 14-2 THE MARGINAL REVENUE PRODUCT OF A VARIABLE INPUT

L	$\frac{\partial X}{\partial L} = 0.75\left(\frac{60}{L}\right)^{0.25}$	$\frac{dR}{dX}$	$\frac{\partial R}{\partial L} = \$1.50\left(\frac{60}{L}\right)^{0.25}$
1	2.09	\$2.00	\$4.18
2	1.76	2.00	3.52
3	1.59	2.00	3.18
4	1.48	2.00	2.96
5	1.40	2.00	2.80
6	1.33	2.00	2.66
7	1.28	2.00	2.56
8	1.24	2.00	2.48
9	1.21	2.00	2.42
10	1.17	2.00	2.34

Marginal revenue product: the monopolist

The firm that sells product X as a monopolist, we know (from Chapters 9 and 12), faces a demand that is less than perfectly elastic. We shall assume (for simplicity) that this demand function is decreasing and linear, or

$$X = j - mP_X \tag{14-26}$$

where X is the quantity demanded and j and m are the parameters of the demand function. The demand equation can be rewritten

$$P_X = \frac{j - X}{m} \tag{14-27}$$

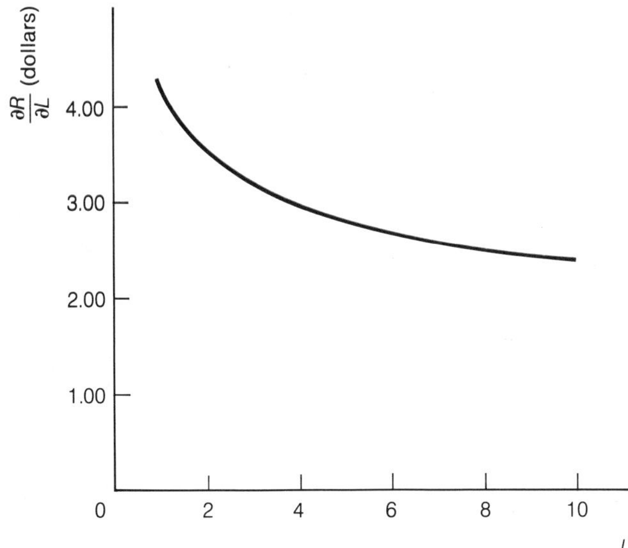

FIGURE 14-2

Recalling our earlier work,[6] the firm's revenue function is

$$R = \frac{jX - X^2}{m} \tag{14-28}$$

and its marginal-revenue function is

$$\frac{dR}{dX} = \frac{j - 2X}{m} \tag{14-29}$$

When the firm's marginal-product function is

$$\frac{\partial X}{\partial L} = a\left(\frac{K}{L}\right)^{1-a} \tag{14-18}$$

its marginal-revenue-product function, employing equations 14-29 and 14-14, is

$$\frac{\partial R}{\partial L} = \frac{\partial X}{\partial L}\frac{dR}{dX} \tag{14-14}$$

$$\frac{\partial R}{\partial L} = a\left(\frac{K}{L}\right)^{1-a}\frac{j - 2X}{m} \tag{14-30}$$

Equation 14-30 has three variables: $\partial R/\partial L$, L, and X, since K is assumed constant. For X, however, we may substitute the right side of equation 14-16 and obtain

$$\frac{\partial R}{\partial L} = a\left(\frac{K}{L}\right)^{1-a}\frac{j - 2(L^aK^{1-a})}{m} \tag{14-31}$$

This last equation, when K is constant, contains only two variables, $\partial R/\partial L$ and L.

Looking back at equation 14-31, we can see that with K constant the marginal product of L $[a(K/L)^{1-a}]$ will decrease as L increases. We can also see that as L increases, K constant, marginal revenue $[j - 2(L^aK^{1-a})]/m$ will decrease. This means that marginal revenue product, equal to marginal product times marginal revenue, must also decrease as L increases. Because both marginal product and marginal revenue decrease as L increases, marginal revenue product decreases as L increases: marginal revenue product is inversely related to L.

As a numerical example of the marginal-revenue-product function confronting the firm that sells its product as a monopolist, let us employ the same production and marginal-product functions we used in our previous examples:

$$X = L^{0.75} \cdot K^{0.25} \tag{14-17}$$

$$\frac{\partial X}{\partial L} = 0.75\left(\frac{60}{L}\right)^{0.25} \tag{14-19}$$

We have assumed that K is fixed and equal to 60. We shall assume that the demand for the monopolist's product is

$$X = 800 - 500P_X \tag{14-32}$$

With this demand equation, the firm's marginal-revenue function is

$$\frac{dR}{dX} = \frac{800 - 2X}{500} \tag{14-33}$$

[6]See pages 205 to 207.

TABLE 14-3 MARGINAL REVENUE PRODUCT OF A MONOPOLIST

L	$\frac{\partial X}{\partial L} = 0.75\left(\frac{60}{L}\right)^{0.25}$	$\frac{dR}{dX} = \frac{800 - 2(L^{0.75}K^{0.25})}{500}$	$\frac{\partial R}{\partial L} = 0.75\left(\frac{60}{L}\right)^{0.25} \frac{800 - 2(L^{0.75}L^{0.25})}{500}$
1	2.09	\$1.589	\$3.32
2	1.76	1.581	2.78
3	1.59	1.575	2.50
4	1.48	1.569	2.32
5	1.40	1.563	2.19
6	1.33	1.557	2.07
7	1.28	1.552	1.97
8	1.24	1.547	1.91
9	1.21	1.542	1.87
10	1.17	1.537	1.80

or, substituting $L^{0.75}K^{0.25}$ (from equation 14-17) for X,

$$\frac{dR}{dX} = \frac{800 - 2(L^{0.75}K^{0.25})}{500} \qquad (14\text{-}34)$$

Marginal revenue product, employing equations 14-14, 14-19, and 14-34, is then

$$\frac{\partial R}{\partial L} = 0.75\left(\frac{60}{L}\right)^{0.25} \frac{800 - 2(L^{0.75}K^{0.25})}{500} \qquad (14\text{-}35)$$

Table 14-3 shows marginal product, marginal revenue, and marginal revenue product as L varies from 1 to 10. Note again that the marginal revenue product of the variable input is inversely related to the quantity of the variable input employed and that the decreases in marginal revenue product become smaller as L increases. Figure 14-3 at the top of the next page has L plotted on the horizontal axis and the marginal revenue product of L on the vertical axis.

Exercise 14-1

In all the questions that follow, assume that the firm employs two inputs, M and N, to produce one product, Y.

1 Write the firm's cost function: $C =$ ____________

2 The marginal product of M is the limit which ____________ / ____________ approaches as ____________ approaches zero, ____________ remaining constant; or, in symbols, ____________ / ____________

3 The firm's total revenue R is equal to ____________ · ____________

a The marginal revenue from the sale of Y is the limit which ____________ / ____________ approaches as ____________ approaches zero; or, in symbols, ____________ / ____________

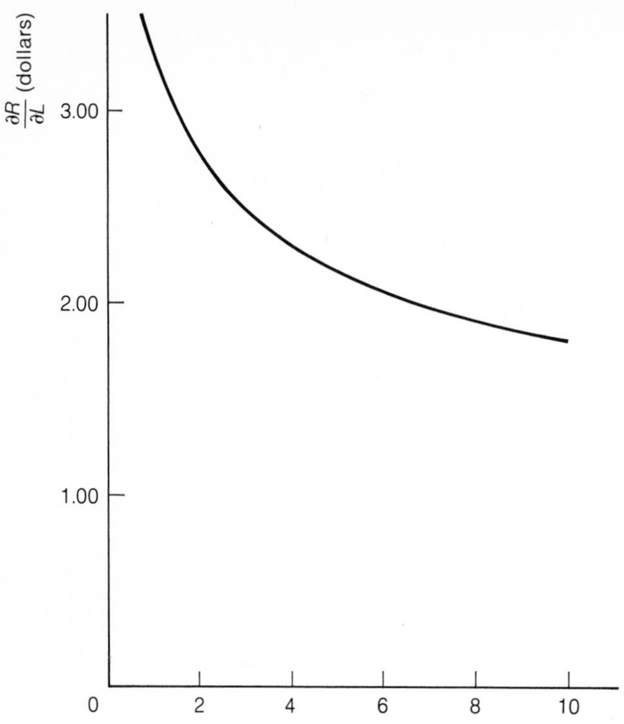

FIGURE 14-3

b The marginal revenue product of *M* is the limit which __________/__________ approaches as __________ approaches zero, __________ remaining constant; or, in symbols, __________/__________

c Show that the marginal revenue product of *M* is equal to the marginal product of *M* multiplied by the marginal revenue from the sale of *Y*.

4 Assume that the variable *A* is a function of two other variables, *B* and *C*; $A = f(B,C)$:

a Define the partial derivative of *A* with respect to *B* and the partial derivative of *A* with respect to *C*.

b When do mathematicians and economists use the symbol ∂ instead of the symbol *d*?

5 If the firm's production function is $Y = M^aN^{1-a}$:

a It is assumed that *a* is less than __________ and greater than __________

b $\partial Y/\partial M =$ __________

c If the firm can sell all the *Y* it wishes at a price of $\bar{P}_Y$, $\partial R/\partial M =$ __________

d If the firm can sell *Y* at a price equal to $(g - Y)/h$, $\partial R/\partial M =$ __________

6 Show that when $Y = M^aN^{1-a}$:

a $\frac{\partial Y}{\partial M} = a\left(\frac{N}{M}\right)^{1-a}$

b $\frac{\partial Y}{\partial N} = (1 - a)\left(\frac{M}{N}\right)^a$

7 Suppose $Y = M^{0.8}N^{0.2}$ and N is fixed at 50.

a $\partial Y/\partial M =$ __________

b If the firm selling Y is a perfect competitor in the product market and can sell Y at a constant price of \$5, $\partial R/\partial M =$ __________

c If the firm producing Y is a monopolist and the demand for Y is $Y = 600 - 30P_Y$, $\partial R/\partial M =$ __________

8 Explain how to find the partial derivative of a function such as $A = f(B,C)$.

MARGINAL RESOURCE COST

A firm that changes its employment of an input such as L, keeping its employment of K constant, finds that the cost of producing its product also changes. The ratio of the change ΔC in the firm's costs to the change ΔL in the employment of L is $\Delta C/\Delta L$. As ΔL approaches zero, the limit which $\Delta C/\Delta L$ approaches is $\partial C/\partial L$. The *marginal resource cost* of input L we define as $\partial C/\partial L$, and

$$\frac{\partial C}{\partial L} = \lim_{\Delta L \to 0} \frac{\Delta C}{\Delta L} \qquad (14\text{-}36)$$

Notice that because the costs of the firm depend not only upon the amount of L employed but also upon the amount of K employed and because a change in cost may result from either a change in L, a change in K, or both, the marginal resource cost of an input is a partial rather than a simple derivative.

In a similar way we define the marginal resource cost of K as the limit which $\Delta C/\Delta K$ approaches as ΔK approaches zero. For the marginal resource cost of K we employ the notation $\partial C/\partial K$. The marginal resource cost of K is

$$\frac{\partial C}{\partial K} = \lim_{\Delta K \to 0} \frac{\Delta C}{\Delta K} \qquad (14\text{-}37)$$

Marginal resource cost: the perfectly competitive employer

A firm that is a perfectly competitive employer of an input finds that the quantity of the input it employs does not affect the price it must pay for the input. The supply of the input to the firm is perfectly elastic. If L is the input, the price P_L of L is

$$P_L = n \qquad (14\text{-}38)$$

where n is a constant and equal to the fixed price of L.

If we substitute n for P_L in the firm's cost function (equation 14-4), we have

$$C = K \cdot P_K + L \cdot n \qquad (14\text{-}39)$$

Holding the quantity of K employed and the price of K constant, we see that the partial derivative of this function with respect to L, $\partial C/\partial L$, is the marginal resource cost of L. When we employ the method used in earlier chapters for finding the simple derivative and remember that $K \cdot P_K$ is assumed to be constant, we have

$$\frac{\partial C}{\partial L} = n \tag{14-40}$$

The marginal resource cost of an input to a firm that employs the input as a perfect competitor is equal to the price of the input.

In Figure 14-4 we have plotted L on the horizontal axis and the price and marginal resource cost of L on the vertical axis. The horizontal curve is the supply curve of L to the firm. A horizontal supply curve means that the firm may employ as much or as little L as it wishes without affecting its price and that the supply of the input to the firm is perfectly elastic. We have assumed that the firm can hire as much L as it wants at a price of \$2.50. The horizontal curve is also a graph of the firm's marginal-resource-cost function. It says that the marginal resource cost is constant and is equal the constant price of L, or \$2.50.

Marginal resource cost: the monopsonist

A firm that is the only employer of an input is a *monopsonist*. A monopsonist finds that the price it must pay for the input is an increasing function of the quantity of the input it employs. We shall assume for simplicity that the relation between the quantity L of the input *supplied* to the firm and the price P_L it must pay for it is not only direct but also linear, or

$$L = v + wP_L \tag{14-41}$$

The parameters in the supply function facing the monopsonist are v and w. The parameter w may be greater than, less than, or equal to 1, but the absolute value of w is, of course, positive.

$$w \gtreqless 1$$

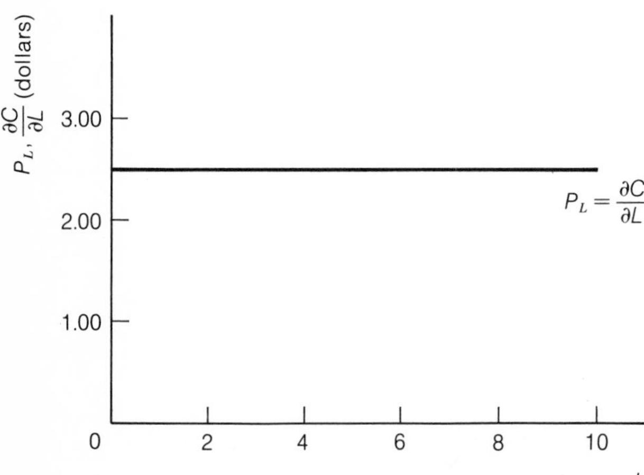

FIGURE 14-4

The parameter v may be positive, negative, or zero.

$$v \gtreqless 0$$

Equation 14-41 may be rewritten

$$P_L = \frac{L - v}{w} \tag{14-42}$$

To find the marginal-resource-cost function we again employ the firm's cost equation:

$$C \equiv K \cdot P_K + L \cdot P_L \tag{14-4}$$

For P_L in the cost equation we substitute the right side of equation 14-42 and obtain

$$C = K \cdot P_K + L \frac{L - v}{w}$$

or

$$C = K \cdot P_K + \frac{L^2}{w} - \frac{vL}{w} \tag{14-43}$$

with K and P_K and therefore $K \cdot P_K$ assumed constant, the partial derivative of this function with respect to L is

$$\frac{\partial C}{\partial L} = \frac{2L}{w} - \frac{v}{w}$$

or

$$\frac{\partial C}{\partial L} = \frac{2L - v}{w} \tag{14-44}$$

As an example, we might have a monopsonist who finds that the supply function for the input L is

$$L = -6.50 + 5P_L$$

which can be rewritten

$$P_L = \frac{L + 6.50}{5} \tag{14-45}$$

Substituting the right side of equation 14-45 in the monopsonist's cost function,

$$C = K \cdot P_K + L \frac{L + 6.50}{5}$$

or

$$C = K \cdot P_K + \frac{L^2 + 6.50L}{5} \tag{14-46}$$

The marginal-resource-cost function is the partial derivative of this cost function with respect to L, or

$$\frac{\partial C}{\partial L} = \frac{2L + 6.50}{5} \tag{14-47}$$

In Figure 14-5 we have plotted the monopsonist's supply function (equation 14-45) and marginal-resource-cost function (equation 14-47). We can see from this graph that both the price the monopsonist must pay for L and the marginal resource cost of L are increasing functions of L. (When the supply of L is a linear function, the marginal-resource-cost function for L will also be linear.)

We can also see in Figure 14-5 that the marginal resource cost of the input (at any positive amount of L) is greater than the price the monopsonist must pay (for that amount of L). Put another way, if we subtract the price of L from the marginal resource cost of L, the difference is positive. To see that this is necessarily true, let us subtract P_L from $\partial C/\partial L$. From equation 14-42 we know that

$$P_L = \frac{L - v}{w} \qquad (14\text{-}42)$$

and from equation 14-44 we know that

$$\frac{\partial C}{\partial L} = \frac{2L - v}{w} \qquad (14\text{-}44)$$

If we subtract the right side of equation 14-42 from the right side of equation 14-44, we find that the difference between P_L and $\partial C/\partial L$ is equal to L/w. We have assumed in writing the supply function for L that w is an *absolute value*. L, the quantity of the input employed, must be either zero or positive; it cannot be less than zero, and so L/w must be positive or zero. The amount by which the marginal resource cost exceeds the price of an input therefore must be positive or zero. And as long as L is *not* zero, L/w is positive. In short, the price

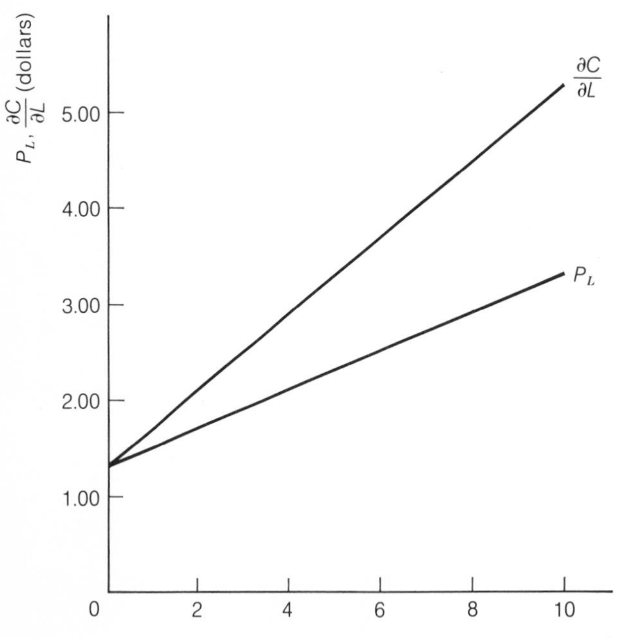

FIGURE 14-5

and marginal resource cost of an input are equal only when the quantity of the input employed is zero; but when the quantity employed is greater than zero, marginal resource cost exceeds price.

Exercise 14-2

In all the questions below it is assumed that the output of product Y is a function of the quantities of inputs M and N employed.

1 The marginal resource cost of M is the limit __________ / __________ approaches as __________ approaches zero, __________ remaining constant; or, in symbols, __________ / __________

2 When the firm employing M is a perfect competitor in the market for M:

a The supply of M to the firm is __________

b The price of M is __________

c The marginal resource cost of M is equal to __________

3 Show that when the firm employing input N is a perfect competitor in the market for N, $\partial C/\partial N = P_N$.

4 Assume a firm may hire as much or as little of input M as it wishes at a price of \$12. The marginal resource cost of M to the firm is equal to \$__________

5 When the firm employing M is a monopsonist, the price the firm must pay for M is an __________ function of __________

6 If the supply function for M facing a monopsonist is $M = r + mP_M$, show that $\partial C/\partial M = (2M - r)/m$.

7 Suppose that the supply function for input N employed by a monopsonist is $N = -40 + 6P_N$. Then $\partial C/\partial N =$ __________

8 Show that when the supply of input M is an increasing and linear function, the marginal resource cost of M is greater than the price of M when the quantity of M employed is greater than zero.

THE PRICE AND EMPLOYMENT OF INPUTS

In the last chapter we examined the marginal-revenue-product and marginal-resource-cost functions of the firm. We employ these tools in this chapter to explain what determines the quantity of an input the individual firm will employ and the price it must pay for that input.

This chapter is divided into two major sections. In the first we look at the firm in the short run. Employing our new tools, we first explain the quantity of a variable input the perfectly competitive employer will hire and the market price of that input, and then we explain the quantity of a variable input a monopsonist will hire and the price he will pay for it. The second section examines the firm in the long run and explains the proportion in which the profit-maximizing firm will employ inputs and the amount of each input it will employ.

EQUILIBRIUM IN THE SHORT RUN

The short run, we recall from Chapter 11, is a period of time during which some of the inputs employed by a firm are variable and some are fixed. We assume throughout this chapter that the firm employs only two inputs, L and K, to produce a single product, X. The firm's production function is

$$X = f(L,K) \tag{15-1}$$

We shall assume that the variable input is L and the fixed input is K in the short run.

Profit maximization

The assumed goal of the firm in the short run (and in the long run) is the maximization of its economic profit π, which is, by definition, equal to the firm's revenue less its costs, or

$$\pi \equiv R - C \tag{15-2}$$

Either a change in revenue or a change in cost will result in a change in profit. The change $\Delta\pi$ in the firm's profit is therefore equal to the change ΔR in revenue less the change ΔC in the costs of the firm.

$$\Delta\pi \equiv \Delta R - \Delta C \tag{15-3}$$

Both a firm's revenue and a firm's costs change when it changes the amount of the variable input L it employs. When we divide equation 15-3 by the change ΔL in the quantity of L employed, we have

$$\frac{\Delta\pi}{\Delta L} \equiv \frac{\Delta R}{\Delta L} - \frac{\Delta C}{\Delta L}$$

If we now let ΔL approach zero, since profit, revenue, and cost are functions of L alone (because the quantity of K is fixed), we may write

$$\frac{d\pi}{dL} \equiv \frac{dR}{dL} - \frac{dC}{dL} \tag{15-4}$$

In equation 15-4, with K fixed, dR/dL is the marginal revenue product of L and dC/dL is the marginal resource cost of L. $d\pi/dL$ is the *marginal profit* of the input L, that is, the ratio of the change in profit to the change in the quantity of L employed as ΔL approaches zero. Equation 15-4 tells us that marginal profit is equal to marginal revenue product less marginal resource cost.

From our work in Chapter 12[1] we know that if a firm is to maximize its profit, $d\pi/dX$ (the firm's marginal profit with respect to its output of X) must be equal to zero. If the firm is to employ the quantity of L that maximizes its profit, the marginal profit of L must also be zero, or

$$\frac{d\pi}{dL} = 0$$

By looking at Figure 15-1 we can see that $d\pi/dL$ must equal zero if a firm is to maximize its profit. On the horizontal axis is plotted the quantity of L employed by the firm, and on the vertical axis is plotted the firm's profit. Where profit is the greatest, the firm employs L_1 of L. The slope of the firm's profit curve at L_1 is equal to zero: it is perfectly flat and has no slope. The slope of this profit curve is simply $d\pi/dL$. If profit is to be a maximum, it is necessary that $d\pi/dL$ equal zero.

When we substitute zero for $d\pi/dL$ in equation 15-4, profits are a maximum when

$$0 = \frac{dR}{dL} - \frac{dC}{dL} \tag{15-5}$$

Profits are a maximum, this equation tells us, when the marginal revenue product

[1]See pages 305 to 307.

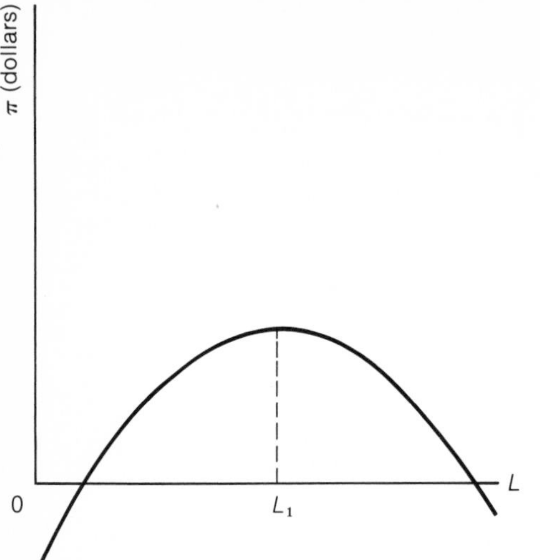

FIGURE 15-1

of the variable input L minus the marginal resource cost of L is equal to zero. Adding dC/dL to both sides of equation 15-5 gives

$$\frac{dC}{dL} = \frac{dR}{dL} \tag{15-6}$$

The firm has hired the quantity of the variable input L that maximizes its profit when the marginal resource cost of L and the marginal revenue product of L are equal.[2]

To ensure that the firm has hired the quantity of L that maximizes its profits rather than the quantity of L that *minimizes* profits it is necessary that the firm's profits would decrease if it hired a greater quantity of L. Looking again at Figure 15-1, we can see that this means that the firm's profit curve must have a negative slope to the right of L_1. Put another way, if the firm were to *increase* the quantity of L it employs beyond L_1, the slope of the profit curve would change from zero to a negative value. The change in the slope would be negative because a change from a zero slope to a less-than-zero slope is a negative change.

For profits to be a maximum it is therefore necessary that the change in the slope of the profit curve be negative when the firm increases the quantity of L it employs. The ratio of the change in the slope of the profit curve to the change in the quantity of L employed must be negative. Since the slope of the profit curve is $d\pi/dL$, we can write the necessary condition as

$$\frac{d\ d\pi/dL}{dL} < 0$$

Mathematicians write the left side of this inequality as $d^2\pi/dL^2$. Using this term, we can say that for profit to be a maximum rather than a minimum a necessary

[2]By a *maximum* profit we mean that if the firm hired a little more or a little less L, the firm's profits would be less; see footnote 6, page 316.

condition is that

$$\frac{d^2\pi}{dL^2} < 0 \qquad (15\text{-}7)$$

The change in the slope of the profit curve divided by the positive change in the employment of the variable input L (as the change in L approaches zero) must be negative.

Since

$$\frac{d^2\pi}{dL^2} \equiv \frac{d^2R}{dL^2} - \frac{d^2C}{dL^2}$$

for $d^2\pi/dL^2$ to be negative, d^2C/dL^2 must be greater than d^2R/dL^2. For the firm to maximize its profit, therefore, it is necessary that

$$\frac{dC}{dL} = \frac{dR}{dL} \qquad (15\text{-}6)$$

and that

$$\frac{d^2C}{dL^2} > \frac{d^2R}{dL^2} \qquad (15\text{-}8)$$

The term d^2C/dL^2 is simply the *slope* of the marginal-resource-cost curve, and d^2R/dL^2 is the *slope* of the marginal-revenue-product curve. In geometric terms, inequality 15-8 is satisfied when the slope of the marginal-resource-cost curve is greater than the slope of the marginal-revenue-product curve.

But for the firm to be in equilibrium it is also necessary (as we learned in Chapters 12 and 13[3]) that its total revenue exceed or equal its total variable cost. In the short run when L is the variable and K the fixed input, the firm's total variable cost equals the quantity of L employed by the firm multiplied by the price it pays for L. If revenue is to exceed or equal total variable cost, it is necessary that

$$R \geqq L \cdot P_L$$

If we divide this last inequality by L, we have

$$\frac{R}{L} \geqq \frac{L \cdot P_L}{L}$$

or

$$\frac{R}{L} \geqq P_L \qquad (15\text{-}9)$$

The term on the left side of inequality 15-9 we define as the *average revenue product of L,* the firm's total revenue divided by the quantity of L employed. The term on the right is, of course, the price of the input L. Inequality 15-9 says that the average revenue product of L must exceed or equal the price of L.

If the price of L exceeds the average revenue product of L or if

$$P_L > \frac{R}{L}$$

[3]See pages 311 to 316.

it means, multiplying both sides of this inequality by L, that

$$P_L \cdot L > R$$

The firm's variable costs exceed its total revenue. And we know that when a firm finds that at its most profitable output total variable cost exceeds revenue, it will produce no output. Should it produce no output, it would employ none of the variable input L.

A firm, then, is maximizing its profit and in equilibrium with respect to the employment of the variable input L when *three* conditions are satisfied. The quantity of L it will employ to maximize its profit is the quantity at which

$$\frac{dC}{dL} = \frac{dR}{dL} \qquad (15\text{-}6)$$

provided that

$$\frac{d^2C}{dL^2} > \frac{d^2R}{dL^2} \qquad (15\text{-}8)$$

and

$$\frac{R}{L} \geqq P_L \qquad (15\text{-}9)$$

We now have all the tools we need to determine what amount of a variable input a firm will employ and the price it will pay for that input in the short run. The firm may be either a perfectly competitive employer of the input or a monopsonist. For each of these two kinds of employers there is an economic model.

The perfectly competitive employer

Let us assume at first that the perfectly competitive employer of the variable input L is also a perfectly competitive seller of product X. The firm's production function we shall assume to be

$$X = L^a K^{1-a} \qquad (15\text{-}10)$$

This is the same production function we employed in Chapter 14.

Since the perfectly competitive employer of L faces a perfectly elastic supply function for L, the price of L to the firm is an exogenous variable.

$$P_L = \bar{P}_L \qquad (15\text{-}11)$$

We shall explain a little later what determines the price the perfectly competitive employer of L has to pay for it. The firm's revenue is

$$R \equiv X \cdot P_X \qquad (15\text{-}12)$$

Costs in the short run are

$$C = F + L \cdot P_L \qquad (15\text{-}13)$$

F is the fixed cost of the firm and is equal to $K \cdot P_K$. For the firm in the short run its fixed cost is a constant and an exogenous variable, or

$$F = \bar{F} \qquad (15\text{-}14)$$

The price at which the firm sells product X is also fixed and an exogenous variable.

$$P_X = \bar{P}_X \tag{15-15}$$

The firm is in equilibrium (maximizing its profit in the short run) when

$$\frac{dC}{dL} = \frac{dR}{dL} \tag{15-6}$$

provided that

$$\frac{d^2C}{dL^2} > \frac{d^2R}{dL^2} \tag{15-8}$$

and

$$\frac{R}{L} \geqq P_L \tag{15-9}$$

Because K is fixed in the short run, we add an equation that says K is an exogenous variable.

$$K = \bar{K} \tag{15-16}$$

This model contains eight equations and two inequalities. It also has eight variables, four of which (P_L, F, P_X, and K) are exogenous and four of which (X, L, C, and R) are endogenous. (We can also find the firm's profit by employing equation 15-2.) To obtain the solution equation for L, we start with the equilibrium equation of the model

$$\frac{dC}{dL} = \frac{dR}{dL} \tag{15-6}$$

For dC/dL we substitute the derivative of the firm's cost function (equation 15-13). dC/dL is equal to P_L, and for P_L we substitute (from equation 15-11) $\bar{P}_L$. For dR/dL we substitute

$$\frac{dX}{dL}\frac{dR}{dX}$$

(from equation 14-9[4]). We now have

$$\bar{P}_L = \frac{dX}{dL}\frac{dR}{dX}$$

For dX/dL we substitute the derivative with respect to L of the firm's production function, $dX/dL = a(K/L)^{1-a}$. For dR/dX we substitute the derivative of the firm's revenue function, $dR/dX = P_X$. Now we have

$$\bar{P}_L = a\left(\frac{K}{L}\right)^{1-a} \cdot P_X$$

Finally, for P_X we substitute (from equation 15-15) $\bar{P}_X$, and for K we substitute (from equation 15-16) $\bar{K}$.

$$\bar{P}_L = a\left(\frac{\bar{K}}{L}\right)^{1-a} \cdot \bar{P}_X \tag{15-17}$$

[4]See pages 357 to 358.

Equation 15-17 can be rewritten to isolate the variable L on the left side and all parameters and exogenous variables on the right side. First, we divide both sides of equation 15-17 by $a\bar{P}_X$ to obtain

$$\frac{\bar{P}_L}{a\bar{P}_X} = \left(\frac{\bar{K}}{L}\right)^{1-a}$$

or

$$\frac{\bar{P}_L}{a\bar{P}_X} = \frac{\bar{K}^{1-a}}{L^{1-a}}$$

Next we divide both sides of the last equation by $\bar{K}^{1-a}$:

$$\frac{\bar{P}_L}{a\bar{P}_X\bar{K}^{1-a}} = \frac{1}{L^{1-a}}$$

Finally we invert both sides of the equation to find

$$L^{1-a} = \frac{a\bar{P}_X\bar{K}^{1-a}}{\bar{P}_L} \tag{15-18}$$

L to the $(1 - a)$th power is alone on the left side. On the right side we have the parameter a and three exogenous variables, $\bar{P}_X$, $\bar{K}$, and $\bar{P}_L$. Equation 15-18 is the solution equation for L. L can be found by using logarithms. Having found L, we can then determine X (from equation 15-1). With L and X determined, we can find R (from equation 15-12) and C (from equation 15-13). (Profit can be computed by employing equation 15-2.)

Numerical example Let us assume that the firm's production function is

$$X = L^{0.75} \cdot K^{0.25} \tag{15-19}$$

and that

$$P_X = \$2 \tag{15-20}$$

$$P_L = \$2.67 \tag{15-21}$$

Employing equation 15-18, we can find the quantity of input L the firm should employ to maximize its profits in the short run if the quantity of K employed by the firm is fixed at 60. Substituting into equation 15-18,

$$L^{1-0.75} = \frac{0.75(\$2)(60^{1-0.75})}{\$2.67}$$

$$L^{0.25} = \frac{0.75(\$2)(60^{0.25})}{\$2.67}$$

Employing logarithms to find L,

$$0.25 \log L = \log 0.75 + \log 2 + 0.25 \log 60 - \log 2.67$$

If we divide through by 0.25, we have

$$\log L = \frac{\log 0.75 + \log 2 + 0.25 \log 60 - \log 2.67}{0.25}$$

$$= \frac{1.87506 + 0.30103 + 0.44454 - 0.42602}{0.25}$$

$$= \frac{0.19461}{0.25}$$

$$= 0.77844$$

The antilog of 0.77844 is 6.004. Rounding therefore gives

$$L = 6$$

The firm will maximize its profits if it employs 6 units of the variable input L.

Just to be sure that the firm is maximizing rather than minimizing its profits, let us check that inequalities 15-8 and 15-9 are satisfied when the firm employs 6 units of L. When the firm employs $6L$, its output of X is 10.67. This we find by employing the firm's product function

$$X = L^{0.75} \cdot K^{0.25} \tag{15-19}$$

Since K is 60 and L is 6,

$$X = 6^{0.75}(60^{0.25})$$

and

$$\begin{aligned} \log X &= 0.75 \log 6 + 0.25 \log 60 \\ &= 0.75(0.77815) + 0.25(1.77815) \\ &= 0.58361 + 0.44454 \\ &= 1.02815 \\ X &= 10.67 \end{aligned}$$

If the firm produces 10.67 units of X, its revenue, employing equation 15-12, is

$$\begin{aligned} R &= 10.67(\$2) \\ &= \$21.33 \end{aligned}$$

R/L is equal to \$21.33 divided by 6 or $\$3.55\frac{1}{2}$; and this is greater than the \$2.67 price of the input L. Inequality 15-9 is therefore satisfied.

But is inequality 15-8 satisfied? The firm's cost function when K is fixed is, employing equation 15-13,

$$C = F + L \cdot P_L \tag{15-13}$$

If P_L is \$2.67, its cost function is

$$C = F + L \cdot \$2.67$$

The first derivative of this cost function with respect to L is

$$\frac{dC}{dL} = \$2.67$$

and the second derivative is

$$\frac{d^2C}{dL^2} = 0$$

The firm's revenue function is

$$R \equiv X \cdot P_X \tag{15-12}$$

Substituting the right side of equation 15-19 for X and \$2 (equation 15-20) for P_X, its revenue function is

$$R = L^{0.25} \cdot K^{0.25} \cdot \$2$$

With K equal to 60,

$$R = L^{0.25}(60^{0.25})(\$2)$$

The first derivative with respect to L of this revenue function[5] is

$$\frac{dR}{dL} = \$1.50\left(\frac{60}{L}\right)^{0.25} \tag{15-22}$$

The derivative of this last equation is the second derivative, d^2R/dL^2, and is equal to

$$-0.375\,\frac{60^{0.25}}{L^{1.25}}$$

We find this second derivative in the following way. First we write equation 15-22 as

$$\frac{dR}{dL} = \$1.50(60^{0.25})(L^{-0.25}) \tag{15-23}$$

Next we multiply the right side of the exponent of L (-0.25) and reduce the exponent of L by 1 to find

$$\frac{d^2R}{dL^2} = -0.25(\$1.50)(60^{0.25})(L^{-1.25})$$

or

$$\frac{d^2R}{dL^2} = -0.375\,\frac{60^{0.25}}{L^{1.25}}$$

Without going any further we can see that when L is equal to 6, the right-hand side of equation 15-23 is *negative*. Inequality 15-8 is satisfied because d^2C/dL^2 (equal to 0) is greater than *any* negative value of d^2R/dL^2.

When the firm employs 6 units of L, its output of X (we determined above) is 10.67 and its revenue is \$21.33. Its costs, employing equation 15-13, are

$$\begin{aligned} C &= F + 6(\$2.67) \\ &= F + \$16 \end{aligned}$$

Its profit is equal to its revenue less its costs, or

$$\begin{aligned} \pi &= \$21.33 - (F + \$16) \\ &= \$5.33 - F \end{aligned}$$

The firm's profit is \$5.33 less the amount of its fixed costs, but its total revenue of \$21.33 is greater than the total variable cost of \$16. Therefore the firm will produce in the short run and employ 6 units of L.

A monopoly seller The model for a firm that is not a perfectly competitive seller of X is similar to the model for the firm that sells X under perfectly competitive conditions. The model is

$$X = L^aK^{1-a} \tag{15-10}$$
$$P_L = \bar{P}_L \tag{15-11}$$
$$R \equiv X \cdot P_X \tag{15-12}$$
$$C = F + L \cdot P_L \tag{15-13}$$
$$F = \bar{F} \tag{15-14}$$

$$P_X = \frac{j - X}{m} \tag{15-24}$$

[5]See equation 14-25.

$$K = \overline{K} \tag{15-16}$$

$$\frac{dC}{dL} = \frac{dR}{dL} \tag{15-6}$$

$$\frac{d^2C}{dL^2} > \frac{d^2R}{dL^2} \tag{15-8}$$

$$\frac{R}{L} \geqq P_L \tag{15-9}$$

Like the model for the perfectly competitive seller of X, this one contains eight equations and two inequalities. It also has eight variables, three of which (P_L, F, and K) are exogenous and five of which (X, L, P_X, C, and R) are endogenous. The only equation which is different is equation 15-24. If the firm sells X as a monopolist, the price of X is no longer exogenous but a decreasing function of X. For simplicity we have assumed that it is also a linear function.

To find the solution value of L we again start with the equilibrium equation (15-6). For dC/dL we substitute $\overline{P}_L$ and for dR/dL we substitute[6]

$$a\left(\frac{K}{L}\right)^{1-a} \frac{j - 2(L^aK^{1-a})}{m}$$

For K we then substitute (from equation 15-16) $\overline{K}$ to obtain

$$P_L = a\left(\frac{\overline{K}}{L}\right)^{1-a} \frac{j - 2(L^a\overline{K}^{1-a})}{m} \tag{15-25}$$

Equation 15-25 contains only one endogenous variable, L. It also contains two exogenous variables (P_L and K) and three parameters (a, j, and m).

A solution equation such as 15-25 with only one unknown, the endogenous variable L, should tell us what the value of L is. However, there is no simple method of finding the equilibrium value of L even though there is a value for L that satisfies equation 15-25 and the two inequalities in the model. To find L, therefore, it is convenient to use graphs and a numerical example. To see how we find L graphically, let us assume that

$$X = L^{0.75} \cdot K^{0.25} \tag{15-19}$$

$$P_L = \$2.50 \tag{15-26}$$

$$P_X = \frac{800 - X}{500} \tag{15-27}$$

The production function (equation 15-19) and the demand function (15-27) are the same functions we employed in Chapter 14[7] to construct the marginal-revenue-product function in Table 14-3 and the marginal-revenue-product curve in Figure 14-3. We have redrawn this marginal-revenue-product curve in Figure 15-2, which also shows the firm's marginal-resource-cost curve. With the price of L an exogenous variable and equal to \$2.50, dC/dL is also equal to \$2.50. The marginal-resource-cost curve is the left side of equation 15-25, and the marginal-revenue-product curve is the right side of equation 15-25. Where these two curves intersect the two sides of the equation are equal: the value which L has at the intersection of the two curves is the L which will maximize the firm's profit in the short run.

[6] See equation 14-31.
[7] See pages 366 to 367.

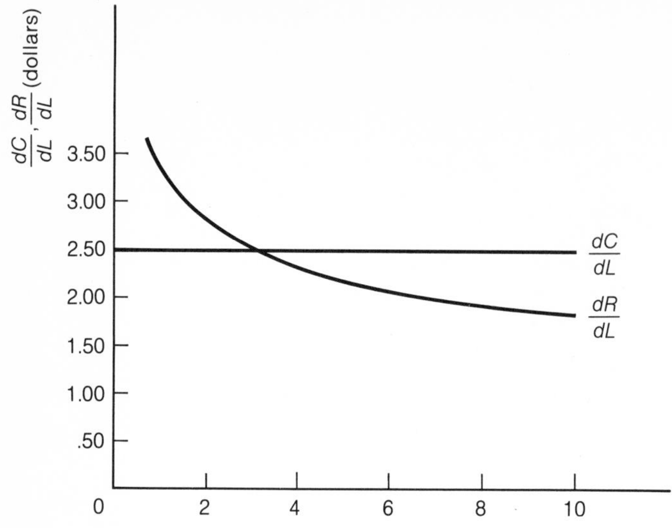

FIGURE 15-2

We can see from the graph that dC/dL and dR/dL are equal at (approximately) 3 units of L. We can check to determine whether 3 units of L satisfies equation 15-25 (when the price of L is \$2.50, K is 60, the parameter a is 0.75, j is 800, and m is 500). Substituting these values into equation 15-25, we have

$$\$2.50 = 0.75\left(\frac{60}{3}\right)^{1-0.75} \frac{800 - 2[10^{0.75}(60^{1-0.75})]}{500}$$

$$= 0.75(20)^{0.25} \frac{800 - 2[10^{0.75}(60^{0.25})]}{500}$$

Looking back to Table 14-3, we can see that $0.75(20^{0.25})$ is equal to 1.59; and that

$$\frac{800 - 2[10^{0.75}(60^{0.25})]}{500}$$

is equal to 1.575. Therefore

$$\$2.50 = 1.59(1.575)$$
$$\$2.50 = \$2.50 \qquad \text{approximately}$$

To determine the values of X, P_X, C, and R we go back to the equations of the model. When L is 3,

$$X = 3^{0.75}(60^{0.25}) = 6.34$$

$$P_X = \frac{800 - 6.34}{500} = \frac{793.64}{500} = \$1.587$$

$$R = 6.34(\$1.587) = \$10.06$$

$$C = F + L \cdot P_L = F + 3(\$2.50) = F + \$7.50$$

$$\pi = \$10.06 - (F + \$7.50) = \$10.06 - F - \$7.50 = \$2.56 - F$$

To be sure that the firm is maximizing profit in the short run we see whether inequalities 15-8 and 15-9 are satisfied. Inequality 15-9 is satisfied because R/L is equal to \$10.06/3, or \$3.35, and is greater than the \$2.50 price of input L. Inequality 15-8 is satisfied because at $3L$ the zero *slope* of the dC/dL curve (which is d^2C/dL^2) is greater than the negative *slope* of the dR/dL curve (which is d^2R/dL^2).

The market price of the input To the individual perfectly competitive employer of an input the price of that input is an exogenous variable. The supply of the input is perfectly elastic to the single employer: it can hire as much or as little of the input as it wishes at a fixed price. This price is determined by the total (or market) demand for and the total (or market) supply of the input. The total demand for the input is the sum of the demands of all employers for the input.

The demand function of the individual employer We already know that the quantity of the variable input L the firm will employ is the quantity at which dC/dL equals dR/dL. Because the individual employer of L finds that dC/dL is equal to the price of L, the firm employs the amount of L at which

$$P_L = \frac{dR}{dL} \tag{15-28}$$

Equation 15-28 is the individual firm's demand function for input L. To this demand function we must, however, attach two conditions: (1) It is the demand function only where the average revenue product R/L of L exceeds or equals the price of L. (2) It is the demand function only where d^2C/dL^2 is greater than d^2R/dL^2. Since d^2C/dL^2 to the perfectly competitive employer of L is zero, i.e., the slope of dC/dL in Figure 15-2 is zero, for d^2R/dL^2 to be less than d^2C/dL^2, d^2R/dL^2 must be negative. The second condition we attach is that equation 15-28 is the firm's demand function only where d^2R/dL^2 is negative.

The firm's demand function for L, therefore, is its marginal-revenue-product function where marginal revenue product is decreasing (d^2R/dL^2 is negative) and average revenue product of L is greater than or equal to the price of L. The firm's marginal-revenue-product function for L is

$$\frac{dR}{dL} = \frac{dX}{dL}\frac{dR}{dX} \tag{15-29}$$

When dX/dL is $a(\overline{K}/L)^{1-a}$, the marginal-revenue-product function for L is

$$\frac{dR}{dL} = a\left(\frac{\overline{K}}{L}\right)^{1-a}\frac{dR}{dX} \tag{15-30}$$

Substituting the right side of equation 15-30 for dR/dL in equation 15-28, the firm's demand function for L can be written[8]

$$P_L = a\left(\frac{\overline{K}}{L}\right)^{1-a}\frac{dR}{dX} \tag{15-31}$$

If this firm is a perfectly competitive seller of X, its demand function for L will

[8]While it is customary in writing a demand function for L to make the quantity of L demanded a function of the price of L, that is, to write $L = f(P_L)$, we can just as well make the price of L depend upon the quantity of L and write $P_L = f(L)$ as we have done in equation 15-31. All that $P_L = f(L)$ says is that the price the firm is willing to pay for L depends upon the quantity of L it employs.

be

$$P_L = a\left(\frac{\overline{K}}{L}\right)^{1-a} \overline{P}_X \qquad (15\text{-}32)$$

where $\overline{P}_X$ is the fixed price at which it is able to sell X. As a numerical example, we might have a firm whose marginal-product function is

$$\frac{dX}{dL} = 0.75\left(\frac{60}{L}\right)^{0.25} \qquad (15\text{-}33)$$

and who sells L at price of \$2. Its demand function for L, then, is

$$P_L = 0.75\left(\frac{60}{L}\right)^{0.25}(\$2)$$

or

$$P_L = \$1.50\left(\frac{60}{L}\right)^{0.25} \qquad (15\text{-}34)$$

Note that this is exactly the same curve as that plotted in Figure 14-2. We can see there that the firm's demand function for L is *not* linear.

When the firm employing L is a monopoly seller of X, its demand for L is

$$P_L = a\left(\frac{\overline{K}}{L}\right)^{1-a} \frac{j - 2X}{m} \qquad (15\text{-}35)$$

where $(j - 2X)/m$ is the marginal revenue from the sale of X [when $P_X = (j - X)/m$ is the demand for X facing the monopolist]. To use our previous numerical example, if

$$\frac{dX}{dL} = 0.75\left(\frac{60}{L}\right)^{0.25} \qquad (15\text{-}33)$$

$$P_X = \frac{800 - X}{500} \qquad (15\text{-}27)$$

then

$$\frac{dR}{dX} = \frac{800 - 2X}{500} \qquad (15\text{-}36)$$

and the firm's demand function for L is

$$P_L = 0.75\left(\frac{60}{L}\right)^{0.25} \frac{800 - 2X}{500}$$

But this last equation contains two endogenous variables, L and X. For X we may substitute the firm's production function, $X = L^{0.75} \cdot 60^{0.25}$, to obtain

$$P_L = 0.75\left(\frac{60}{L}\right)^{0.25} \frac{800 - 2(L^{0.75})(60^{0.25})}{500} \qquad (15\text{-}37)$$

This is the same function we plotted in Figure 15-2. Again we can observe that this demand function for L is not *linear.*

The total demand for the input The firms employing an input such as L do not all produce the same product. The same input is used to produce a number of different products. Some firms use L to produce X, some use it to produce Y, some use it to produce Z, and so forth. Since some of these firms sell their products in perfectly competitive markets and some are monopolists, there is no simple connection between the total demand for L and the *number* of different employers of L. Employers have different demands for L because they produce different products and sell them under different competitive conditions.

The total demand for L, however, is the sum of the demands of all the firms using L to produce a product. The demand of each firm is a decreasing function. We may reason that because each firm's demand for L is a decreasing function of the price of L, the sum of such demands is also a decreasing function. The sum of these demands is the total or market demand for L and is a decreasing function of the price of L. We should not, however, expect this total demand for L to be a linear function because (as we noted above) the demands of the firm are not linear functions. The demand for L in the market will be decreasing and nonlinear. But for simplicity we shall assume that the demand for L *is* linear as well as a decreasing function.

If we let D_L be the total quantity of L demanded, we have a total demand for L that is

$$D_L = g - hP_L \tag{15-38}$$

Assuming that the market-supply function for L is increasing and linear, or

$$S_L = r + sP_L \tag{15-39}$$

we have two functional equations in a perfectly competitive market for L. The parameters g, h, and s are positive, but r may (and probably does) have a negative value.

The price of L will be the price at which

$$D_L = S_L \tag{15-40}$$

Solving for P_L, we substitute $g - hP_L$ for D_L and $r + sP_L$ for S_L in equation 15-40 and write

$$\begin{aligned} g - hP_L &= r + sP_L \\ g - r &= sp_L + hP_L \\ &= P_L(s + h) \end{aligned}$$

$$P_L = \frac{g - r}{s + h} \tag{15-41}$$

If the price of L is not to be negative—a nonsense answer—we must assume (as we did in Chapter 8) that the value of the parameter g is greater than the value of r. This means that if the price of L were zero, the quantity demanded at this price g would be greater than the quantity supplied r.

As a numerical example, suppose that

$$\begin{aligned} D_L &= 150 - 10P_L \\ S_L &= 70 + 20P_L \end{aligned}$$

The market price of L (using equation 15-40) is the price at which

$$\begin{aligned} 150 - 10P_L &= 70 + 20P_L \\ 80 &= 30P_L \\ P_L &= \tfrac{80}{30} \\ &= \$2.67 \end{aligned}$$

This might be the \$2.67 price for L which we used above in our example of the firm selling X under perfectly competitive conditions.

To take another example, assume that

$$D_L = 200 - 20P_L$$
$$S_L = 75 + 30P_L$$

Then the equilibrium price of L is the price which satisfies the equation

$$200 - 20P_L = 75 + 30P_L$$
$$125 = 50P_L$$
$$P_L = \tfrac{125}{50}$$
$$= \$2.50$$

And this could be the \$2.50 assumed above as the price at which the firm monopolizing the sale of X was able to employ L.

Exercise 15-1

Assume in the questions that follow that the firm's production function is $Y = f(M,N)$, M is the variable, and N the fixed input in the short run.

1 The goal of the firm in the short run is the maximization of its economic profit. Profit is a maximum:

a When $d\pi/dM =$ ___________

b Or when ___________ = ___________
Provided that:

c ___________ > ___________

d And ___________ $\geqq$ ___________

2 Show that for profit to be a maximum in the short run:
a $d\pi/dM$ must equal zero.
b dC/dM must equal dR/dM.
c R/M must exceed or equal the price of M.
d d^2C/dM^2 must exceed d^2R/dM^2.

3 If $Y = M^a \cdot N^{1-a}$, $a < 1$, and $N = \bar{N}$:

a The marginal product of M, dY/dM, = ___________
b When the price of Y is constant and equal to $\bar{P}_Y$, the marginal-revenue product of M, dR/dM, = ___________
c When the price at which the firm can employ M is constant and equal to $\bar{P}_M$, the marginal resource cost of M, dC/dM, = ___________
d Show that with $P_Y = \bar{P}_Y$ and $P_M = \bar{P}_M$, the firm maximizes its profit when the quantity of M it employs satisfies the equation

$$M^{1-a} = \frac{a\bar{P}_Y\bar{N}^{1-a}}{\bar{P}_M}$$

4 Suppose that

$$Y = M^{0.5} \cdot N^{0.5}$$
$$N = 100$$
$$P_Y = \$18$$
$$P_M = \$3$$
$$P_N = \$10$$

a The quantity of M that maximizes the firm's profit in the short run is ________. (The log of 3 is 0.47712, the log of 100 is 2.00000, and 2.95424 is the log of 900.)

b When the firm employs this quantity of M:

(1) $X =$ ________

(2) $R =$ ________

(3) $C =$ ________

(4) $\pi =$ ________

(5) $R/M =$ ________ and is ________ P_M.

(6) $d^2C/dM^2 =$ ________

(7) d^2R/dM^2 is ________ and, therefore, ________ d^2C/dM^2.

5 Assume $Y = M^a N^{1-a}$, $a < 1$, $N = \bar{N}$, $P_Y = (j - Y)/m$, and $P_M = \bar{P}_M$.

a $dR/dM =$ ________

b Show that to maximize its profits in the short run this monopoly seller of Y should employ an amount of M that satisfies the equation

$$\bar{P}_L = a\left(\frac{\bar{N}}{M}\right)^{1-a} \frac{j - 2(M^a\bar{N}^{1-a})}{m}$$

6 Again suppose that

$Y = M^{0.5} \cdot N^{0.5}$

$N = 100$

$P_N = \$10$

$P_M = \$3$

$$P_Y = \frac{1{,}400 - Y}{200}$$

a We have plotted the marginal-revenue-product function on the graph below. Plot the marginal-resource-cost function on this same graph.

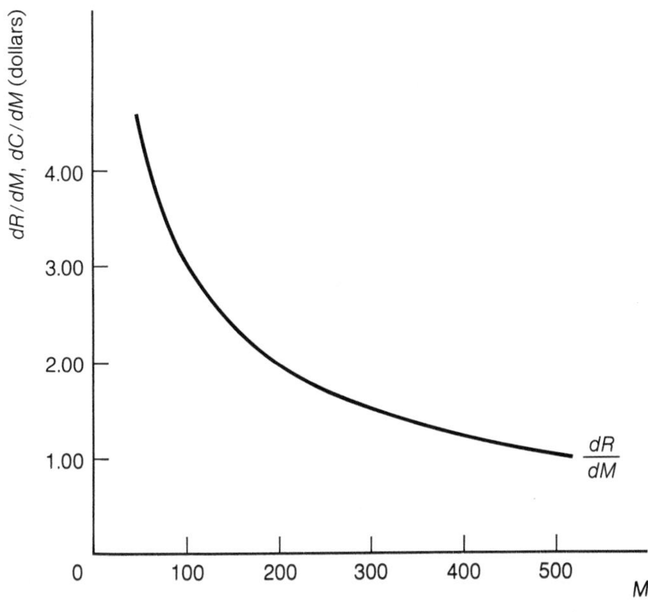

FIGURE 15-A

b The firm maximizes its profit in the short run when M is __________

c When the firm employs this quantity of M:

(1) $Y =$ __________

(2) $P_Y = \$$__________

(3) $R = \$$__________

(4) $C = \$$__________

(5) $\pi = \$$__________

(6) $R/M = \$$__________ and is __________ than P_M.

(7) The slope of the marginal-resource-cost curve is __________ than the slope of the marginal-revenue-product curve.

7 The demand function of the individual perfectly competitive employer of input M can be written either as:

a $P_M =$ __________

b Or $P_M =$ __________ · __________

c Where R/M is __________ and where __________ is greater than __________

8 Suppose that a firm which employs input M under perfectly competitive conditions is also a perfectly competitive seller of product Y and that $P_Y = \$18$. If the production function is $Y = M^{0.5} \cdot N^{0.5}$ and $N = 100$, its demand function for M is $P_M =$ __________

9 If a perfectly competitive employer of M is a monopoly seller of Y and if

$Y = M^{0.5} \cdot N^{0.5}$

$N = 100$

$P_Y = \dfrac{1{,}400 - Y}{200}$

The demand function for M will be $P_M =$ __________

10 If the total demand for input M is $D_M = 2{,}000 - 200P_M$, and if the total supply is $S_M = -3{,}000 + 600P_M$:

a $P_M = \$$__________

b $D_M = S_M =$ __________

The monopsonist

A monopsonist is the sole employer of an input. He may sell X in a perfectly competitive market or monopolize the sale of X. For each of these situations we have a model. Because both models result in solution equations that are not easily solved algebraically, we shall use graphs to find the quantity of L the firm should employ to maximize its profits.

The perfectly competitive seller of *X* This model, like the two previous ones, contains eight equations and two inequalities.

$$X = L^a K^{1-a} \tag{15-10}$$

$$P_L = \frac{L - v}{w} \tag{15-42}$$

$$R \equiv X \cdot P_X \tag{15-12}$$

$$C = F + L \cdot P_L \tag{15-13}$$

$$F = \bar{F} \tag{15-14}$$

$$P_X = \bar{P}_X \tag{15-15}$$

$$K = \bar{K} \tag{15-16}$$

$$\frac{dC}{dL} = \frac{dR}{dL} \tag{15-6}$$

$$\frac{d^2C}{dL^2} > \frac{d^2R}{dL^2} \tag{15-8}$$

$$\frac{R}{L} \geqq P_L \tag{15-9}$$

Equation 15-42, which is identical with equation 14-42, tells us that the price of the input L is an increasing and linear function of the quantity of L employed by the monopsonist. Because this monopsonist is a perfectly competitive seller of X, the price of X is an exogenous variable (equation 15-15). This model has five endogenous variables (X, L, P_L, R, and C) and three exogenous variables (F, P_X, and K). (We can also find the firm's profit by subtracting C from R.)

Earlier[9] we found that the marginal-resource-cost function of the monopsonist was

$$\frac{dC}{dL} = \frac{2L - v}{w} \tag{15-43}$$

His marginal-revenue-product function, because he sells his product competitively, is

$$\frac{dR}{dL} = a\left(\frac{\bar{K}}{L}\right)^{1-a} \cdot \bar{P}_X \tag{14-14}$$

Setting dC/dL equal to dR/dL, we have

$$\frac{2L - v}{w} = a\left(\frac{\bar{K}}{L}\right)^{1-a} \cdot \bar{P}_X \tag{15-44}$$

Equation 15-44 is our solution equation for L, but it is not easy to find the algebraic value of L. We therefore resort to the use of a graph and curves to determine the approximate equilibrium value of L.

Let us assume that the firm's production function is

$$X = L^{0.75} \cdot 60^{0.25}$$

and that the firm is able to sell its product at a price which is

$$P_X = \$2 \tag{15-20}$$

The firm's marginal-revenue-product function (the right side of equation 15-44) is

$$\frac{dR}{dL} = 0.75\left(\frac{60}{L}\right)^{0.25} (\$2)$$

[9] See pages 371 to 372.

or

$$\frac{dR}{dL} = \$1.50 \left(\frac{60}{L}\right)^{0.25} \tag{15-22}$$

This is the same marginal-revenue-product function plotted in Figure 14-2; it is redrawn in Figure 15-3.

Suppose that the supply of L function facing the monopsonist is

$$P_L = \frac{L - (-1.2)}{4} \tag{15-45}$$

The firm's marginal-resource-cost function then is

$$\frac{dC}{dL} = \frac{2L + 1.2}{4} \tag{15-46}$$

Equations 15-45 and 15-46 are both plotted in Figure 15-3.

We can see in Figure 15-3 that dR/dL and dC/dL are equal at (approximately) 5 units of L, where marginal revenue product and marginal resource cost are both \$2.80. We can now use our solution equation (equation 15-44) to check this result. When L is 5,

$$\frac{2(5) - (-1.2)}{4} = 0.75 \left(\frac{60}{5}\right)^{0.25} (\$2)$$

$$\frac{10 + 1.2}{4} = \$1.50(12)^{0.25}$$

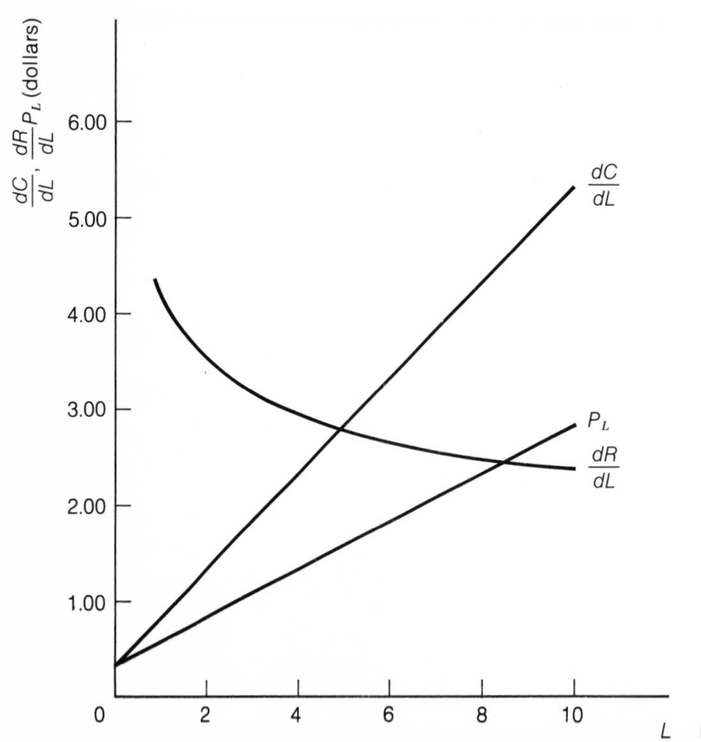

FIGURE 15-3

$$\$2.80 = \$1.50(1.86)$$
$$\$2.80 = \$2.80 \qquad \text{approximately}$$

Having found L to be approximately 5, we can determine from the equations in the model the values of the other endogenous variables.

$$P_L = \frac{5-(-1.2)}{4} = \frac{6.2}{4} = \$1.55$$

$$X = 5^{0.75}(60^{0.25}) = 9.30$$
$$R = 9.30(\$2) = \$18.60$$
$$C = F + 5(\$1.55) = F + \$7.75$$
$$\pi = \$18.60 - F - \$7.75 = \$11.85 - F$$

The firm's average-revenue product R/L is \$18.60/5, or \$3.72, and is greater than the price of L (\$1.55). At 5 units of L in Figure 15-3 the positive *slope* of the marginal-resource-cost curve (d^2C/dL^2) is greater than the negative *slope* of the marginal-revenue-product curve (d^2R/dL^2). Inequalities 15-9 and 15-8 are therefore satisfied.

The monopoly seller of *X* We may now change the model to reflect the assumption that the monopsonistic employer of L is also a monopolistic seller of X and make the price of X a decreasing and linear function of the quantity of X supplied by the firm. The model is now

$$X = L_a K^{1-a} \tag{15-10}$$

$$P_L = \frac{L-v}{w} \tag{15-42}$$

$$R \equiv X \cdot P_X \tag{15-12}$$

$$C = F + L \cdot P_L \tag{15-13}$$

$$F = \bar{F} \tag{15-14}$$

$$P_X = \frac{j-X}{m} \tag{15-24}$$

$$K = \bar{K} \tag{15-16}$$

$$\frac{dC}{dL} = \frac{dR}{dL} \tag{15-6}$$

$$\frac{d^2C}{dL^2} > \frac{d^2R}{dL^2} \tag{15-8}$$

$$\frac{R}{L} \geqq P_L \tag{15-9}$$

Like our other three models, this one contains eight equations and two inequalities. It differs from the previous model because equation 15-24 makes the price of X a function of X rather than an exogenous variable. This model has only two exogenous variables (F and K). The other six variables (X, L, P_L, R, C, and P_X) are endogenous.

The firm's marginal-resource-cost function (as in the previous model) is

$$\frac{dC}{dL} = \frac{2L-v}{w} \tag{15-43}$$

But its marginal-revenue-product function, employing our earlier work,[10] is now

$$\frac{dR}{dL} = a\left(\frac{\bar{K}}{L}\right)^{1-a} \frac{j - 2L^a\bar{K}^{1-a}}{m}$$

Setting dC/dL equal to dR/dL gives us

$$\frac{2L - v}{w} = a\left(\frac{\bar{K}}{L}\right)^{1-a} \frac{j - 2L^a\bar{K}^{1-a}}{m} \qquad (15\text{-}47)$$

Equation 15-47 is the solution equation for L; but, as in the solution equation for the last model (15-44), there is no simple algebraic means of finding the value of L that satisfies this equation. Again we resort to a graph and curves to find the approximate value of L at which the marginal revenue product and the marginal resource cost of L are equal.

To illustrate how we find the equilibrium value of L with curves, assume that the firm's production function is again

$$X = L^{0.75} \cdot 60^{0.25}$$

The supply function for L confronting the monopsonist is

$$P_L = \frac{L - (-3.6)}{5} \qquad (15\text{-}48)$$

And the demand function for his product as a monopolist is

$$P_X = \frac{800 - X}{500} \qquad (15\text{-}27)$$

The firm's marginal-resource-cost function is

$$\frac{dC}{dL} = \frac{2L + 3.6}{5} \qquad (15\text{-}49)$$

This function and the supply function (equation 15-48) are plotted in Figure 15-4 together with the firm's marginal-revenue-product function, which is

$$\frac{dR}{dL} = 0.75\left(\frac{60}{L}\right)^{0.25} \frac{800 - 2L^{0.75} \cdot 60^{0.25}}{500} \qquad (15\text{-}50)$$

We can see in Figure 15-4 that marginal revenue product and marginal resource cost are both \$2.32 when the firm employs approximately 4 units of L. Using the solution equation (15-47) to test this result,

$$\frac{2(4) - (-3.6)}{5} = 0.75\left(\frac{60}{4}\right)^{0.25} \frac{800 - 2(4)^{0.75}(60^{0.25})}{500}$$

$$\frac{8 + 3.6}{5} = 1.48(1.569)$$

$$\frac{11.6}{5} = 2.32 \qquad \text{approximately}$$

$$\$2.32 = \$2.32 \qquad \text{approximately}$$

When L is 4,

$$X = 4^{0.75}(60^{0.25}) = 7.87$$

[10]See equation 14-31.

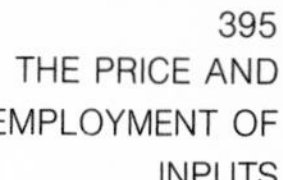

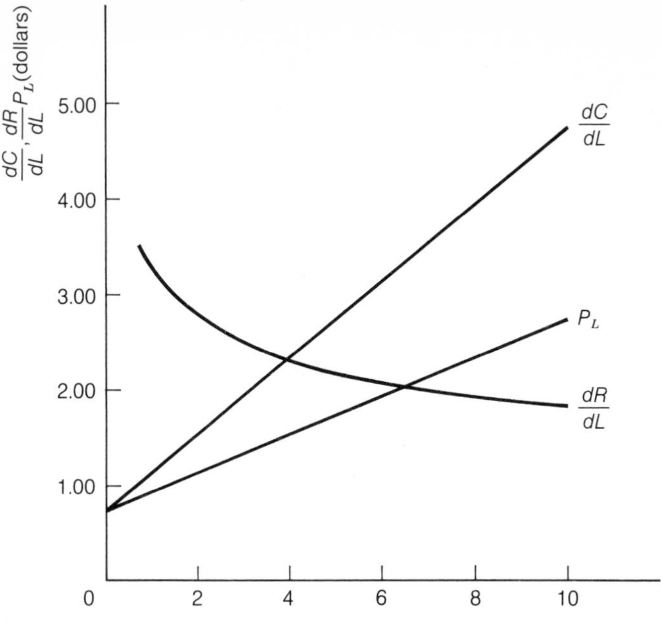

FIGURE 15-4

$$P_L = \frac{4 - (-3.6)}{5} = \frac{4 + 3.6}{5} = \frac{7.6}{5} = \$1.52$$

$$P_X = \frac{800 - 7.87}{500} = \frac{792.13}{500} = \$1.58 \qquad \text{approximately}$$

$$R = 7.87(\$1.58) = \$12.43$$

$$C = F + 4(\$1.52) = F + \$6.08$$

$$\pi = \$12.43 - F - \$6.08 = \$6.37 + F$$

The two inequalities in the model are satisfied. When L is 4, R/L is \$12.43/4, or \$3.10¾, and this is greater than the \$1.52 price of L. And when L is 4, the positive *slope* of the marginal-resource-cost curve (d^2C/dL^2) is greater than the negative *slope* of the marginal-revenue-product curve (d^2R/dL^2).

Exercise 15-2

1 Assume $Y = M^a \cdot N^{1-a}$, $a < 1$, $P_M = (M - b)/c$, $P_Y = \bar{P}_Y$, and $N = \bar{N}$.

a $dC/dM =$ ____________

b $dY/dM =$ ____________

c $dR/dY =$ ____________

d $dR/dM =$ ____________

e To maximize his short-run profit this monopsonist who sells Y in a perfectly competitive market should employ the quantity of M that satisfies the equation

____________ = ____________ provided that:

(1) $R/M \geqq$ __________

(2) d^2C/dM^2 __________ d^2R/dM^2

2 If

$$Y = M^{0.5} \cdot N^{0.5}$$

$$P_M = \frac{M + 100}{200}$$

$$P_Y = \$18$$

$$N = 100$$

$$P_N = \$20$$

then:

a $dR/dM =$ __________

b $dC/dM =$ __________

c The marginal-revenue-product function has been plotted on the graph below. Plot on this same graph the supply function and the marginal-resource-cost function for *M*.

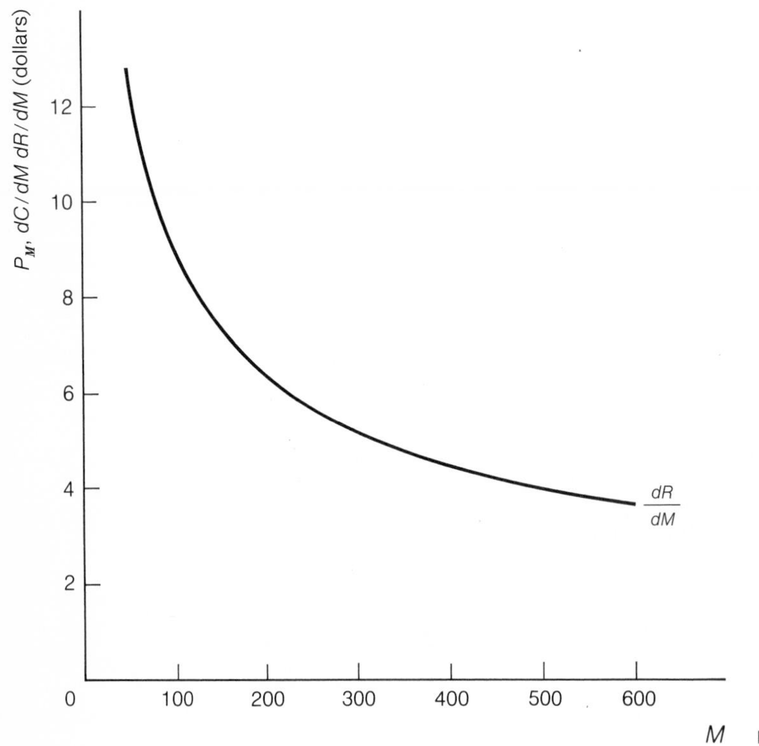

FIGURE 15-B

d To maximize his profits in the short run this monopsonist selling *Y* in a perfectly competitive market should employ __________ units of *M* and set the price of *M* at $__________

e If the firm employs this quantity of M:

(1) $Y =$ ____________

(2) $R =$ $____________

(3) $C =$ $____________

(4) $\pi =$ $____________

3 Assuming that $Y = M^a \cdot N^{1-a}$, $a < 1$, $P_M = (M - b)/c$, $P_Y = (g - Y)/h$, and $N = \bar{N}$:

a $dC/dM =$ ____________

b $dY/dM =$ ____________

c $dR/dY =$ ____________

d $dR/dM =$ ____________

e To maximize his short-run profit this monopsonist who monopolizes the sale of Y should employ the quantity of M that satisfies the equation ____________ = ____________ provided that:

(1) ____________

(2) ____________

4 If we assume that

$$Y = M^{0.5} \cdot N^{0.5}$$

$$P_M = \frac{M + 32}{100}$$

$$P_Y = \frac{22{,}440 - Y}{500}$$

$$N = 100$$

$$P_N = \$20$$

then:

a $dR/dM =$ ____________

b $dC/dM =$ ____________

c The marginal-revenue-product function has been plotted on the graph on the next page. Plot on this graph the supply function and the marginal-resource-cost function for M.

d To maximize his profits in the short run a monopsonist who monopolizes the sale of Y should employ ____________ units of M and set the price of M at $____________.

e If the firm employs this quantity of M:

(1) $Y =$ ____________

(2) $P_Y =$ $____________

(3) $R =$ $____________

(4) $C =$ $____________

(5) $\pi =$ $____________

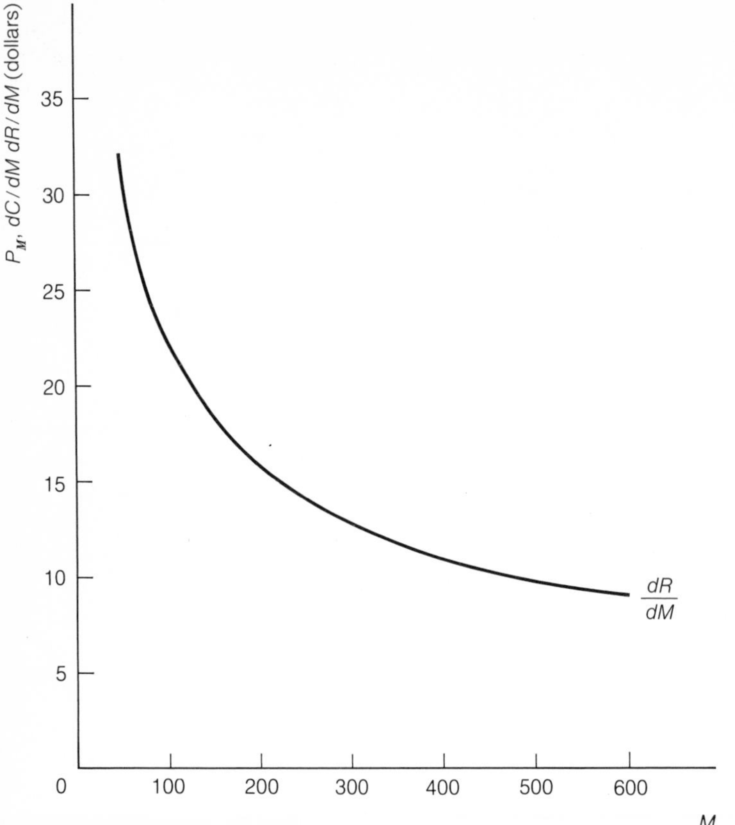

FIGURE 15-C

EQUILIBRIUM IN THE LONG RUN

In the long run a firm has no fixed inputs and no fixed costs. All its inputs and all its costs are variable. But the goal of the firm in the long run, we assume, is the same as its goal in the short run—maximization of its economic profit.

If a firm is to maximize its profit in the long run, it must produce whatever output it decides to produce at the lowest possible cost. The *least-cost combination* of inputs is the combination of inputs that enables the firm to minimize the cost of producing a given output. To maximize its profits a firm must employ inputs in the least-cost combination. But it must also determine what output to produce and therefore what quantity of each input to employ.

The first thing we determine in this section is the *proportion* in which a firm must employ inputs if it is to produce an output at the least cost, and the second is the *amount* of each input the firm must employ if it is to maximize its profit.

The least-cost combination of inputs

Assuming that the firm employs two inputs, L and K, both of which are variable, to produce a single product X, the firm's cost function is

$$C \equiv L \cdot P_L + K \cdot P_K \tag{15-51}$$

We can see in equation 15-51 that a firm's cost depends upon the quantities of L and K employed and the prices the firm pays for L and K. If the firm changed by very small amounts the quantities of L and K it employs, cost would also change by a very small amount equal to dC. This small change in cost would equal the small change dL in the quantity of L employed multiplied by the marginal resource cost of L *plus* the small change dK in the quantity of K employed multiplied by the marginal resource cost of L. In mathematical terms we can say

$$dC \equiv dL \frac{\partial C}{\partial L} + dK \frac{\partial C}{\partial K} \qquad (15\text{-}52)$$

where $\partial C/\partial L$ and $\partial C/\partial K$ are the marginal resource costs of L and K, respectively.[11]

If the cost of producing a given output is a minimum (or a maximum), any further very small change in either L or K will not bring a further change in costs. We show mathematically that costs must neither increase nor decrease by writing

$$dC = 0 \qquad (15\text{-}53)$$

For the cost of producing a given output to be a minimum, dC in equation 15-52 must be zero and we can write

$$0 = dL \frac{\partial C}{\partial L} + dK \frac{\partial C}{\partial K} \qquad (15\text{-}54)$$

Subtracting $dK\ \partial C/\partial K$ from both sides of equation 15-54 leaves us with

$$-dK \frac{\partial C}{\partial K} = dL \frac{\partial C}{\partial L}$$

Dividing through by dL,

$$-\frac{dK}{dL} \frac{\partial C}{\partial K} = \frac{\partial C}{\partial L}$$

And dividing through by $\partial C/\partial K$ gives us the equation we have been looking for.

$$-\frac{dK}{dL} = \frac{\partial C/\partial L}{\partial C/\partial K} \qquad (15\text{-}55)$$

Let us set equation 15-55 aside for a minute and return to the firm's production function

$$X = f(L,K) \qquad (15\text{-}1)$$

in which L and K are both variable. When the firm changes its employment of L and K by small amounts, the firm's output will also change by a small amount dX. This small change in the firm's output will be equal to the small change in L times the marginal product of L *plus* the small change in K times the marginal product of K, or

$$dX = dL \frac{\partial X}{\partial L} + dK \frac{\partial X}{\partial K} \qquad (15\text{-}56)$$

[11] dC, dL, and dK are very small changes in C, L, and K, respectively, and are approximately equal to ΔC, ΔL, and ΔK, respectively. We assume that the changes in L and K are so very small that $dL = \Delta L$, $dK = \Delta K$, and, as a result, $dC = \Delta C$.

To produce any *given* (or fixed) output, the output of the firm must remain constant: there must be no change in X. To keep X constant it is therefore necessary that

$$dX = 0 \tag{15-57}$$

Substituting zero for dX in equation 15-56, we have

$$0 = dL\,\frac{\partial X}{\partial L} + dK\,\frac{\partial X}{\partial K} \tag{15-58}$$

which can be rewritten

$$-dK\,\frac{\partial X}{\partial K} = dL\,\frac{\partial X}{\partial L} \tag{15-59}$$

Dividing through by dL, we have

$$-\frac{dK}{dL}\frac{\partial X}{\partial K} = \frac{\partial X}{\partial L} \tag{15-60}$$

and dividing through by $\partial X/\partial K$ gives another equation we have been looking for.

$$-\frac{dK}{dL} = \frac{\partial X/\partial L}{\partial X/\partial K} \tag{15-61}$$

Equation 15-61 tells us that if the firm's output is constant, when L and K change by small amounts, the ratio of the change in K to the change in L equals the marginal product of L divided by the marginal product of K. The minus sign preceding the left side of the equations means that an increase in K must be accompanied by a decrease in L (and vice versa) if the output of the firm is to remain unchanged.

Now let us combine equations 15-55 and 15-61. Since the left sides of these two equations are equal to $-dK/dL$, we can set the right sides equal to each other.

$$\frac{\partial C/\partial L}{\partial C/\partial K} = \frac{\partial X/\partial L}{\partial X/\partial K} \tag{15-62}$$

If we multiply through by $\partial X/\partial K$, we have

$$\frac{\partial C/\partial L}{\partial C/\partial K}\frac{\partial X}{\partial K} = \frac{\partial X}{\partial L}$$

When we divide both sides by $\partial C/\partial L$, we obtain

$$\frac{\partial X/\partial K}{\partial C/\partial K} = \frac{\partial X/\partial L}{\partial C/\partial L} \tag{15-63}$$

What does equation 15-63 tell us? It says that if the firm is to produce any given output at the least cost, the inputs L and K must be combined in such a way that *the marginal product $\partial X/\partial K$ of K divided by the marginal resource cost $\partial C/\partial K$ of K is equal to the marginal product $\partial X/\partial L$ of L divided by the marginal resource cost $\partial C/\partial L$ of L*. The least-cost combination of (any number of) inputs is the combination in which the ratio of the marginal product of an input to its marginal resource cost is the same for all inputs.

A special case: the perfectly competitive employer A firm that is a perfectly competitive employer of an input (we learned in Chapter 14) finds that the marginal resource cost of an input is equal to the price of that input. Assuming the firm employing L and K is a perfectly competitive employer of both L and K, then

$$\frac{\partial C}{\partial K} = P_K$$

$$\frac{\partial C}{\partial L} = P_L$$

For $\partial C/\partial K$ and $\partial C/\partial L$ in equation 15-63, therefore, we may substitute P_K and P_L, respectively, and write

$$\frac{\partial X/\partial K}{P_K} = \frac{\partial X/\partial L}{P_L} \qquad (15\text{-}64)$$

To minimize the cost of producing a given output, the perfectly competitive employer of inputs must combine L and K so that the marginal product of K divided by its price is equal to the marginal product of L divided by its price. Equation 15-64 is nothing more than a special case of equation 15-63; it applies only when the firm employs inputs in perfectly competitive markets.

Numerical examples Let us look at two numerical examples of the least-cost combination of inputs. In both examples the firm's production function is

$$X = L^{0.75} \cdot K^{0.25} \qquad (15\text{-}19)$$

Example 1 The firm in this example is a perfectly competitive employer of both L and K, and

$$P_L = \$1$$
$$P_K = \$2$$

The firm wishes to produce 30 units of X at the lowest possible cost. Substituting 30 for X in equation 15-19,

$$30 = L^{0.75} \cdot K^{0.25} \qquad (15\text{-}65)$$

and

$$K^{0.25} = \frac{30}{L^{0.75}} \qquad (15\text{-}66)$$

$$L^{0.75} = \frac{30}{K^{0.25}} \qquad (15\text{-}67)$$

The marginal-product functions for L and K are

$$\frac{\partial X}{\partial L} = 0.75\left(\frac{K}{L}\right)^{0.25} \qquad (15\text{-}68)$$

$$\frac{\partial X}{\partial K} = 0.25\left(\frac{L}{K}\right)^{0.75} \qquad (15\text{-}69)$$

Substituting in equation 15-64,

$$\frac{0.75(K/L)^{0.25}}{\$1} = \frac{0.25(L/K)^{0.75}}{\$2}$$

$$0.75\,\frac{K^{0.25}}{L^{0.25}} = 0.125\,\frac{L^{0.75}}{K^{0.75}}$$

Substituting from equation 15-66,

$$0.75 \frac{30/L^{0.75}}{L^{0.25}} = 0.125 \frac{L^{0.75}}{(30/L^{0.75})^3}$$

We can solve for L in this last equation with the help of logarithms.

$$\log 0.75 + \log 30 - 0.75 \log L - 0.25 \log L = \log 0.125 + 0.75 \log L - 3(\log 30 - 0.75 \log L)$$

$$\log L = \log 30 + \frac{\log 0.75 - \log 0.125}{4}$$

$$= 1.47712 + 0.1945375 = 1.6716575$$

$$L = 46.95$$

Having found L, we can find K by using equation 15-66 and logarithms.

$$K = 7.821$$

If we substitute 46.95 and 7.821 for L and K, respectively, in equation 14-65, we find that the firm's output is the 30 we wished it to be. Employing equations 15-68 and 15-69, we find

$$\frac{\partial X}{\partial L} = 0.4792$$

$$\frac{\partial X}{\partial K} = 0.9584$$

Equation 15-64 is satisfied since

$$\frac{0.4792}{\$1} = \frac{0.9584}{\$2}$$

The firm is able to produce $30X$ because

$$\begin{aligned} 30 &= 46.95^{0.75}(7.821^{0.25}) \\ &= 17.94(1.672) \\ &= 30 \end{aligned}$$

And the total cost of producing $30X$ is

$$\begin{aligned} C &= 46.95(\$1) + 7.821(\$2) \\ &= \$46.95 + \$15.64 \\ &= \$62.59 \end{aligned}$$

Example 2 The firm in this example is a monopsonistic employer of both L and K, and

$$P_L = \tfrac{1}{2}L \qquad (15\text{-}70)$$

$$P_K = \tfrac{1}{5}K \qquad (15\text{-}71)$$

This firm also wishes to produce 30 units of X at the lowest possible cost, and so again

$$30 = L^{0.75} \cdot K^{0.25} \qquad (15\text{-}65)$$

$$K^{0.25} = \frac{30}{L^{0.75}} \qquad (15\text{-}66)$$

$$L^{0.75} = \frac{30}{K^{0.25}} \qquad (15\text{-}67)$$

$$\frac{\partial X}{\partial L} = 0.75\left(\frac{K}{L}\right)^{0.25} \tag{15-68}$$

$$\frac{\partial X}{\partial K} = 0.25\left(\frac{L}{K}\right)^{0.75} \tag{15-69}$$

Given the supply functions for the two inputs (equations 15-70 and 15-71) we can determine the marginal-resource-cost functions for L and K by employing equation 15-42.

$$\frac{\partial C}{\partial L} = L \tag{15-72}$$

$$\frac{\partial C}{\partial K} = \frac{2}{5}K \tag{15-73}$$

Now we have all information we need to apply equation 15-64.

$$\frac{0.75(K/L)^{0.25}}{L} = \frac{0.25(L/K)^{0.75}}{{}^{2}\!/_{5}K}$$

$$\frac{3(K^{0.25}/L^{0.25})}{L} = \frac{L^{0.75}/K^{0.75}}{{}^{2}\!/_{5}K}$$

Substituting from equation 15-66,

$$\frac{3\left(\dfrac{30/L^{0.75}}{L^{0.25}}\right)}{L} = \frac{L^{0.75}/(30/L^{0.75})^{3}}{{}^{2}\!/_{5}(30/L^{0.75})^{4}}$$

Skipping several intermediate steps, this last equation can be reduced to

$$L^{8} = {}^{6}\!/_{5}(30^{8})$$

Now we employ logarithms.

$$8 \log L = \log 1.2 + 8 \log 30$$

$$\begin{aligned}\log L &= \frac{\log 1.2 + 8 \log 30}{8}\\ &= \frac{0.07918 + 11.81696}{8}\\ &= \frac{11.89614}{8}\\ &= 1.48702\end{aligned}$$

$$L = 30.69$$

Substituting 30.69 for L into equation 15-66 and again employing logarithms,

$$K = 28.02$$

When we substitute 30.69 and 28.02 for L and K, respectively, in equation 15-65, we find

$$30 = (30.69)^{0.75}(28.02)^{0.25}$$

Equations 15-68 and 15-69 enable us to find the marginal products of L and K.

$$\frac{\partial X}{\partial L} = 0.7331$$

$$\frac{\partial X}{\partial K} = 0.2676$$

Equation 15-64 is satisfied because

$$\frac{0.7331}{L} = \frac{0.2676}{\frac{2}{5}K}$$

$$\frac{0.7331}{30.69} = \frac{0.2676}{\frac{2}{5}(28.02)}$$

$$\frac{0.7331}{30.69} = \frac{0.2676}{11.21}$$

$$0.0239 = 0.0239 \qquad \text{approximately}$$

When the firm employs these quantities of L and K, it sets their prices at

$$P_L = \tfrac{1}{2}L = \tfrac{1}{2}(30.69) = \$15.345$$
$$P_K = \tfrac{1}{5}K = \tfrac{1}{5}(28.02) + \$11.208$$

The total cost of producing the 30 units of X is a minimum and is equal to

$$\begin{aligned} C &= \$15.345(30.69) + \$11.208(28.02) \\ &= \$470.94 + \$314.05 \\ &= \$784.99 \end{aligned}$$

Profit maximization in the long run

We saw in the first section of this chapter that to maximize its profit in the short run the firm must equate the marginal resource cost and the marginal revenue product of the variable input; or, where L is the variable input, it is necessary that

$$\frac{\partial C}{\partial L} = \frac{\partial R}{\partial L} \qquad (15\text{-}6a)$$

provided that

$$\frac{\partial^2 C}{\partial L^2} > \frac{\partial^2 R}{\partial L^2} \qquad (15\text{-}8a)$$

and

$$\frac{R}{L} > P_L \qquad (15\text{-}9)$$

To maximize its profit in the long run when no inputs are fixed and *both* L and K are variable inputs it is necessary that the marginal resource cost of *each* input equal its marginal revenue product, or, using symbols when L and K are two variable inputs, that

$$\frac{\partial C}{\partial L} = \frac{\partial R}{\partial L} \qquad (15\text{-}6a)$$

$$\frac{\partial C}{\partial K} = \frac{\partial R}{\partial K} \qquad (15\text{-}6b)$$

and that

$$\frac{\partial^2 C}{\partial L^2} > \frac{\partial^2 R}{\partial L^2} \qquad (15\text{-}8a)$$

$$\frac{\partial^2 C}{\partial K^2} > \frac{\partial^2 R}{\partial K^2} \tag{15-8b}$$

If the firm is to employ these quantities of L and K, it must not find that its profit is negative.[12] If it hired these amounts of L and K and found it had a loss (because its costs exceed its revenue) it would maximize its profit (minimize its loss) by closing down, producing no output, and employing no amount of either L or K. In short, the profit-maximizing firm must have a revenue greater than or equal to its costs. It is also necessary, therefore, that

$$R \geqq C \tag{15-74}$$

or, substituting the right side of the firm's cost function (equation 15-51) for C, that

$$R \geqq L \cdot P_L + K \cdot P_K \tag{15-75}$$

The perfectly competitive employer For the firm that is a perfectly competitive employer of both L and K we may rewrite equations 15-6*a* and 15-6*b*. Because the marginal resource cost of L is equal to its price and the marginal resource cost of K is equal to its price, the perfectly competitive employer of inputs is maximizing its profit in the long run when

$$P_L = \frac{\partial R}{\partial L} \tag{15-76a}$$

$$P_K = \frac{\partial R}{\partial K} \tag{15-76b}$$

The perfectly competitive employer of L and K maximizes its profit when the price of L equals its marginal revenue product and the price of K equals its marginal revenue product, provided that inequalities 15-8*a* and 15-8*b* and inequality 15-75 are satisfied.

For $\partial^2 C/\partial L^2$ and $\partial^2 C/\partial L^2$ in inequalities 15-8*a* and 15-8*b* we may substitute zero because, as we learned earlier, the slopes of the marginal-resource-cost curves are zero when the firm hires inputs under perfectly competitive conditions. Thus

$$0 > \frac{\partial^2 R}{\partial L^2} \tag{15-77a}$$

$$0 > \frac{\partial^2 R}{\partial K^2} \tag{15-77b}$$

For the firm's profit to be a maximum rather than a minimum, the slopes of the marginal-revenue-product curves for both L and K must be negative.

The profit-maximizing output If a firm employs the quantities of L and K that satisfy equations 15-6*a* and 15-6*b*, it also produces an *output of X* that maximizes its profit, the amount of X at which the marginal cost of X and the marginal revenue from X are equal.

When a firm employs two inputs, L and K, it is able to change its output of

[12] In addition to inequalities 15-8*a* and 15-8*b*, a more complicated inequality must be satisfied if profit is to be a maximum. This inequality is beyond the scope of the mathematics in this book, and we shall simply assume that it is satisfied.

X only by changing the amount of L, the amount of K, or the amount of both L and K it employs. Let us consider input L first and multiply equation 15-6*a* by $\partial L/\partial X$, the inverse of the marginal product of input L.

$$\frac{\partial C}{\partial L} = \frac{\partial R}{\partial L} \tag{15-6a}$$

$$\frac{\partial C}{\partial L}\frac{\partial L}{\partial X} = \frac{\partial R}{\partial L}\frac{\partial L}{\partial X}$$

$$\frac{\partial C}{\partial X_L} = \frac{\partial R}{\partial X} \tag{15-78a}$$

The marginal cost of X *by varying* L, equation 15-78*a* tells us, is equal to the marginal revenue from the sale of X.

In a similar way, if we multiply 15-6*b* by $\partial K/\partial X$, the inverse of the marginal product of K, we have

$$\frac{\partial C}{\partial K} = \frac{\partial R}{\partial K} \tag{15-6b}$$

$$\frac{\partial C}{\partial K}\frac{\partial K}{\partial X} = \frac{\partial R}{\partial K}\frac{\partial K}{\partial X}$$

$$\frac{\partial C}{\partial X_K} = \frac{\partial R}{\partial X} \tag{15-78b}$$

The marginal cost of X *by varying* K is equal to the marginal revenue from the sale of X.

Thus if the marginal cost of X by varying either L or K is equal to marginal revenue, the marginal cost of X—no matter whether X and the cost of X are varied by changing L or K—must be equal to the marginal revenue from X.

Summary

To maximize its profit in the long run the firm must produce any output it might decide to produce by combining L and K in the least-cost combination, i.e., so that

$$\frac{\partial X/\partial L}{\partial C/\partial L} = \frac{\partial X/\partial K}{\partial C/\partial K} \tag{15-63}$$

The marginal product of L divided by its marginal resource cost must equal the marginal product of K divided by its marginal resource cost.

Let us multiply equation 15-63 by marginal revenue, dR/dX. The result,

$$\frac{\dfrac{\partial X}{\partial L}\dfrac{dR}{dX}}{\dfrac{\partial C}{\partial L}} = \frac{\dfrac{\partial X}{\partial K}\dfrac{dR}{dX}}{\dfrac{\partial C}{\partial K}}$$

and, employing equations 14-9 and 14-12,

$$\frac{\partial R/\partial L}{\partial C/\partial L} = \frac{\partial R/\partial K}{\partial C/\partial K} \tag{15-79}$$

We recognize $\partial R/\partial L$ and $\partial R/\partial K$ as the marginal revenue product of L and the marginal revenue product of K, respectively. Equation 15-79 tells us that the least-cost combination of the inputs is also the combination of L and K in which the marginal revenue product of L divided by its marginal resource cost is equal to the marginal revenue product of K divided by its marginal research cost.

We now combine this new equation for the least-cost combination of inputs (equation 15-79) with the expressions for the most profitable amounts of inputs (equations 15-6*a* and 15-6*b*) to obtain a single equation which will tell us when the firm is employing inputs in the best proportion *and* in the best amounts.

If, to maximize profits, $\partial R/\partial L$ must equal $\partial C/\partial L$, then the *ratio* of $\partial R/\partial L$ to $\partial C/\partial L$ must be equal to 1. [3 is equal to 3; and the ratio of 3 to 3 (3/3) is equal to 1.] Similarly, if $\partial R/\partial K$ must equal $\partial C/\partial K$ to maximize profits, then the *ratio* of $\partial R/\partial K$ to $\partial C/\partial K$ must equal 1. In terms of equations, then, it is necessary that

$$\frac{\partial R/\partial L}{\partial C/\partial L} = 1 \tag{15-80}$$

and

$$\frac{\partial R/\partial K}{\partial C/\partial K} = 1 \tag{15-80a}$$

If these two ratios are both equal to 1, we may write

$$\frac{\partial R/\partial L}{\partial C/\partial L} = \frac{\partial R/\partial K}{\partial C/\partial K} = 1 \tag{15-81}$$

The firm is employing inputs in the least-cost combination and employing the quantity of each input that maximizes its profit when *the ratio of the marginal revenue product of each input to its marginal resource cost is equal to* 1. When equation 15-81 is satisfied, so are expressions 15-6*a*, 15-6*b*, and 15-79 (and 15-63 as well).

When the firm employs L and K in perfectly competitive markets, we may substitute the price of L for the marginal resource cost of L and the price of K for the marginal resource cost of K and rewrite equation 15-81 as

$$\frac{\partial R/\partial L}{P_L} = \frac{\partial R/\partial K}{P_K} = 1 \tag{15-82}$$

The perfectly competitive employer of inputs employs inputs in the least-cost combination and in amounts that maximize its profit when the ratio of the marginal revenue product of each input to its price is equal to 1.

We provide no numerical examples of the employment of L and K that maximizes profit in the long run, because the arithmetic involved is far too complex. We cannot plot the marginal revenue product of either L or K on a two-dimensional graph because each depends upon the quantity of both L and K employed by the firm. Profit maximization must remain without numerical examples.

Exercise 15-3

1 In the long run the firm seeking to maximize its profits must determine:

a In what ____________ to employ inputs if it wishes to produce any given output at the ____________ cost.

b The total ____________ of each input to employ.

2 Assume the firm's production function is $Y = M^a \cdot N^{1-a}$ and that a is less than 1.

a The firm's total cost function is $C =$ __________

b A small change in the firm's costs is dC, and $dC =$ __________

c If the cost of producing a given output is to be a minimum, it is necessary that $dC =$ __________

d Substituting your answer in part *c* above for dC in your answer to part *b*, the cost of producing a given output is a minimum when:

(1) $\_\_\_\_\_\_\_\_ = d\_\_\_\_ \frac{\partial}{\partial\_\_} + d\_\_\_\_ \frac{\partial}{\partial\_\_}$

(2) Or when $-\frac{d}{d\_\_} = \frac{\partial \quad / \partial}{\partial\_\_/\partial\_\_}$

3 When Y is a function of M and N:

a Any small change in the firm's output is dY, and

$dY = d\_\_\_\_ \frac{\_\_}{\_\_} + d\_\_\_\_ \frac{\_\_}{\_\_}$

b To produce a given output, there must be no change in the firm's output. dY must equal __________.

c Combining your answers to parts *a* and *b* above, when the firm produces a given output:

(1) $\_\_\_\_\_\_\_\_ = d\_\_\_\_ \frac{\partial}{\partial\_\_} + d\_\_\_\_ \frac{\partial}{\partial\_\_}$

(2) $-\frac{d}{d\_\_} = \frac{\partial \quad / \partial}{\partial\_\_/\partial\_\_}$

4 Employing your final answers in questions 2 and 3, the firm produces a given output at the least cost when:

a $\frac{\partial \quad / \partial}{\partial\_\_/\partial\_\_} = \frac{\partial \quad / \partial}{\partial\_\_/\partial\_\_}$

b Or when

$\frac{\partial \quad / \partial}{\partial\_\_/\partial\_\_} = \frac{\partial \quad / \partial}{\partial\_\_/\partial\_\_}$

c Or if the firm employs M and N in perfectly competitive markets, when

$\frac{\partial \quad / \partial}{\_\_\_\_} = \frac{\partial \quad / \partial}{\_\_\_\_}$

5 Suppose

$Y = M^{0.5} \cdot N^{0.5}$
$P_M = \$2$
$P_N = \$2/9$

and the firm wishes to produce $75Y$ at the least cost.

a $\partial Y/\partial M =$ __________, and $\partial Y/\partial N =$ __________

b $\partial C/\partial M = \$$__________, and $\partial C/\partial N = \$$__________

c The firm should employ __________ M and __________ N.

d If it employs these quantities of M and N:

(1) $\partial Y/\partial M =$ __________

(2) $\partial Y/\partial N =$ ______

e The marginal product of each input divided by its price is ______

6 Suppose

$$Y = M^{0.5} \cdot N^{0.5}$$
$$P_M = \tfrac{1}{128}M$$
$$P_N = 2N$$

a The marginal-resource-cost functions are:

(1) $\partial C/\partial M =$ ______

(2) $\partial C/\partial N =$ ______

b The marginal-product functions are:

(1) $\partial Y/\partial M =$ ______

(2) $\partial Y/\partial N =$ ______

c If the firm wishes to produce 64Y at the least cost, it should employ ______ M and ______ N.

d When it employs these quantities of M and N:

(1) $\partial Y/\partial M =$ ______

(2) $\partial Y/\partial N =$ ______

(3) $\partial C/\partial M =$ $ ______

(4) $\partial C/\partial N =$ $ ______

e The ratio of the marginal product to marginal resource cost for both inputs is equal to ______ / $ ______

f The firm will set the price of:

(1) M at $ ______

(2) N at $ ______

g The total cost of producing the 64Y will be $ ______

7 A firm employing two variable inputs, M and N, in the long run maximizes its profit:

a When:

(1) ______ = ______

(2) ______ = ______

b Or if it is a perfectly competitive employer of M and N, when:

(1) ______ = ______

(2) ______ = ______

c Provided that:

(1) ______

(2) ______

d And ______

8 Demonstrate that when a firm employs the quantities of M and N that maximize its profit in the long run, the marginal cost of producing its product and the marginal revenue from its sale are equal.

9 Prove that when the ratio of the marginal revenue product of each input to its marginal resource cost is equal to 1, the firm is employing inputs in the least-cost combination and in quantities that maximize its long-run profits.

ANSWERS TO EXERCISES

Exercise 1-1

1 variable

2 values

3 a change in; *a*. change in, *R*; *b*. 0.10; *c*. -0.05

4 *ceteris paribus*

5 equal to; *a*. side, member, right side, right member; *b*. terms, variables, parameters; *c*. plus, minus

6 *a*. functional, behavioral; *b*. definitional, identity; *c*. equilibrium

7 *a*. (1) function, (2) functional notation, (3) change; *b*. (1) 70, (2) 80, (3) 20, (4) -40, (5) shift, change

8 $\equiv$, definitional, identity

9 what the magnitude of particular variables will be

10 -40, -120

Exercise 1-2

1 *a*. $W < Z$; *b*. $W > Z$; *c*. $W \geqq Z$; *d*. $W \leqq Z$

2 first, an equation in which the greatest exponent is 1 and the variables are not multiplied by each other

3 second-degree, nonlinear, curvilinear

4 *a*. first; *b*. first; *c*. first; *d*. second; *e*. first

5 *a.* zero; *b.* W; *c.* slope

6 *a.* −100; *b.* 166⅔; *c.* 0.6; *d.* (1) the point at which the curve crosses the U axis, (2) the slope of the curve

7 *a.* (1) $c + e(Z + \Delta Z)$, (2) $e\,\Delta Z$, (3) e; *b.* (1) $g[-h(Q + \Delta Q)]$, (2) $-h\,\Delta Q$, (3) $-h$; *c.* (1) $-100 + 0.6(T + \Delta T)$, (2) $0.6\Delta T$, (3) 0.6; *d.* (1) $150 - 3(V + \Delta V)$, (2) $-3\Delta V$, (3) −3

9 *a.* the first and second ones; *b.* $U = -100, 75, 80, -10$; $\Delta U/\Delta T = 0.5, 0.6, -0.3, -0.2$

Exercise 1-3

1 equations, system, equations

2 *a.* endogenous; *b.* exogenous, ‾

3 equal, variables, different, consistent

4 *a.* they are the same equation; *b.* they are not consistent; *c.* they are not consistent; *d.* they are the same equation

5 *a.* closed, three; *b.* $\frac{a + c}{b + e}$; *c.* (1) $\frac{\Delta a}{b + e}$, (2) $\frac{1}{b + e}$

6 *a.* 22; *b.* 34; *c.* (1) −2, (2) −4

7 *a.* open, four; *b.* G, exogenous; *c.* (1) Y, I, (2) S, Y, (3) I, S; *d.* (1) $\frac{a + I + \bar{G}}{c}$, (2) $-a + cY - \bar{G}$, (3) $I + \bar{G}$

8 *a.* (1) $I + 50$, (2) $S - 50$, (3) $\frac{I + 60}{0.2}$; *b.* (1) 10, (2) −10, (3) 10/0.2; *c.* (1) −10, (2) −10, (3) −10/0.2

Exercise 2-1

1 *a.* Y; *b.* $C + I$; *c.* $C + S$; $Y - C$

2 *a.* $D = Y$; *b.* $C + S = C + S$; *c.* $I = S$

3 *a.* greater than zero; *b.* less than 1; *c.* less than 1

4 *a.* $\Delta C/\Delta Y$; *b.* $\Delta S/\Delta Y$; *c.* C/Y; *d.* S/Y

6 *a.* $-100 + 0.20Y$; *b.* 0.80; *c.* 0.20; *d.* (1) 1.3, (2) −0.3; *e.* 100

9 −10, 0, 10, 20, 30; *b.* $C = 20 + 0.9Y$; *c.* $S = -20 + 0.1Y$

10 *a.* $150/Y + 0.7$; *b.* $-150/Y + 0.3$

Exercise 2-2

1 $C = C_0 + bY$, $I = \bar{I}$, $D \equiv C + I$, $D = Y$

2 *a.* C, D, Y; *b.* I; *c.* behavioral, definitional, equilibrium

4 $S = -C_0 + (1 - b)Y$, $I = \bar{I}$, $S = I$, 3, S, Y

6 *a.* 450; *b.* 400; *c.* 50; *d.* 450

7 *a.* k_C, $\Delta Y^*/\Delta C_0$; *b.* k_I, $\Delta Y^*/\Delta \bar{I}$

9 *a.* increase, 25; *b.* decrease, 45; *c.* increase, 20; *d.* decrease, 15

10 *a.* +10; *b.* −7.2

Exercise 2-3

1 increasing, linear, national income

2 *a*. autonomous; *b*. induced; *c*. marginal propensity, invest, *m*

3 *a*. 0.0625; *b*. 5; *c*. increase, 1; *d*. decrease, 2.5

4 $C = C_0 + bY$, $I = I_0 + mY$, $D \equiv C + I$, $Y = D$, C, I, D, Y

5 $S = -C_0 + (1 - b)Y$, $I = I_0 + mY$, $S = I$

7 *a*. 400; *b*. 330; *c*. 70; *d*. 70; *e*. 400

8 *a*. $\Delta Y^*/\Delta C_0$, K_C; *b*. $\Delta Y^*/\Delta I_0$, K_I

10 *a*. $3\frac{1}{3}$; *b*. increase, 70; *c*. decrease, 20; *d*. increase, 60; *e*. decrease, 80

Exercise 2-4

1 $C = C_0 + bY$, $D \equiv C + I$, $D = Y$, $I = I_0 - ji$, $i = \bar{i}$, C, Y, I, D

2 *a*. the interest rate; *b*. interest rate = investment; *c*. $-j$

3 *a*. increase, 8; *b*. decrease, 12

5 *a*. 820; *b*. 736; *c*. 84; *d*. 820; *e*. 84

7 *a*. 5; *b*. −20

8 *a*. decrease, 15; *b*. increase, 25; *c*. decrease, 40; *d*. increase, 30

9 *a*. −1%; *b*. $+1\frac{1}{3}$%

10 −15

Exercise 3-1

1 *a*. Tx, Tr; *b*. Y, T; *c*. Y_d, C; *d*. $\Delta C/\Delta Y_d$; *e*. $\Delta S/\Delta Y_d$; *f*. C/Y_d; *g*. S/Y_d

2 *a*. $-40 + 0.4Y_d$; *b*. 0.6; *c*. 0.4

3 *a*. 550; *b*. 370; *c*. 180

4 *a*. C_0 is greater than zero, and b and $1 - b$ are less than 1

6 *a*. (1) $30/Y_d + 0.7$ (2) $-30/Y_d + (0.3)$; *b*. 0.76, 0.24

7 D

8 C, I, G

10 exogenous

Exercise 3-2

1 *a*. $Y_d \equiv Y - T$, $D \equiv C + I + G$, $D = Y$; *b*. (1) 330; (2) 300; (3) 260; (4) 40; (5) 330

4 (2) 10, 5, 4, 3, $2\frac{1}{2}$, 2; (3) −9, −4, −3, −2, $-1\frac{1}{2}$, −1

5 *a*. increase, $33\frac{1}{3}$; *b*. decrease, $42\frac{6}{7}$; *c*. increase, 100

Exercise 3-3

1 taxes are a function of national income instead of being exogenous

2 *a*. $\Delta T/\Delta Y$; *c*. autonomous taxes

3 $C = C_0 + bY_d$, $T = T_0 + tY$, $I = \bar{I}$, $G = \bar{G}$, $Y_d \equiv Y - T$, $D \equiv C + I + G$, $Y = D$; *a*. C, Y_d, T, Y, D; *b*. Y_d, C

5 *a.* $-100 + 0.25Y_d$; *b.* (1) 450, (2) 310, (3) 170, (4) 280, (5) 450, (6) -30; *c.* surplus, 110; *d.* $-30 + 170 = 80 + 60 = 140$

6 *a.* 2; *b.* $-1\frac{1}{4}$

8 *a.* 2; *b.* 2

9 *a.* -27; *b.* $+54$; *c.* -81; *d.* -121.5 (all approximate)

11 because the MPC is less than 1

12 the greater the value of *t*, the smaller are k_T and k_G

Exercise 4-1

1 *a.* undistributed, personal; *b.* personal, personal, NNP, NI, PI

2 *a.* Y_d, *T*; *b.* *C, I, G, X, M*

3 $\bar{X}$, $\bar{G}$, $\bar{I}$

4 *a.* C_0, bY_d; *b.* I_0, *ji*; *c.* T_0, *tY*; *d.* N_0, *mY*

5 *a.* autonomous, greater than, equal to; *b.* *M, Y,* marginal propensity, import; *c.* zero, one

6 *Y, D*; *a.* *S, T, M, I, G, X*; *b.* *S, T, I, G, X, M*

7 Y_d, *C*

8 $C_0 + bY_d$, $I_0 - ji$, $T_0 + tY$, $N_0 + mY$, $Y - T$, $\bar{I}$, $\bar{G}$, $\bar{X}$, $C + I + G + X - M$, *D, Y*; *a.* *C*, Y_d, *T, Y, I, M, D*; *c.* $b - bt - m$, 1

9 *a.* 160; *b.* 84; *c.* 76; *d.* 107; *e.* 12; *f.* 19; *g.* 160; *h.* -31

10 *a.* 72; *b.* 72; *c.* 1; *d.* 1

Exercise 4-2

1 the ratio the change in equilibrium national income resulting from a change in exogenous exports to the change in exogenous exports

3 *a.* 1.67; *b.* increase, 15; *c.* decrease, 25

5 *a.* decrease, 20; *b.* increase, 11.25; *c.* decrease, 266.67; *d.* increase, 40

6 a. $X - M$; *b.* $\Delta X - \Delta M$

8 $b - bt - m < 1$, $m > 0$, $0 < b < 1$, and $0 < t < 1$

10 *a.* increase, 22; *b.* decrease, 1.5; *c.* decrease, 0.5625; *d.* decrease, 0.5; *e.* increase, .1333; *f.* increase, 1

Exercise 5-1

1 M_c, M_d

2 *a.* constant; *b.* M_d

3 *a.* 340; *b.* increase, 40

4 (3) 300, 400, 450, 1,000, 280, 3,000

5 (3) 3, $3\frac{1}{3}$, 6, $6\frac{2}{3}$, 8, 10, 12; (4).9,000, 10,000, 14,400, 16,000, 16,000, 15,000, 12,000

6 10,800, 8,000, 5,600, 4,000, 3,000, 1,667, 600

7 $-2{,}000$, 1,067, -400, $+1{,}600$, $+66\frac{2}{3}$

9 *a.* buy government securities; lower the discount rate

10 *a.* to increase demand deposits; *b.* to decrease demand deposits

11 *a.* 100; *b.* $13\frac{1}{3}$

Exercise 5-2

1 L_t, L_a

2 kY; *a.* $0 < k < 1$

3 $L_0 - ni$; *a.* $L_0 > 0$; *b.* $n > 0$

4 *a.* (1) 0, (2) 20; *b.* $6\frac{2}{3}$; *c.* (1) 0.3, (2) −300; *d.* $0.3Y + 20 - 200i$

5 *a.* 160; *b.* 182.5; *c.* 212.5

6 *a.* decrease, 12.5; *b.* decrease, 2.5

Exercise 5-3

1 M_0, L

2 *a.* M_c, r, R; *b.* Y; *c.* M_0

3 $L_t + L_a$, kY, $L_0 - ni$, $M_0 = L$, $\bar{Y}$, $\bar{M}_0$

5 *a.* 5; *b.* (1) 90, (2) 35, (3) 125

7 *a.* increase, 3.3; *b.* decrease, 1.5; *c.* decrease, 10; *d.* decrease, 1.67

Exercise 6-1

1 Y, D, L, M

2 $C_0 + bYd$, $I_0 - ji$, $\bar{G}$, $C + I + G$, $Y - T$, $\bar{T}$, D; *a.* 8, C_0, b, I_0, j; *b.* open

4 *a.* $(160 - 0.2Y)/600$; *b.* $(160 - 600i)/0.2$; *c.* $-0.2\Delta Y^*/600$; *d.* $-600\Delta i^*/0.2$

5 (i_c^*) 10, 9, 8, 7, 6, 5, 4, 3, 2; (Y_c^*) 500, 530, 560, 590, 620, 650, 680, 710, 740

6 $-0.0003\frac{1}{3}$

Exercise 6-2

1 $L_t + L_a$, kY, $L_0 - ni$, $\bar{M}_0$, $L = M_0$; *a.* 6, k, L_0, n; *b.* open

3 *a.* $(1Y - 26)/600$; *b.* $(26 + 600i)/0.1$; *c.* $0.1\ \Delta Y^*/600$; *d.* $600\ \Delta i^*/0.1$

4 *a.* (i_m^*) 10, 9, 8, 7, 6, 5, 4, 3, 2; (Y_m^*) 860, 800, 740, 680, 620, 560, 500, 440, 380

5 $+0.0001\frac{2}{3}$

Exercise 6-3

1 $C + I + G$, Y, $L_t + L_a$, $\bar{M}_0$

3 *a.* $D \equiv C + I + G$, $Y = D$, $L \equiv L_t + L_a$, $Y_d \equiv Y - T$, $L = M_0$; *b.* 6, 620; *d.* 6, 620

4 *a.* 545; *b.* 516; *c.* 4; *d.* 620; *e.* 62; *f.* 24; *g.* 86; *h.* 620, 620; *i.* 86, 86

5 *a.* less than; *b.* greater than; *c.* less than; *d.* greater than

Exercise 6-4

2 *a.* (1) −1.67, (2) −100, (3) −100, (4) −80, (5) +10, (6) −10, (7) +10; *b.* (1) +1.78, (2) +106.7, (3) +106.7, (4) +85.3, (5) +10.7, (6) +10.7, (7) −10.7; *c.* (1) +2.22, (2) −66.7, (3) −66.7, (4) −53.3, (5) −13.2, (6) −6.67, (7) −13.2

3 *a.* +2.22; *b.* +133.3

4 *a.* −1.11; *b.* +33.3

6 *a.* −24; *b.* −24; *c.* +30

Exercise 7-1

1 an increase in the national income of an economy

2 *a.* natural resources, *b.* labor force, *c.* capital, *d.* technology; constant, capital

3 investment, I

4 capital-output ratio; *a.* K/P; *b.* $1/r$; *c.* constant, greater; *d.* K, P; *e.* $1/r$, $1/r$

5 *a.* (1) 4,000, (2) 750, (3) 400, (4) 150; *b.* 5; *c.* 4

6 *a.* $\Delta Y/Y$; *b.* $\Delta P/P$; *c.* $\Delta I/I$

7 *a.* 8.5; *b.* 20; *c.* 5; *d.* 30; *e.* 100; *f.* 8

8 b, $1 - b$; *a.* zero; *b.* zero; *c.* b; *d.* $1 - b$; *e.* b; *f.* $1 - b$; *g.* equal; *h.* equal

9 *a.* (1) $C + I$, (2) $C + S$, $C + I$, (3) S, I; *b.* (1) $C + I + G$, (2) $C + S + T$, $C + I + G$, (3) $S + G$, $I + G$

10 *a.* $I/(1 - b)$; *b.* $\Delta(I + G)/(1 - b)$

11 P, Y^*, ΔP, ΔY^*

Exercise 7-2

1 $P = Y$, $\Delta P = \Delta Y$, $\Delta I/(1 - b)$, $I/(1 - b)$, $(1/r)I$; *a.* P, Y^*, ΔP, ΔY^*, I, ΔI, b, r; *b.* open, cannot

3 *a.* 2; *b.* 2; *c.* (P) 5,000, 5,100, 5,202, (Y^*) 5,000, 5,100, 5,202, (C) 4,500, 4,590, 4,681.8, (S) 500, 510, 520.2, (I) 500, 510, 520.2

4 *a.* (P) 5,000, 5,100, (Y^*) 5,000, 5,250; (C) 4,500, 4,725, (S) 500, 525, (I) 500, 525; (1) 2, (2) inflation; *b.* (P) 5,000, 5,100, (Y^*) 5,000, 5,050, (C) 4,500, 4,545, (S) 500, 505, (I) 500, 505; (1) 1, (2) unemployment

Exercise 7-3

1 P, Y^*, $\Delta P = \Delta Y^*$, $\Delta(I + G)/(1 - b + bt)$, $(I + G)/(1 - b + bt)$, $(1/r)(I + G)$; *a.* P, Y^*, ΔP, ΔY^*, $I + G$, $\Delta(I + G)$, b, r, t; *b.* $\Delta P/P$, $\Delta Y^*/Y$, $\Delta(I + G)/(I + G)$

3 *a.* 8; *b.* 8; *c.* (P) 1,000, 1,080, 1,166.4, (Y^*) 1,000, 1,080, 1,166.4, (T) 400, 432, 466.6, (Y_d) 600, 648, 699.8, (C) 360, 388.8, 419.9, (S) 240, 259.2, 279.9, ($I + G$) 640, 691.2, 756.5; *d.* 8, *e.* 8

4 *a.* (P) 1,000, 1,080, (Y^*) 1,000, 1,050, (T) 400, 420, (Y_d) 600, 630 (C) 360, 378, (S) 240, 252, ($I + G$) 640, 672; *b.* (1) 5, (2) unemployment; *c.* (P) 1,000, 1,080, (Y^*) 1,000, 1,100, (T) 400, 440, (Y_d) 600, 660, (C) 360, 396, (S) 240, 264, ($I + G$) 640, 704; *d.* 8, inflation

5 *a.* capital-output ratio; *b.* percentage of national income saved

6 *a.* increases in productivity capacity; *b.* increases national income

7 *a.* *I* must increase by increasing amounts; *b.* they will increase by increasing amounts

8 *a.* it will decline; *b.* they will decline

Exercise 8-1

1 *a.* it is greater than zero; *b.* $\Delta D/\Delta P$; *c.* (1) physical units, (2) physical units, (3) physical units per dollar, (4) dollars; *d.* $-b$, law of demand

2 *a.* 100 bales; *b.* \$5; *c.* decreases by 20 bales; *d.* 20, 40, 60; *f.* $-1/20$

3 *a.* it may be greater than, less than, or equal to zero; *b.* it is positive; *c.* $\Delta S/\Delta P$; *d.* there is a direct relationship between price and quantity supplied

4 -40 bales; *b.* \$1.33; *c.* decreases by 30 bales; *d.* 80, 110, 140; *f.* $1/30$

5 *a.* $D = S$

6 *a.* 2.80; *b.* 44

7 *a.* competitive; *b.* product, service of a resource; *c.* market (total)

8 time

9 equilibrium price, equilibrium quantity

10 substitute the price in either the demand or supply equation

Exercise 8-2

1 *a.* *a*; *b.* *c*

2 *a.* positive; *b.* negative

4 Both *b* and *e* are positive numbers, and $1/(b + e)$ is therefore positive; *a.* when demand increases, Δa is positive and $\Delta a/(b + e)$ and $e\,\Delta a/b + e$ are therefore positive; *b.* when supply decreases, Δc is negative; therefore, $-\Delta c/(b + e)$ is positive, and $b\,\Delta a/(b + e)$ is negative

5 *a.* $+0.80$, $+24$; *b.* -2.00, -60; *c.* -0.40, $+8$; *d.* $+1.20$, -24

7 *a.* -0.40, $+28$; *b.* $+1.40$, $+22$; *c.* -1.00, -40; *d.* -2.10, -38

8 *a.* if $\Delta a > \Delta c$; *b.* if the absolute value of Δc is greater than the absolute value of Δa; *c.* if $e\,\Delta a > b\,\Delta c$; *d.* if the absolute value of $e\,\Delta a$ is greater than the absolute value of $b\,\Delta c$

10 *a.* if $\Delta a = \Delta c$, then $\Delta a - \Delta c = 0$ and $\Delta P^* = 0$; *b.* if $e\,\Delta a = -b\,\Delta c$, then $\Delta Q^* = 0$

Exercise 9-1

1 $\dfrac{100 \text{ cartons} - D}{20 \text{ cartons/dollar}}$

2 *a.* $P \cdot D$; *b.* $\Delta R/\Delta D$

3 *a.* $\dfrac{1}{b}(aD - D^2) = \dfrac{aD - D^2}{b}$; *b.* $\dfrac{1}{b}(a - 2D - \Delta D)$

4 *a.* $\dfrac{100 \text{ cartons } D - D^2}{20 \text{ cartons/dollar}}$; *b.* $\dfrac{1}{20 \text{ cartons/dollar}}(100 \text{ cartons} - 2D - \Delta D)$

5 *a.* 1; *b.* 60; *c.* 105; *d.* 80. *e.* 0.95; *f.* −1.05

7 increases, maximum, decreases

8 positive, zero, negative

Exercise 9-2

1 *a.* larger; *b.* $(1/b)(a - 2D)$; *c.* limit, derivative

2 *a.* $\frac{1}{20 \text{ cartons/dollar}}$ (100 cartons − $2D$); $\frac{1}{20 \text{ cartons/dollar}}$ (100 cartons − $2D$)

3 limit, ΔD, zero

4 *a.* $Y + \Delta Y$; *b.* Y; *c.* the value of C when $Y = Y + \Delta Y$, the value of C when $Y = Y$; *d.* ΔY; ΔY

5 *a.* h; *b.* zero; *c.* $3aY^2 - 2bY$; *d.* $2aY$; *e.* naY^{n-1}

6 *a.* $12X^3$; *b.* zero; *c.* −12; *d.* $6X^2 - 30X$; *e.* $8X$

7 *a.* b; *b.* b; *c.* equal

8 third, first-degree equation

Exercise 9-3

1 *a.* dR/dD; *b.* total revenue

2 $\frac{a}{b} - \frac{2}{b}D = \frac{1}{b}(a - 2D)$; *a.* first; *b.* straight line; *c.* $\frac{1}{2}a$; *d.* (1) $\frac{1}{2}a$, negative, (2) $\frac{1}{2}a$, positive

4 *a.* $\frac{1}{20 \text{ cartons/dollar}}$ (100 cartons − $2D$); *b.* 5; *c.* 100, *d.* zero; *e.* 50, 2.50

5 dR/dD; *a.* positive; *b.* negative; *c.* zero

6 *a.* $=$; *b.* $>$

7 *a.* less than 40 tons; *b.* greater than 40 tons; *c.* equal to 40 tons

Exercise 9-4

1 *a.* the ratio of the relative change in quantity demanded to the relative change in price as the change in price approaches zero; *b.* $(dD/D)/(dP/P)$

2 $(dD/dP)(P/D)$

3 *a.* −20 cartons/dollar; *b.* (−20 cartons/dollar)(P/D); *c.* (1) −1, (2) $-\frac{2}{3}$, (3) $-1\frac{1}{2}$

4 negative, pure

5 *a.* elastic; *b.* inelastic; *c.* unitary elastic

6 *a.* k; *b.* vertical; *c.* zero

7 *a.* K; *b.* horizontal; *c.* infinity (an indefinitely large number)

8 $(dS/S)/(dP/P)$, $(dS/dP)(P/S)$; *a.* (1) greater than 1, (2) less than 1, (3) equal to 1; *b.* positive, pure; *c.* (1) zero, k, (2) infinity, K

9 *a.* 30 cartons/dollar; *b.* (30 cartons/dollar)(P/S); *c.* 1.3

Exercise 9-5

2 *a*. infinity; *b*. zero; *c*. one; *d*. price

3 *a*. infinity; *b*. zero; *c*. one; *d*. price

4 *a*. 12; *b*. infinity

5 9, less than

6 *a*. elastic, positive; *b*. inelastic, negative; *c*. unitary elastic, zero

7 *a*. greater than, 50; *b*. less than, 50; *c*. equal to, 50

8 *a*. equal to; *b*. less than

Exercise 10-1

1 *a*. P_X, P_Y, I, T; *b*. P_X, P_Y, I, T; *c*. P_X, P_Y, I; *d*. indifference curves

2 the different combinations of X and Y that give the consumer the same utility

3 $-dY/dX$, marginal rate of substitution of X for Y; *a*. negative; *b*. decreases; *c*. convex to the origin

4 *a*. $\bar{U} = f(X,Y)$; *b*. $<$; *c*. $>$

5 intersect, closer

6 $P_X \cdot X + P_Y \cdot Y = I$; *a*. I/P_X; *b*. I/P_Y; *c*. $-P_X/P_Y$; *d*. $I - P_X(g)$

8 *a*. $16\frac{2}{3}$; *b*. $12\frac{1}{2}$; *c*. $-\frac{3}{4}$; *d*. $9\frac{1}{2}$, $8\frac{2}{3}$

9 Maximum, *a*. $-dY/dX = -P_XP_Y$; *b*. $P_X \cdot X + P_Y \cdot Y = I$

10 *a*. (1) the maximum quantity of Y he can buy, (2) the maximum quantity of X he can buy; *b*. C; *c*. they are on lower indifference curves than C; *d*. they are not on his budget line; *e*. X_4 of X and Y_3 of Y

Exercise 10-2

1 *a*. I, P_Y, P_X; *b*. P_X, increases; *d*. complement of X; does

2 *a*. $dD_Y/dP_X < 0$; *b*. $dD_Y/dP_X > 0$; *c*. $dDY/dP_X = 0$

3 *a*. $dD_X/dI > 0$; *b*. $dD_X/dI < 0$

4 *a*. P_X, P_Y, I; *b*. I, increases; *c*. inferior; *d*. normal

5 *a*. I, decreases, decreases; *b*. normal; *c*. normal

6 *a*. P_X; *b*. P_X, increases; *c*. complement; *d*. does not

7 *a*. increases; *b*. decreases; *c*. increases

8 perfectly inelastic

9 *a*. $\Delta I/P_X$; *b*. $\Delta I/P_Y$

10 decreases, remains constant

Exercise 11-1

1 *a*. $Y = f(N,R)$; *b*. (1) $\bar{Y} = f(\bar{N},\bar{R})$, (2) $Y = f(N,R)$; *c*. $Y = f(N,\bar{R})$

2 *a*. fixed, fixed; *b*. variable, variable; *c*. partly fixed and partly variable, variable

3 $C = N \cdot P_N + R \cdot P_R$; *a*. $\bar{C} = \bar{N} \cdot \bar{P}_N + \bar{R} \cdot \bar{P}_R$; *b*. $C = N \cdot \bar{P}_N + \bar{R} \cdot \bar{P}_R$; *c*. $C = N \cdot \bar{P}_N + R \cdot \bar{P}_R$

4 *a*. fixed, do not; *b*. variable, do; *c*. total cost

5 *a*. fixed, fixed, *b*. variable, variable; *c*. variable, partly fixed and partly variable

6 *a*. F; *b*. $F + V$; *c*. V

7 *a*. F/X; *b*. V/X; *c*. C/X, F/X, V/X

8 *a*. F/X, A_F; *b*. V/X, A_V; *c*. F/X, V/X, A_F, A_V

9 *a*. (1) 40, (2) 30, (3) 70; *b*. (1) 2, (2) 1.50, (3) 3.50; *c*. (1) 5, (2) 5, (3) $5/3$, $1.66\frac{2}{3}$

10 $\Delta C/\Delta X$, ΔX, dC/dX

Exercise 11-2

1 *a*. F, V; *b*. A_F, A_V

2 *a*. $aX^3 - bX^2 + cX + \bar{F}$; *b*. $\bar{F}/X$; *c*. $aX^2 - bX + c$; *d*. $aX^2 - bX + c + \bar{F}/X$

3 greater than

4 *a*. decreases; *b*. decreases, increases; *c*. decreases, increases; greater than

5 *a*. 600, 225; *b*. $X^3 - 15X^2 + 200X + 300$; *c*. $300/X$; *d*. $X^2 - 15X + 200$; *e*. $X^2 - 15X + 200 + 300/X$

6 *a*. 300; *b*. 750; *c*. 1,050; *d*. 60; *e*. 150; *f*. 210

7 *a*. 7.5; *b*. an output greater than 7.5

8 *a*. zero; *b*. F

Exercise 11-3

1 *a*. $3aX^2 - 2bX + c$; *b*. marginal cost, dC/dX; *c*. $\Delta C/\Delta X$, ΔX

2 *a*. $3X^2 - 30X + 200$; *b*. (1) $6X - 30$, (2) 5; *c*. $X^3 - 15X^2 + 200X$; *d*. $3X^2 - 30X + 200$; *e*. equal to

3 *a*. dF/dX, dV/dX; *b*. zero; *c*. dV/dX

4 *a*. dC/dL; *b*. $\bar{P}_L$

5 *a*. marginal product; *b*. $2aL - 3bL^2$; *c*. increases, decreases

6 *a*. dC/dX, marginal cost; *b*. $\dfrac{\bar{P}_L}{dX/dL}$; *c*. it decreases and then increases

8 *a*. 7.5; *b*. 143.75; *c*. 143.75

10 *a*. 9.25; *b*. 179.20; *c*. 179.18

Exercise 11-4

1 $eX^3 - fX^2 + gX$; *a*. third; *b*. greater than

2 *a*. $eX^2 - fX + g$; *b*. $3eX^2 - 2fX + g$

4 *a*. $6X^2 - 25X + 40$; *b*. $18X^2 - 50X + 40$; *c*. (1) $2\frac{1}{12}$, (2) 13.96; *d*. M_r; *e*. (1) $36X - 50$, (2) 1.39, (3) 5.28

5 *a*. decreases, increases; *b*. decreases, increases; *c*. economies, scale, diseconomies, scale

6 less than, greater than

Exercise 12-1

1 $R - C$

2 output

3 increases, maximum, decreases

4 *a.* zero; *b.* $d\pi/dX$, zero

6 negative; *a.* $d\pi/dX$, negative; *b.* $d\pi/dX$, dX, negative; *c.* $d^2\pi/dX^2$, negative

8 *a.* V, P, A_V; *b.* $R < V$, $P < A_V$

9 *a.* C, P, A_C; *b.* $R < C$, $P < A_C$

Exercise 12-2

1 *a.* $aX^3 - bX^2 + cX + \bar{F}$; *b.* $(A - X)/B$; *c.* $X \cdot P$; *d.* $R - C$; *e.* $dC/dX = dR/dX$

2 *a.* d^2C/dX^2, d^2R/dX^2; *b.* R, V

3 $\dfrac{-\beta \pm \sqrt{\beta^2 - 4\alpha\gamma}}{2\alpha}$

4 *a.* $3aX^2 - 2bX + c$; *b.* $A/B - (2/B)X$; *c.* (1) $3aX^2 - 2bX + c$, $A/B - (2/B)X$, (2) $3X^2 + (2/B - 2b)X + (c - A/B)$;
d. $\dfrac{(2/B - 2b) \pm \sqrt{(2/B - 2b)^2 - 4\,(3a)(c - A/B)}}{2(3a)}$

5 d^2C/dX^2, d^2R/dX^2, R, V

6 $(A - X)/B$; *b.* $aX^3 - bX^2 + cX + \bar{F}$; *c.* R, $X \cdot P$; *d.* π, $R - C$; *e.* dividing R by X; *f.* dividing π by X

7 *a.* zero; *b.* zero; *c.* 50; *d.* −50

8 *a.* 12; *b.* 55; *c.* 660; *d.* 616; *e.* 44

9 *a.* 12; *b.* 55; *c.* 660; *d.* 716; *e.* −56

Exercise 12-3

1 $eX^3 - fX^2 + gX$; *b.* $P = (A - X)/B$; *c.* $R \equiv X \cdot P$; *d.* $\pi \equiv R - C$; *e.* $dC/dX = dR/dX$; *f.* $d^2C/dX^2 > d^2R/dX^2$; *g.* $R \geqq C$

2 *a.* 15; *b.* 770; *c.* 11,550; *d.* 11,212.5; *e.* 337.5

3 *a.* zero; *b.* zero; *c.* zero; *d.* zero

Exercise 13-1

1 *fixed*, $\bar{N}$

2 *a.* profits, positive; *b.* profits, negative; *c.* profits, zero

3 perfectly; *a.* $\bar{P}$; *b.* P

4 the same

5 constant, entry, exit, long-run, functions

6 less than; *a.* $A - BP$; *b.* $(A - D)/B$

Exercise 13-2

1 a. (1) C, (2) $\bar{P}$, (3) $x \cdot P$, (4) $R - C$, (5) $dC/dx = dR/dx$; b. (1) $d^2C/dx > d^2R/dx^2$, (2) $R \geqq V$; c. 5, 1, 4

3 profit is a minimum rather than a maximum

4 $b/2a$; a. $c - b^2/4a$; b. zero

5 a. $0.6x^2 - 10x + 45$; b. 13.75, 12.5; c. P; d. (1) $0.6x^2 - 10x + 45$, P, (2) $0.6x^2 - 10x + 45 - P$;

e. $\dfrac{10 \pm \sqrt{2.4P - 8}}{1.2}$; f. $\dfrac{10 \pm \sqrt{2.4P - 8}}{1.2}$, 13.75

6 a. (1) 13, (2) 213.20, 204.40, 8.80; b. (1) 15, (2) 450, 250, 200; c. (1) zero, (2) zero, 25, −25

7 a. $\bar{N}$; b. D; c. S, D; d. P

8 a. $\bar{N}\dfrac{2b + \sqrt{4b^2 - 12(c - P)}}{6a} = A - BP$; b. A/B

9 a. $80\dfrac{10 + \sqrt{2.4P - 8}}{1.2}$, 13.75; b. (1) 45, (2) 22.60, (3) 1,120, (4) 14, 316.40, 223.80, 92.60

Exercise 13-3

1 a. $ex^3 - fx^2 + gx$; b. $\bar{P}$; c. $x \cdot P$; d. $R - C$; e. $dC/dx = dR/dx$; f. d^2C/dx^2, d^2R/dx^2; g. R, C

2 $\dfrac{2f + \sqrt{4f^2 - 12e(g - P)}}{6a}$, $g - \dfrac{f^2}{4e}$

3 $\dfrac{6 + \sqrt{4.8P - 108}}{2.4}$, 24.375

4 a. (1) 3.75, (2) 91.40625, 91.40625, 0; b. (1) 0, (2) 0, 0, 0; c. (1) 4, (2) 100.80., 97.60., 3.20

5 a. (1) R, C, (2) R/x, C/x, (3) P, average; b. dC/dx, dR/dx, dC/dx, P, minimum average cost; c. dC/dx, average cost, price; d. price, minimum, average

6 a. $g - f^2/4e$; b. $N(f/2e)$; c. $A - BP$; d. S, D

7 a. $2e/f - (A - Bg) + fB/2$; b. $g - f^2/4e$; c. $A - Bg + Bf^2/4e$

8 a. 52; b. 195; c. 24.375; d. (1) 3.75, (2) 91.40625, 91.40625, 0

Exercise 14-1

1 $M \cdot P_M + N \cdot P_N$

2 $\Delta Y/\Delta M$, ΔM, N, $\partial Y/\partial M$

3 Y, P_Y; a. $\Delta R/\Delta Y$, ΔY, dR/dY; b. $\Delta R/\Delta M$, ΔM, N, dR/dM

4 a. the limit which $\Delta A/\Delta B$ approaches as ΔB approaches zero, C remaining constant, the limit which $\Delta A/\Delta C$ approaches as ΔC approaches zero, B remaining constant; b. to indicate a partial derivative and that one variable is a function of more than one other variable

5 a. one, zero; b. $a(N/M)^{1-a}$; c. $a(N/M)^{1-a}\overline{P_Y}$; d. $a(N/M)^{1-a}\,\dfrac{g - 2Y}{h}$

7 a. $0.8(50/M)^{0.2}$; b. $4(50/M)^{0.2}$; c. $0.8(50/M)^{0.2}\,\dfrac{600 - 2Y}{30}$

8 to find $\partial A/\partial B$, treat C as a constant and find the simple derivative of A with respect to B

Exercise 14-2

1 $\Delta C/\Delta M$, ΔM, N, $\partial C/\partial M$

2 a. perfectly elastic; b. constant; c. its price

4 12

5 increasing, the quantity of M employed

7 $(2N + 40)/6$

Exercise 15-1

1 a. zero; b. dC/dM, dR/dM; c. d^2C/dM^2, d^2R/dM^2; d. R/M, P_M

3 $a(N/M)^{1-a}$; b. $a(N/M)^{1-a}\,\bar{P}_Y$; c. $\bar{P}_M$

4 a. 900; b. (1) 300, (2) 5,400, (3) 3,700, (4) 1,700, (5) 6, greater than, (6) zero, (7) negative, less

5 a. $a\left(\dfrac{\bar{N}}{M}\right)^{1-a}\dfrac{j - 2(M^a \cdot \bar{N}^{1-a})}{m}$

6 b. 10; c. (1) 100, (2) 6.50, (3) 650, (4) 1,300, (5) −650, (6) 6.50, greater than, (7) greater than

7 a. dR/dM; b. $a\left(\dfrac{\bar{N}}{M}\right)^{1-a}\dfrac{dR}{dY}$; c. P_M, d^2C/dM^2, d^2R/dM^2

8 $9\left(\dfrac{100}{M}\right)^{0.5}$

9 $0.5\left(\dfrac{100}{M}\right)^{0.5}\dfrac{1{,}400 - 2Y}{200}$

10 a. 6.25; b. 750

Exercise 15-2

1 a. $(2M - b)/c$; b. $a(\bar{N}/M)^{1-a}$; c. $\bar{P}_Y$; d. $a(\bar{N}/M)^{1-a} \cdot \bar{P}_Y$; e. $(2M - b)/c = a(\bar{N}/M)^{1-a} \cdot \bar{P}_Y$, (1) P_M, (2) $>$

2 a. $9(100/M)^{0.5}$; b. $(2M + 100)/200$; d. 400, 2.50; e. (1) 200, (2) 3,600, (3) 3,000, (4) 600

3 a. $(2M - b)/c$; b. $a(\bar{N}/M)^{1-a}$; c. $\dfrac{g - 2M^a \cdot \bar{N}^{1-a}}{h}$;

d. $a\left(\dfrac{\bar{N}}{M}\right)^{1-a} - \dfrac{g - 2M^a \cdot \bar{N}^{1-a}}{h}$;

e. $\dfrac{2M - b}{c}$, $a\left(\dfrac{\bar{N}}{M}\right)^{a} - \dfrac{g - 2M^a \cdot \bar{N}^{1-a}}{h}$,

(1) $d^2C/dM^2 > d^2R/dM^2$, (2) $R/M \geqq P_M$

4 a. $0.5\left(\dfrac{100}{M}\right)^{0.5}\dfrac{22{,}440 - 2M^{0.5} \cdot 100^{0.5}}{500}$; b. $\dfrac{2M + 32}{100}$; d. 484, 516;

e. (1) 220, (2) 44.40, (3) 9,768, (4) 3,135.20, (5) 6,632.80

Exercise 15-3

1 *a.* proportion, least; *b.* amount

2 *a.* $M \cdot P_M + N \cdot P_N$; *b.* $dM\ \partial C/\partial M + dN\ \partial C/\partial N$; *c.* zero; *d.* (1) $0 = dM\ \partial C/\partial M + dN\ \partial C/\partial N$,

(2) $-\dfrac{dN}{dM} = \dfrac{\partial C/\partial M}{\partial C/\partial N}$

3 *a.* $dM\ \partial Y/\partial M + dN\ \partial Y/\partial N$; *b.* zero; *c.* (1) $0 = dM\ \partial Y/\partial M + dN\ \partial Y/\partial N$,

(2) $-\dfrac{dN}{dM} = \dfrac{\partial Y/\partial M}{\partial Y/\partial N}$

4 *a.* $\dfrac{\partial C/\partial M}{\partial C/\partial N} = \dfrac{\partial Y/\partial M}{\partial Y/\partial N}$; *b.* $\dfrac{\partial Y/\partial N}{\partial C/\partial N} = \dfrac{\partial Y/\partial M}{\partial C/\partial M}$; *c.* $\dfrac{\partial Y/\partial N}{P_N} = \dfrac{\partial Y/\partial M}{P_M}$

5 *a.* $0.5(N/M)^{0.5}$, $0.5(M/N)^{0.5}$; *b.* 2, $2/9$; *c.* 225, 25; *d.* $3/2$, $1/6$; *e.* $3/4$

6 *a.* (1) $\frac{1}{64}M$, (2) $4N$; *b.* (1) $0.5(N/M)^{0.5}$, (2) $0.5(M/N)^{0.5}$; *c.* 256, 16; *d.* (1) $1/8$, (2) 2, (3) 4, (4) 64; *e.* $1/32$; *f.* (1) 2, (2) 32; *g.* 1,024

7 *a.* (1) $\partial C/\partial M = \partial R/\partial M$, (2) $\partial C/\partial N = \partial R/\partial N$; *b.* (1) $P_M = \partial R/\partial M$, (2) $P_N = \partial R/\partial N$; *c.* (1) $\partial^2 C/\partial M^2 > \partial^2 R/\partial M^2$, (2) $\partial^2 C/\partial N^2 > \partial^2 R/\partial N^2$; *d.* $R \geqq M \cdot P_M + N \cdot P_N$